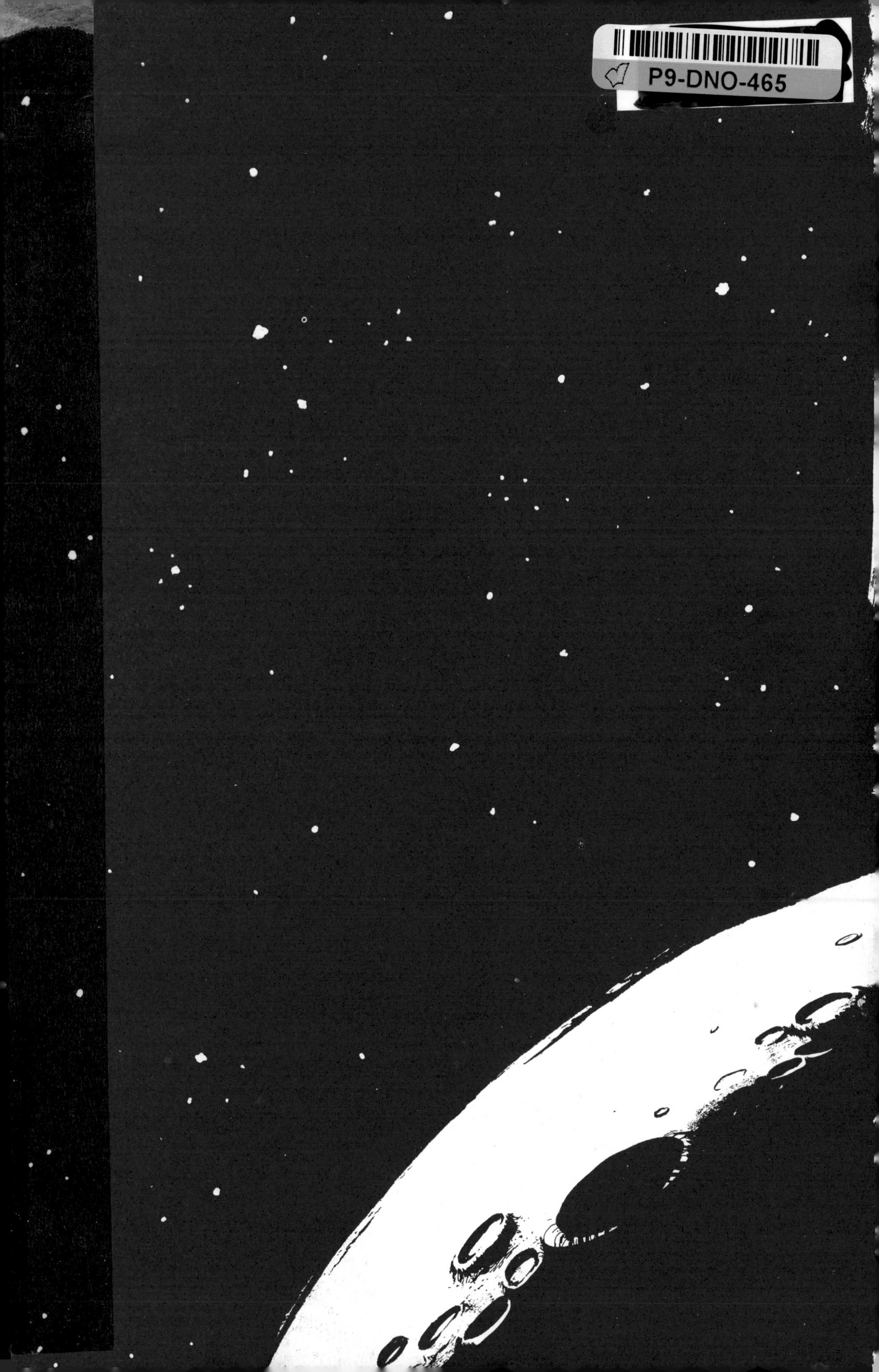

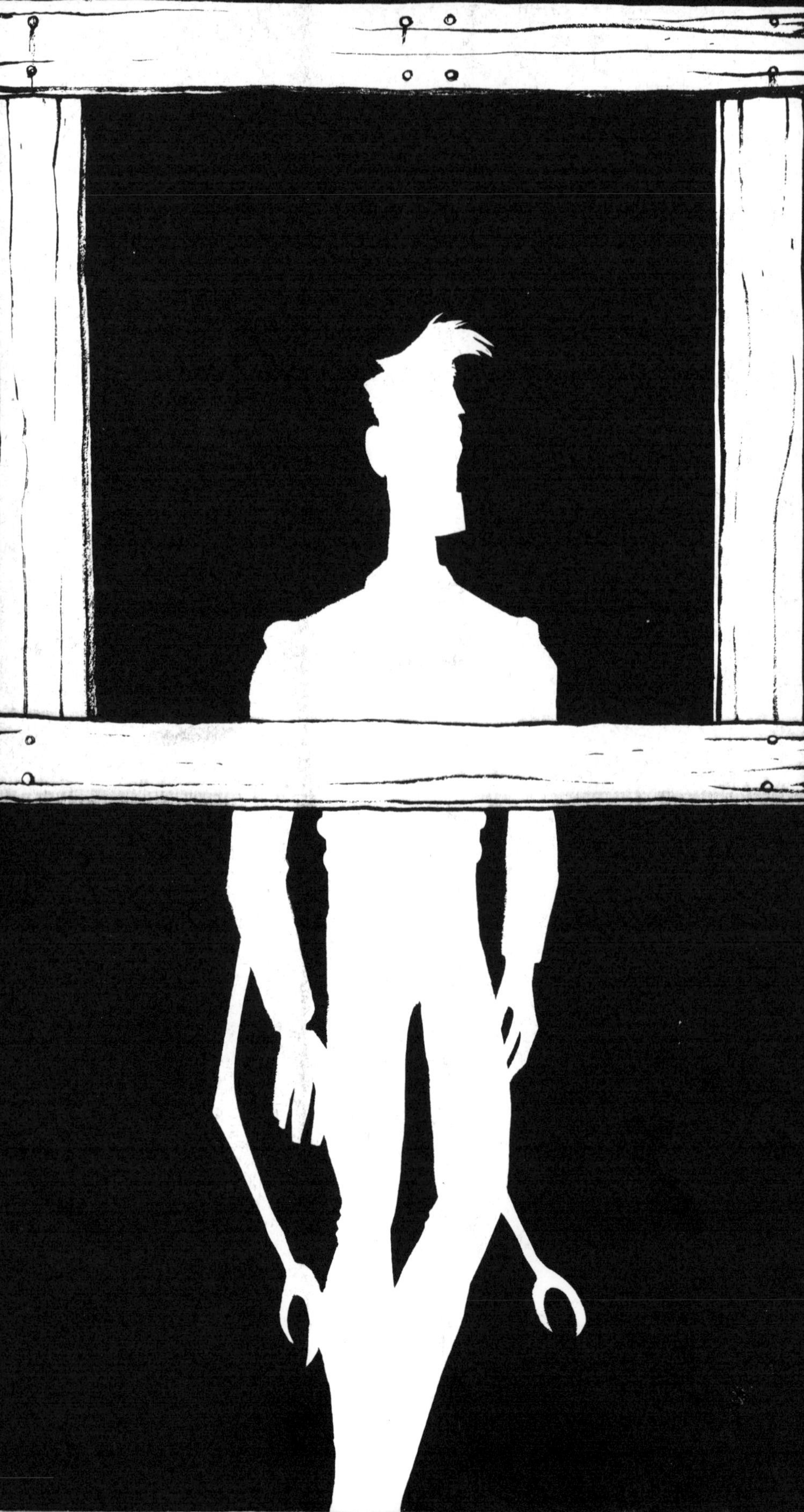

creature Tech

By DOUG Ten NapeL

lettered by JENNIFER BARKER
font by BLAMBOT!

foreword by TERRY MATTINGLY

original publication edited by
CHRIS STAROS

original art direction by
BRETT WARNOCK

Image Comics, Inc.

Robert Kirkman – Chief Operating Officer
Erik Larsen – Chief Financial Officer
Todd McFarlane – President
Marc Silvestri – Chief Executive Officer
Jim Valentino – Vice-President

Eric Stephenson – Publisher
Todd Martinez – Sales & Licensing Coordinator
Betsy Gomez – PR & Marketing Coordinator
Sarah deLaine – Administrative Assistant
Tyler Shainline – Production Manager
Drew Gill – Art Director
Jonathan Chan – Production Artist
Monica Howard – Production Artist
Vincent Kukua – Production Artist
Kevin Yuen – Production Artist

http://www.imagecomics.com

image

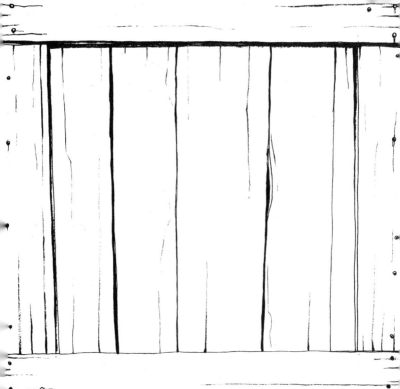

FOREWORD

YOU ARE IN A MOVIE THEATER.

SUDDENLY, A GIANT SHARK RISES OUT OF A SILENT SEA. IN SHOCK, A MAN RETREATS INTO THE BOAT'S CABIN AND QUIETLY MENTIONS THE NEED FOR A BIGGER BOAT.

AN ARCHETYPAL VILLAIN DRESSED IN BLACK ARMOR CLINCHES HIS FIST AT A WOUNDED YOUNG MAN AND PROCLAIMS, "I AM YOUR FATHER."

A GIANT BROADSWORD IS THROWN, SLOWLY TUMBLING, AGAINST A BLUE-GRAY SKY AND THEN LANDS, THRUST INTO A SCOTTISH BATTLEFIELD WITH ITS HANDLE POINTING TOWARD HEAVEN -- THE HILT FORMING A CROSS IN HONOR OF A FALLEN HERO.

THE SHOWER CURTAIN IS JERKED TO ONE SIDE. A WOMAN RAISES HER HANDS IN DEFENSE. A KNIFE RISES, THEN FALLS. THE WOMAN'S MOUTH FREEZES IN A SCREEN. SHE CLUTCHES THE CURTAIN AND FALLS, THE CURTAIN RINGS POPPING OFF IN RAPID FIRE. BLOOD SWIRLS IN THE WATER AS IT RUSHES DOWN THE DRAIN.

A CUSTODIAN TOSSES A CHILD'S SLED INTO A FIREPLACE TO BURN WITH OTHER OBJECTS DISCARDED FROM A MAN'S RICH, TUMULTUOUS LIFE. THE FLAMES LICK AT ITS NAME -- ROSEBUD.

THERE ARE MOMENTS IN MOVIES THAT LOCK INTO THE VIEWER'S MIND AS SINGULAR IMAGES. THE FILM ITSELF RUSHES ON, OF COURSE, IN WAVES OF IMAGERY, MUSIC, SOUND EFFECTS AND DIALOGUE. BUT THE FROZEN IMAGE REMAINS, AS IF WRAPPED IN AN UNSEEN MENTAL FRAME. IN HINDSIGHT, IT IS EASY TO IMAGINE AN ARTIST SITTING AT HIS EASEL, USING A PENCIL OR A PEN TO CREATE THAT SINGULAR IMAGE THAT WILL FRAME THIS MOMENT AS IT COMES TO VIEWERS THROUGH A CAMERA LENS.

THEN THE ARTIST DRAWS ANOTHER IMAGE, AIMING THE MOMENTUM OF THE MOVIE TOWARD ANOTHER ESTABLISHING SHOT, ANOTHER INK-AND-PAPER MAP TO LEAD THE DIRECTOR AND CINEMATOGRAPHER TO THE NEXT CRUCIAL FRAME, THE NEXT SYMBOLIC IMAGE. THE ACTION AND IMAGERY CONTINUE BETWEEN THESE FROZEN MOMENTS, BUT IT'S CLEAR THAT THE VISUAL STORYTELLERS ARE SWINGING LIKE TRAPEZE ARTISTS BETWEEN THESE TENT POLES IN THE IMAGINATION.

THE MOVIE, IN OTHER WORDS, IS UNFOLDING IN THE SPACES BETWEEN THESE STORYBOARDS, BETWEEN THESE FRAMED MOMENTS.

THIS IS PRECISELY WHAT DREW "MORIARTY" MCWEENY WAS TALKING ABOUT IN HIS 2002 AINTITCOOL.COM REVIEW OF THE FIRST EDITION OF DOUG TENNAPEL'S "CREATURE TECH," THIS VERY STRANGE BOOK THAT YOU CURRENTLY ARE HOLDING IN YOUR HANDS. ONLY HE DIDN'T REFER TO THIS BLACK-AND-WHITE OPUS AS A BOOK. NO, THIS IS WHAT HE WROTE:

"SIMPLY PUT, CREATURE TECH IS THE BEST AMERICAN ANIMATED FILM SINCE THE IRON GIANT. YES, BETTER THAN TOY STORY 2. BETTER THAN SHREK. BETTER THAN ANYTHING FROM ANY STUDIO. I KNOW... IT'S A GRAPHIC NOVEL... BUT WHEN YOU READ THIS THING, THERE'S NO DOUBT WHAT IT IS. IT'S A MOVIE THAT JUST HAPPENS TO BE IN PRINT. IT'S THE COMPLETE STORYBOARD, EVERY FRAME. ... NO MATTER HOW STRANGE IT GETS, NO MATTER HOW DARING A MOMENT TENNAPEL GOES FOR, THE THING ALWAYS ENTERTAINS. EVERY PANEL IS WORTH LOOKING AT."

IT'S ALREADY A MOVIE, NO MATTER WHAT HAPPENS IN THE MASS-MEDIA FUTURE OF THIS BIZARRE MODERN MYTH (AND THAT'S A COMPLIMENT). THE FACT THAT A GRAPHIC NOVEL COULD LEAP FROM STORYBOARDS TO CELLULOID SHOULD NOT SURPRISE ANYONE WHO UNDERSTANDS HOW MOVIES ARE BEING MADE TODAY. HOWEVER, THIS IS A TREND WITH DEEP ROOTS IN HOLLYWOOD HISTORY.

YOU SEE, ALFRED HITCHCOCK WAS FAMOUS FOR HAVING HIS PLOTS FINE TUNED IN STORYBOARDS AND THIS CAN BE SEEN IN SEQUENCE AFTER SEQUENCE IN WORKS SUCH AS ROPE, VERTIGO, NORTH BY NORTHWEST, REAR WINDOW AND, OF COURSE, PSYCHO. STEPHEN SPIELBERG AND GEORGE LUCAS ARE ALSO KNOWN FOR THEIR USE OF STORYBOARDS AND OPENLY TALK ABOUT THE IMPACT OF COMIC BOOKS ON THEIR CELLULOID VISIONS. IF YOU PURCHASE THE VISTA EDITION OF M. NIGHT SHYAMALAN'S THE SIXTH SENSE, A SET OF STORYBOARD IMAGES ARE INCLUDED IN THE PACKAGE -- COMPLETING THE ARTISTIC CIRCLE BACK TO THE WRITER-DIRECTOR'S MASTER, WHICH IS, OF COURSE, HITCHCOCK.

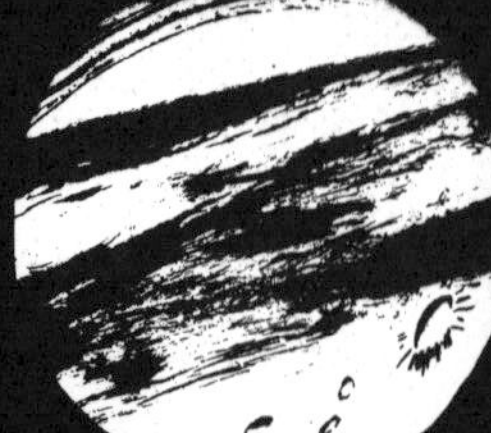

BUT THE CIRCLE GOES BACK FURTHER THAN THAT, STRESSED MEDIA-STUDIES PROFESSOR ALEX WAINER, A FORMER COLLEAGUE OF MINE. BOB KANE AND OTHER PIONEERS OF COMIC-BOOK ART STUDIED THE STILL IMAGES CAPTURED INSIDE THE ORSON WELLES MASTERPIECE CITIZEN KANE AS THEY WERE CONCEIVING THEIR OWN UNIQUE BRAND OF VISUAL STORYTELLING. SO THE STORYBOARDS SHAPED THE MOVIE, THEN THE MOVIE ACHIEVED ICONIC STATUS AND HELPED SHAPED THE EARLY COMICS. TODAY, IT IS IMPOSSIBLE TO IMAGINE THE MODERN MOVIE INDUSTRY WITHOUT THE VAST AND GROWING INFLUENCE OF THE PARALLEL UNIVERSE THAT IS BUILT ON COMICS, VIDEO GAMES AND, ULTIMATELY, GRAPHIC NOVELS. AND WHAT ABOUT MUSIC VIDEOS? WHAT ABOUT THE VISUAL STORYTELLING IN A SERIES LIKE LOST?

"TO STATE THE OBVIOUS, CREATURE TECH ALREADY FEELS LIKE A MOVIE, EVEN AT THE STAGE OF INK ON PAPER," SAID WAINER. "THE ART FUNCTIONS AS THE STORYBOARDS, BUT THERE IS MORE TO THE BOOK THAN THAT. IT'S LIKE A TREE, WITH TENNAPEL ADDING RING AFTER RING OF STORYTELLING ONE INSIDE THE OTHER, RINGS OF TRULY BIZARRE WIT, ACTION, THEOLOGY AND THEN THE CHARACTERS THEMSELVES. ...

"THUS, THE BOOK HAS LAYERS OF MEANING. THERE'S THE FLAT-OUT FREAKISHLY ABSURD PLOT OF SCIENTIFIC INVESTIGATION OF BIZARRE ARTIFACTS, WITHIN WHICH IS A LOVE STORY, THE ENDEARING PORTRAIT OF SMALL TOWN TYPES, A FATHER-SON TALE PITTING FAITH AGAINST SCIENCE AND ULTIMATELY, AT ITS CORE, THE JOURNEY OF A MAN WHO FINDS HIS EMPIRICAL WORLD VIEW CHANGING WHEN HE RECEIVES A NEW HEART."

OF COURSE, IT HELPS TO KNOW THAT EARLY ON THE WORLD-WEARY DR. MICHAEL ONG IS, LITERALLY, REBORN WHEN A PARASITE -- HIS SYMBIOTE -- ATTACHES ITSELF TO THE YOUNG SCIENTIST'S CHEST LIKE A BREASTPLATE AND TAKES THE PLACE OF HIS CRUSHED HEART. BY THE END OF THE TALE, THIS ALIEN HAS USED ITS OWN MORAL FREE AGENCY TO SAVE THE DOUBTER'S LIFE -- BODY AND SOUL -- AND DEFEAT AN INCARNATION OF ABSOLUTE EVIL.

ALONG THE WAY THERE ARE IMAGES OF GREAT BEAUTY THAT ARE MORE THAN THE SUM OF THEIR PARTS. THERE IS THE LEAPING SILHOUETTE OF THE SECURITY OFFICER NAMED BLUE, A GIANT MANTID GENETICALLY ENGINEERED BY GOVERNMENT RESEARCHERS OUT OF A CHUNK OF AMBERLITH, AS HE RUSHES TO THE DEFENSE OF THE RURAL WARRIORS WHO HAVE WELCOMED HIM INTO THEIR GOOD-OLD-BOYS FRATERNITY. THERE IS THE RIPPLE OF SHADOW THAT SPLITS THE CHEEK OF KATIE, THE SAD LOCAL GIRL WITH THE AMBLYOPIC EYE AND THE ATROPHIED HAND. THERE IS THE MAD SCIENTIST WITH THE DEMONIC HAND, WHO, AS HE FALLS TO HIS DEATH, CHEERFULLY SINGS A LINE FROM THE BLOOD, SWEAT & TEARS HIT "SPINNING WHEEL," KNOWING THAT WHEN HE HITS THE GROUND HE WILL BE RAISED FROM THE DEAD BY THE HOLY BLOOD ON THE SHROUD IN WHICH HE IS WRAPPED.

BUT THE BOOK BEGINS AND ENDS WITH A MAN WITH A FRAGILE HEART.

YOU ARE IN A MOVIE THEATER. THE CURTAIN RISES AND, WITH PEN AND INK, TENNAPEL BEGINS HANGING HIS FRAMED IMAGES ON THE SCREEN. EVERY NOW AND THEN THE READER HAS THE OPTION TO HIT PAUSE AND STOP THE ACTION TO STUDY A STARK IMAGE.

HERE IS ONE. WE SEE A YOUNG MAN, STANDING AND GAZING AT HIS OWN CHEST. HE IS STUNNED. HE IS CONFUSED. INSTEAD OF BEING DEAD, HE NOW FACES A LIFE IN WHICH HE IS DEPENDENT ON THIS MYSTERIOUS CREATURE THAT HAS BOTH WOUNDED HIM AND SAVED HIS LIFE. THE READER WILL FLIP MANY PAGES BEFORE DR. ONG HAS GRASPED WHAT HAS HAPPENED AND BE THANKFUL FOR THIS CHANCE TO BE -- DARE I SAY IT -- BORN AGAIN.

AS TENNAPEL'S STORY MOVES INTO ITS FINAL ACT, DR. ONG RECEIVES YET ANOTHER LIFE-CHANGING SHOCK. BECAUSE OF HIS DEEPENING UNION WITH THE SYMBIOTE, HE IS GRANTED A VISION OF GOOD FRIDAY RITES ON THE ALIEN'S HOME PLANET, WHERE ONE OF THESE CREATURES WAS NAILED TO A RECTANGLE, SUSPENDED ON A SHAFT OF WOOD AND LEFT TO DIE ON BEHALF OF THE OTHER MEMBERS OF HIS SPECIES. THUS, THE BELIEVERS WEAR SMALL RECTANGLES AROUND THEIR NECKS, ON CHAINS, IN MEMORY OF THIS SACRIFICE.

THIS IS ONE DEFINING IMAGE IN A MOVIE, FRAMING AN ACT OF UNSPEAKABLE MERCY.

THE MOVIE IS ALREADY PLAYING IN VERY INTIMATE THEATERS, FOR THOSE WITH EYES TO SEE.

TERRY MATTINGLY

DIRECTOR, THE WASHINGTON JOURNALISM CENTER
COLUMNIST, SCRIPPS HOWARD NEWS SERVICE
EDITOR, GETRELIGION.ORG

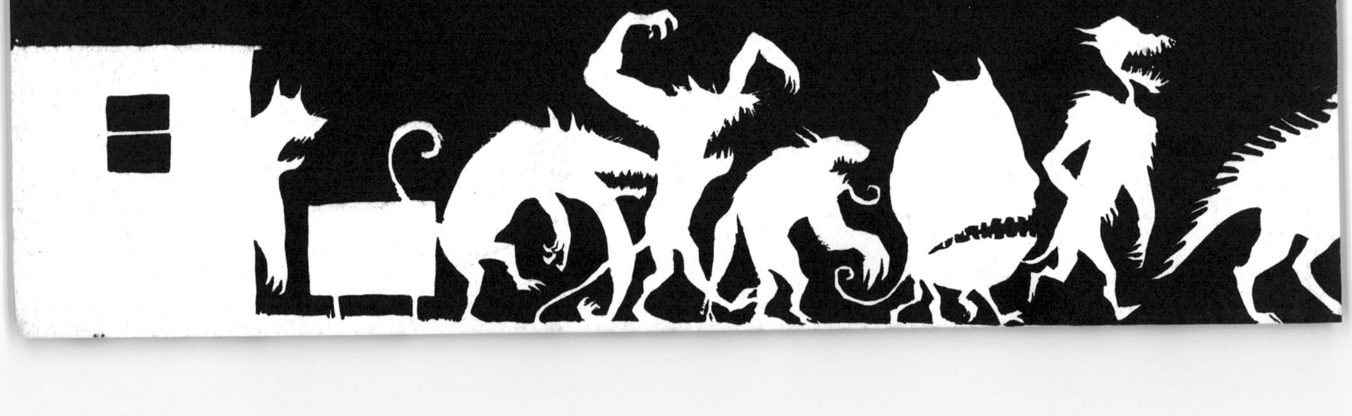

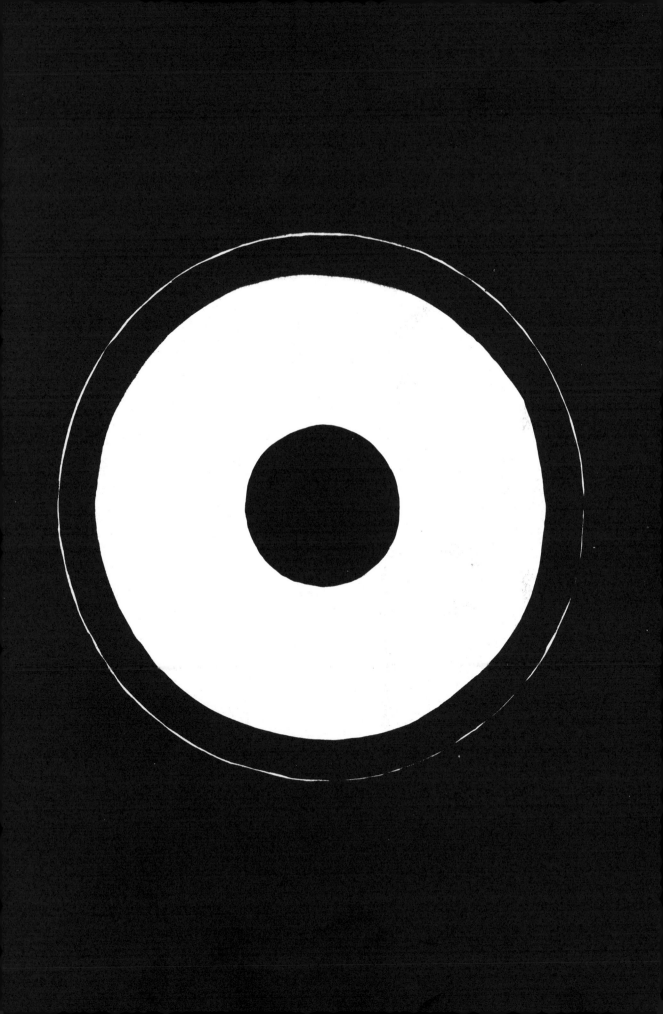

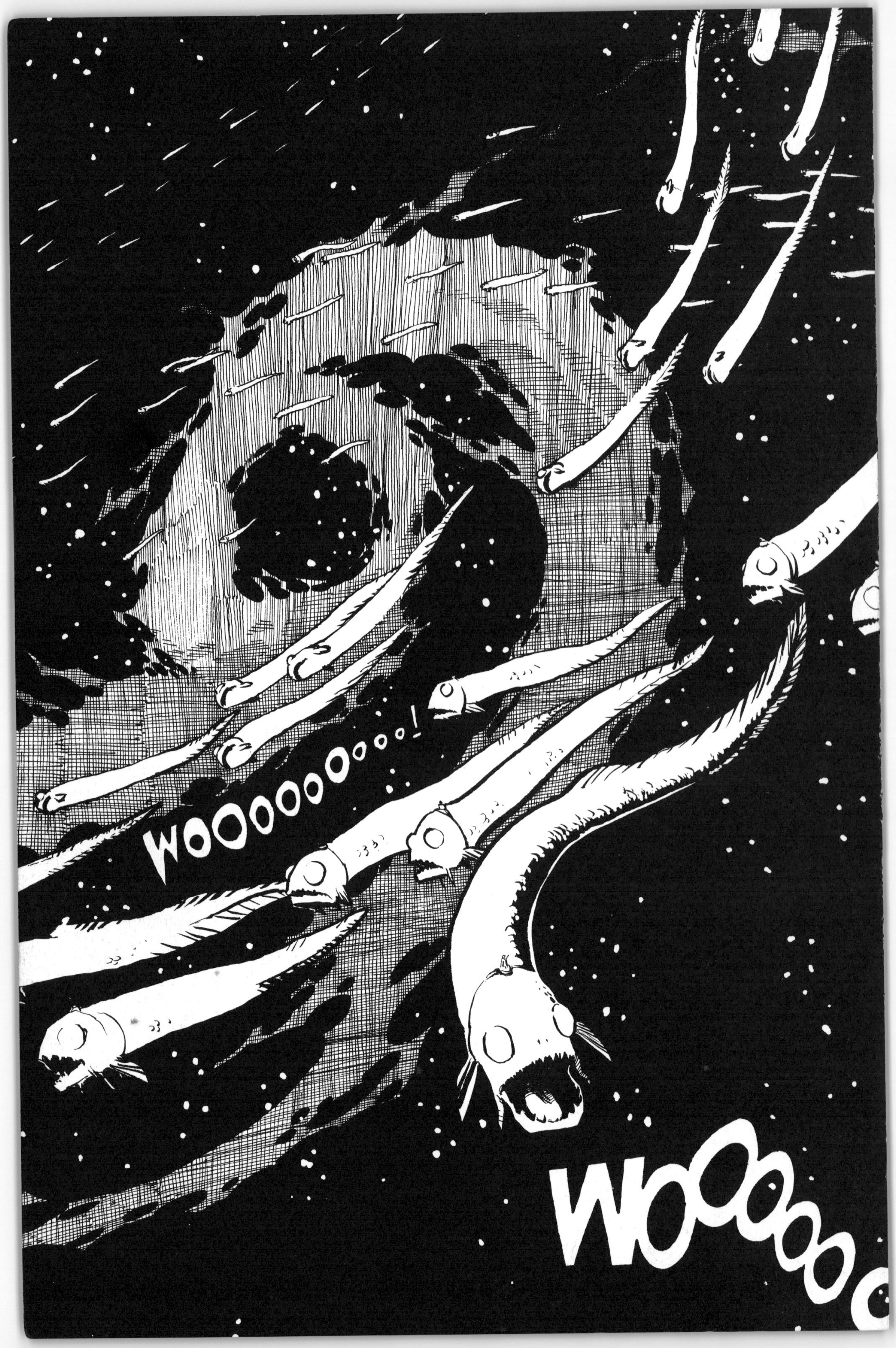
WOOOOOOOooo!
WOOOOOO

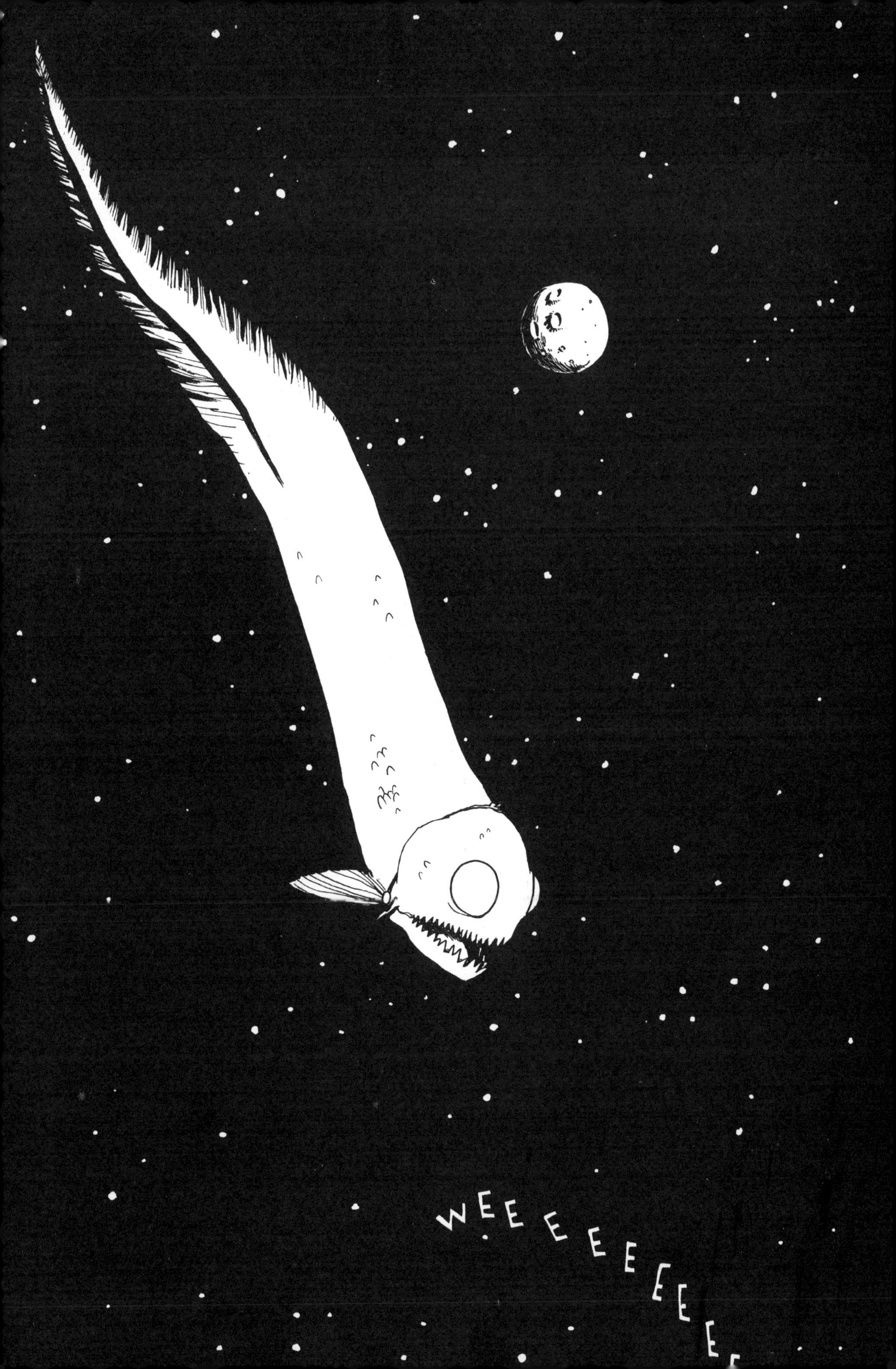
WEEEEEEEE

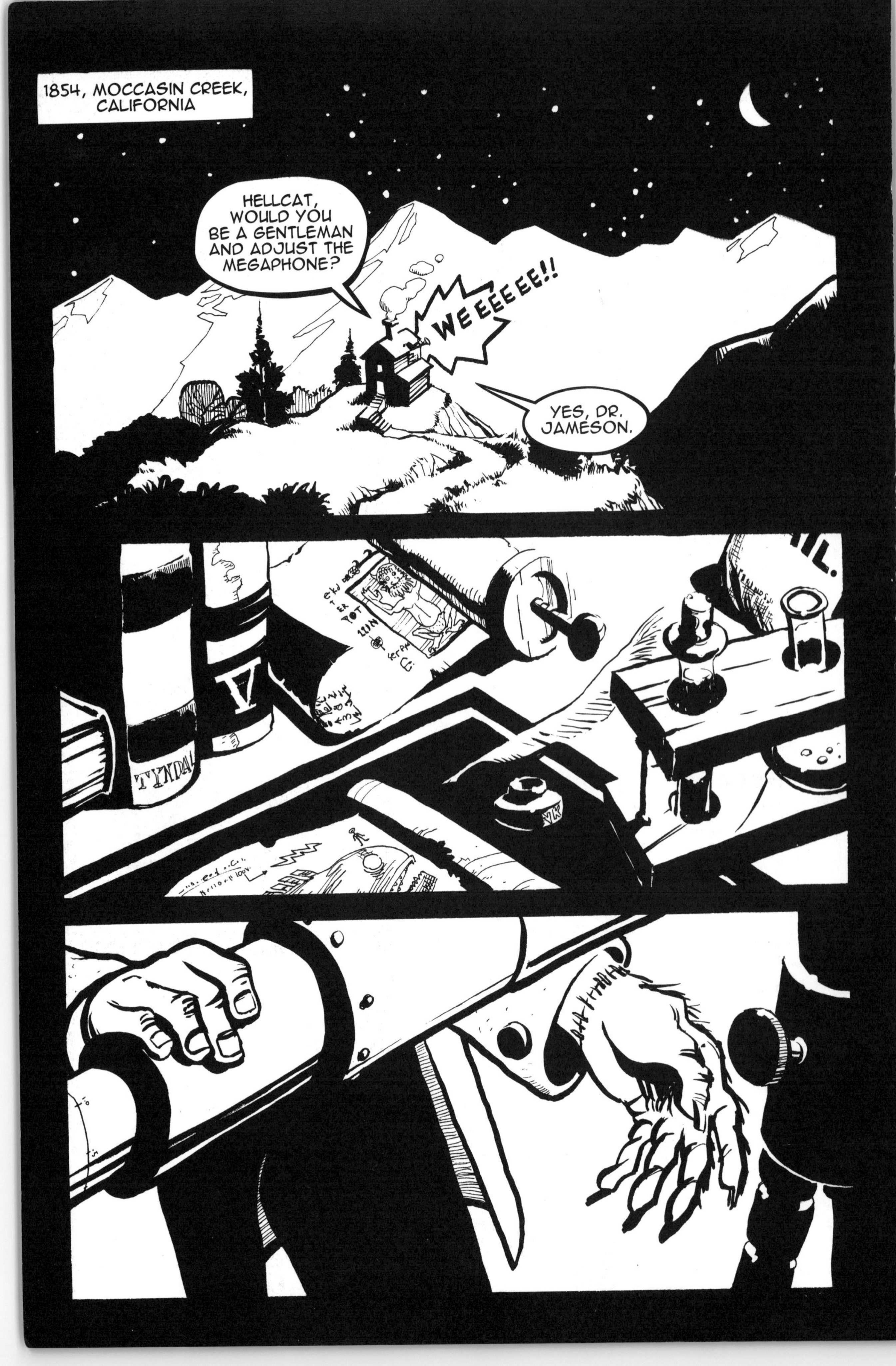

1854, MOCCASIN CREEK, CALIFORNIA
HELLCAT, WOULD YOU BE A GENTLEMAN AND ADJUST THE MEGAPHONE?
WEEEEEE!!
YES, DR. JAMESON.

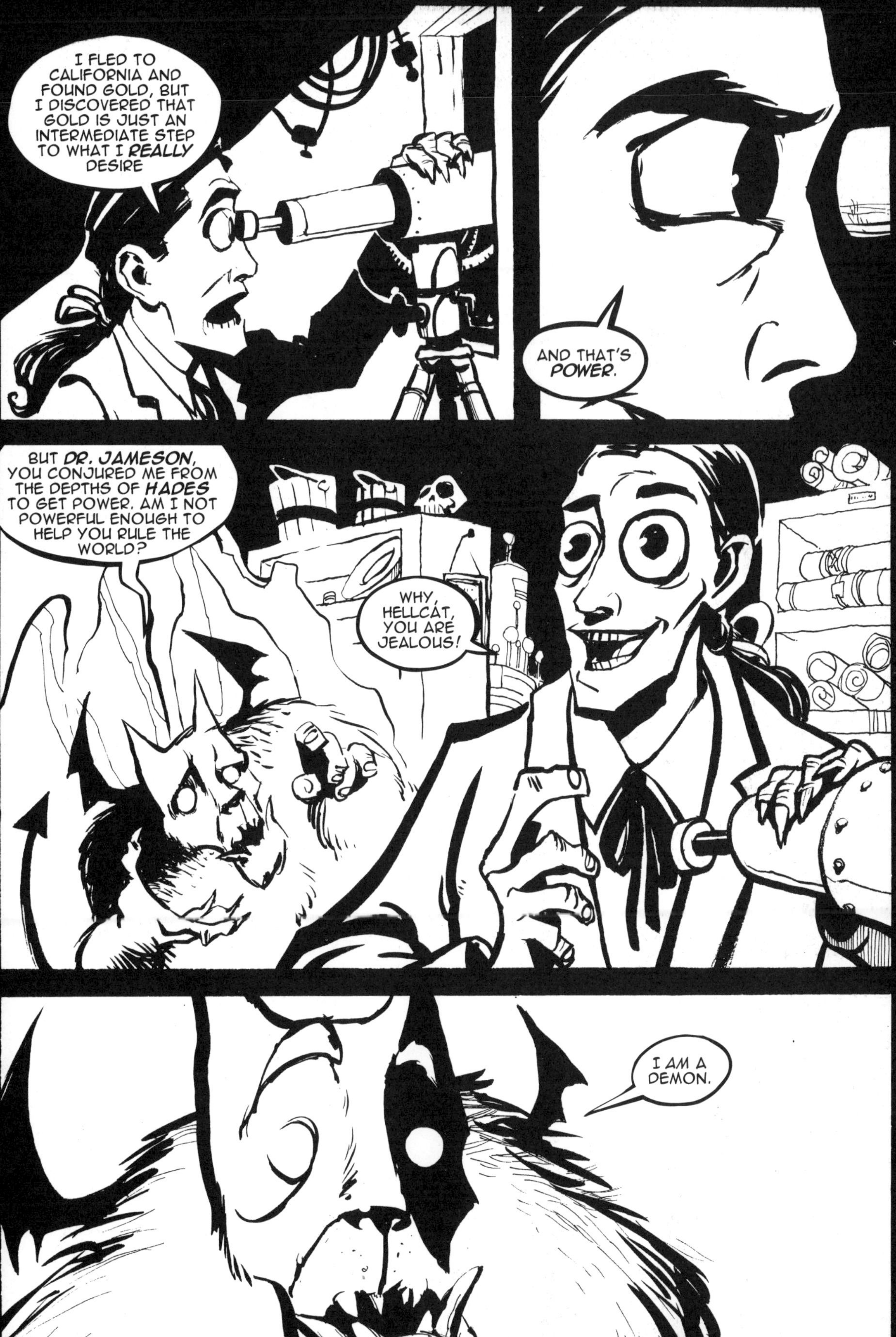
I FLED TO CALIFORNIA AND FOUND GOLD, BUT I DISCOVERED THAT GOLD IS JUST AN INTERMEDIATE STEP TO WHAT I *REALLY* DESIRE
AND THAT'S *POWER*.
BUT *DR. JAMESON*, YOU CONJURED ME FROM THE DEPTHS OF *HADES* TO GET POWER. AM I NOT POWERFUL ENOUGH TO HELP YOU RULE THE WORLD?
WHY, HELLCAT, YOU ARE JEALOUS!
I AM A DEMON.

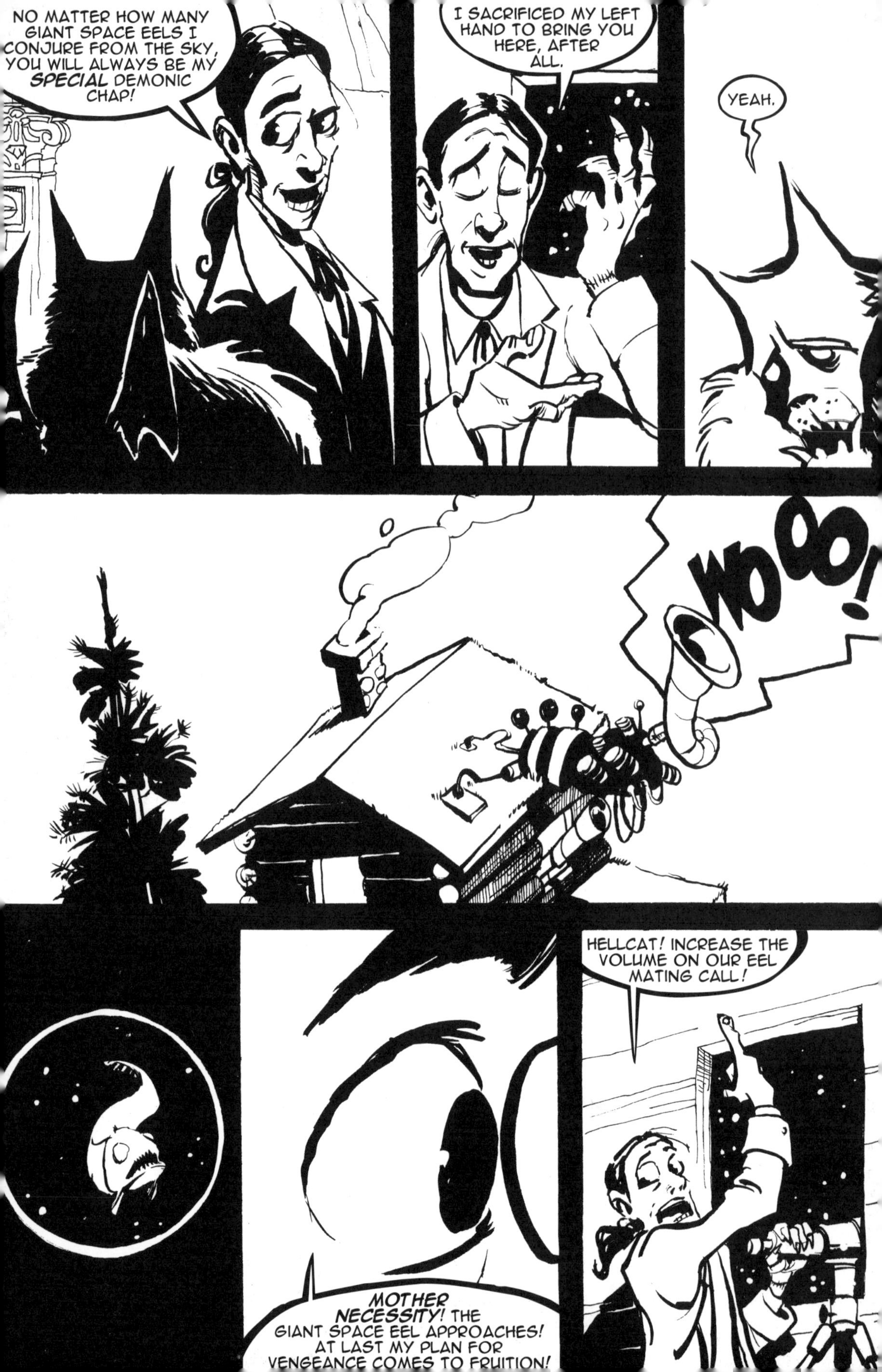
NO MATTER HOW MANY GIANT SPACE EELS I CONJURE FROM THE SKY, YOU WILL ALWAYS BE MY SPECIAL DEMONIC CHAP!
I SACRIFICED MY LEFT HAND TO BRING YOU HERE, AFTER ALL.
YEAH.
WOOO!
MOTHER NECESSITY! THE GIANT SPACE EEL APPROACHES! AT LAST MY PLAN FOR VENGEANCE COMES TO FRUITION!
HELLCAT! INCREASE THE VOLUME ON OUR EEL MATING CALL!

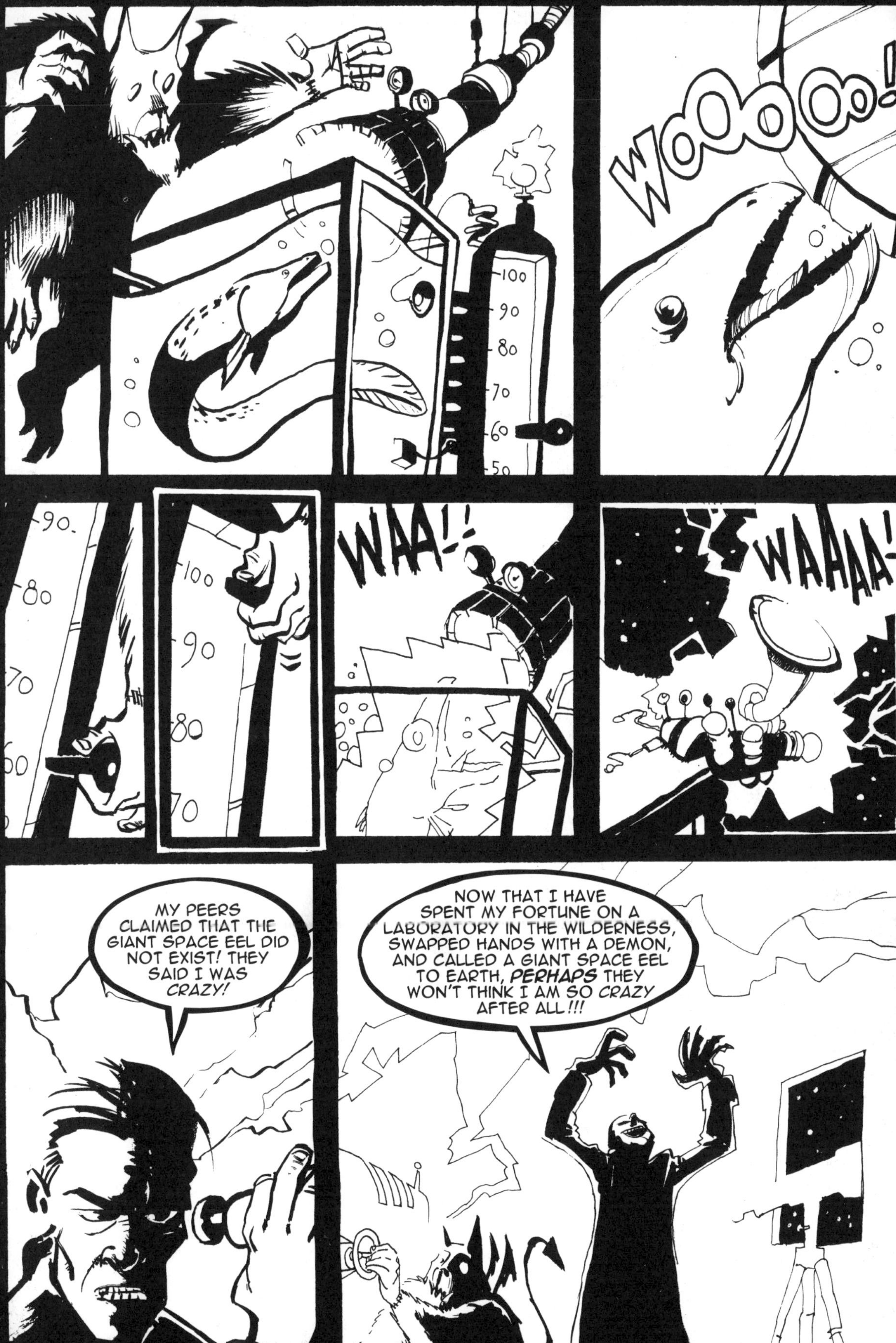
100
90
80
70
60
50
WOOOOO!
90
80
70
60
100
90
80
70
WAA!!
WAAAA!
MY PEERS CLAIMED THAT THE GIANT SPACE EEL DID NOT EXIST! THEY SAID I WAS CRAZY!
NOW THAT I HAVE SPENT MY FORTUNE ON A LABORATORY IN THE WILDERNESS, SWAPPED HANDS WITH A DEMON, AND CALLED A GIANT SPACE EEL TO EARTH, PERHAPS THEY WON'T THINK I AM SO CRAZY AFTER ALL!!!

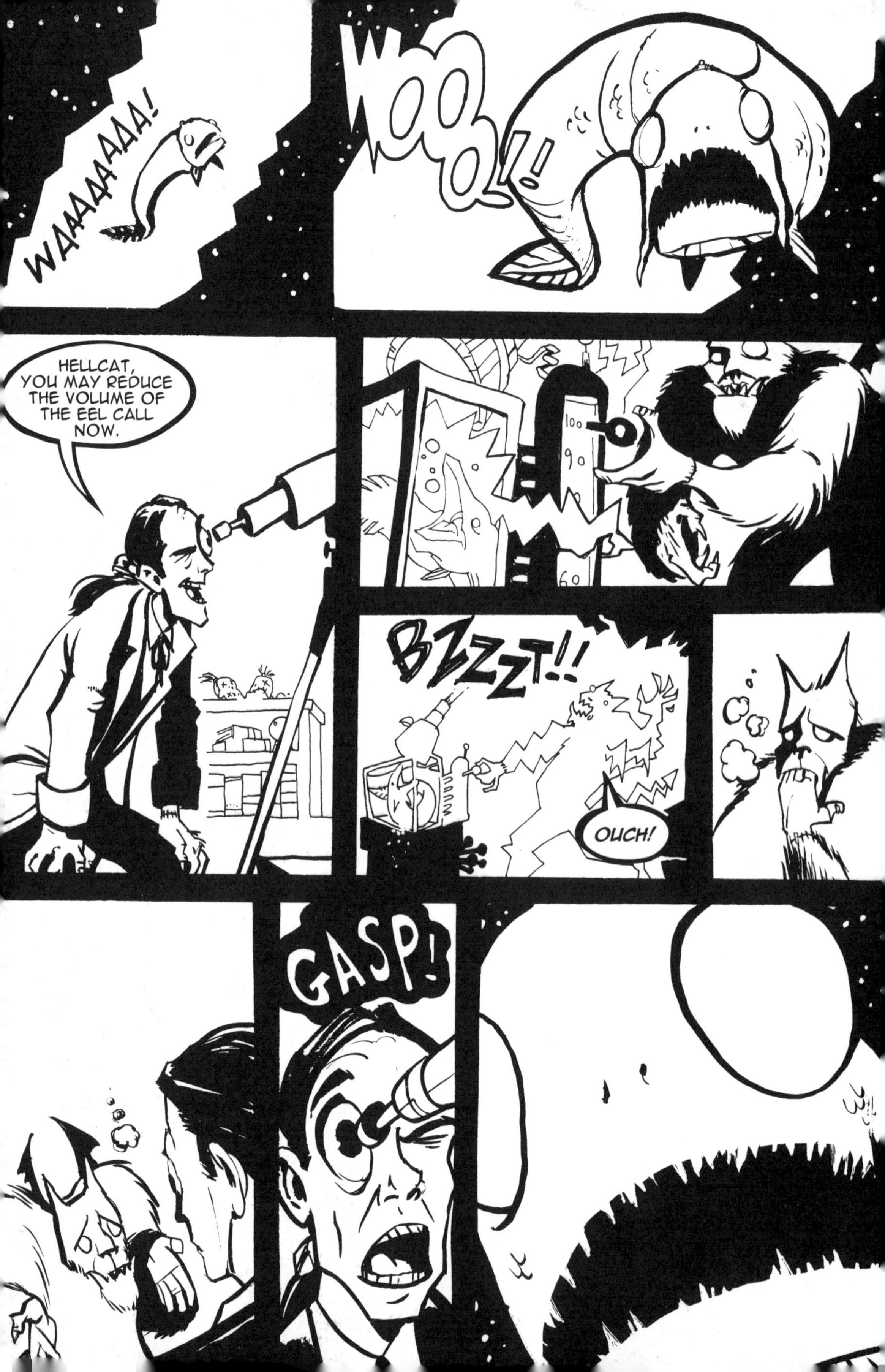
WAAAAAAAA!
WOOO!!
HELLCAT, YOU MAY REDUCE THE VOLUME OF THE EEL CALL NOW.
BZZZT!!
OUCH!
GASP!

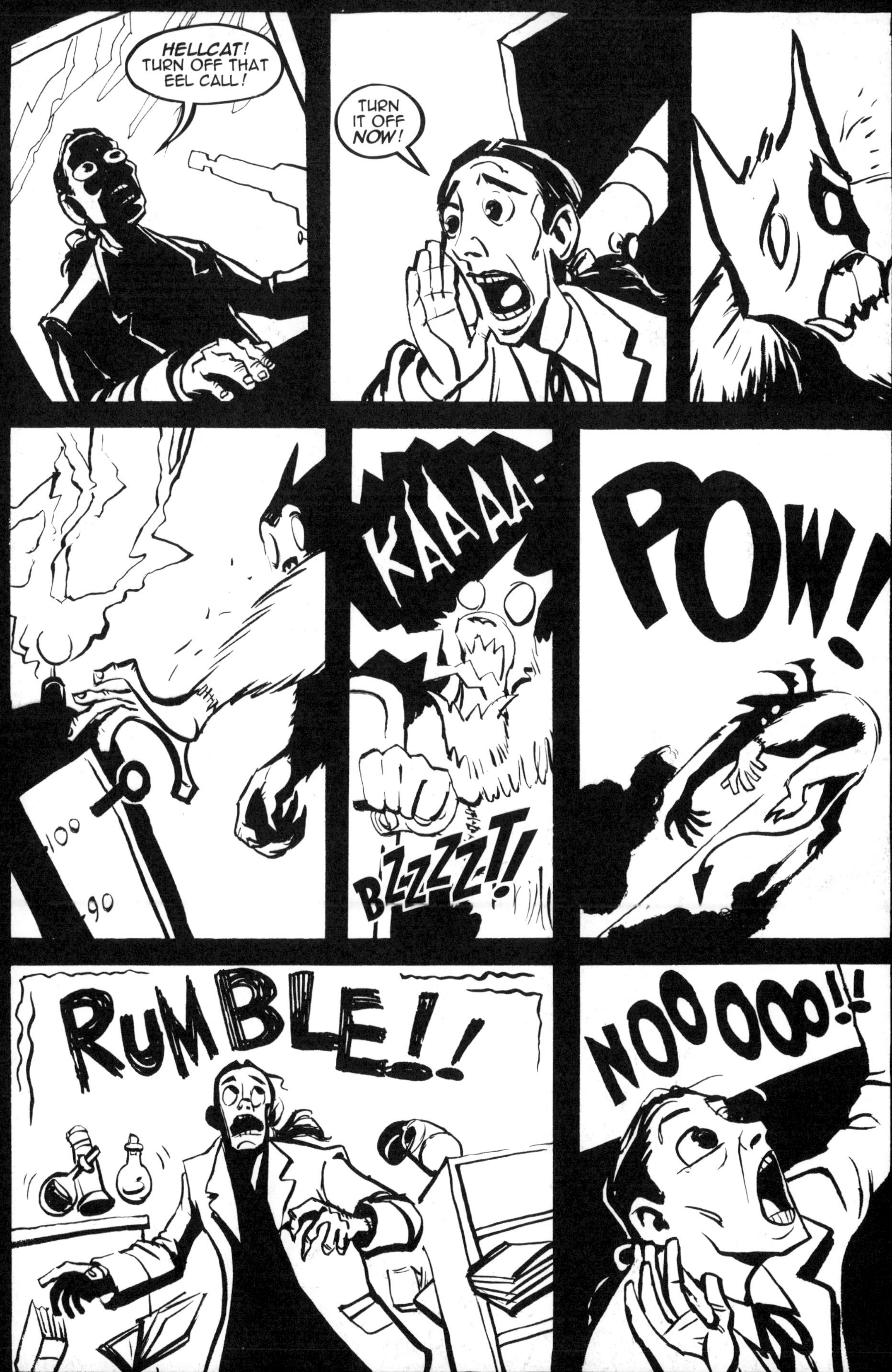
HELLCAT! TURN OFF THAT EEL CALL!
TURN IT OFF NOW!
KAAAA-
BZZZZT!!
POW!!
RUMBLE!!
NOOOOO!!!

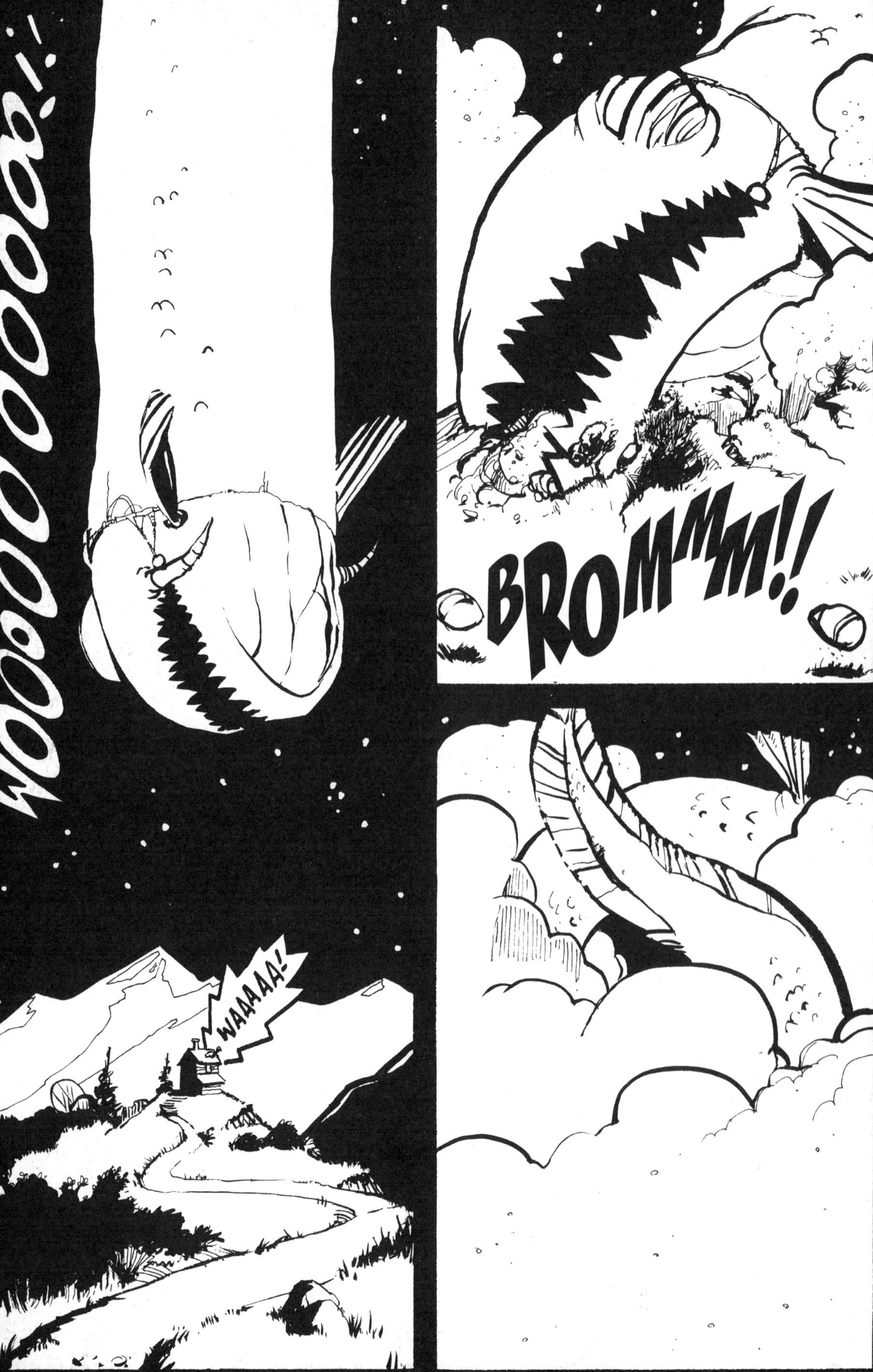
WAAAAA!
BROMMMM!!

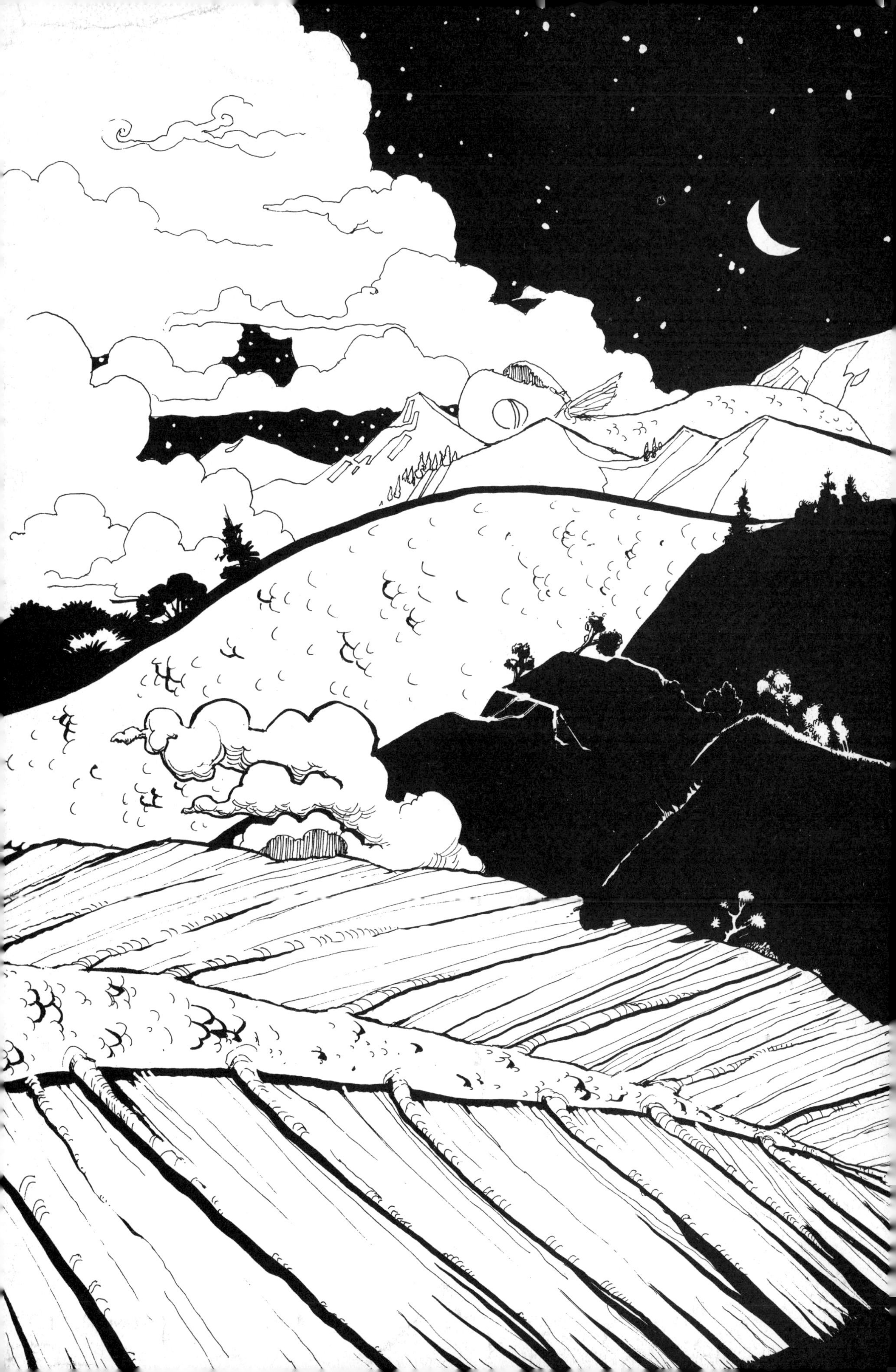

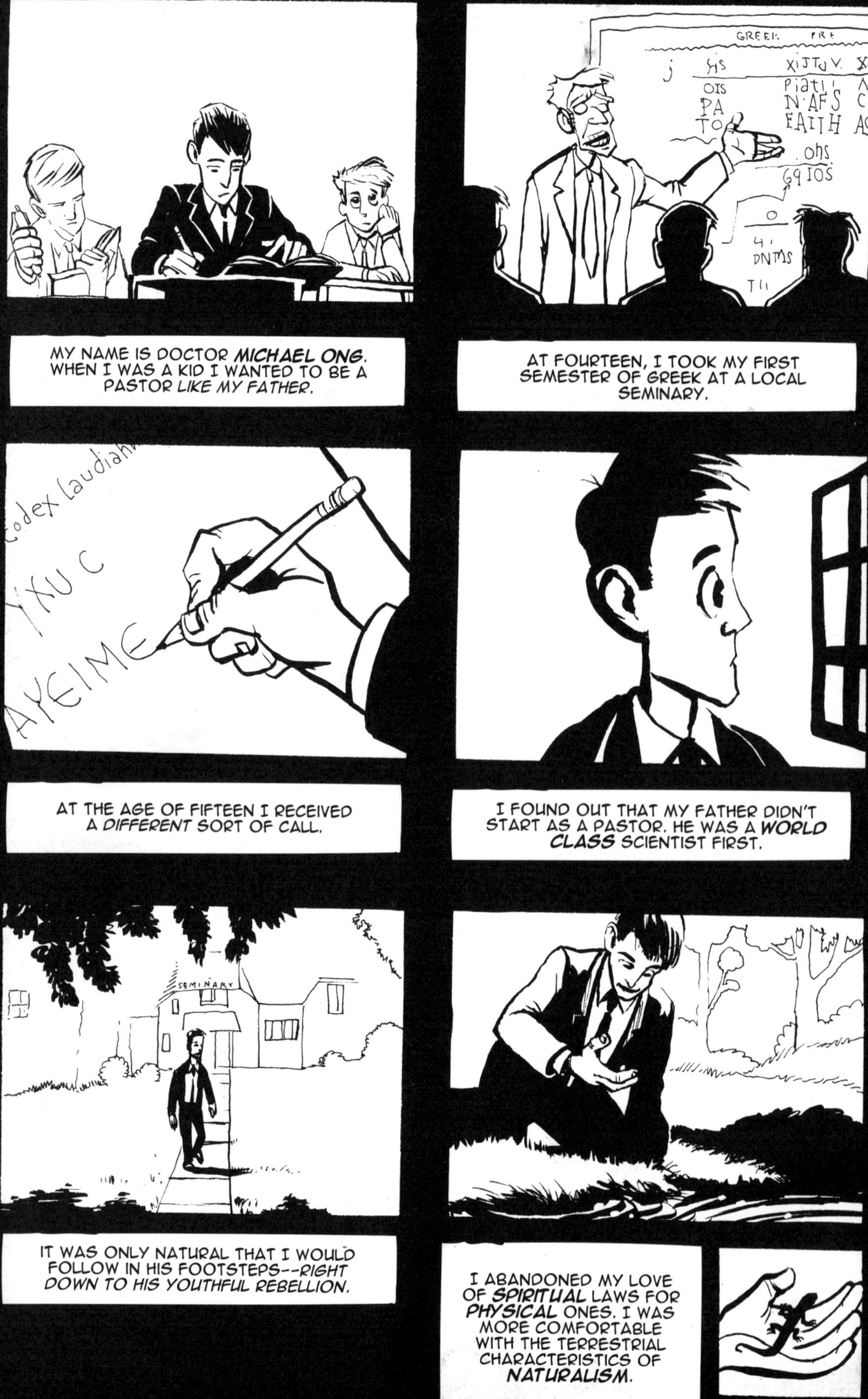
MY NAME IS DOCTOR MICHAEL ONG. WHEN I WAS A KID I WANTED TO BE A PASTOR LIKE MY FATHER.
AT FOURTEEN, I TOOK MY FIRST SEMESTER OF GREEK AT A LOCAL SEMINARY.
AT THE AGE OF FIFTEEN I RECEIVED A DIFFERENT SORT OF CALL.
I FOUND OUT THAT MY FATHER DIDN'T START AS A PASTOR. HE WAS A WORLD CLASS SCIENTIST FIRST.
SEMINARY
IT WAS ONLY NATURAL THAT I WOULD FOLLOW IN HIS FOOTSTEPS--RIGHT DOWN TO HIS YOUTHFUL REBELLION.
I ABANDONED MY LOVE OF SPIRITUAL LAWS FOR PHYSICAL ONES. I WAS MORE COMFORTABLE WITH THE TERRESTRIAL CHARACTERISTICS OF NATURALISM.

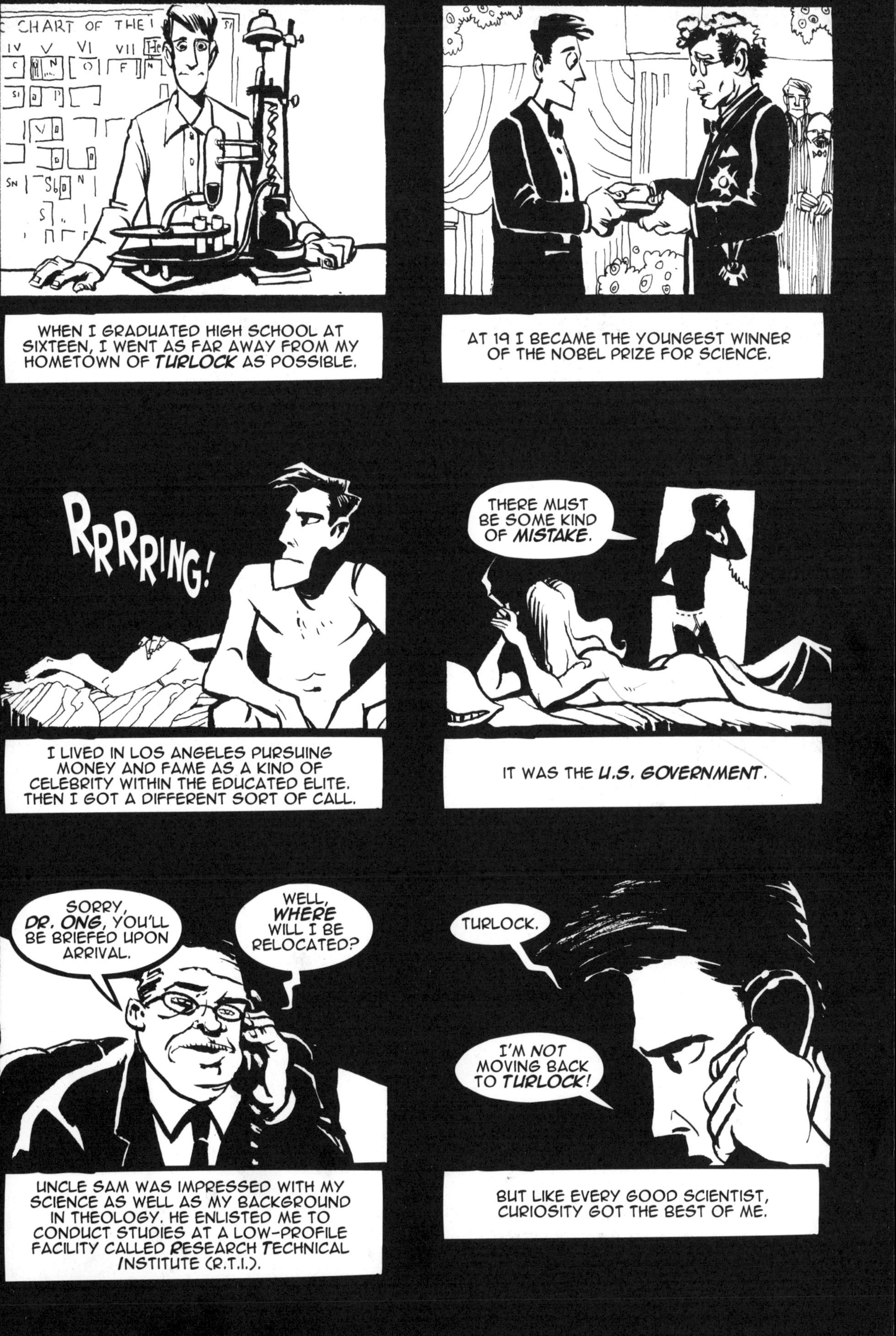
CHART OF THE
WHEN I GRADUATED HIGH SCHOOL AT SIXTEEN, I WENT AS FAR AWAY FROM MY HOMETOWN OF *TURLOCK* AS POSSIBLE.
AT 19 I BECAME THE YOUNGEST WINNER OF THE NOBEL PRIZE FOR SCIENCE.
RRRRING!
I LIVED IN LOS ANGELES PURSUING MONEY AND FAME AS A KIND OF CELEBRITY WITHIN THE EDUCATED ELITE. THEN I GOT A DIFFERENT SORT OF CALL.
THERE MUST BE SOME KIND OF *MISTAKE*.
IT WAS THE *U.S. GOVERNMENT*.
SORRY, *DR. ONG*, YOU'LL BE BRIEFED UPON ARRIVAL.
WELL, *WHERE* WILL I BE RELOCATED?
UNCLE SAM WAS IMPRESSED WITH MY SCIENCE AS WELL AS MY BACKGROUND IN THEOLOGY. HE ENLISTED ME TO CONDUCT STUDIES AT A LOW-PROFILE FACILITY CALLED *R*ESEARCH *T*ECHNICAL *I*NSTITUTE (R.T.I.).
TURLOCK.
I'M *NOT* MOVING BACK TO *TURLOCK*!
BUT LIKE EVERY GOOD SCIENTIST, CURIOSITY GOT THE BEST OF ME.

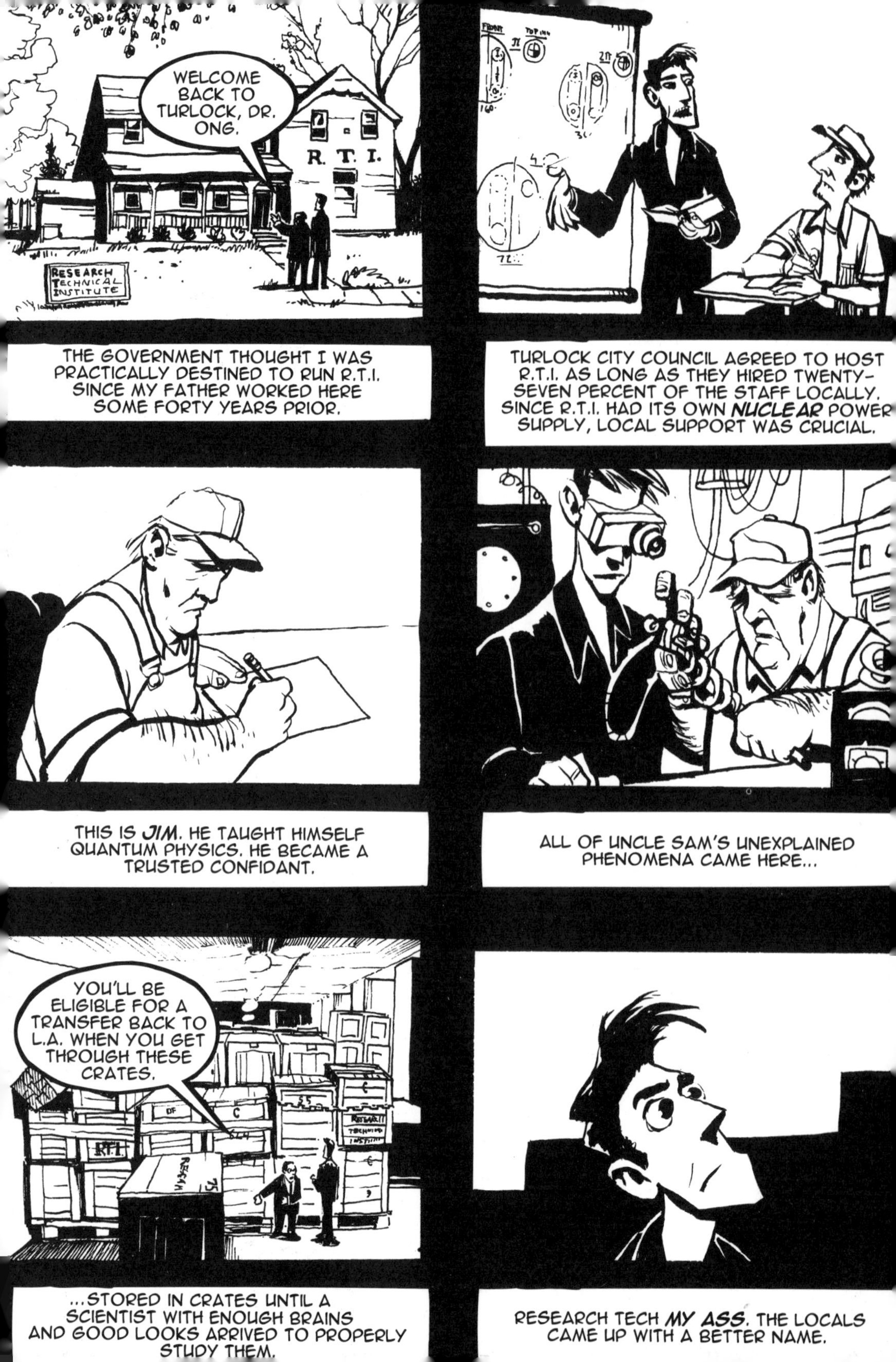
WELCOME BACK TO TURLOCK, DR. ONG.
R. T. I.
RESEARCH TECHNICAL INSTITUTE
THE GOVERNMENT THOUGHT I WAS PRACTICALLY DESTINED TO RUN R.T.I. SINCE MY FATHER WORKED HERE SOME FORTY YEARS PRIOR.
TURLOCK CITY COUNCIL AGREED TO HOST R.T.I. AS LONG AS THEY HIRED TWENTY-SEVEN PERCENT OF THE STAFF LOCALLY. SINCE R.T.I. HAD ITS OWN *NUCLEAR* POWER SUPPLY, LOCAL SUPPORT WAS CRUCIAL.
THIS IS *JIM*. HE TAUGHT HIMSELF QUANTUM PHYSICS. HE BECAME A TRUSTED CONFIDANT.
ALL OF UNCLE SAM'S UNEXPLAINED PHENOMENA CAME HERE...
YOU'LL BE ELIGIBLE FOR A TRANSFER BACK TO L.A. WHEN YOU GET THROUGH THESE CRATES.
RTI
...STORED IN CRATES UNTIL A SCIENTIST WITH ENOUGH BRAINS AND GOOD LOOKS ARRIVED TO PROPERLY STUDY THEM.
RESEARCH TECH *MY ASS*. THE LOCALS CAME UP WITH A BETTER NAME.

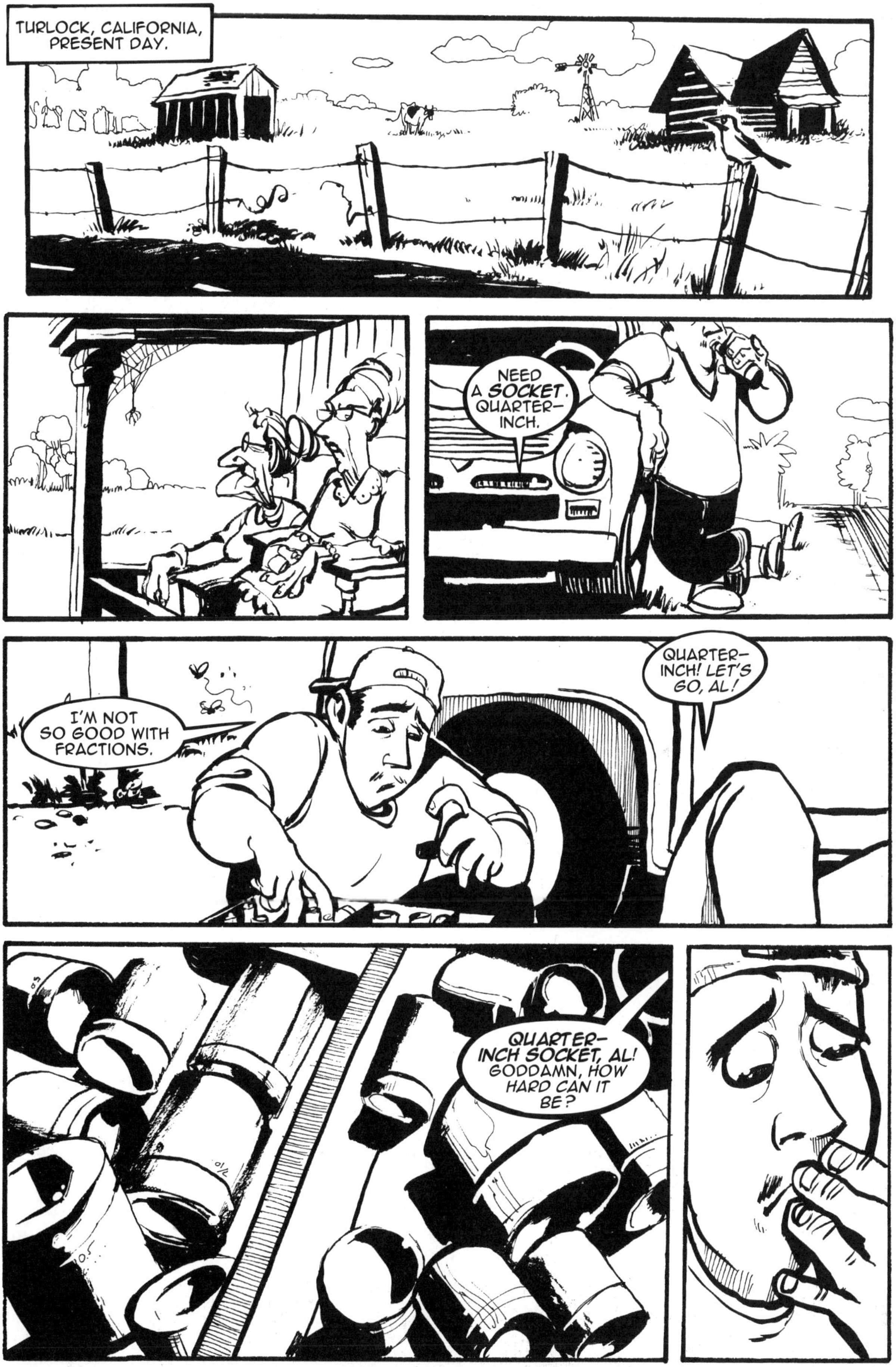
TURLOCK, CALIFORNIA, PRESENT DAY.
NEED A SOCKET. QUARTER-INCH.
I'M NOT SO GOOD WITH FRACTIONS.
QUARTER-INCH! LET'S GO, AL!
QUARTER-INCH SOCKET, AL! GODDAMN, HOW HARD CAN IT BE?

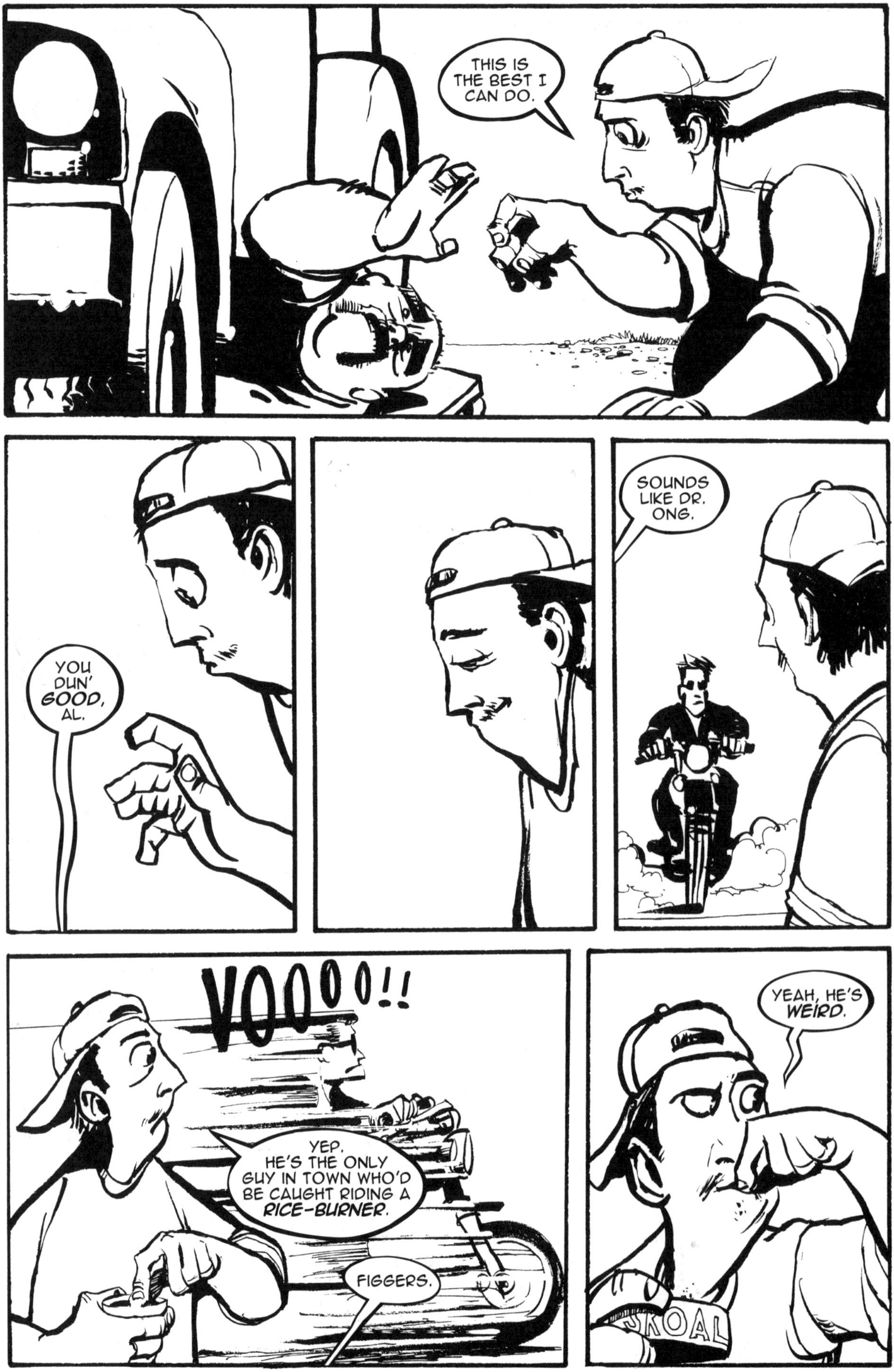
THIS IS THE BEST I CAN DO.
YOU DUN' GOOD, AL.
SOUNDS LIKE DR. ONG.
VOOOO!!
YEP. HE'S THE ONLY GUY IN TOWN WHO'D BE CAUGHT RIDING A RICE-BURNER.
FIGGERS.
YEAH, HE'S WEIRD.
SKOAL

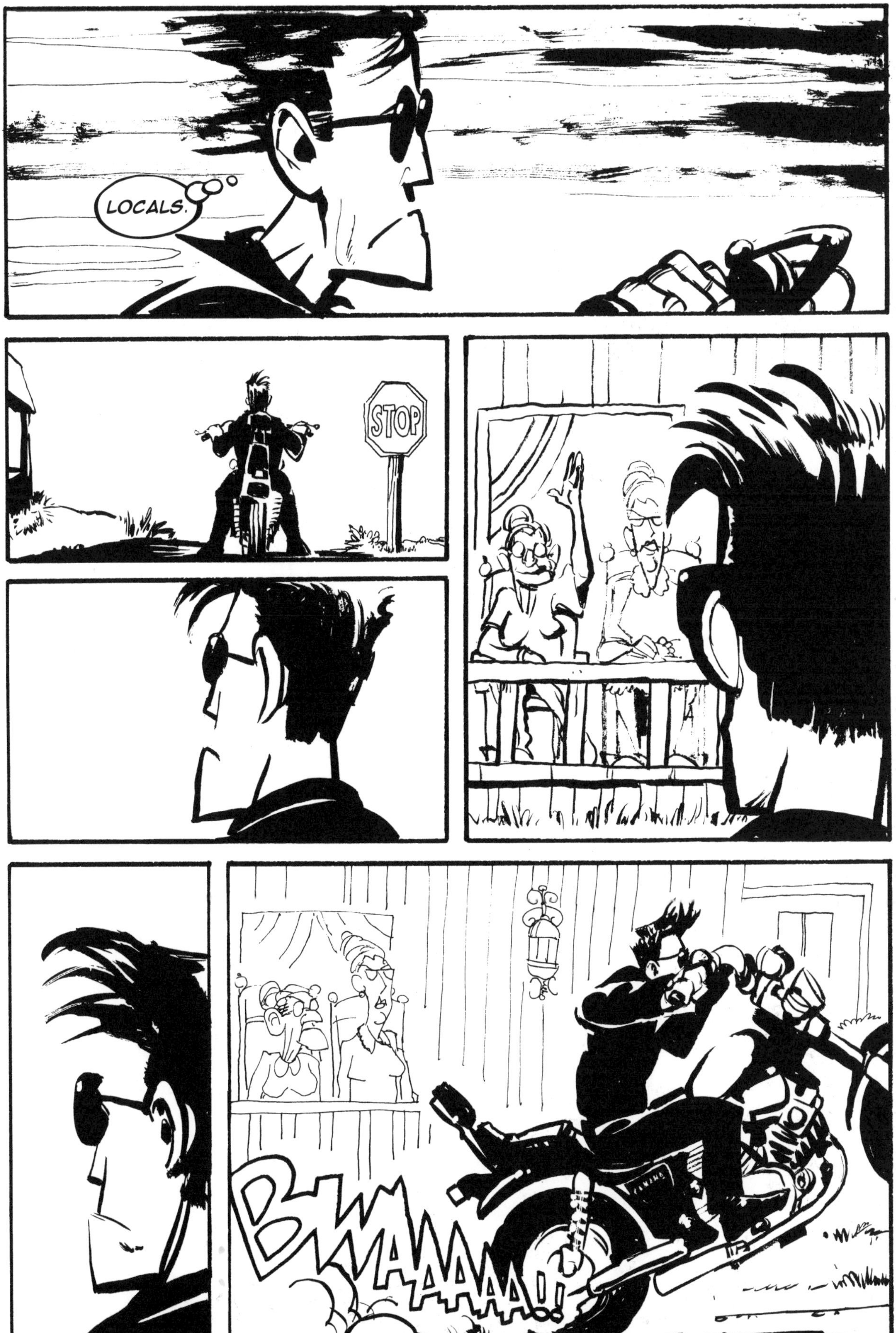
LOCALS.
STOP
BWAAAAAA!!

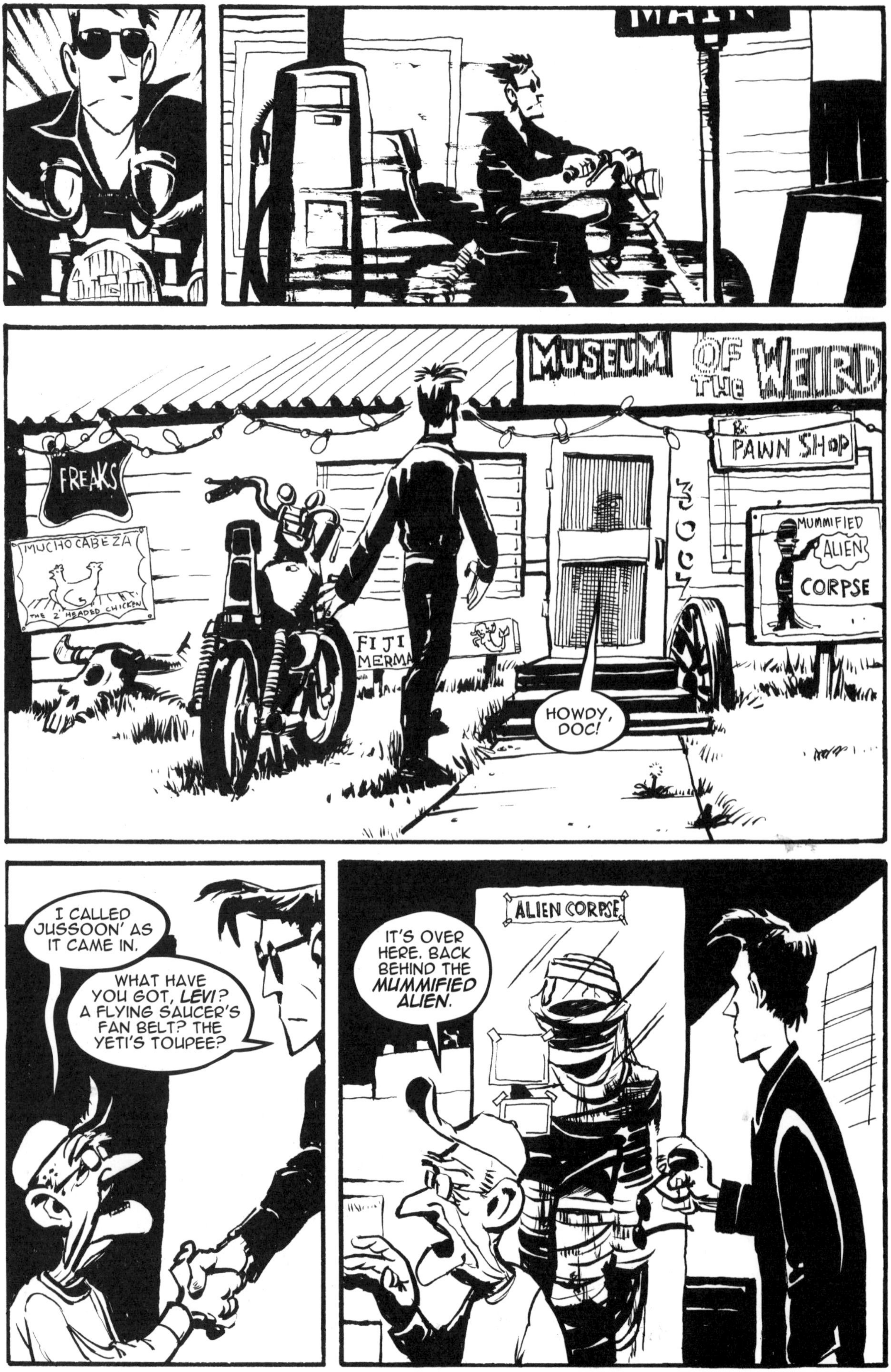

MUSEUM OF THE WEIRD
FREAKS
PAWN SHOP
MUCHO CABEZA
THE 2 HEADED CHICKEN
MUMMIFIED ALIEN CORPSE
FIJI MERMA
HOWDY, DOC!
I CALLED JUSSOON' AS IT CAME IN.
WHAT HAVE YOU GOT, *LEVI*? A FLYING SAUCER'S FAN BELT? THE YETI'S TOUPEE?
ALIEN CORPSE
IT'S OVER HERE. BACK BEHIND THE *MUMMIFIED ALIEN*.

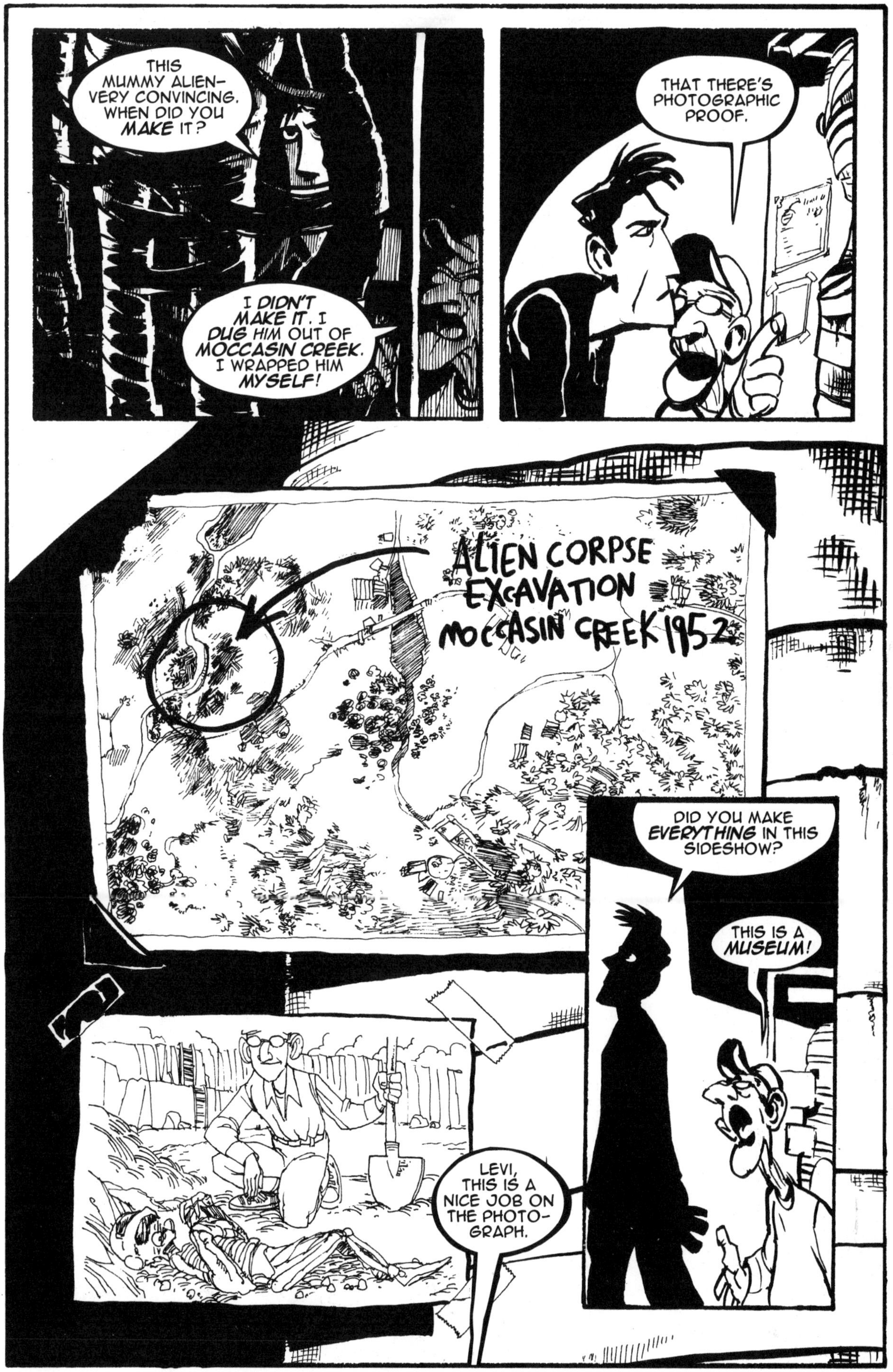
THIS MUMMY ALIEN— VERY CONVINCING. WHEN DID YOU MAKE IT?
I DIDN'T MAKE IT. I DUG HIM OUT OF MOCCASIN CREEK. I WRAPPED HIM MYSELF!
THAT THERE'S PHOTOGRAPHIC PROOF.
ALIEN CORPSE EXCAVATION MOCCASIN CREEK 1952
DID YOU MAKE EVERYTHING IN THIS SIDESHOW?
THIS IS A MUSEUM!
LEVI, THIS IS A NICE JOB ON THE PHOTOGRAPH.

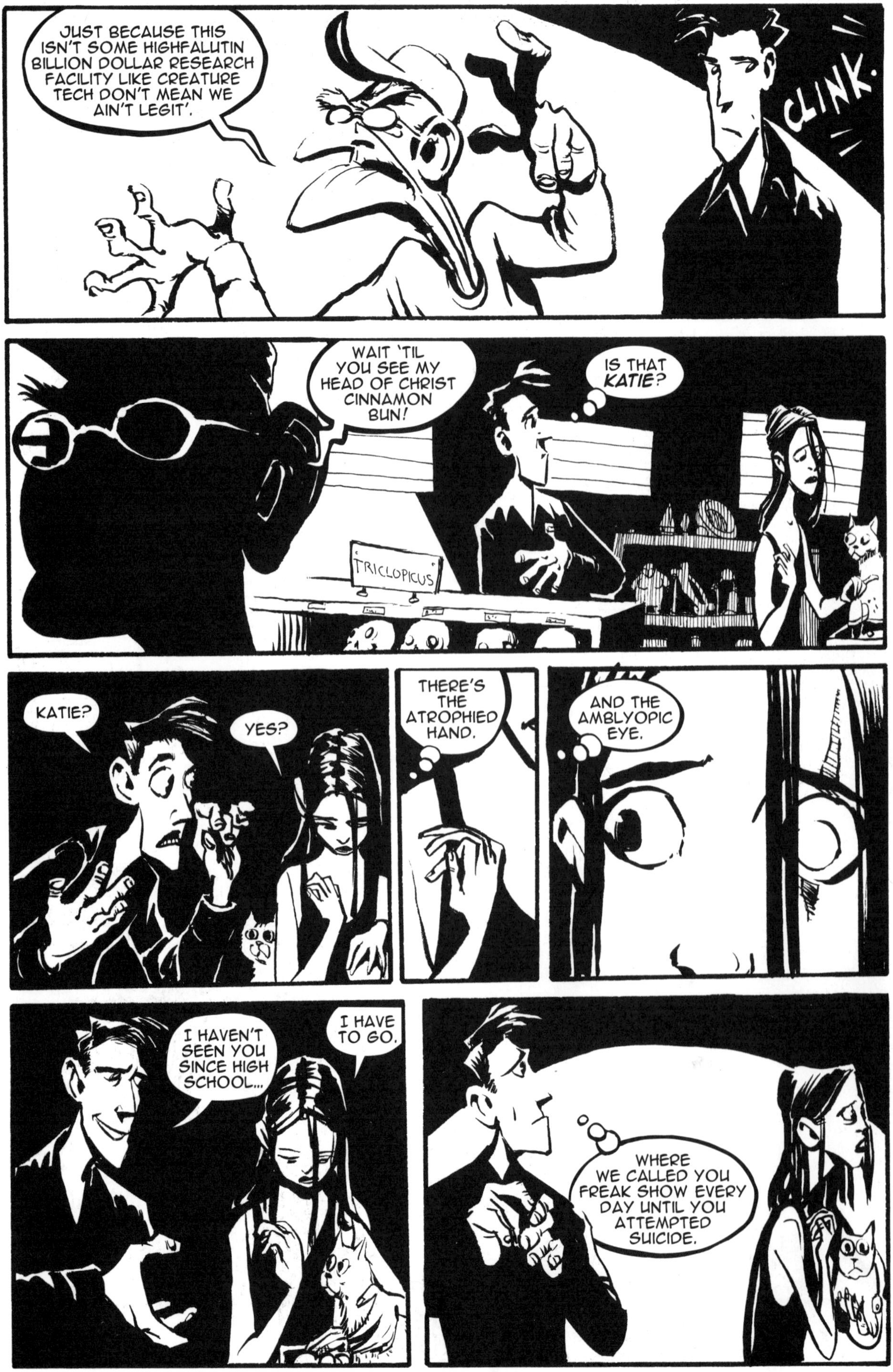
JUST BECAUSE THIS ISN'T SOME HIGHFALUTIN BILLION DOLLAR RESEARCH FACILITY LIKE CREATURE TECH DON'T MEAN WE AIN'T LEGIT'.
CLINK.
WAIT 'TIL YOU SEE MY HEAD OF CHRIST CINNAMON BUN!
IS THAT *KATIE*?
TRICLOPICUS
KATIE?
YES?
THERE'S THE ATROPHIED HAND.
AND THE AMBLYOPIC EYE.
I HAVEN'T SEEN YOU SINCE HIGH SCHOOL...
I HAVE TO GO.
WHERE WE CALLED YOU FREAK SHOW EVERY DAY UNTIL YOU ATTEMPTED SUICIDE.

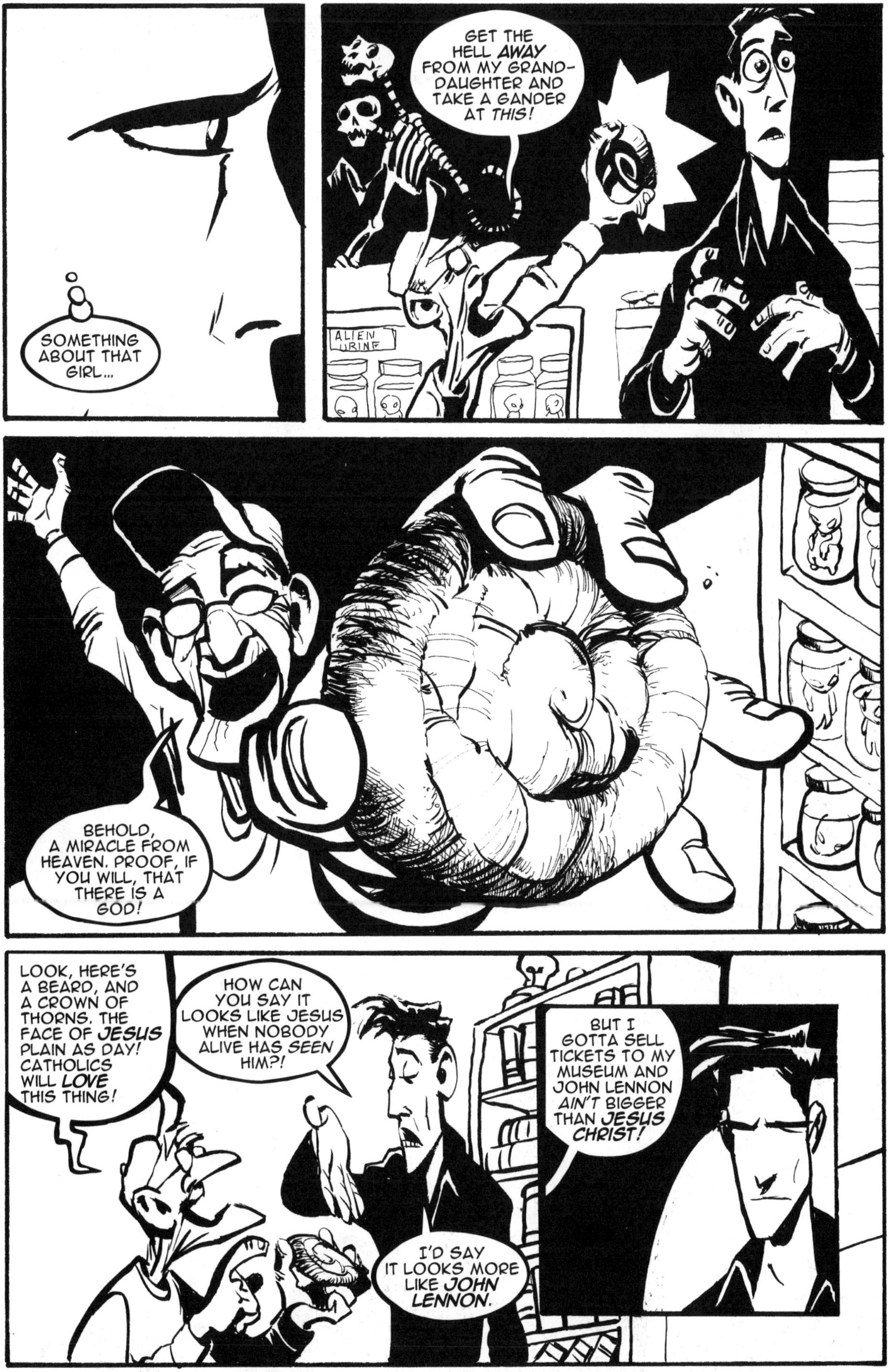

SOMETHING ABOUT THAT GIRL...
GET THE HELL AWAY FROM MY GRAND-DAUGHTER AND TAKE A GANDER AT THIS!
ALIEN URINE
BEHOLD, A MIRACLE FROM HEAVEN. PROOF, IF YOU WILL, THAT THERE IS A GOD!
LOOK, HERE'S A BEARD, AND A CROWN OF THORNS. THE FACE OF JESUS PLAIN AS DAY! CATHOLICS WILL LOVE THIS THING!
HOW CAN YOU SAY IT LOOKS LIKE JESUS WHEN NOBODY ALIVE HAS SEEN HIM?!
I'D SAY IT LOOKS MORE LIKE JOHN LENNON.
BUT I GOTTA SELL TICKETS TO MY MUSEUM AND JOHN LENNON AIN'T BIGGER THAN JESUS CHRIST!

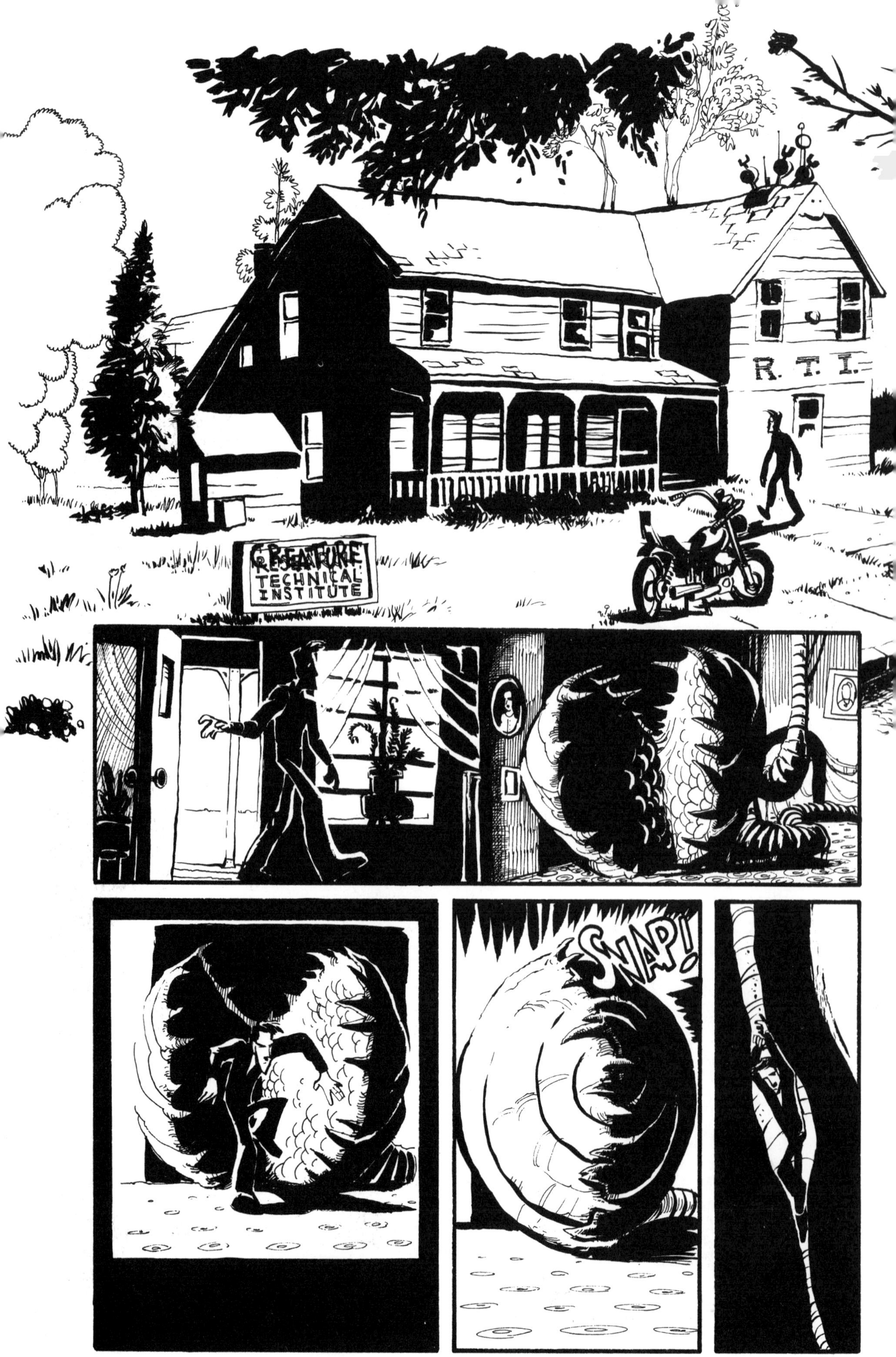

R. T. I.
CREATURE
RESEARCH
TECHNICAL
INSTITUTE
SNAP!

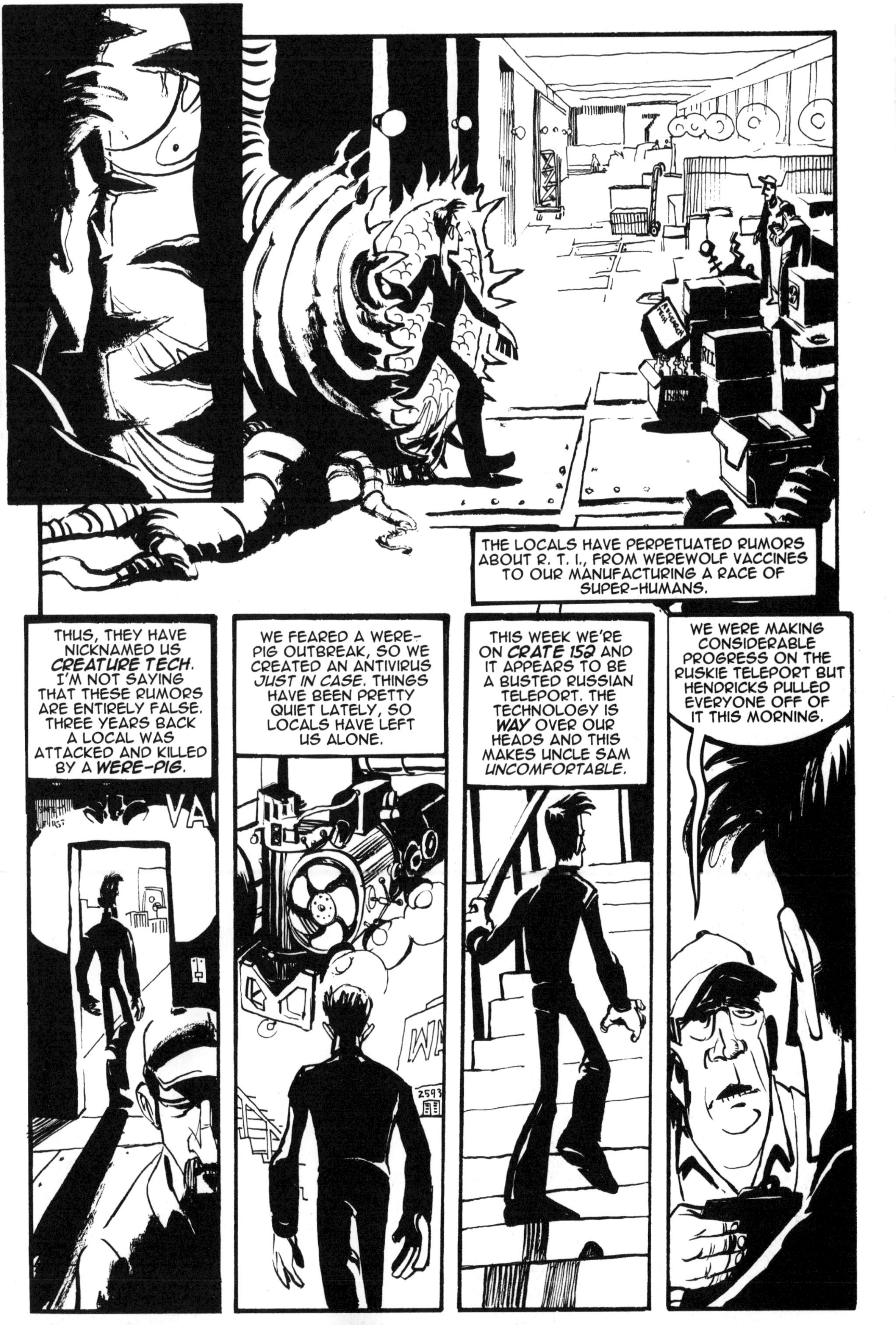
THE LOCALS HAVE PERPETUATED RUMORS ABOUT R. T. I., FROM WEREWOLF VACCINES TO OUR MANUFACTURING A RACE OF SUPER-HUMANS.
THUS, THEY HAVE NICKNAMED US CREATURE TECH. I'M NOT SAYING THAT THESE RUMORS ARE ENTIRELY FALSE. THREE YEARS BACK A LOCAL WAS ATTACKED AND KILLED BY A WERE-PIG.
WE FEARED A WERE-PIG OUTBREAK, SO WE CREATED AN ANTIVIRUS JUST IN CASE. THINGS HAVE BEEN PRETTY QUIET LATELY, SO LOCALS HAVE LEFT US ALONE.
THIS WEEK WE'RE ON CRATE 152 AND IT APPEARS TO BE A BUSTED RUSSIAN TELEPORT. THE TECHNOLOGY IS WAY OVER OUR HEADS AND THIS MAKES UNCLE SAM UNCOMFORTABLE.
WE WERE MAKING CONSIDERABLE PROGRESS ON THE RUSKIE TELEPORT BUT HENDRICKS PULLED EVERYONE OFF OF IT THIS MORNING.

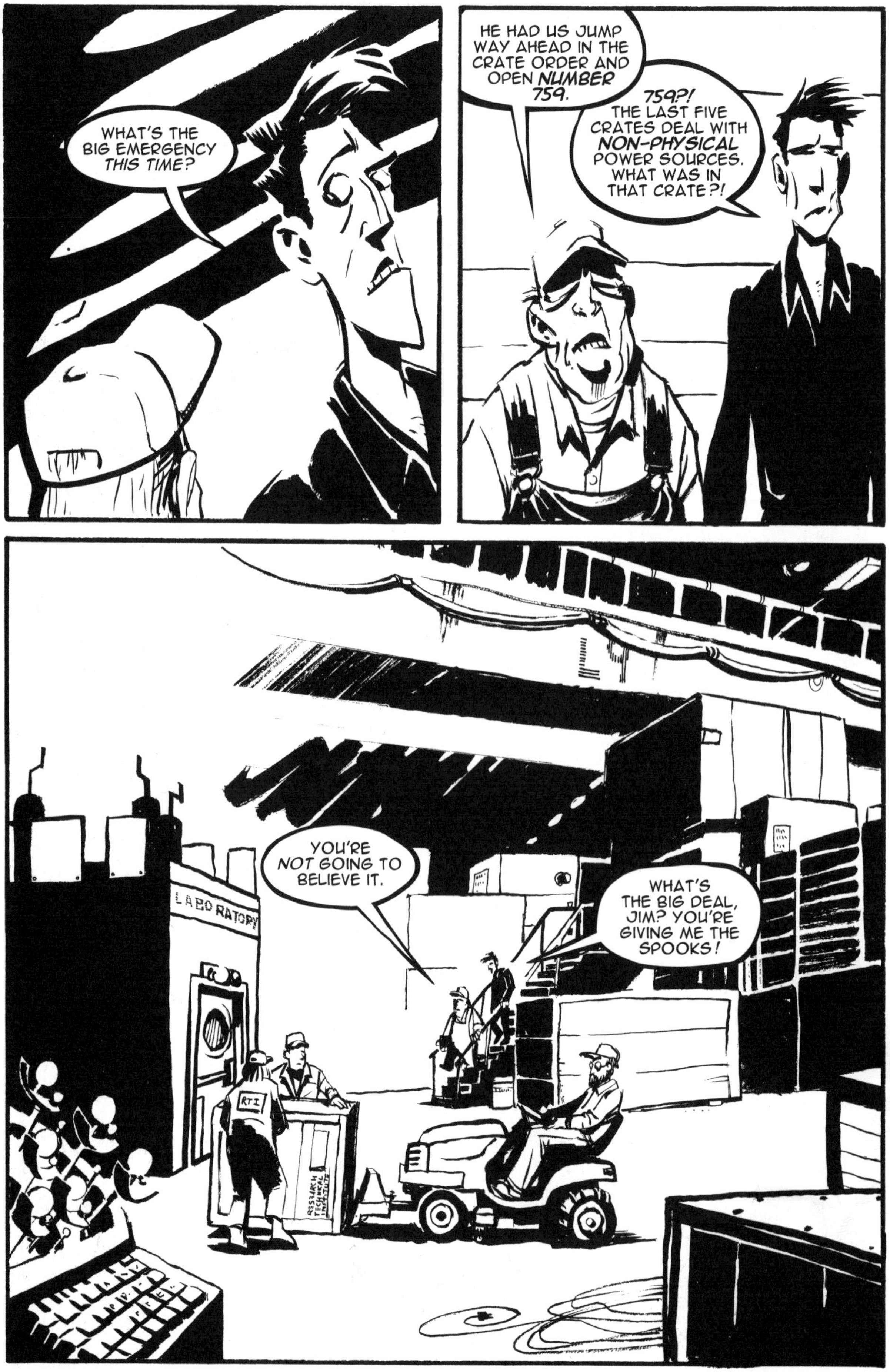
WHAT'S THE BIG EMERGENCY *THIS TIME?*
HE HAD US JUMP WAY AHEAD IN THE CRATE ORDER AND OPEN ***NUMBER* 759.**
759?! THE LAST FIVE CRATES DEAL WITH ***NON-PHYSICAL*** POWER SOURCES. WHAT WAS IN THAT CRATE?!
LABORATORY
RTI
YOU'RE *NOT* GOING TO BELIEVE IT.
WHAT'S THE BIG DEAL, JIM? YOU'RE GIVING ME THE SPOOKS!

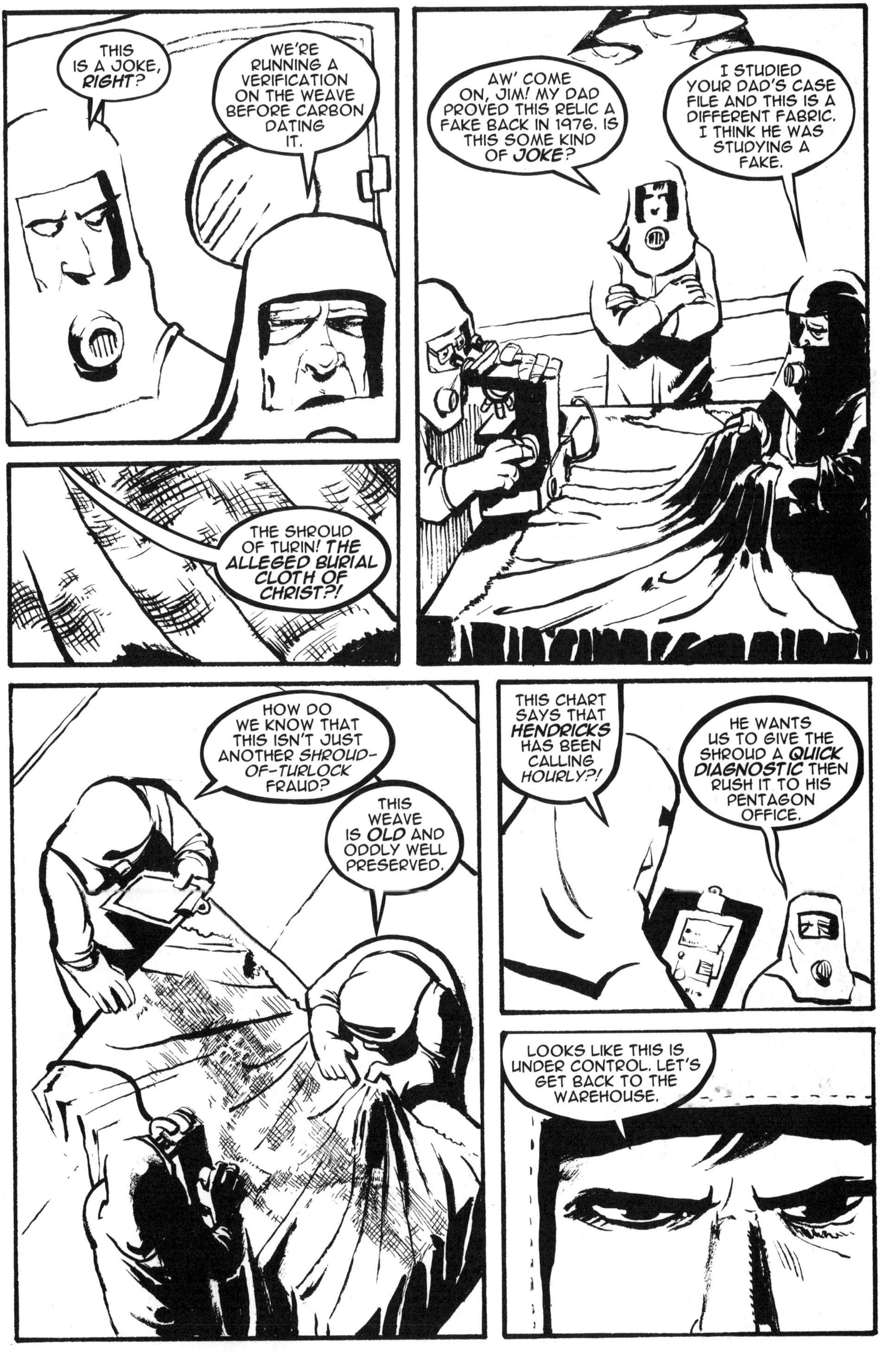

THIS IS A JOKE, RIGHT?
WE'RE RUNNING A VERIFICATION ON THE WEAVE BEFORE CARBON DATING IT.
THE SHROUD OF TURIN! THE ALLEGED BURIAL CLOTH OF CHRIST?!
AW' COME ON, JIM! MY DAD PROVED THIS RELIC A FAKE BACK IN 1976. IS THIS SOME KIND OF JOKE?
I STUDIED YOUR DAD'S CASE FILE AND THIS IS A DIFFERENT FABRIC. I THINK HE WAS STUDYING A FAKE.
HOW DO WE KNOW THAT THIS ISN'T JUST ANOTHER SHROUD-OF-TURLOCK FRAUD?
THIS WEAVE IS OLD AND ODDLY WELL PRESERVED.
THIS CHART SAYS THAT HENDRICKS HAS BEEN CALLING HOURLY?!
HE WANTS US TO GIVE THE SHROUD A QUICK DIAGNOSTIC THEN RUSH IT TO HIS PENTAGON OFFICE.
LOOKS LIKE THIS IS UNDER CONTROL. LET'S GET BACK TO THE WAREHOUSE.

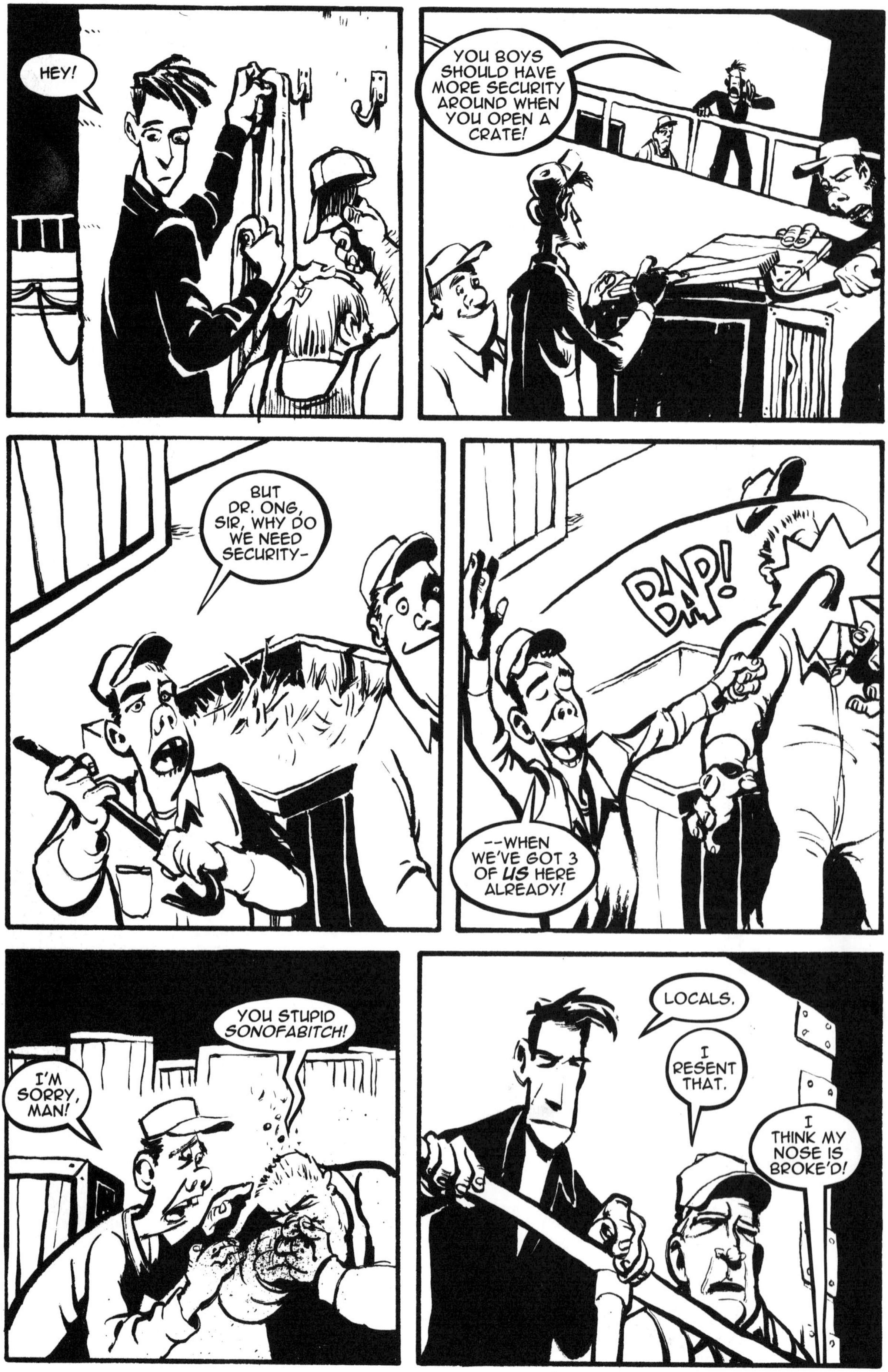
HEY!
YOU BOYS SHOULD HAVE MORE SECURITY AROUND WHEN YOU OPEN A CRATE!
BUT DR. ONG, SIR, WHY DO WE NEED SECURITY-
BAP!
--WHEN WE'VE GOT 3 OF *US* HERE ALREADY!
YOU STUPID SONOFABITCH!
I'M SORRY, MAN!
LOCALS.
I RESENT THAT.
I THINK MY NOSE IS BROKE'D!

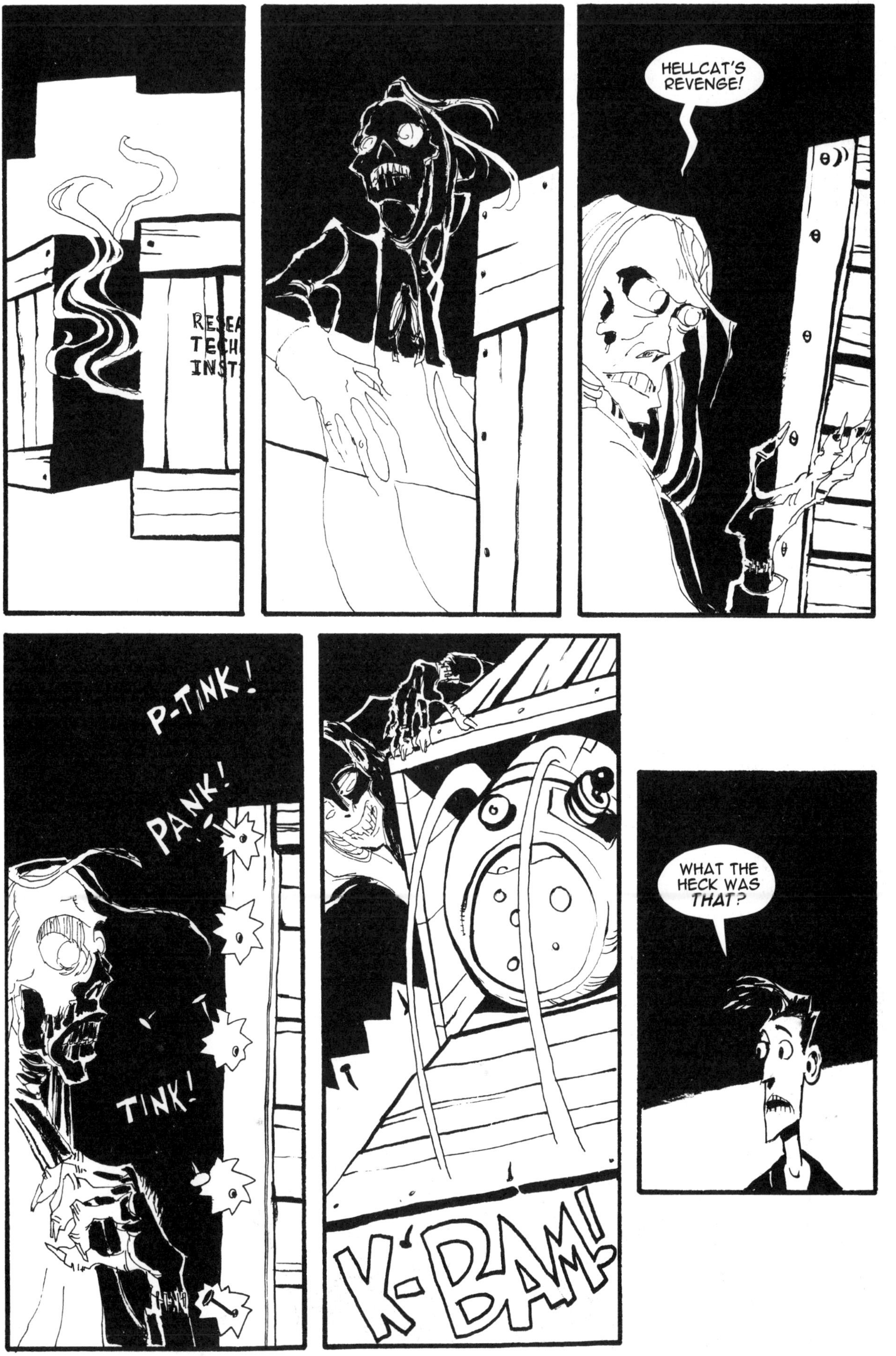
RESEA
TECH
INST
HELLCAT'S REVENGE!
P-TINK!
PANK!
TINK!
K-BAM!
WHAT THE HECK WAS *THAT*?

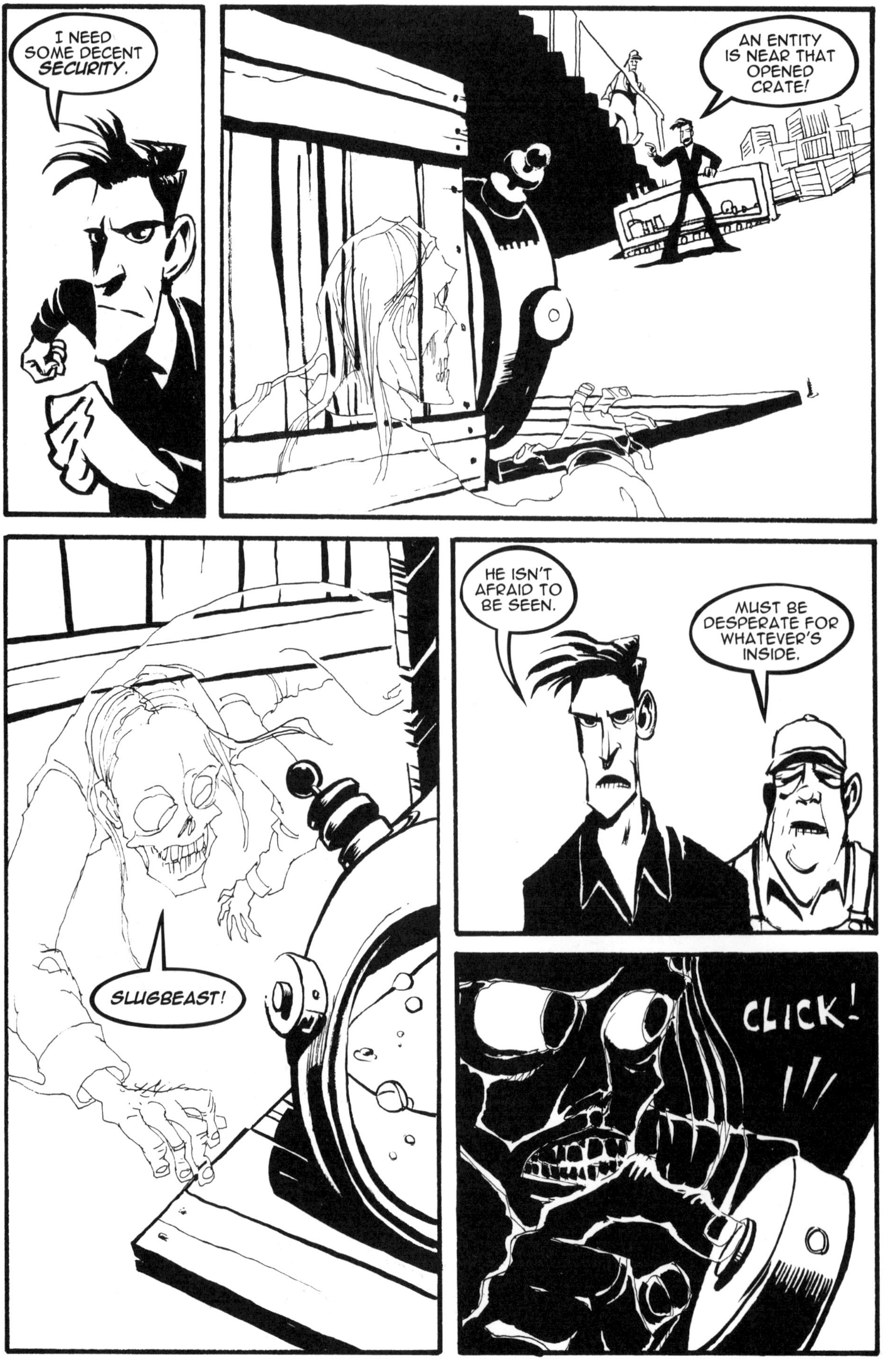
I NEED SOME DECENT SECURITY.
AN ENTITY IS NEAR THAT OPENED CRATE!
SLUGBEAST!
HE ISN'T AFRAID TO BE SEEN.
MUST BE DESPERATE FOR WHATEVER'S INSIDE.
CLICK!

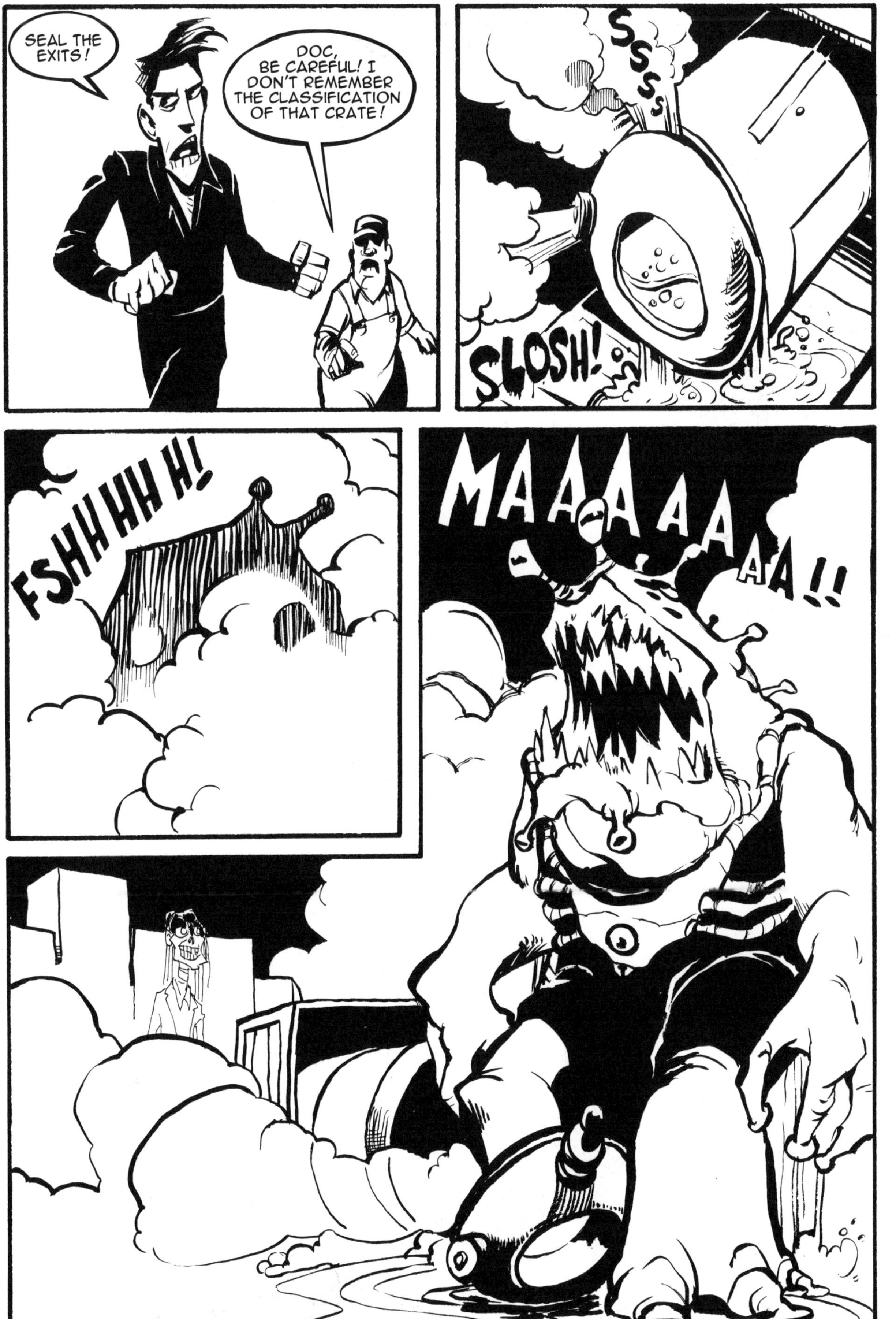
SEAL THE EXITS!
DOC, BE CAREFUL! I DON'T REMEMBER THE CLASSIFICATION OF THAT CRATE!
SSSS
SLOSH!
FSHHHH H!
MAAAAAAAA!!

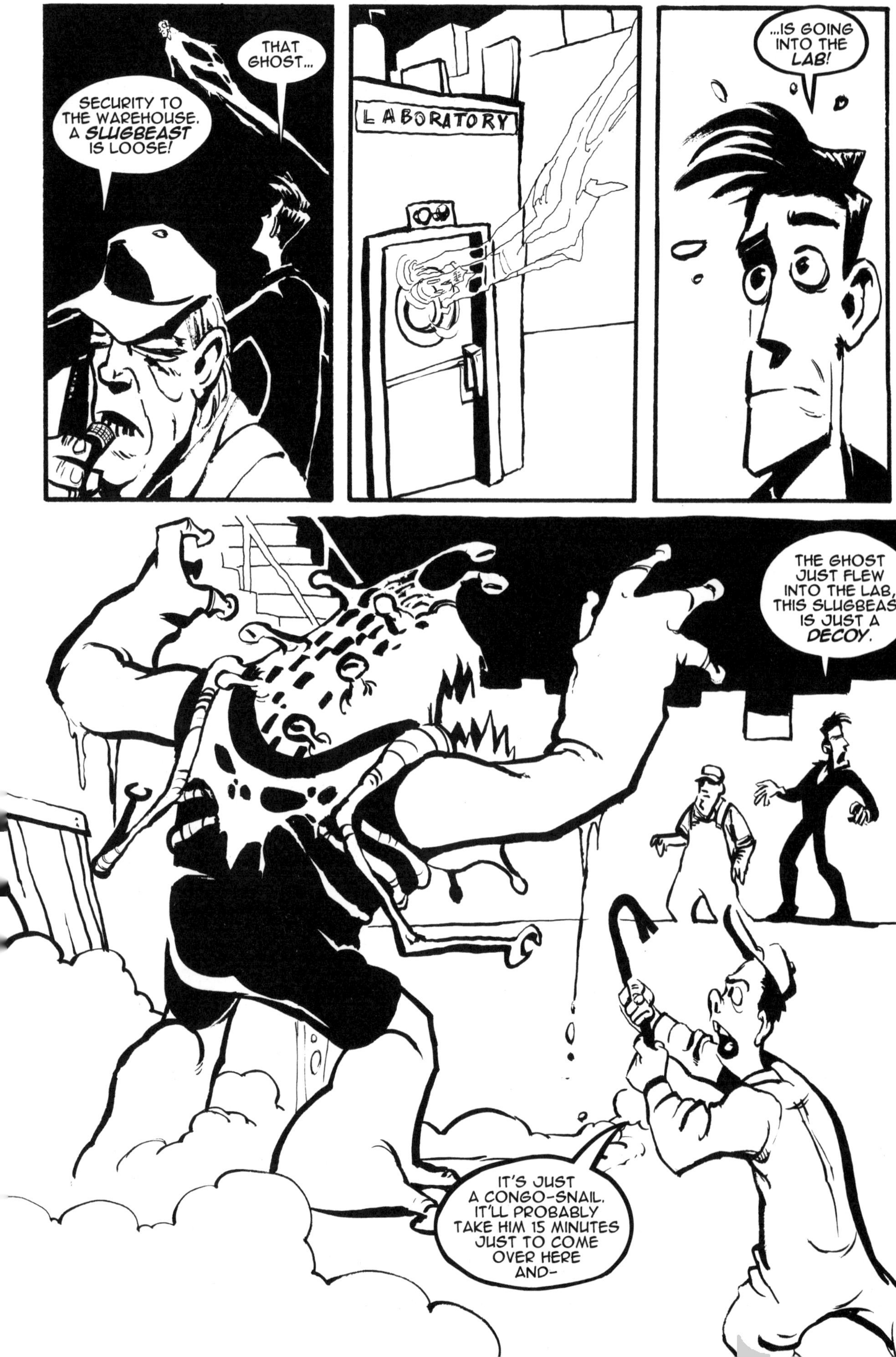
THAT GHOST...
SECURITY TO THE WAREHOUSE. A SLUGBEAST IS LOOSE!
LABORATORY
...IS GOING INTO THE LAB!
THE GHOST JUST FLEW INTO THE LAB, THIS SLUGBEAST IS JUST A DECOY.
IT'S JUST A CONGO-SNAIL. IT'LL PROBABLY TAKE HIM 15 MINUTES JUST TO COME OVER HERE AND-

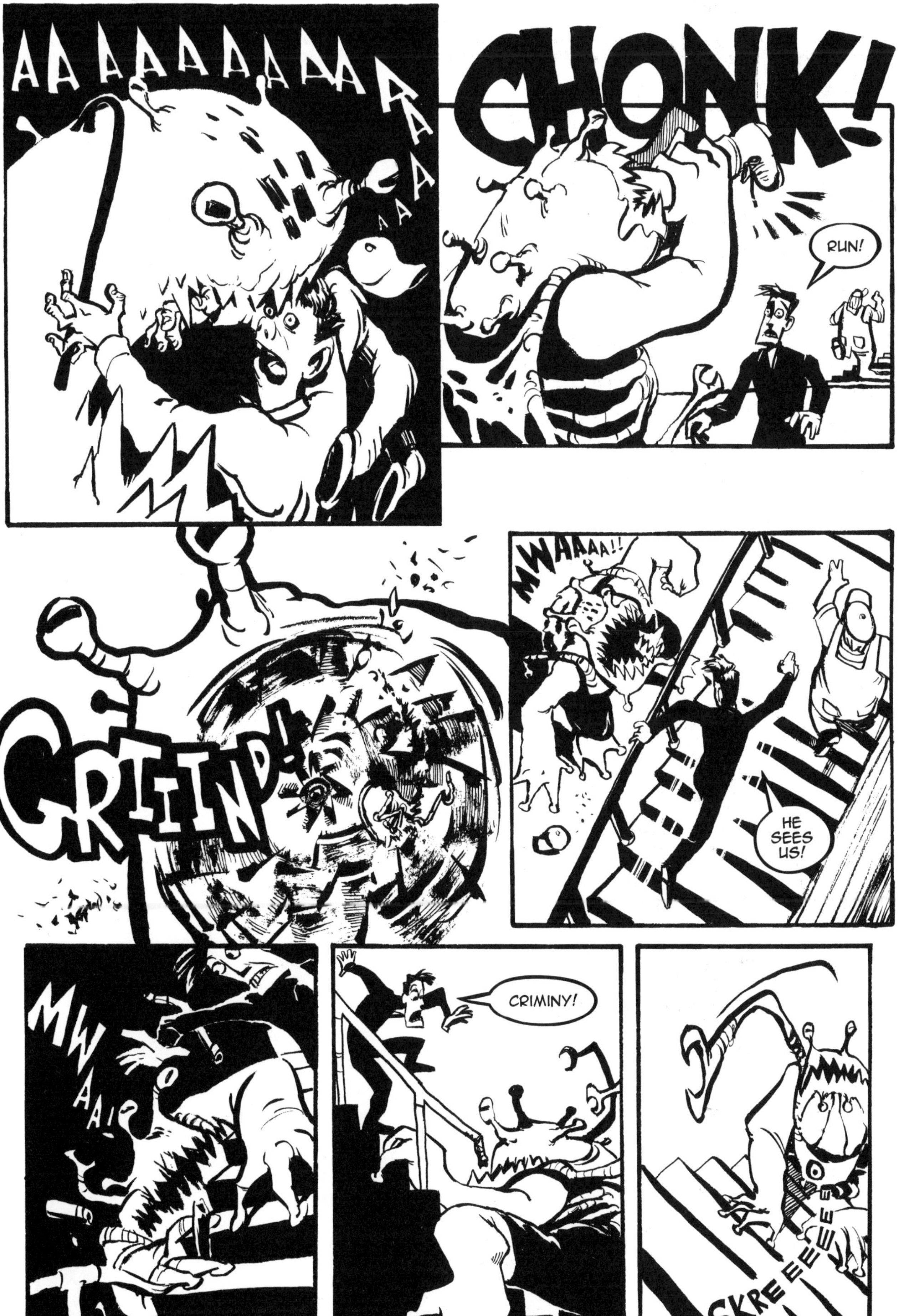
AAAAAAAAAAARAAAAA
CHONK!
RUN!
GRIIIND!
MWAAAA!!
HE SEES US!
MWAAA!
CRIMINY!
SKREEEEEEEEE

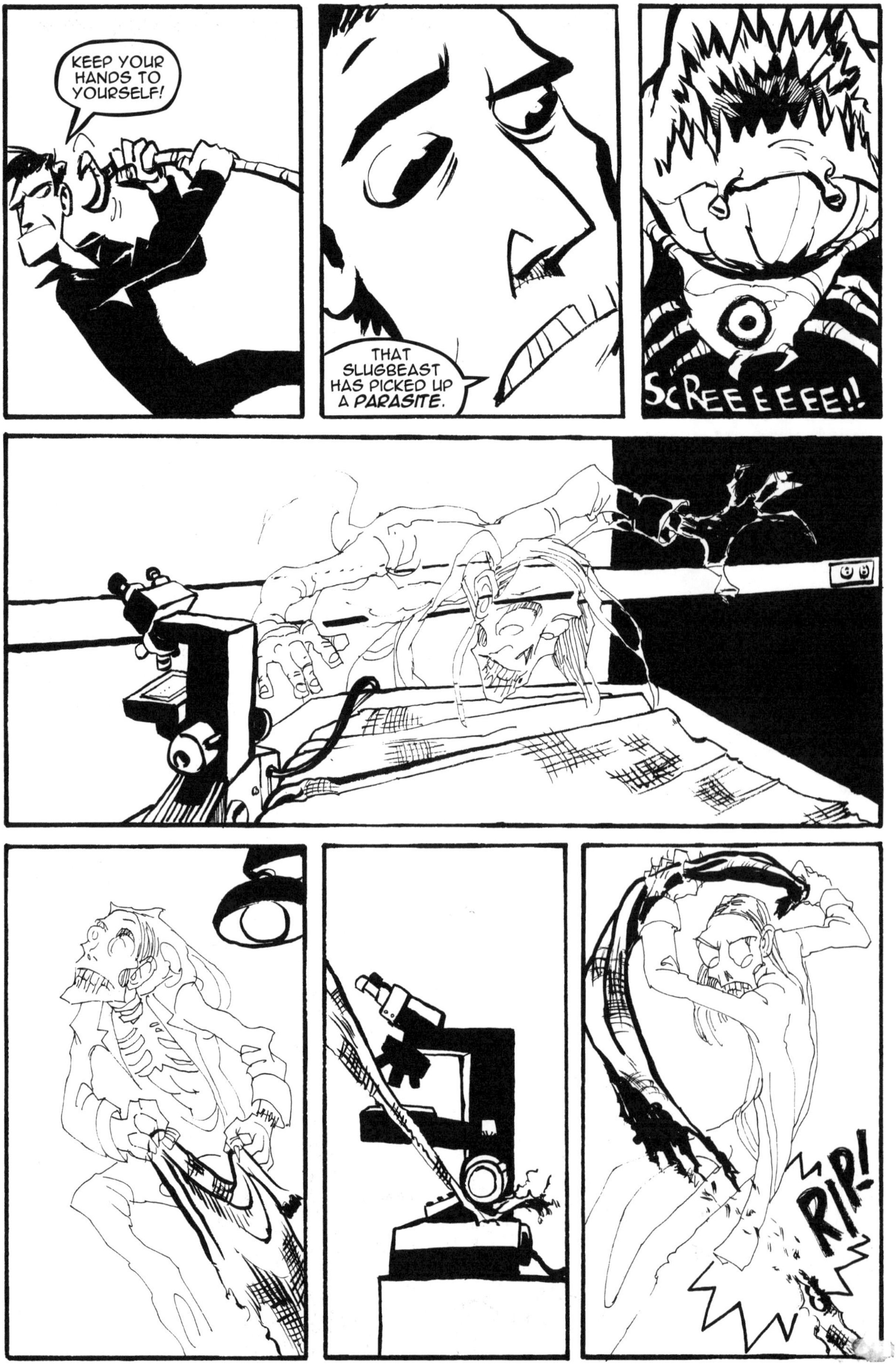

KEEP YOUR HANDS TO YOURSELF!
THAT SLUGBEAST HAS PICKED UP A *PARASITE*.
SCREEEEEEE!!
RIP!

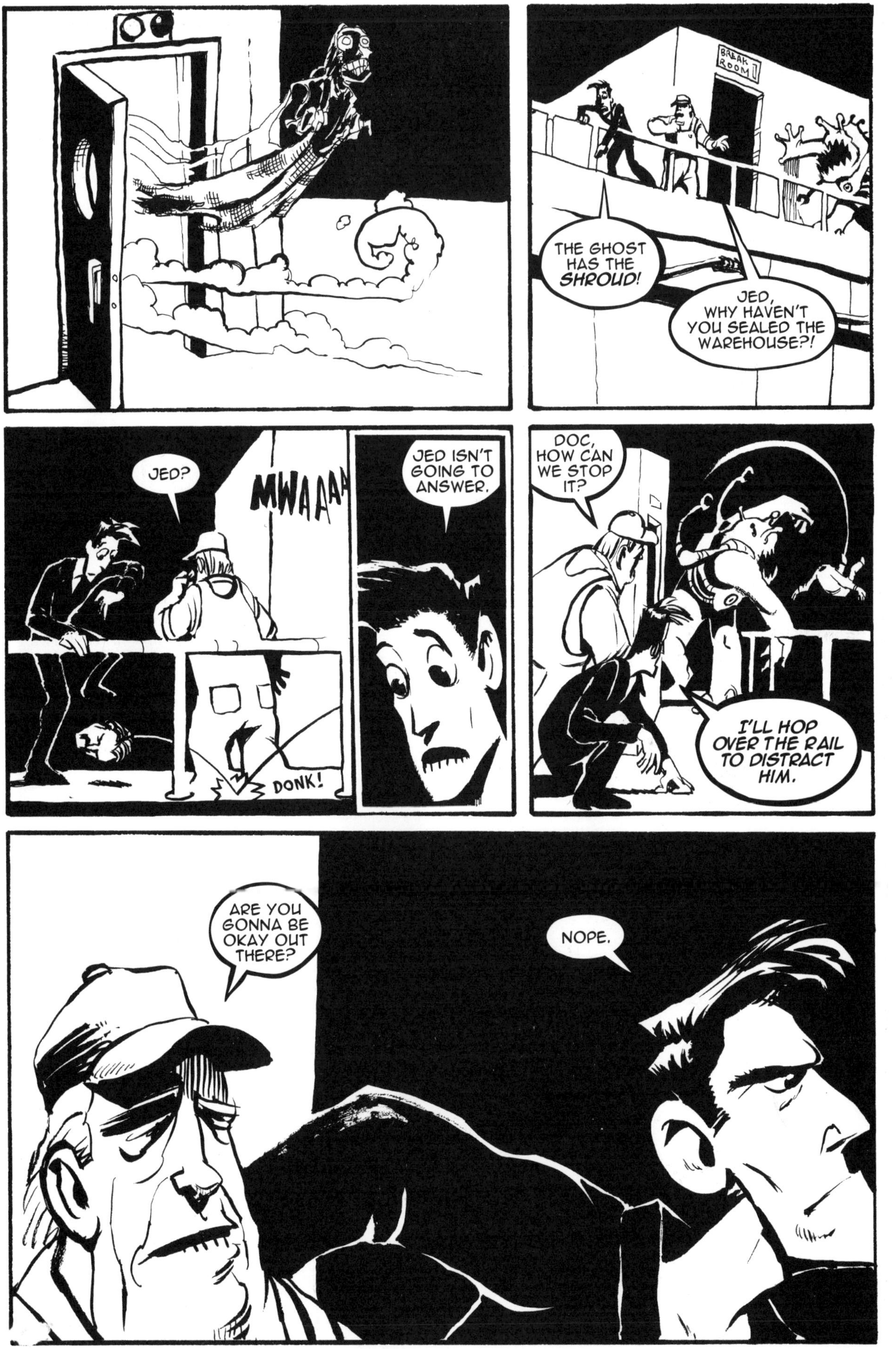
THE GHOST HAS THE SHROUD!
JED, WHY HAVEN'T YOU SEALED THE WAREHOUSE?!
JED?
MWAAAA
DONK!
JED ISN'T GOING TO ANSWER.
DOC, HOW CAN WE STOP IT?
I'LL HOP OVER THE RAIL TO DISTRACT HIM.
ARE YOU GONNA BE OKAY OUT THERE?
NOPE.

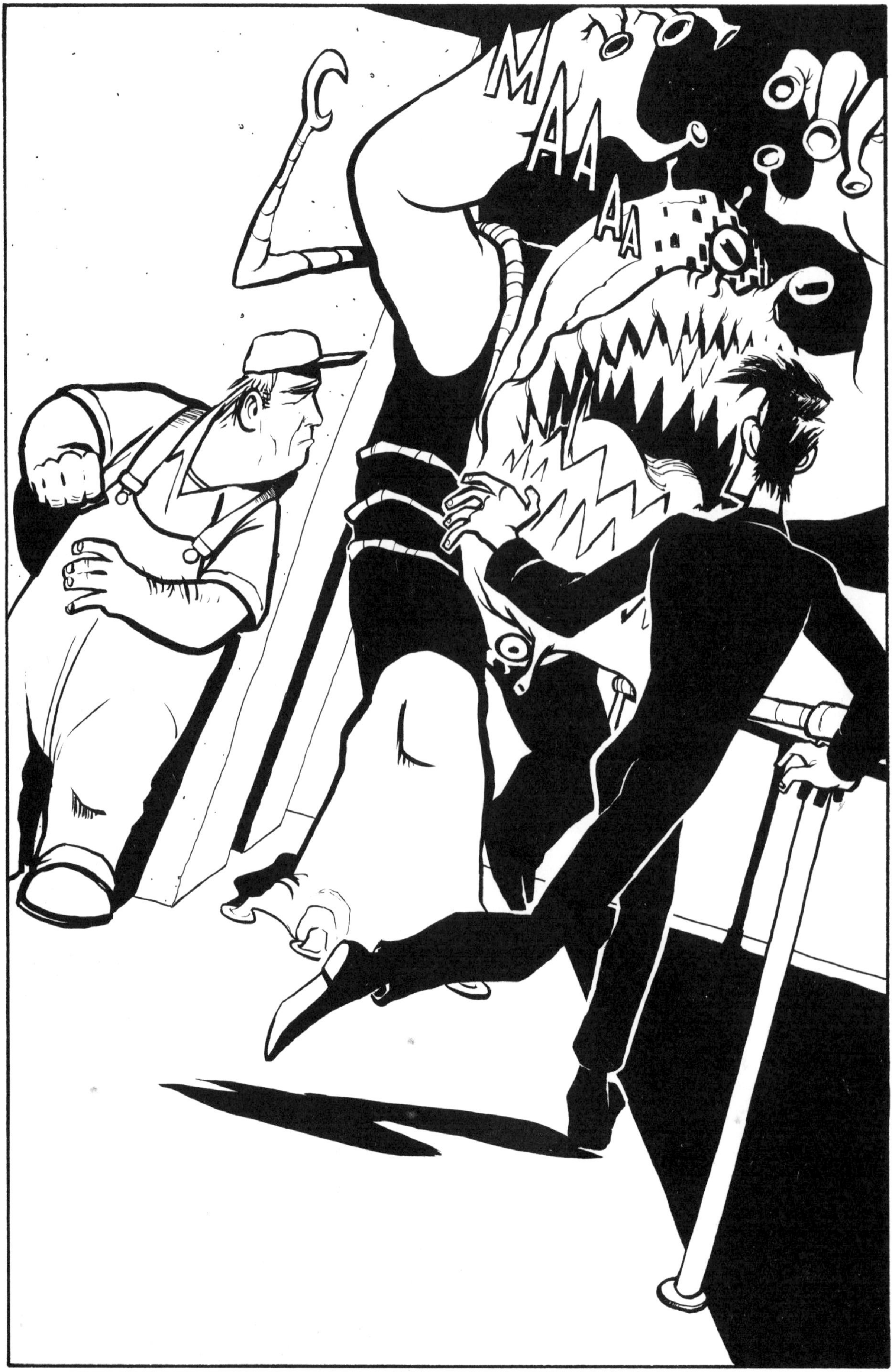
MAAAAA

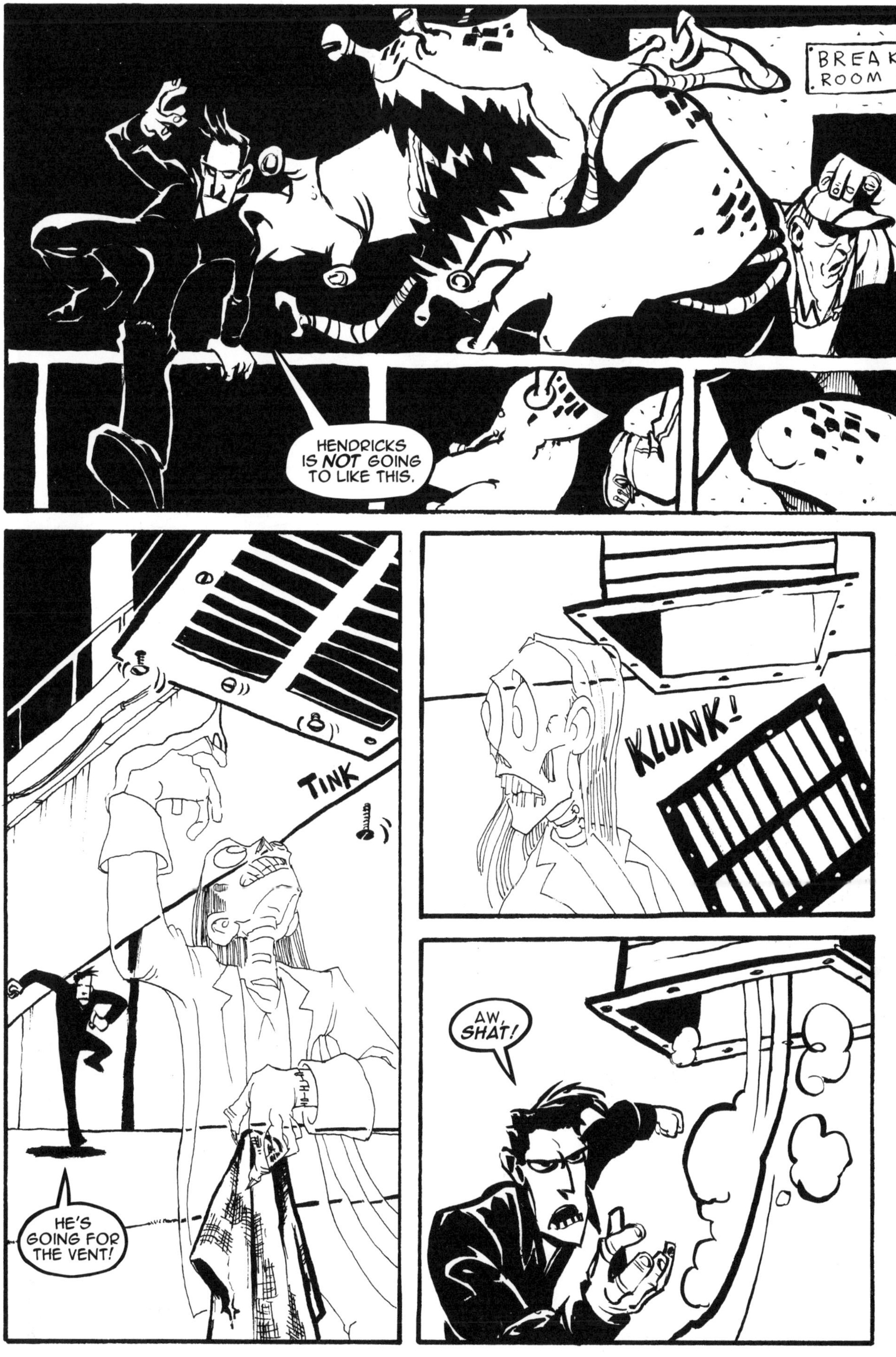

BREAK ROOM
HENDRICKS IS **NOT** GOING TO LIKE THIS.
TINK
HE'S GOING FOR THE VENT!
KLUNK!
AW, SHAT!

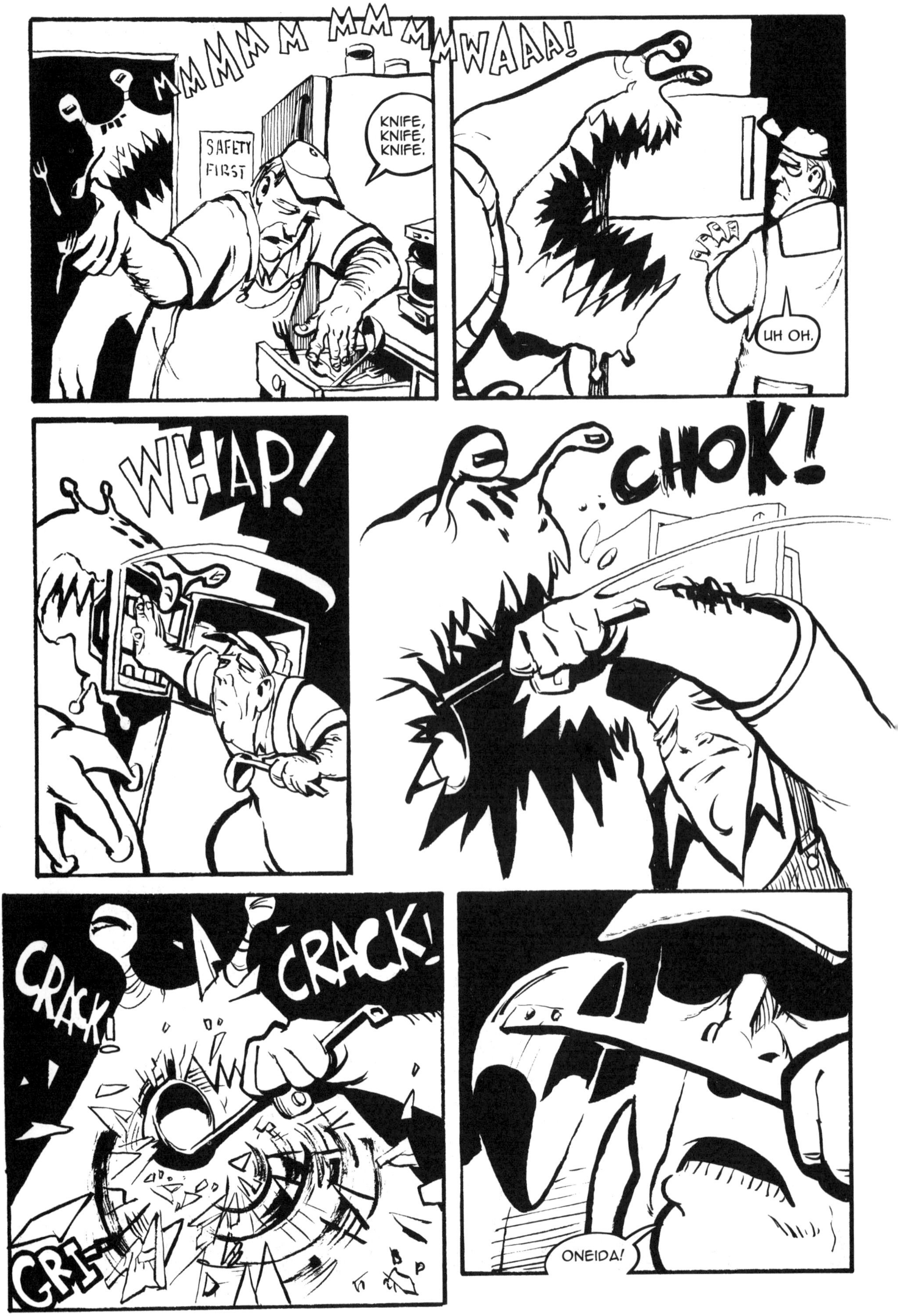
MMMMM M MM MMWAAA!
SAFETY FIRST
KNIFE, KNIFE, KNIFE.
UH OH.
WHAP!
CHOK!
CRACK!
CRACK!
CRI-
ONEIDA!

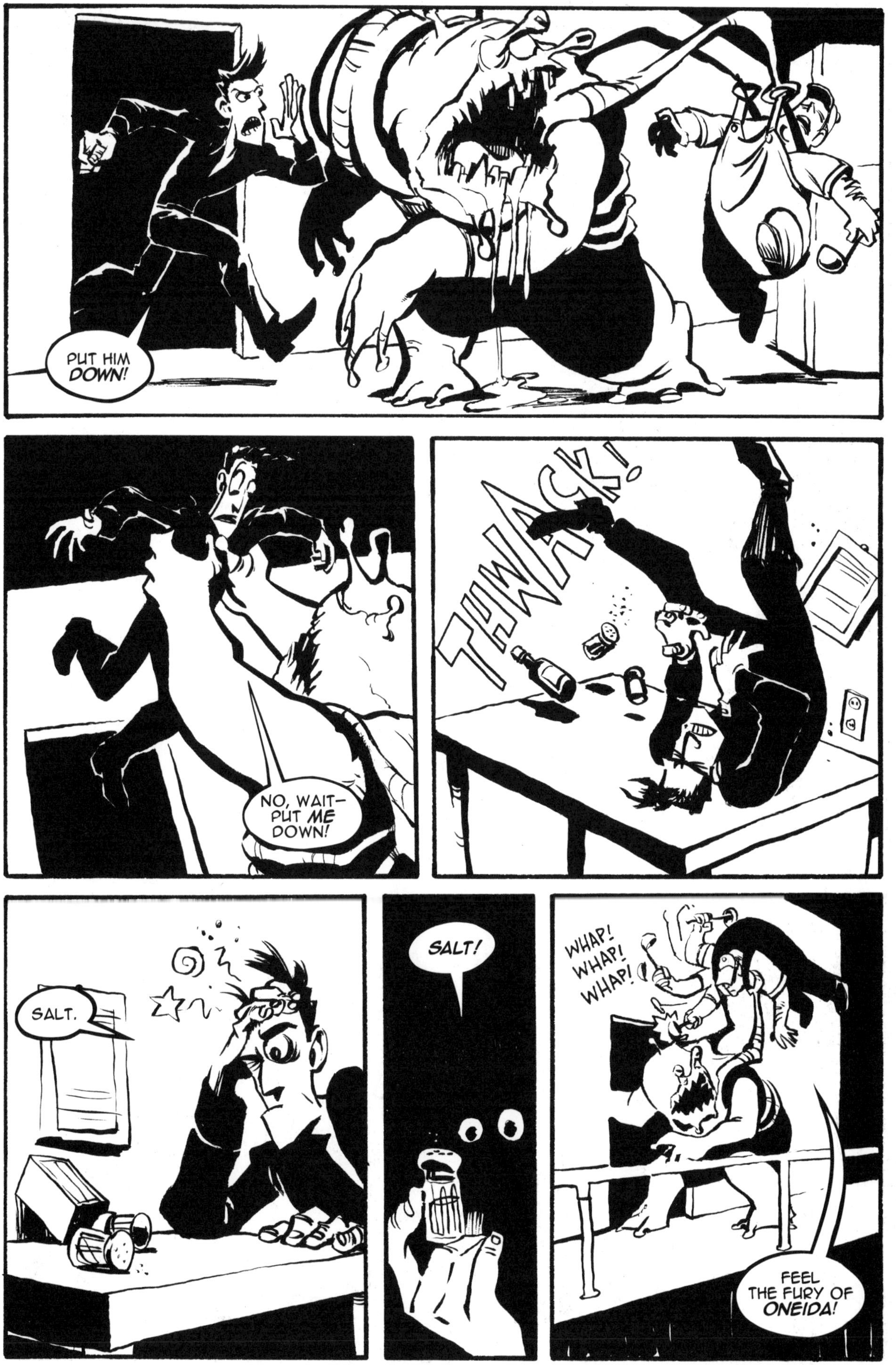
PUT HIM DOWN!
NO, WAIT-PUT ME DOWN!
THWACK!
SALT.
SALT!
WHAP! WHAP! WHAP!
FEEL THE FURY OF ONEIDA!

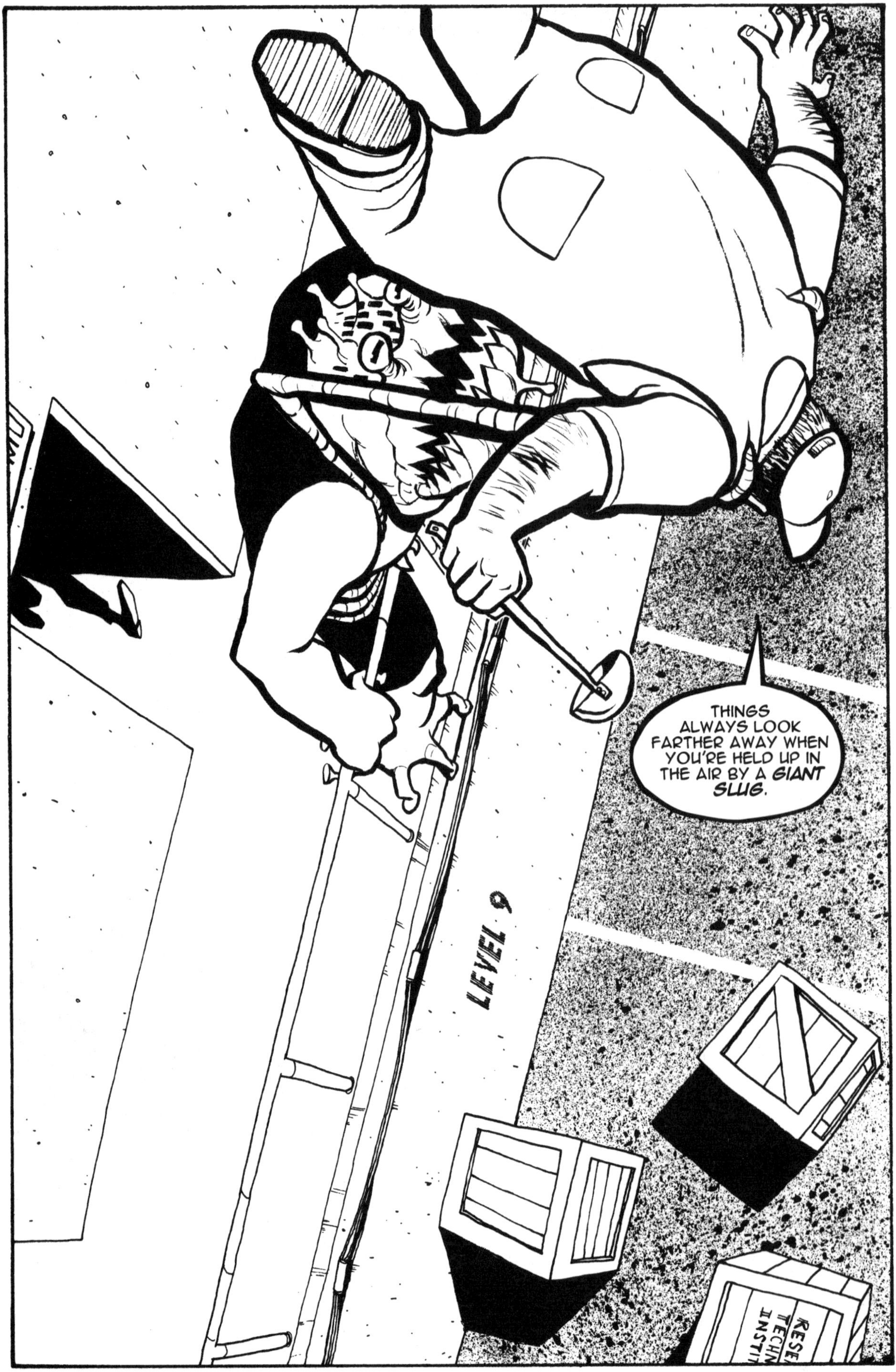
THINGS ALWAYS LOOK FARTHER AWAY WHEN YOU'RE HELD UP IN THE AIR BY A *GIANT SLUG*.
LEVEL 9

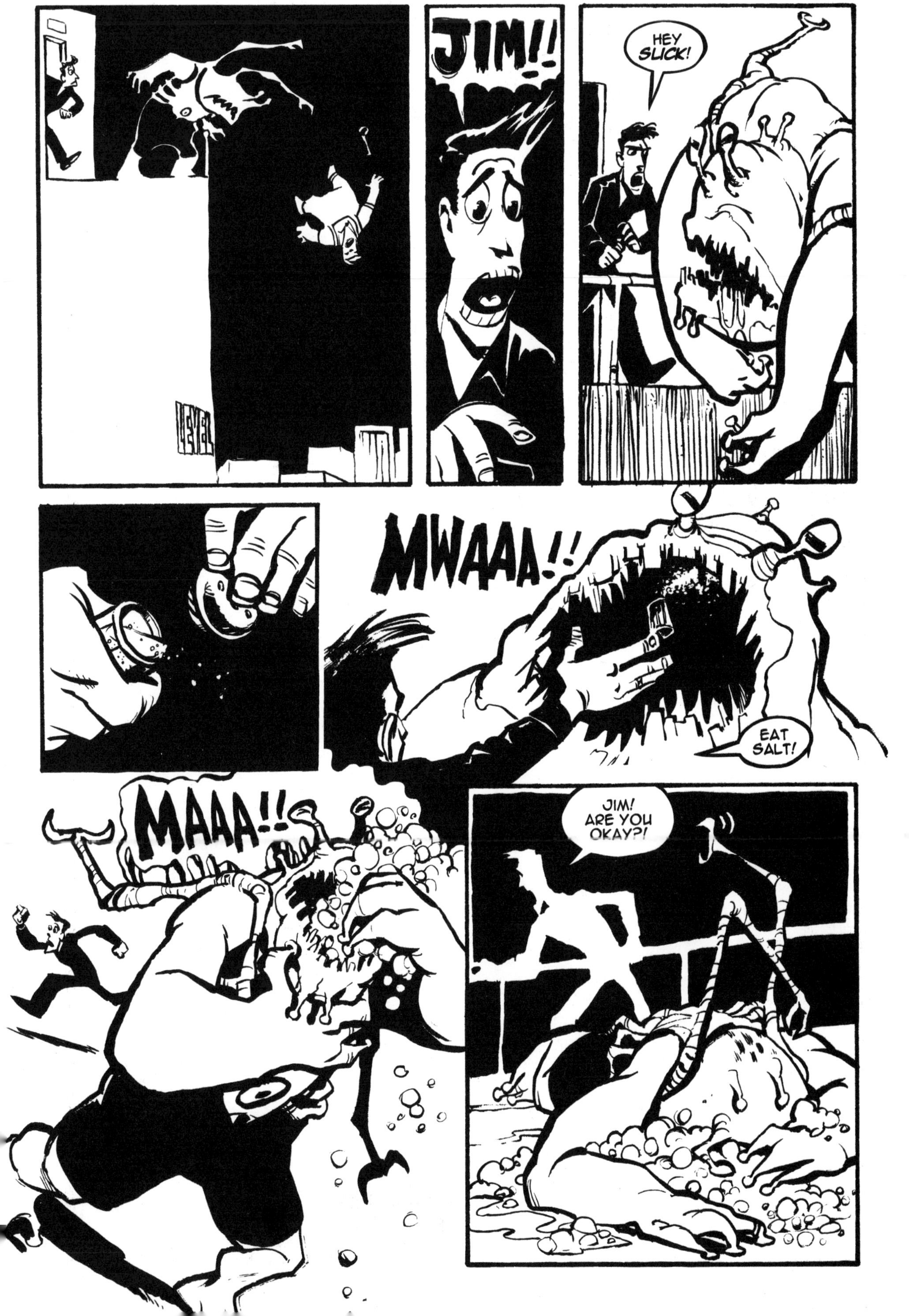

LEVEL
JIM!!
HEY SLICK!
MWAAA!!
EAT SALT!
MAAA!!
JIM! ARE YOU OKAY?!

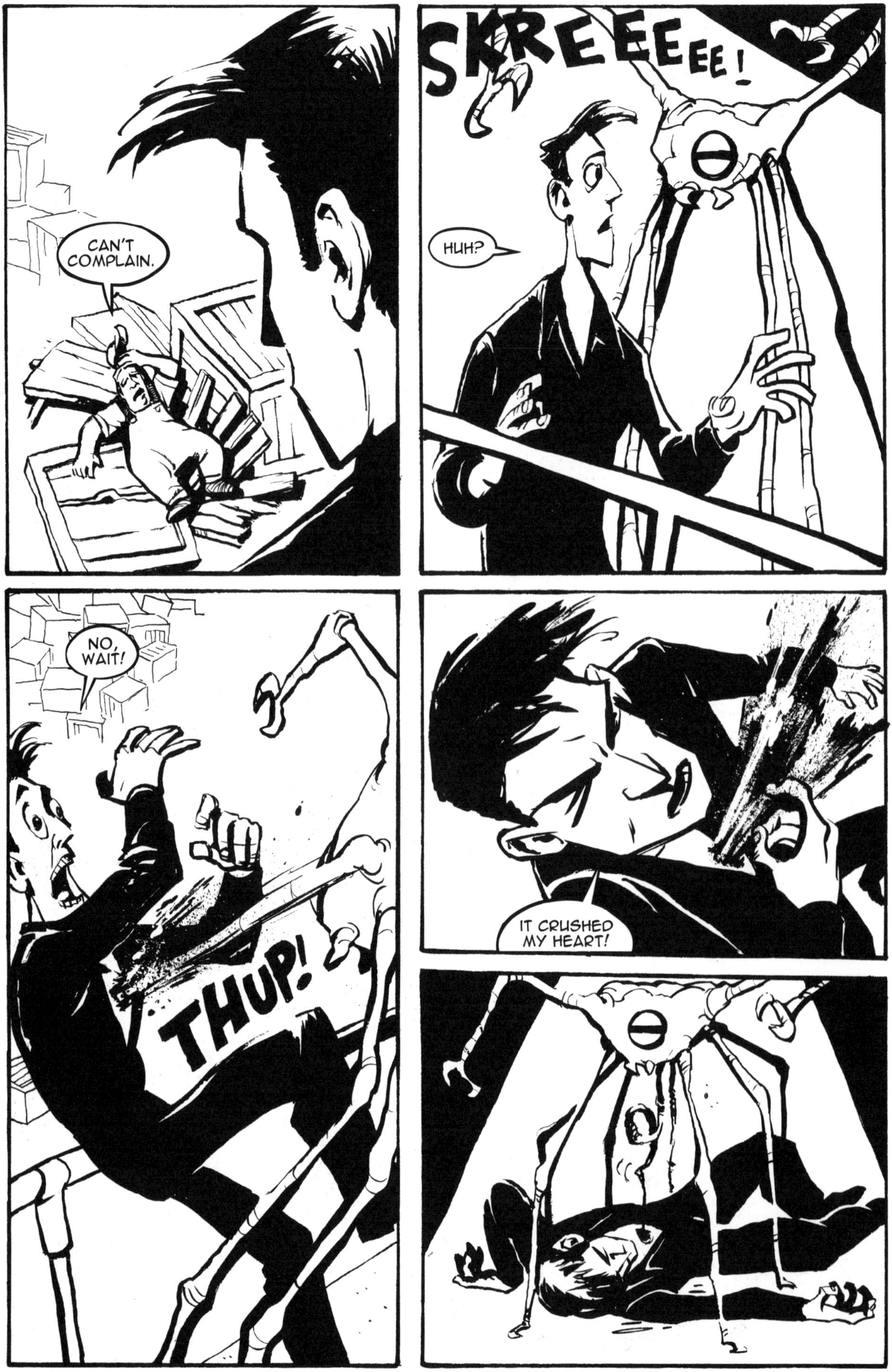
CAN'T COMPLAIN.
SKREEEEEE!
HUH?
NO, WAIT!
THUP!
IT CRUSHED MY HEART!

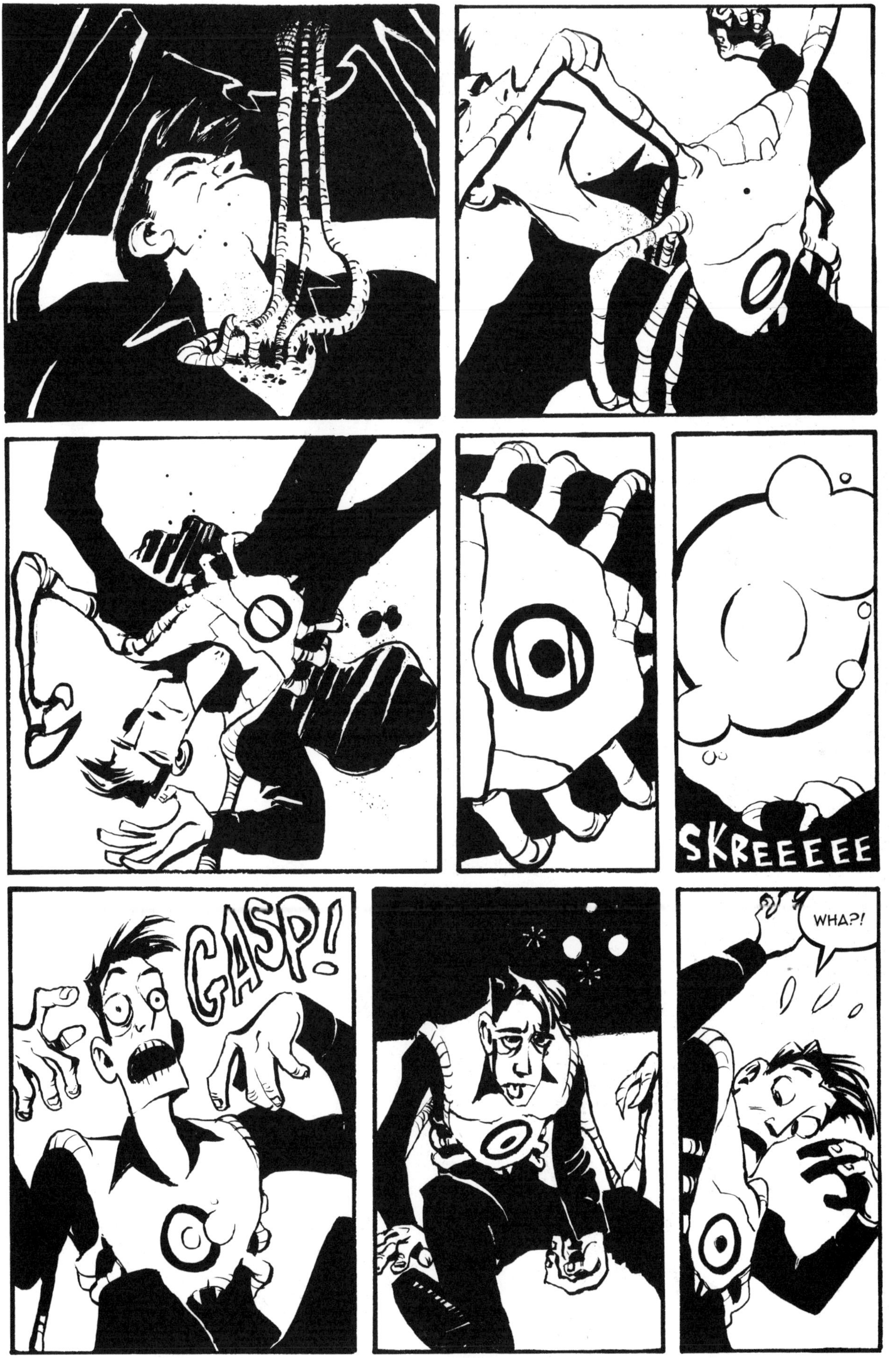
SKREEEEEE
GASP!
WHA?!

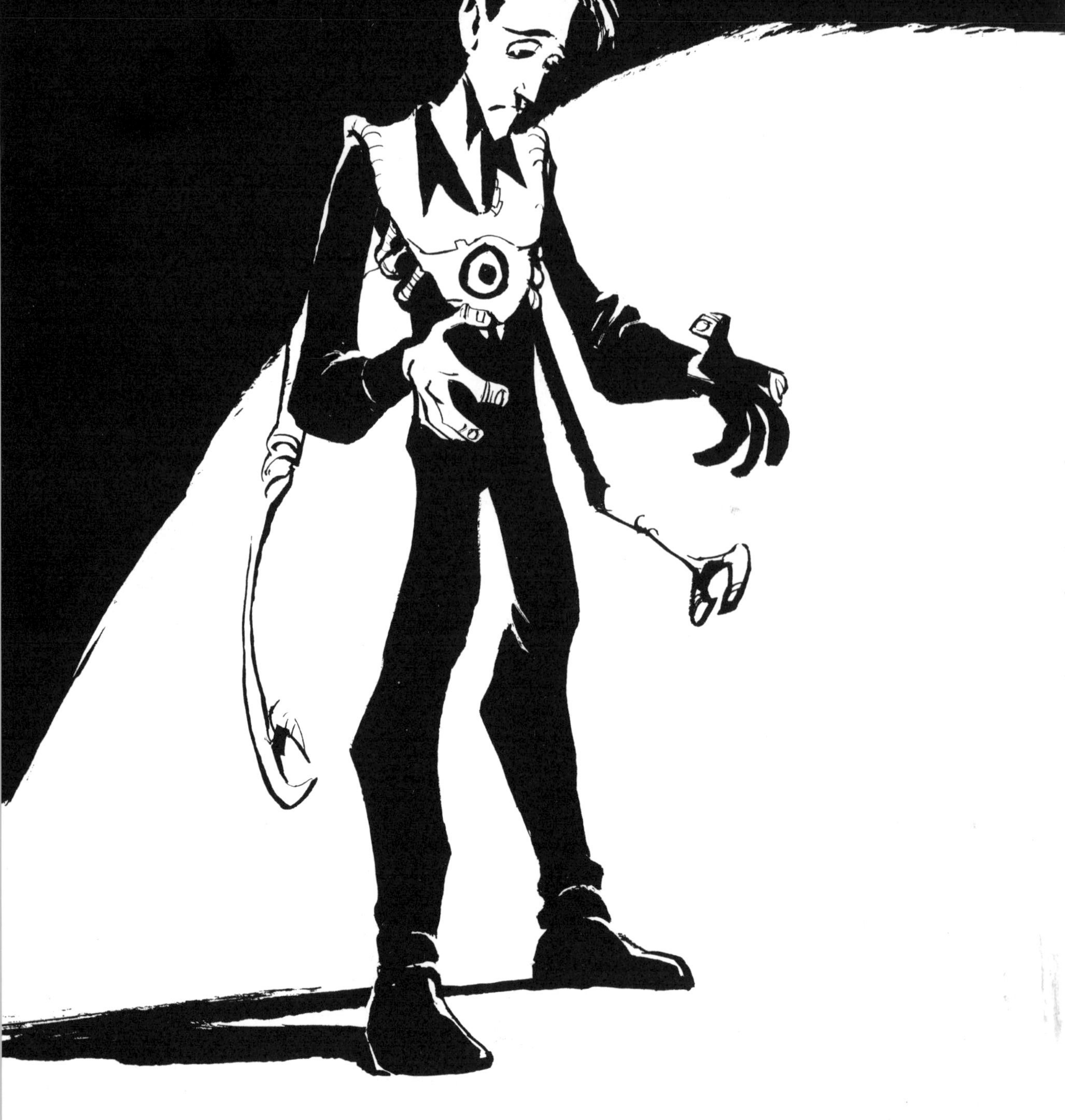

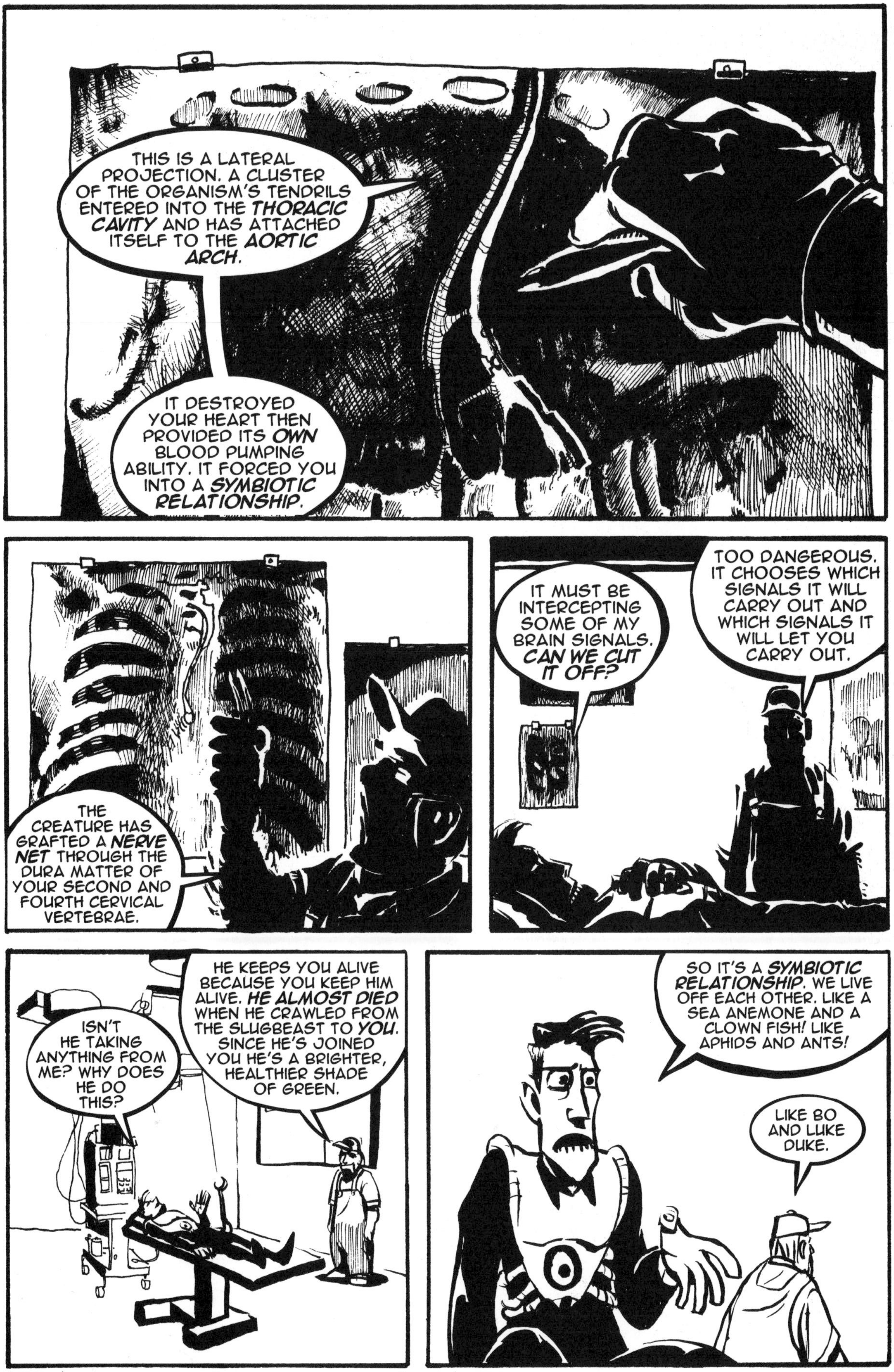
THIS IS A LATERAL PROJECTION. A CLUSTER OF THE ORGANISM'S TENDRILS ENTERED INTO THE THORACIC CAVITY AND HAS ATTACHED ITSELF TO THE AORTIC ARCH.
IT DESTROYED YOUR HEART THEN PROVIDED ITS OWN BLOOD PUMPING ABILITY. IT FORCED YOU INTO A SYMBIOTIC RELATIONSHIP.
THE CREATURE HAS GRAFTED A NERVE NET THROUGH THE DURA MATTER OF YOUR SECOND AND FOURTH CERVICAL VERTEBRAE.
IT MUST BE INTERCEPTING SOME OF MY BRAIN SIGNALS. CAN WE CUT IT OFF?
TOO DANGEROUS. IT CHOOSES WHICH SIGNALS IT WILL CARRY OUT AND WHICH SIGNALS IT WILL LET YOU CARRY OUT.
ISN'T HE TAKING ANYTHING FROM ME? WHY DOES HE DO THIS?
HE KEEPS YOU ALIVE BECAUSE YOU KEEP HIM ALIVE. HE ALMOST DIED WHEN HE CRAWLED FROM THE SLUGBEAST TO YOU. SINCE HE'S JOINED YOU HE'S A BRIGHTER, HEALTHIER SHADE OF GREEN.
SO IT'S A SYMBIOTIC RELATIONSHIP. WE LIVE OFF EACH OTHER. LIKE A SEA ANEMONE AND A CLOWN FISH! LIKE APHIDS AND ANTS!
LIKE BO AND LUKE DUKE.

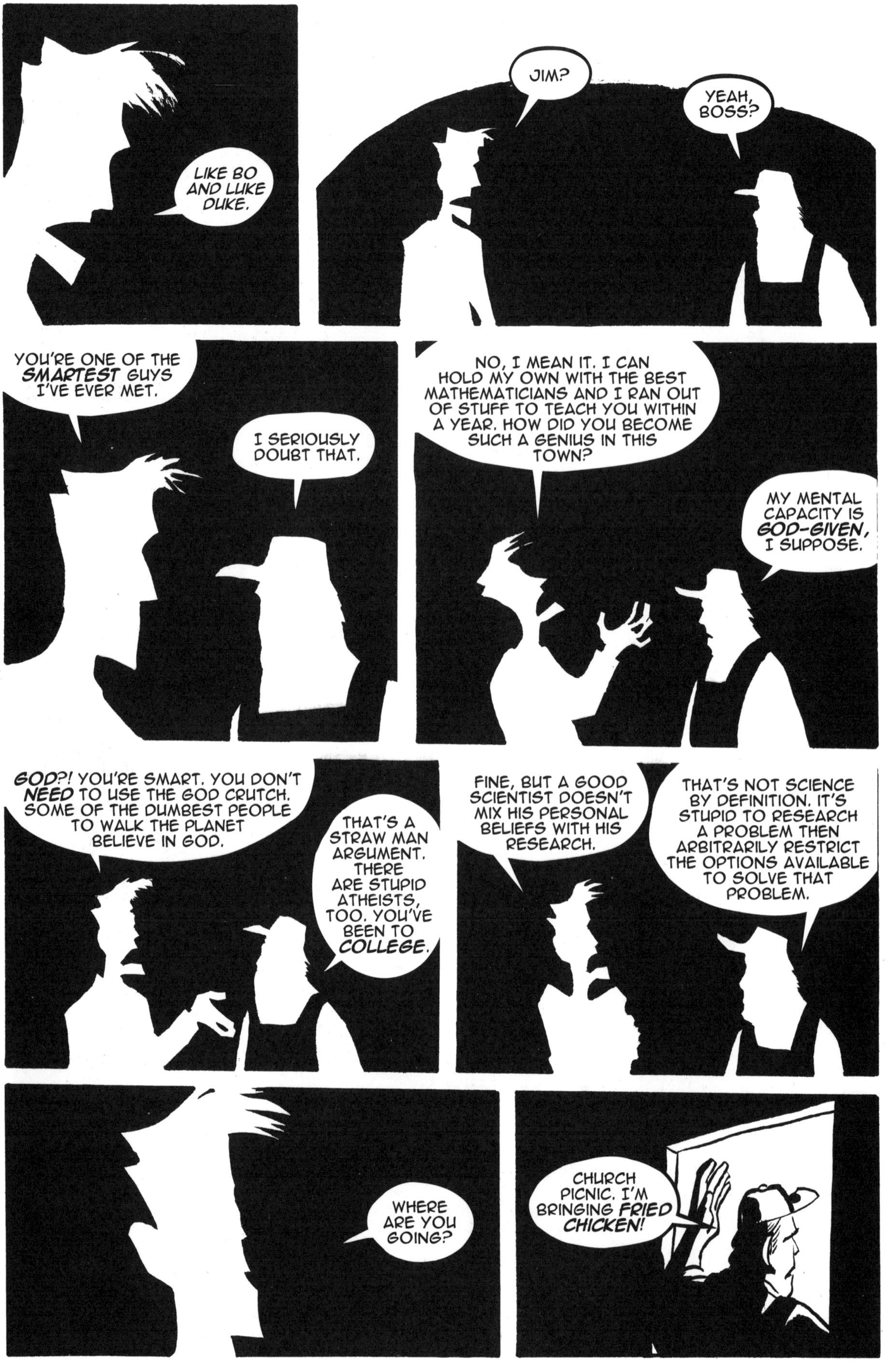
LIKE BO AND LUKE DUKE.
JIM?
YEAH, BOSS?
YOU'RE ONE OF THE SMARTEST GUYS I'VE EVER MET.
I SERIOUSLY DOUBT THAT.
NO, I MEAN IT. I CAN HOLD MY OWN WITH THE BEST MATHEMATICIANS AND I RAN OUT OF STUFF TO TEACH YOU WITHIN A YEAR. HOW DID YOU BECOME SUCH A GENIUS IN THIS TOWN?
MY MENTAL CAPACITY IS GOD-GIVEN, I SUPPOSE.
GOD?! YOU'RE SMART. YOU DON'T NEED TO USE THE GOD CRUTCH. SOME OF THE DUMBEST PEOPLE TO WALK THE PLANET BELIEVE IN GOD.
THAT'S A STRAW MAN ARGUMENT. THERE ARE STUPID ATHEISTS, TOO. YOU'VE BEEN TO COLLEGE.
FINE, BUT A GOOD SCIENTIST DOESN'T MIX HIS PERSONAL BELIEFS WITH HIS RESEARCH.
THAT'S NOT SCIENCE BY DEFINITION. IT'S STUPID TO RESEARCH A PROBLEM THEN ARBITRARILY RESTRICT THE OPTIONS AVAILABLE TO SOLVE THAT PROBLEM.
WHERE ARE YOU GOING?
CHURCH PICNIC. I'M BRINGING FRIED CHICKEN!

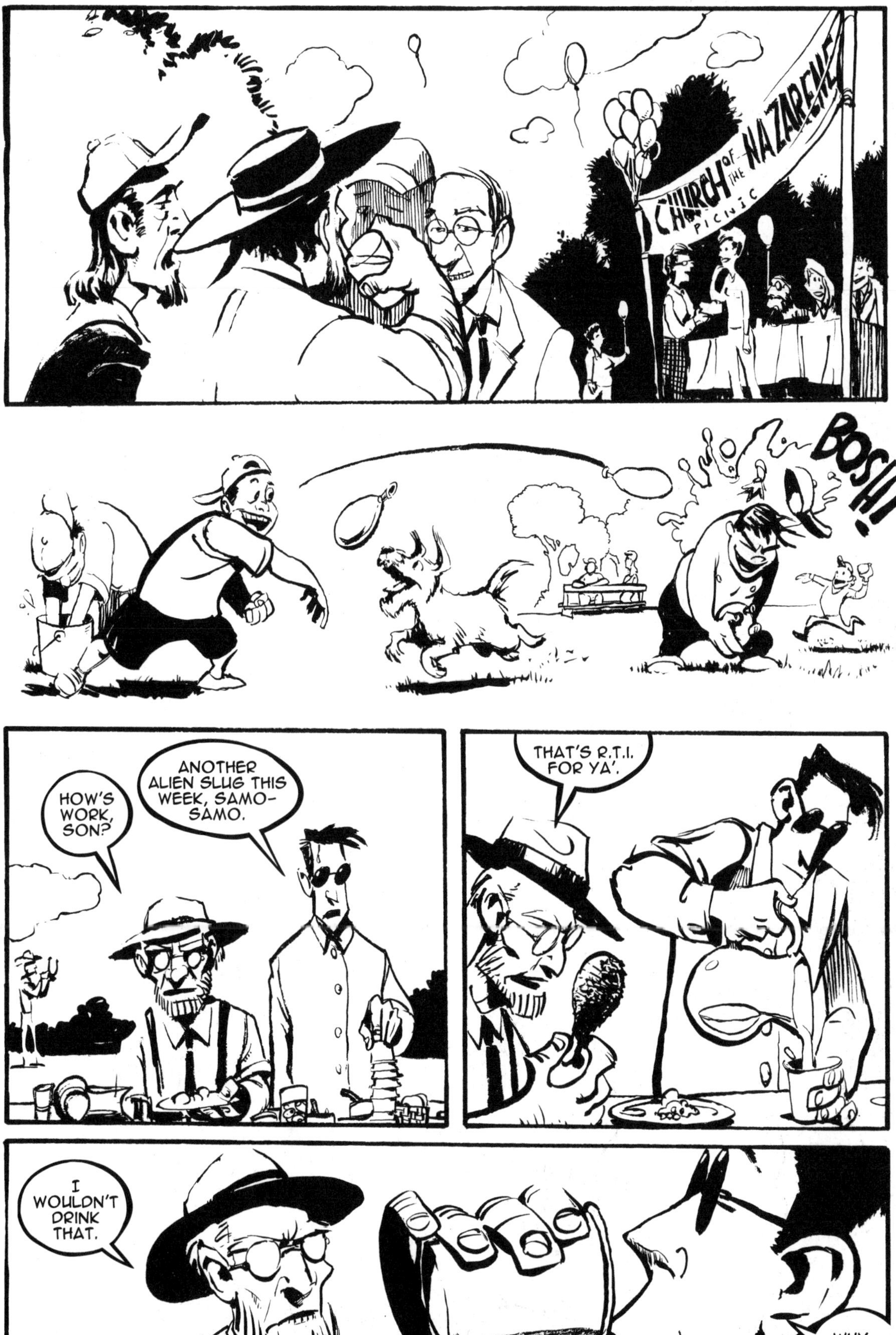
CHURCH OF THE NAZARENE PICNIC
BOSH!!
HOW'S WORK, SON?
ANOTHER ALIEN SLUG THIS WEEK, SAMO-SAMO.
THAT'S R.T.I. FOR YA'.
I WOULDN'T DRINK THAT.
WHY NOT?

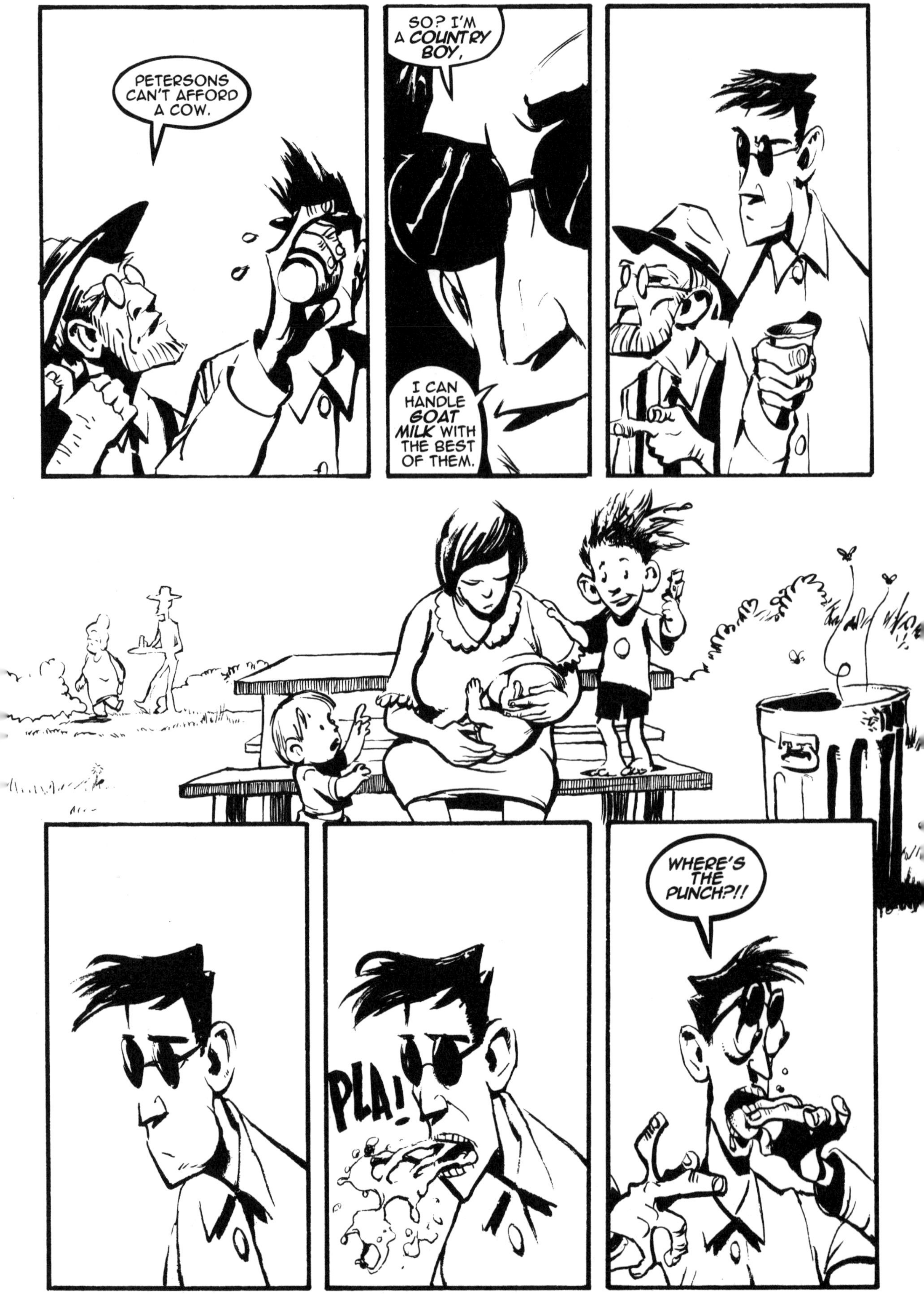
PETERSONS CAN'T AFFORD A COW.
SO? I'M A COUNTRY BOY,
I CAN HANDLE GOAT MILK WITH THE BEST OF THEM.
PLA!
WHERE'S THE PUNCH?!!

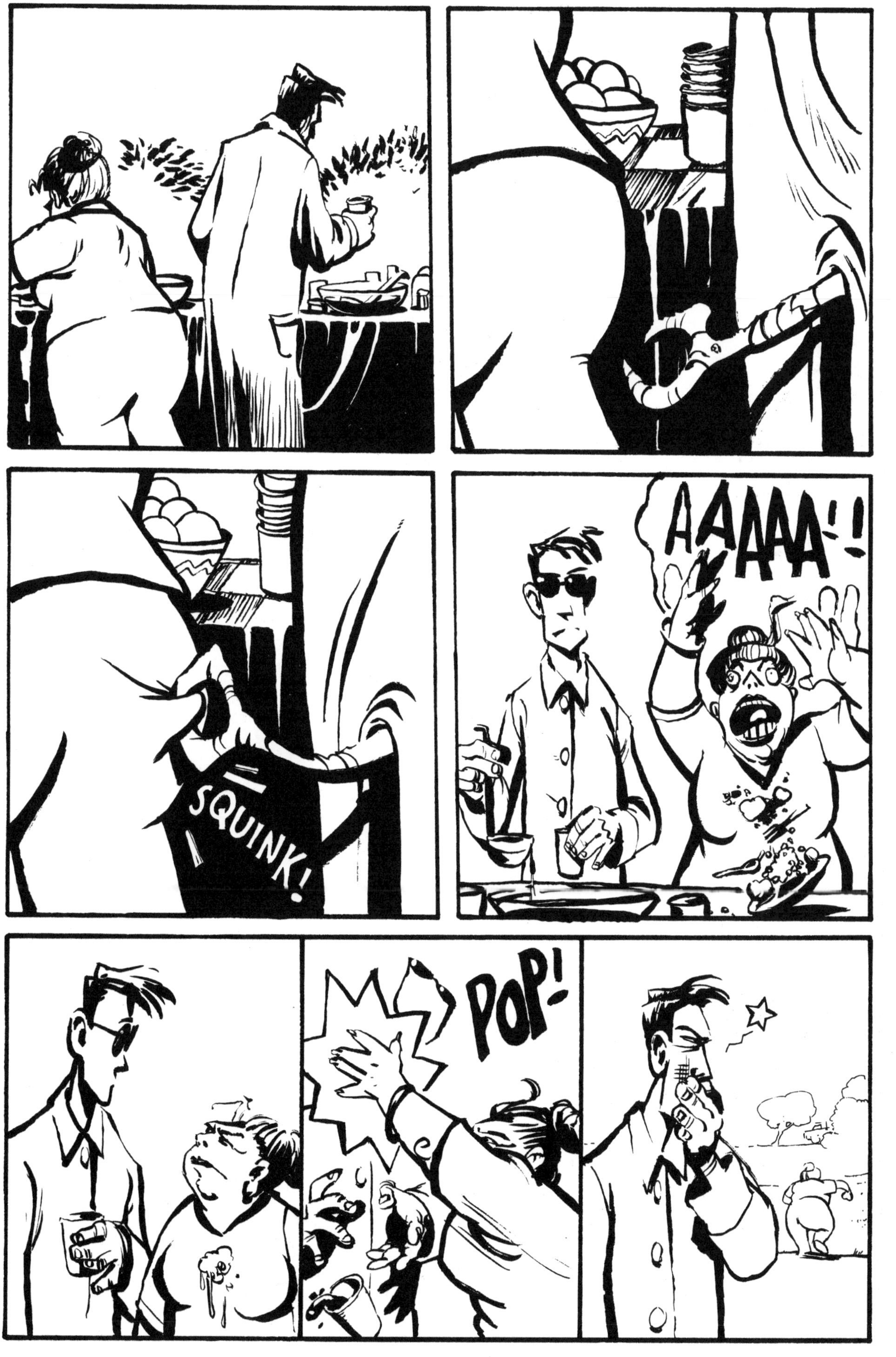
SQUINK!
AAAAA!!
POP!

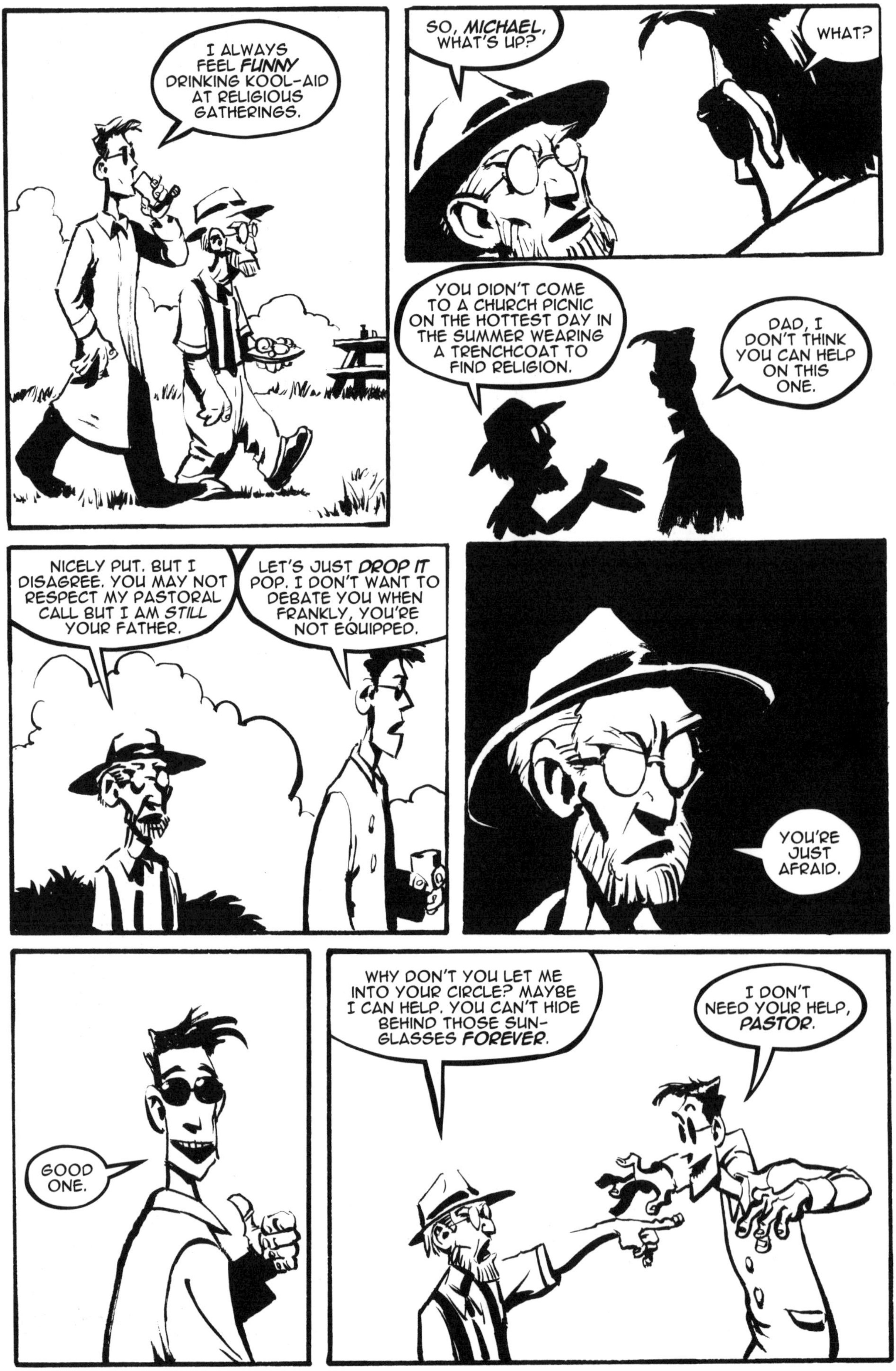
I ALWAYS FEEL FUNNY DRINKING KOOL-AID AT RELIGIOUS GATHERINGS.
SO, MICHAEL, WHAT'S UP?
WHAT?
YOU DIDN'T COME TO A CHURCH PICNIC ON THE HOTTEST DAY IN THE SUMMER WEARING A TRENCHCOAT TO FIND RELIGION.
DAD, I DON'T THINK YOU CAN HELP ON THIS ONE.
NICELY PUT. BUT I DISAGREE. YOU MAY NOT RESPECT MY PASTORAL CALL BUT I AM STILL YOUR FATHER.
LET'S JUST DROP IT POP. I DON'T WANT TO DEBATE YOU WHEN FRANKLY, YOU'RE NOT EQUIPPED.
YOU'RE JUST AFRAID.
GOOD ONE.
WHY DON'T YOU LET ME INTO YOUR CIRCLE? MAYBE I CAN HELP. YOU CAN'T HIDE BEHIND THOSE SUN-GLASSES FOREVER.
I DON'T NEED YOUR HELP, PASTOR.

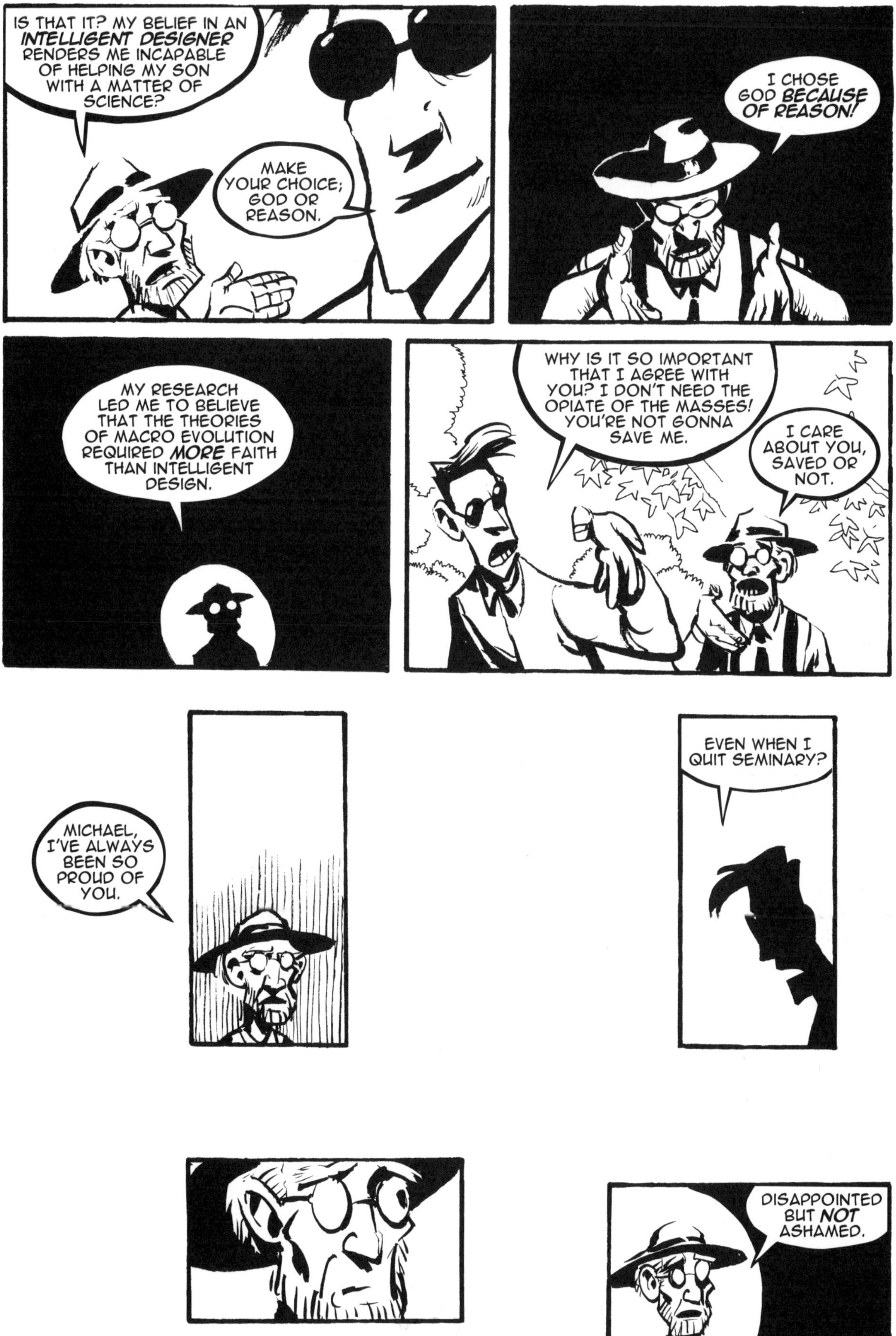
IS THAT IT? MY BELIEF IN AN *INTELLIGENT DESIGNER* RENDERS ME INCAPABLE OF HELPING MY SON WITH A MATTER OF SCIENCE?
MAKE YOUR CHOICE; GOD OR REASON.
I CHOSE GOD *BECAUSE OF REASON!*
MY RESEARCH LED ME TO BELIEVE THAT THE THEORIES OF MACRO EVOLUTION REQUIRED *MORE* FAITH THAN INTELLIGENT DESIGN.
WHY IS IT SO IMPORTANT THAT I AGREE WITH YOU? I DON'T NEED THE OPIATE OF THE MASSES! YOU'RE NOT GONNA SAVE ME.
I CARE ABOUT YOU, SAVED OR NOT.
MICHAEL, I'VE ALWAYS BEEN SO PROUD OF YOU.
EVEN WHEN I QUIT SEMINARY?
DISAPPOINTED BUT *NOT* ASHAMED.

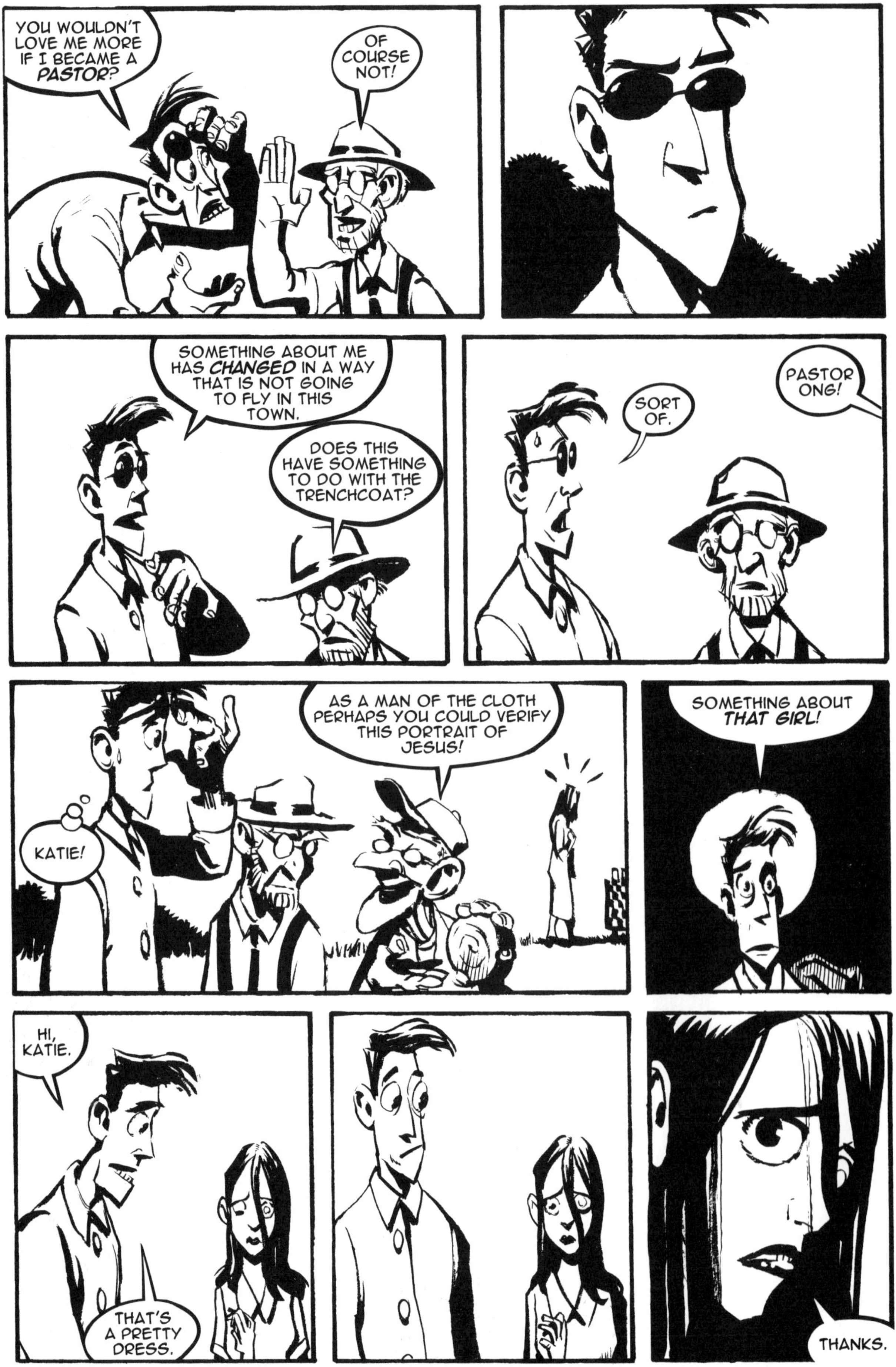
YOU WOULDN'T LOVE ME MORE IF I BECAME A PASTOR?
OF COURSE NOT!
SOMETHING ABOUT ME HAS CHANGED IN A WAY THAT IS NOT GOING TO FLY IN THIS TOWN.
DOES THIS HAVE SOMETHING TO DO WITH THE TRENCHCOAT?
SORT OF.
PASTOR ONG!
KATIE!
AS A MAN OF THE CLOTH PERHAPS YOU COULD VERIFY THIS PORTRAIT OF JESUS!
SOMETHING ABOUT THAT GIRL!
HI, KATIE.
THAT'S A PRETTY DRESS.
THANKS.

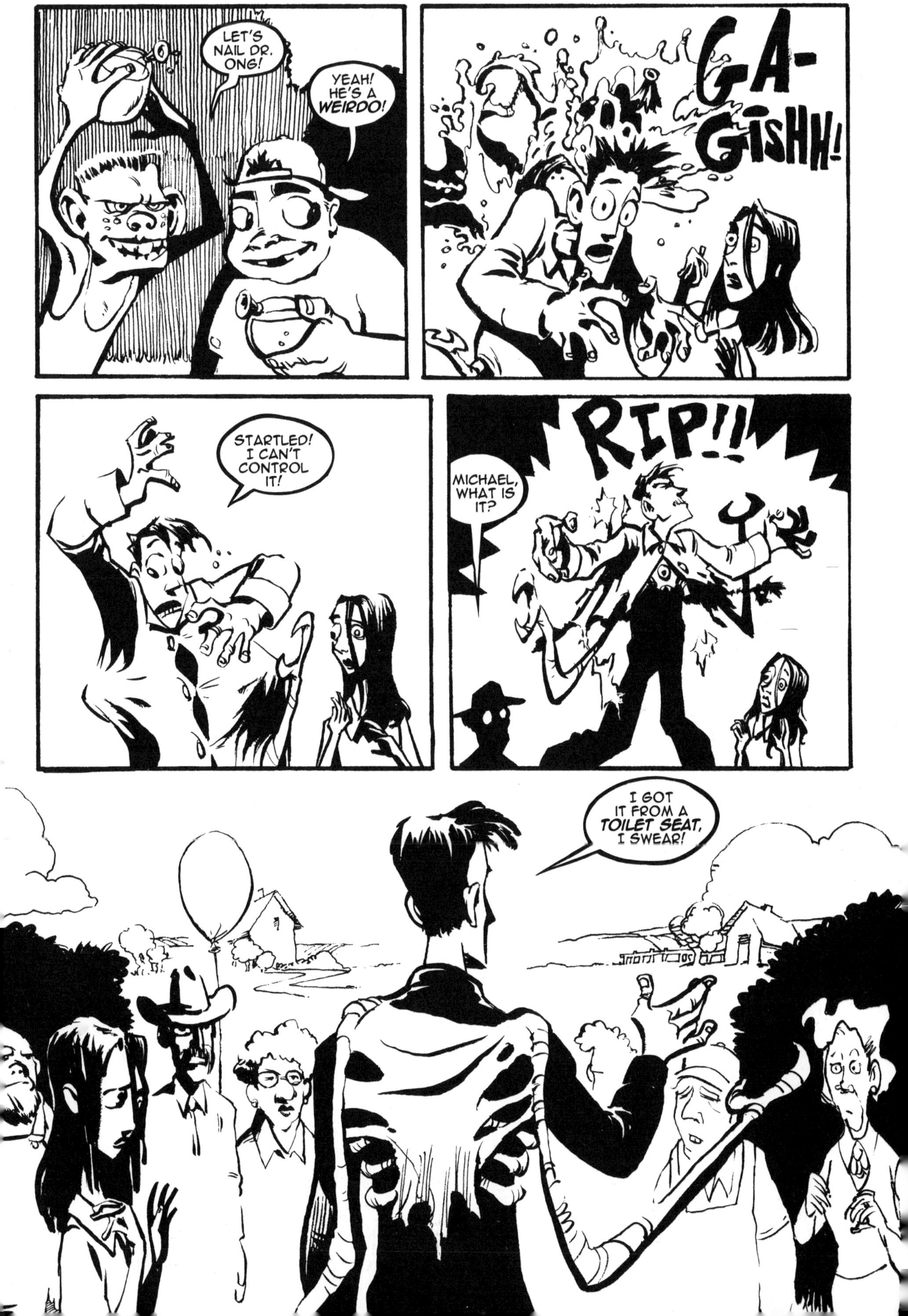

LET'S NAIL DR. ONG!
YEAH! HE'S A WEIRDO!
GA-GISHH!
STARTLED! I CAN'T CONTROL IT!
RIP!!!
MICHAEL, WHAT IS IT?
I GOT IT FROM A TOILET SEAT, I SWEAR!

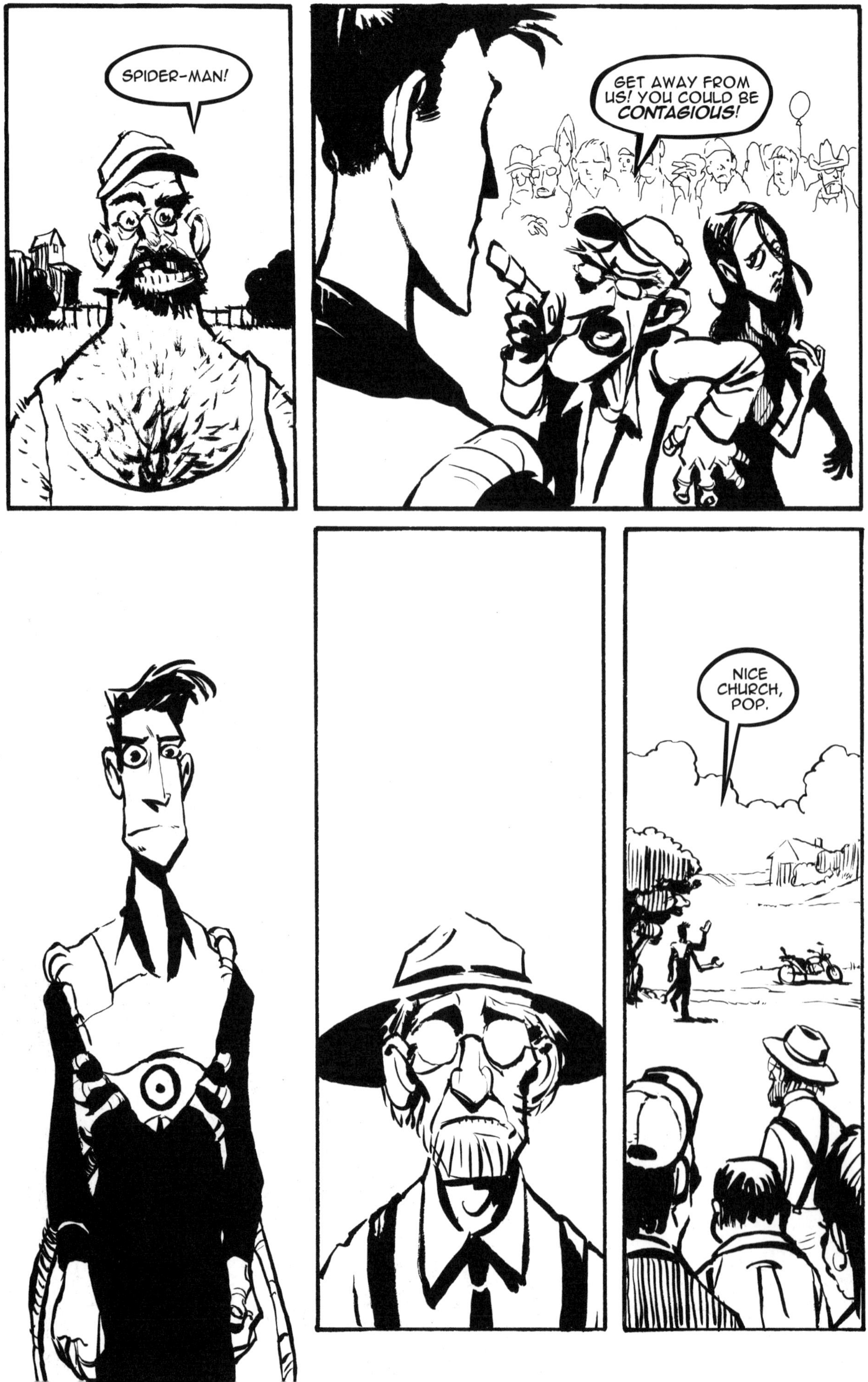
SPIDER-MAN!
GET AWAY FROM US! YOU COULD BE CONTAGIOUS!
NICE CHURCH, POP.

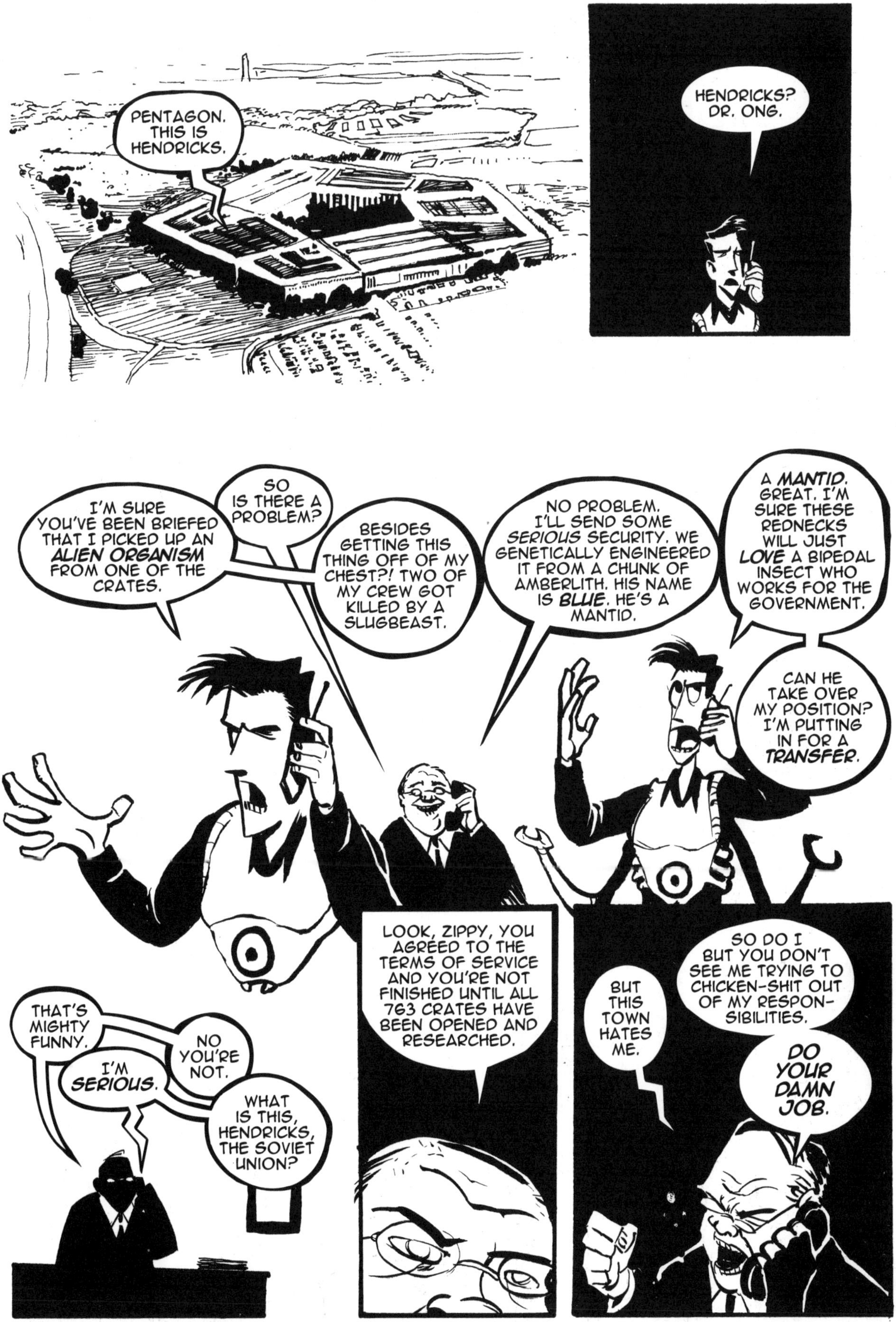
PENTAGON. THIS IS HENDRICKS.
HENDRICKS? DR. ONG.
I'M SURE YOU'VE BEEN BRIEFED THAT I PICKED UP AN ALIEN ORGANISM FROM ONE OF THE CRATES.
SO IS THERE A PROBLEM?
BESIDES GETTING THIS THING OFF OF MY CHEST?! TWO OF MY CREW GOT KILLED BY A SLUGBEAST.
NO PROBLEM. I'LL SEND SOME SERIOUS SECURITY. WE GENETICALLY ENGINEERED IT FROM A CHUNK OF AMBERLITH. HIS NAME IS BLUE. HE'S A MANTID.
A MANTID. GREAT. I'M SURE THESE REDNECKS WILL JUST LOVE A BIPEDAL INSECT WHO WORKS FOR THE GOVERNMENT.
CAN HE TAKE OVER MY POSITION? I'M PUTTING IN FOR A TRANSFER.
THAT'S MIGHTY FUNNY.
I'M SERIOUS.
NO YOU'RE NOT.
WHAT IS THIS, HENDRICKS, THE SOVIET UNION?
LOOK, ZIPPY, YOU AGREED TO THE TERMS OF SERVICE AND YOU'RE NOT FINISHED UNTIL ALL 763 CRATES HAVE BEEN OPENED AND RESEARCHED.
BUT THIS TOWN HATES ME.
SO DO I BUT YOU DON'T SEE ME TRYING TO CHICKEN-SHIT OUT OF MY RESPON-SIBILITIES.
DO YOUR DAMN JOB.

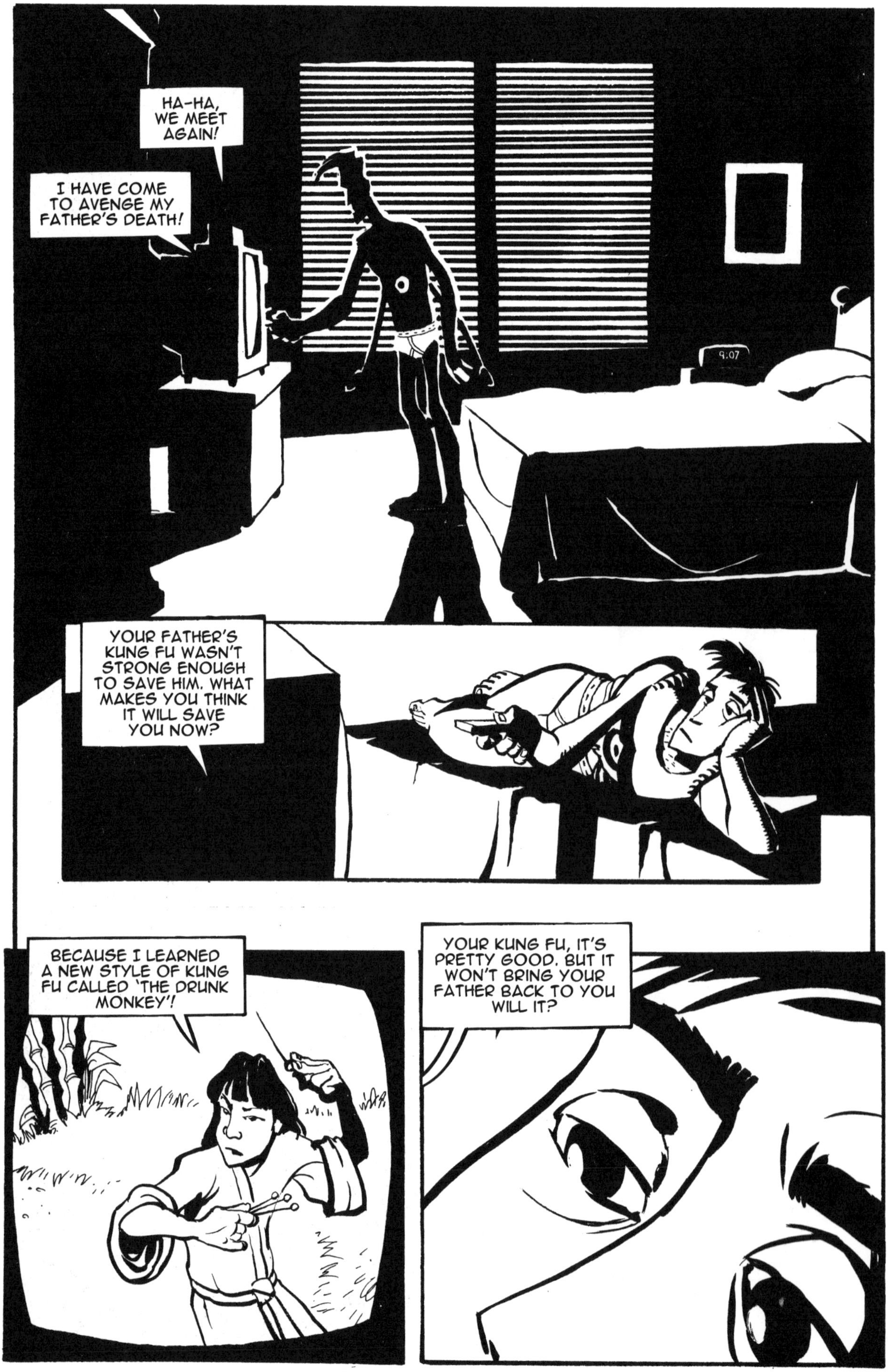
HA-HA, WE MEET AGAIN!
I HAVE COME TO AVENGE MY FATHER'S DEATH!
9:07
YOUR FATHER'S KUNG FU WASN'T STRONG ENOUGH TO SAVE HIM. WHAT MAKES YOU THINK IT WILL SAVE YOU NOW?
BECAUSE I LEARNED A NEW STYLE OF KUNG FU CALLED 'THE DRUNK MONKEY'!
YOUR KUNG FU, IT'S PRETTY GOOD. BUT IT WON'T BRING YOUR FATHER BACK TO YOU WILL IT?

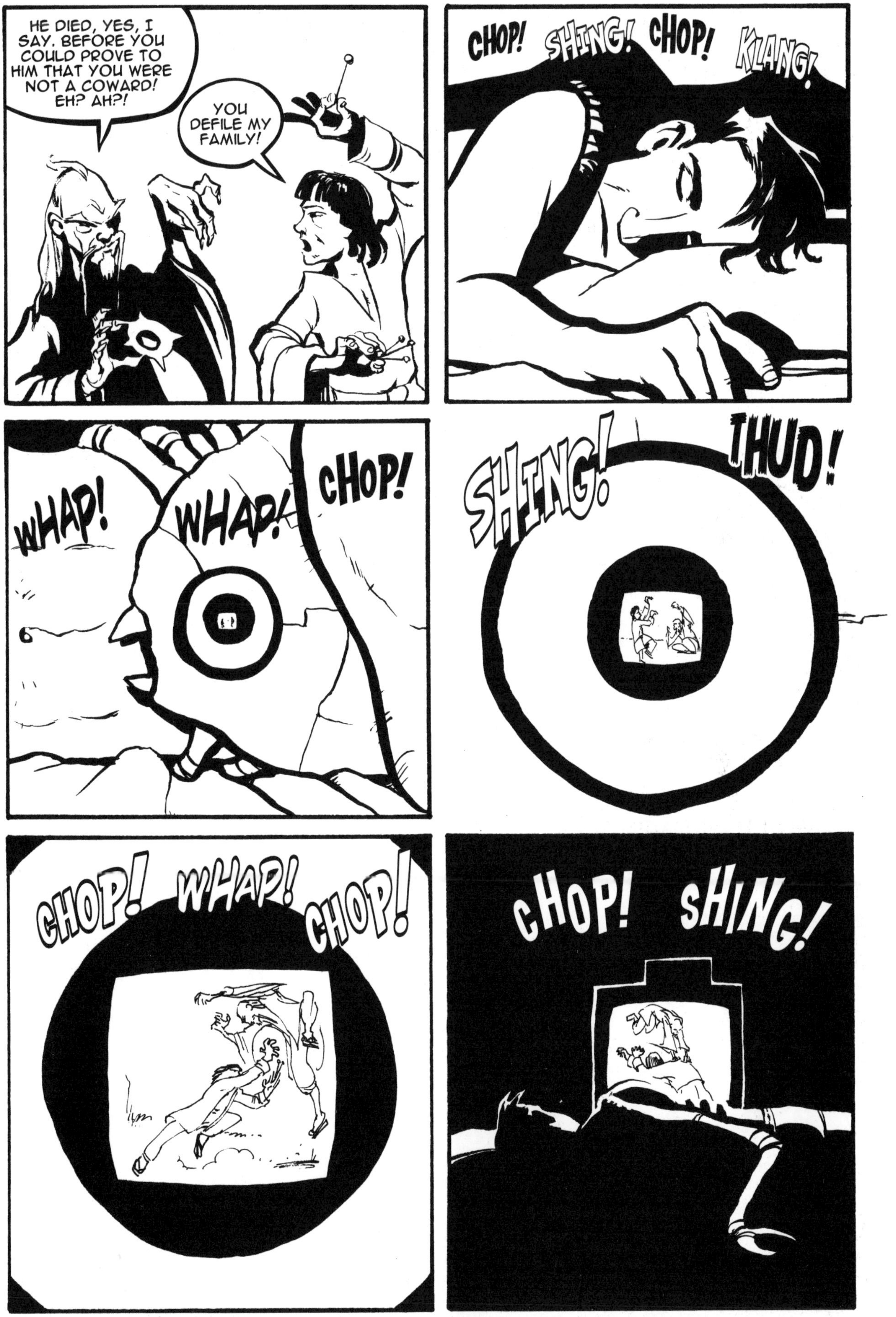
HE DIED, YES, I SAY. BEFORE YOU COULD PROVE TO HIM THAT YOU WERE NOT A COWARD! EH? AH?!
YOU DEFILE MY FAMILY!
CHOP! SHING! CHOP! KLANG!
WHAP! WHAP! CHOP!
SHING! THUD!
CHOP! WHAP! CHOP!
CHOP! SHING!

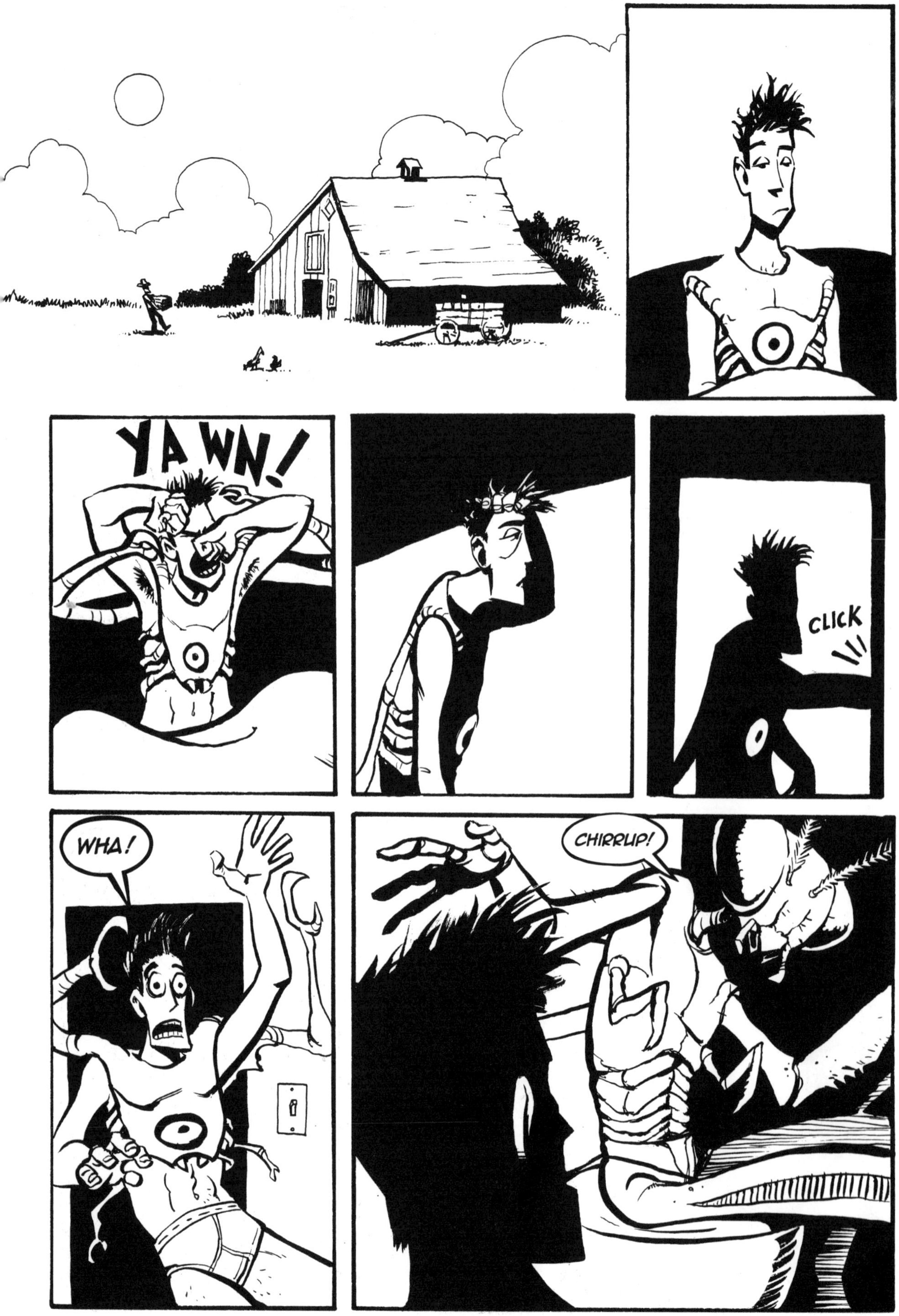
YAWN!
CLICK
WHA!
CHIRRUP!

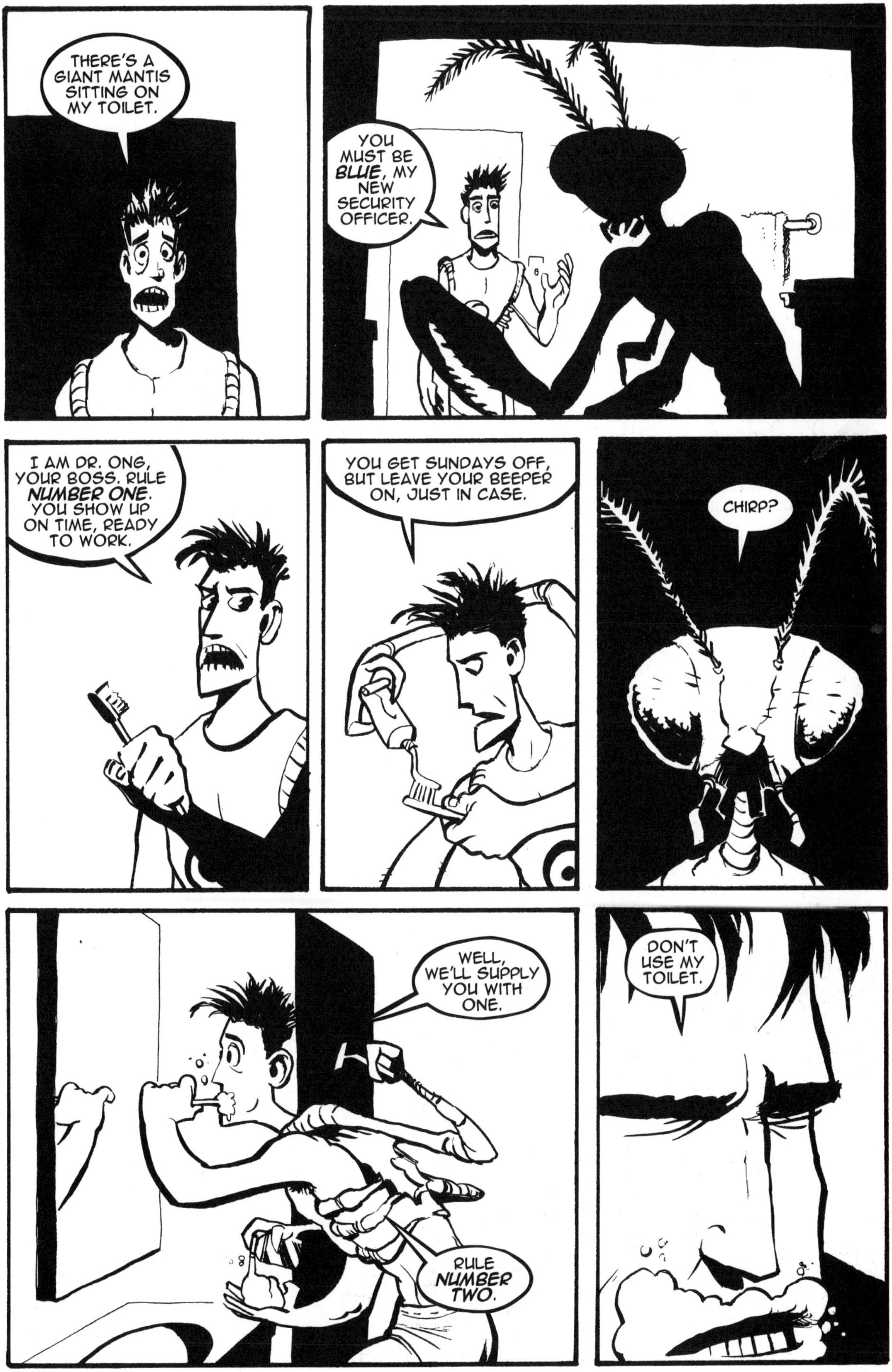
THERE'S A GIANT MANTIS SITTING ON MY TOILET.
YOU MUST BE BLUE, MY NEW SECURITY OFFICER.
I AM DR. ONG, YOUR BOSS. RULE NUMBER ONE. YOU SHOW UP ON TIME, READY TO WORK.
YOU GET SUNDAYS OFF, BUT LEAVE YOUR BEEPER ON, JUST IN CASE.
CHIRP?
WELL, WE'LL SUPPLY YOU WITH ONE.
RULE NUMBER TWO.
DON'T USE MY TOILET.

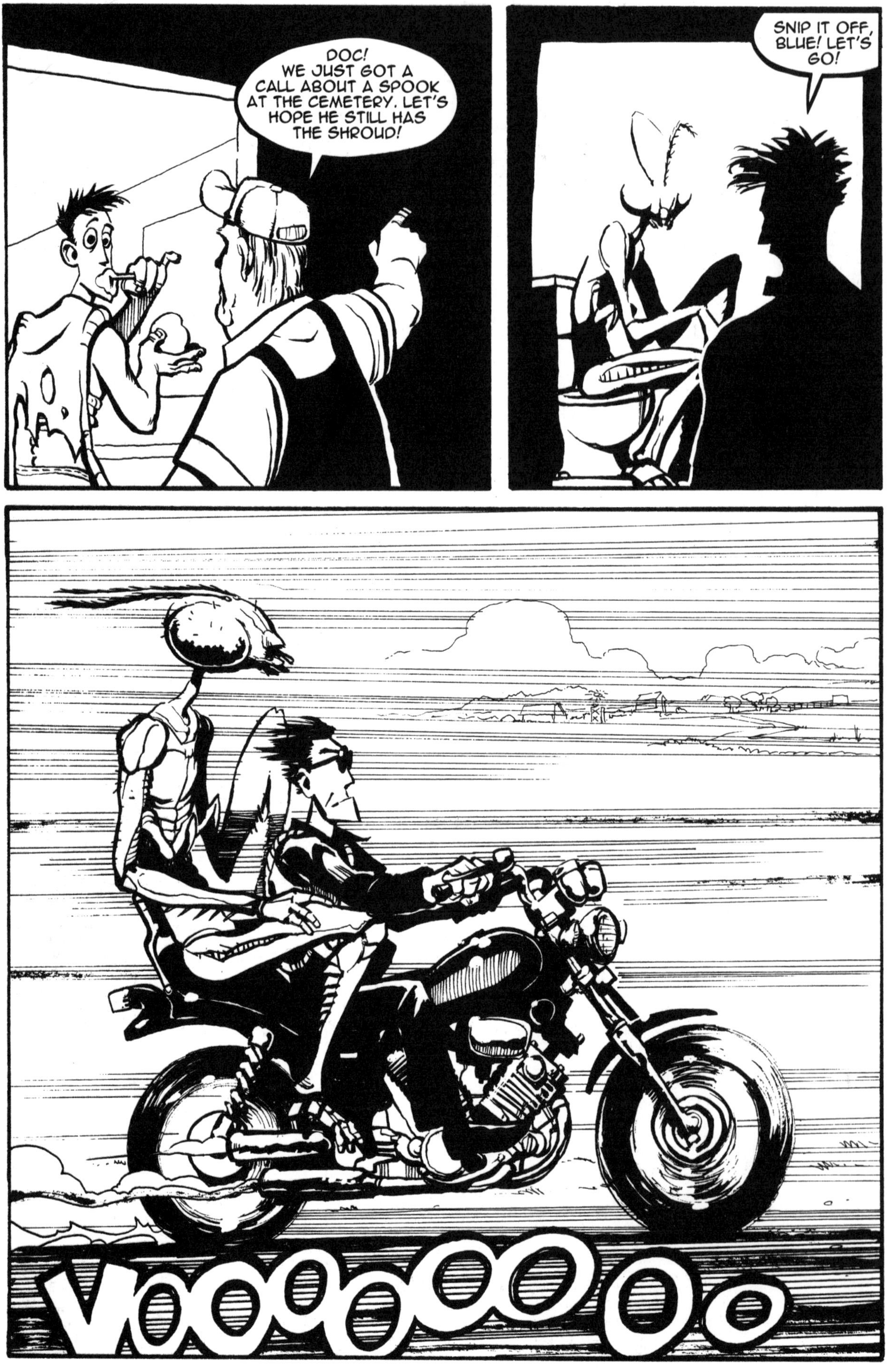
DOC! WE JUST GOT A CALL ABOUT A SPOOK AT THE CEMETERY. LET'S HOPE HE STILL HAS THE SHROUD!
SNIP IT OFF, BLUE! LET'S GO!
VOOOOOOOOO

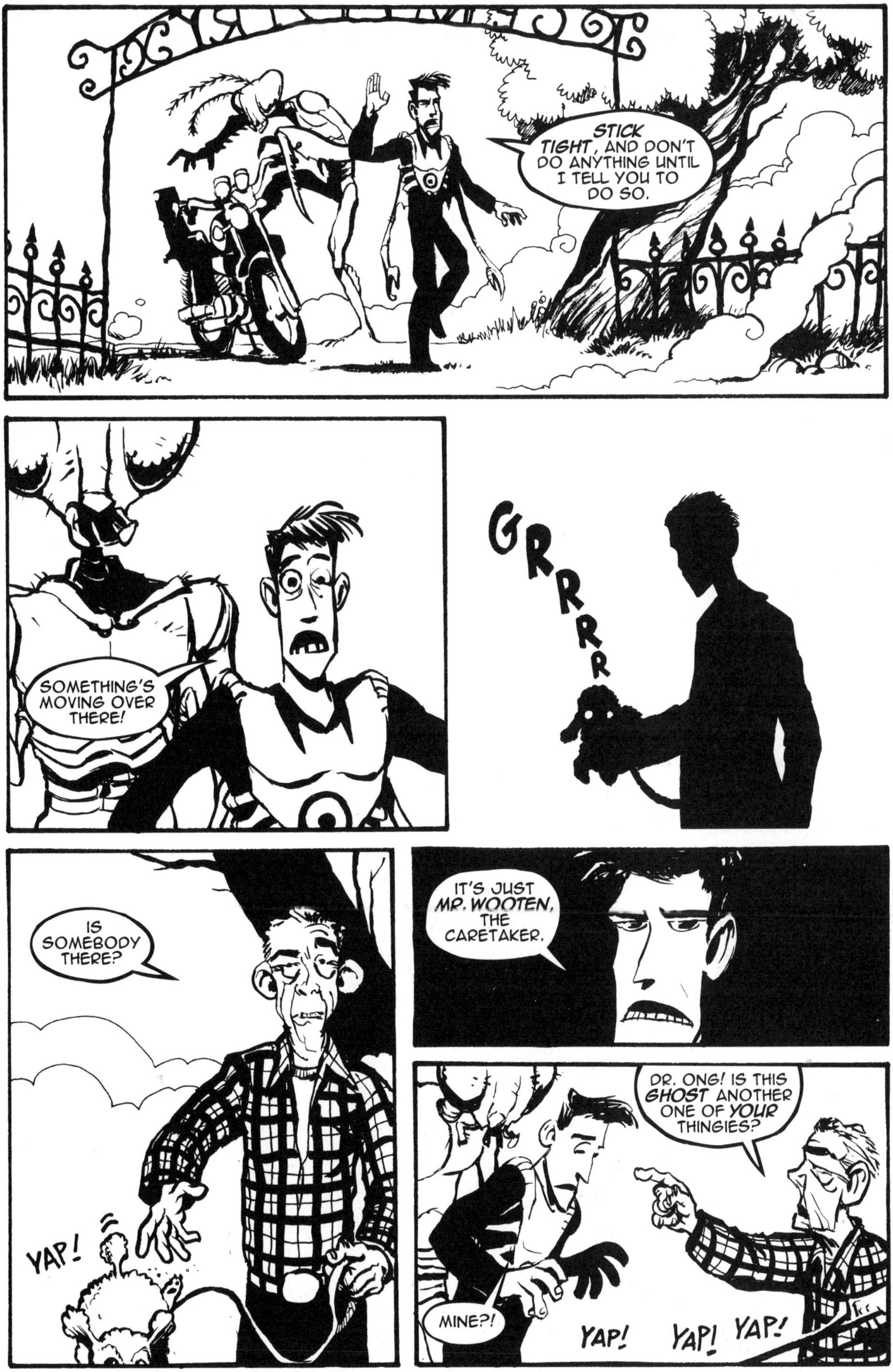
STICK TIGHT, AND DON'T DO ANYTHING UNTIL I TELL YOU TO DO SO.
SOMETHING'S MOVING OVER THERE!
GRRRR
IS SOMEBODY THERE?
YAP!
IT'S JUST MR. WOOTEN, THE CARETAKER.
DR. ONG! IS THIS GHOST ANOTHER ONE OF YOUR THINGIES?
MINE?!
YAP!
YAP!
YAP!

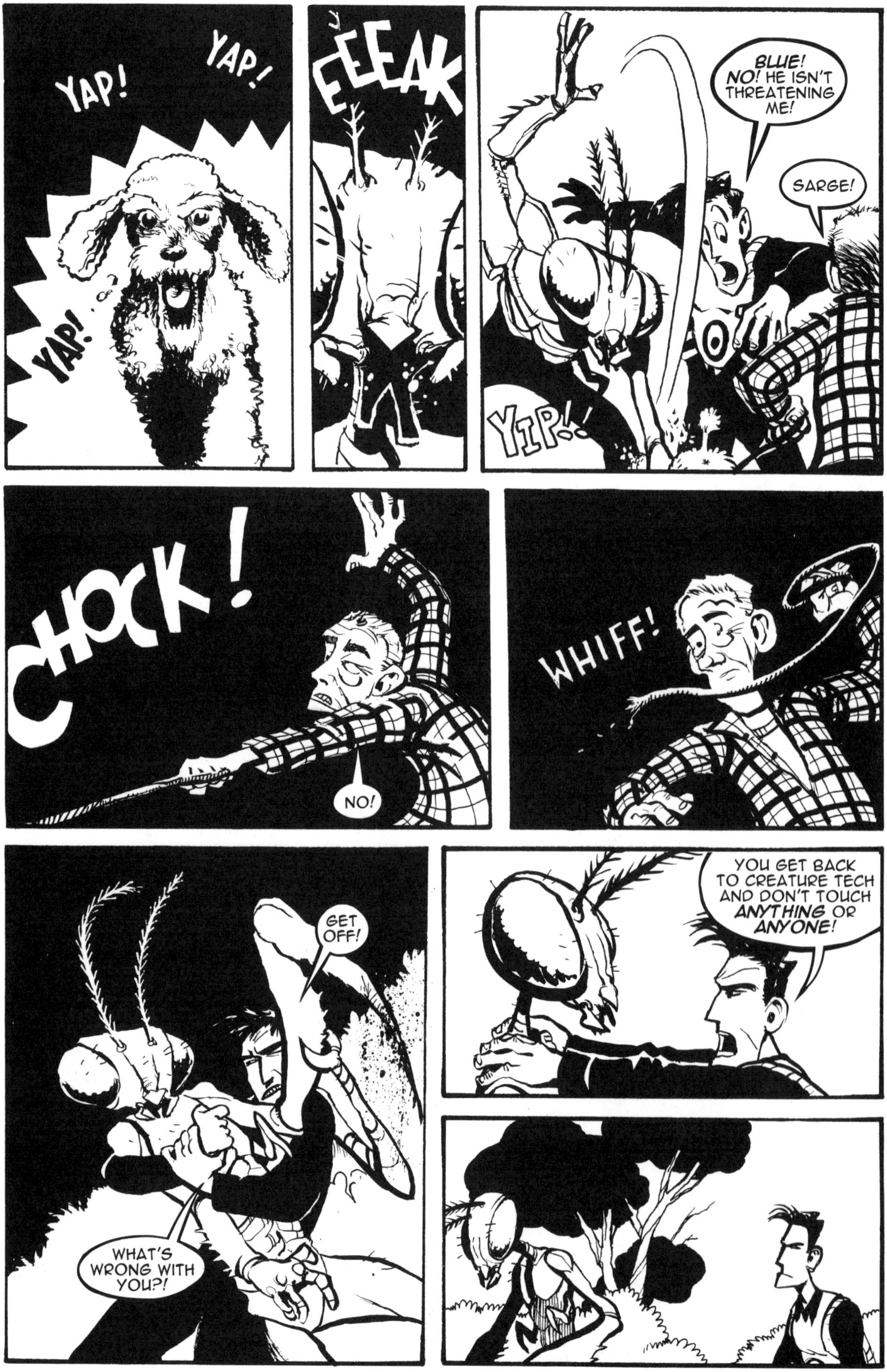
YAP!
YAP!
YAP!
EEEAK
BLUE! NO! HE ISN'T THREATENING ME!
SARGE!
YIP!!
CHOCK!
NO!
WHIFF!
GET OFF!
WHAT'S WRONG WITH YOU?!
YOU GET BACK TO CREATURE TECH AND DON'T TOUCH ANYTHING OR ANYONE!

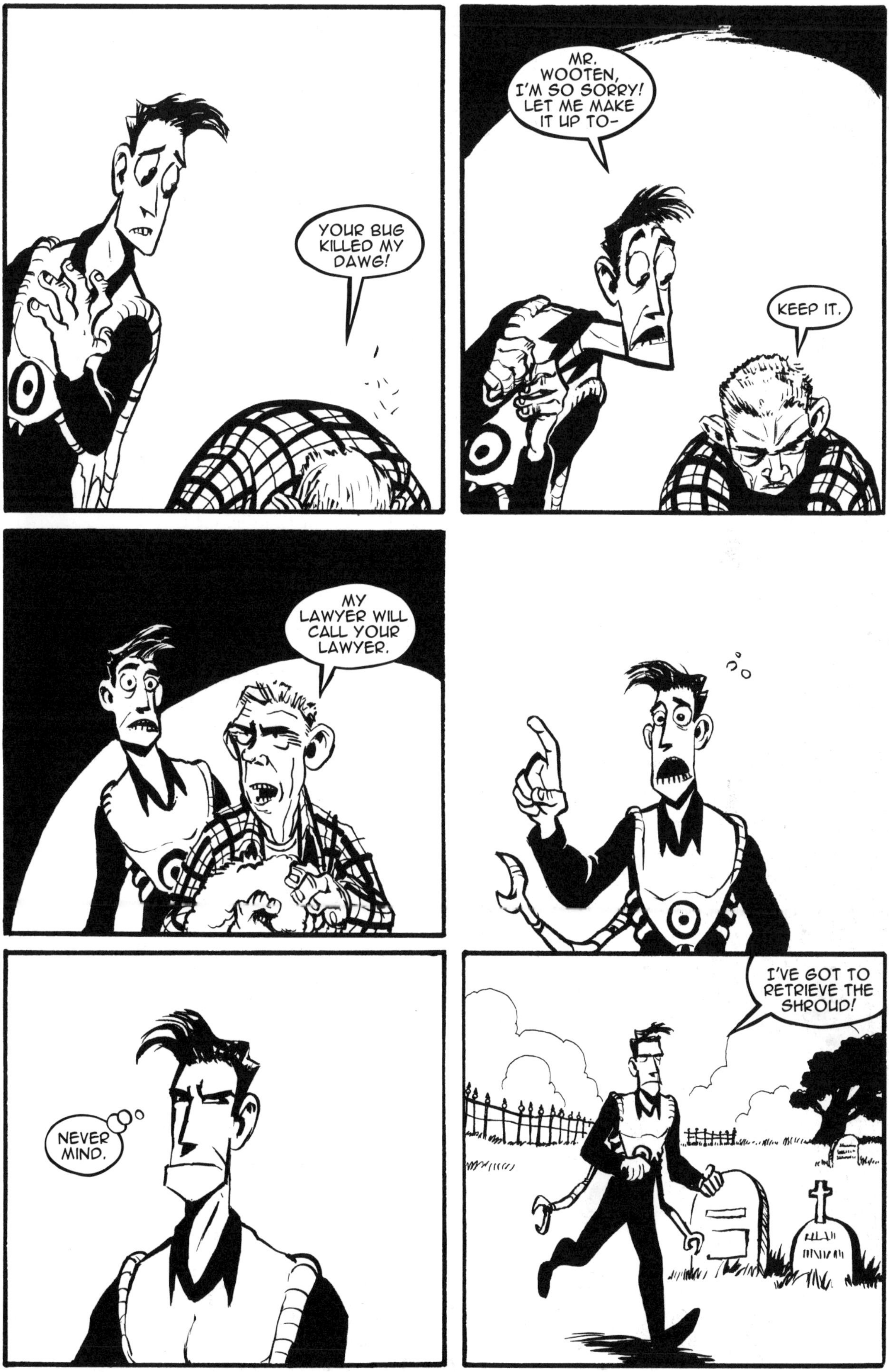
YOUR BUG KILLED MY DAWG!
MR. WOOTEN, I'M SO SORRY! LET ME MAKE IT UP TO-
KEEP IT.
MY LAWYER WILL CALL YOUR LAWYER.
NEVER MIND.
I'VE GOT TO RETRIEVE THE SHROUD!

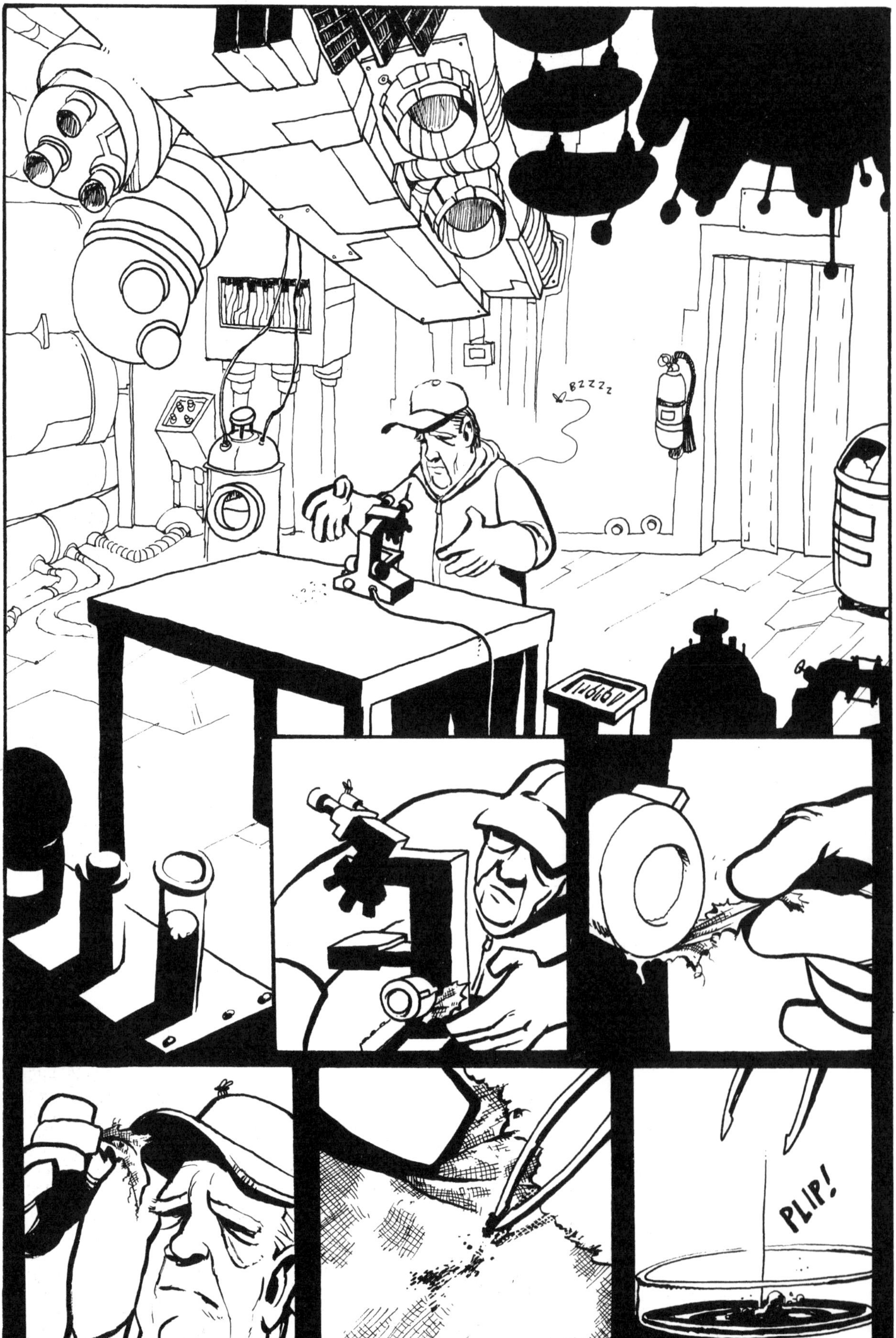
BZZZZ
PLIP!

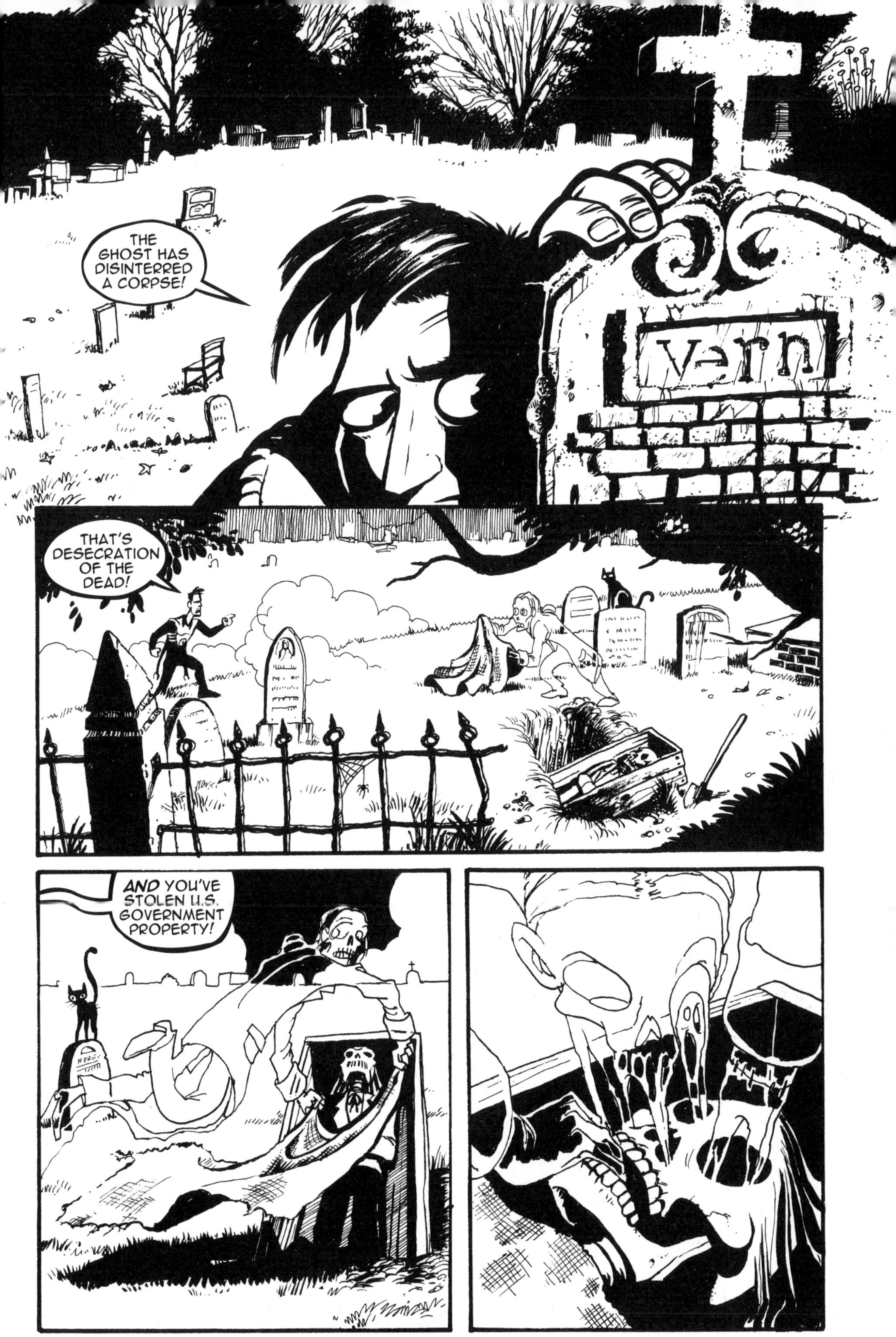
THE GHOST HAS DISINTERRED A CORPSE!
Vern
THAT'S DESECRATION OF THE DEAD!
AND YOU'VE STOLEN U.S. GOVERNMENT PROPERTY!

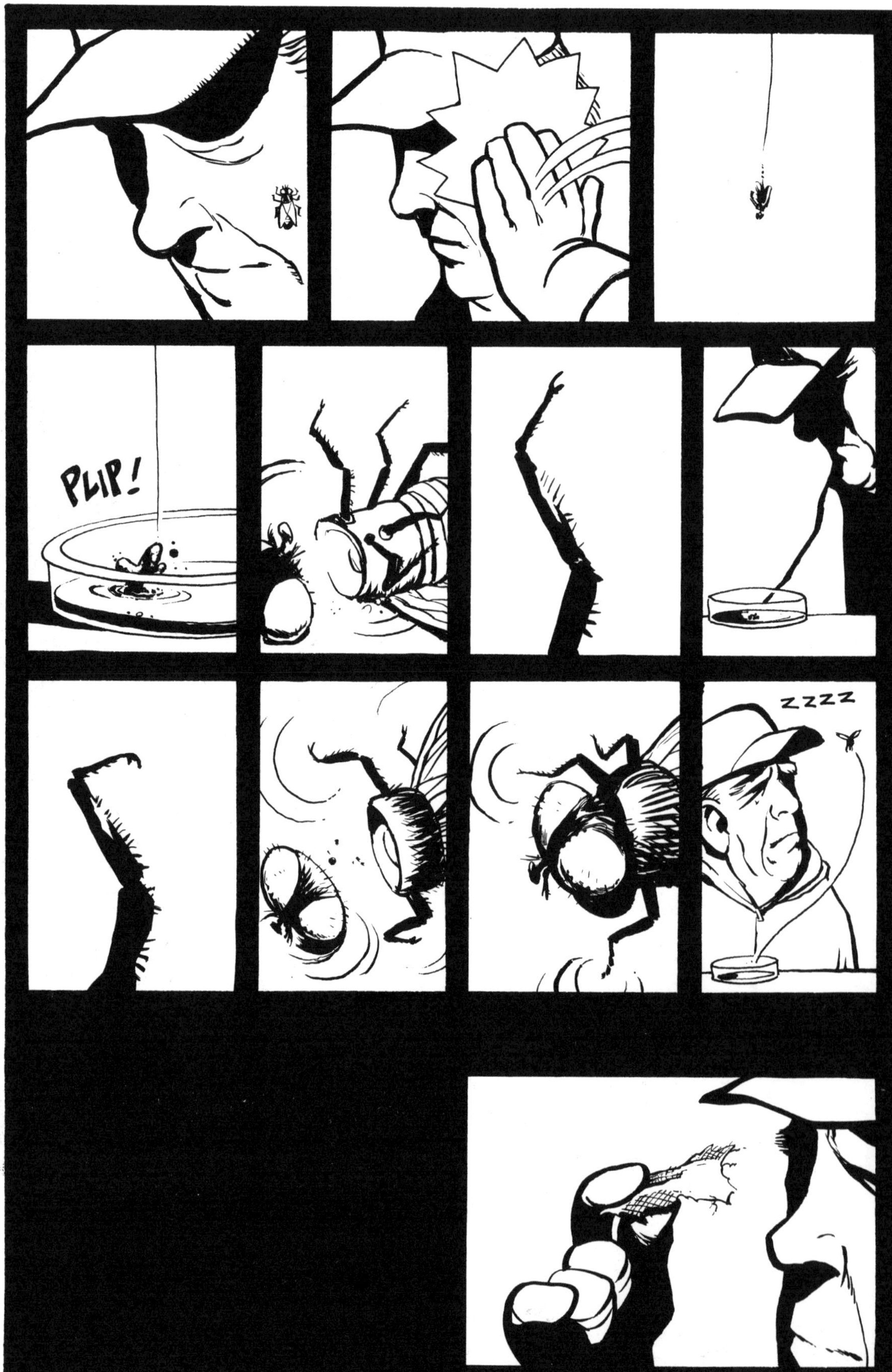
PLIP!
ZZZZ

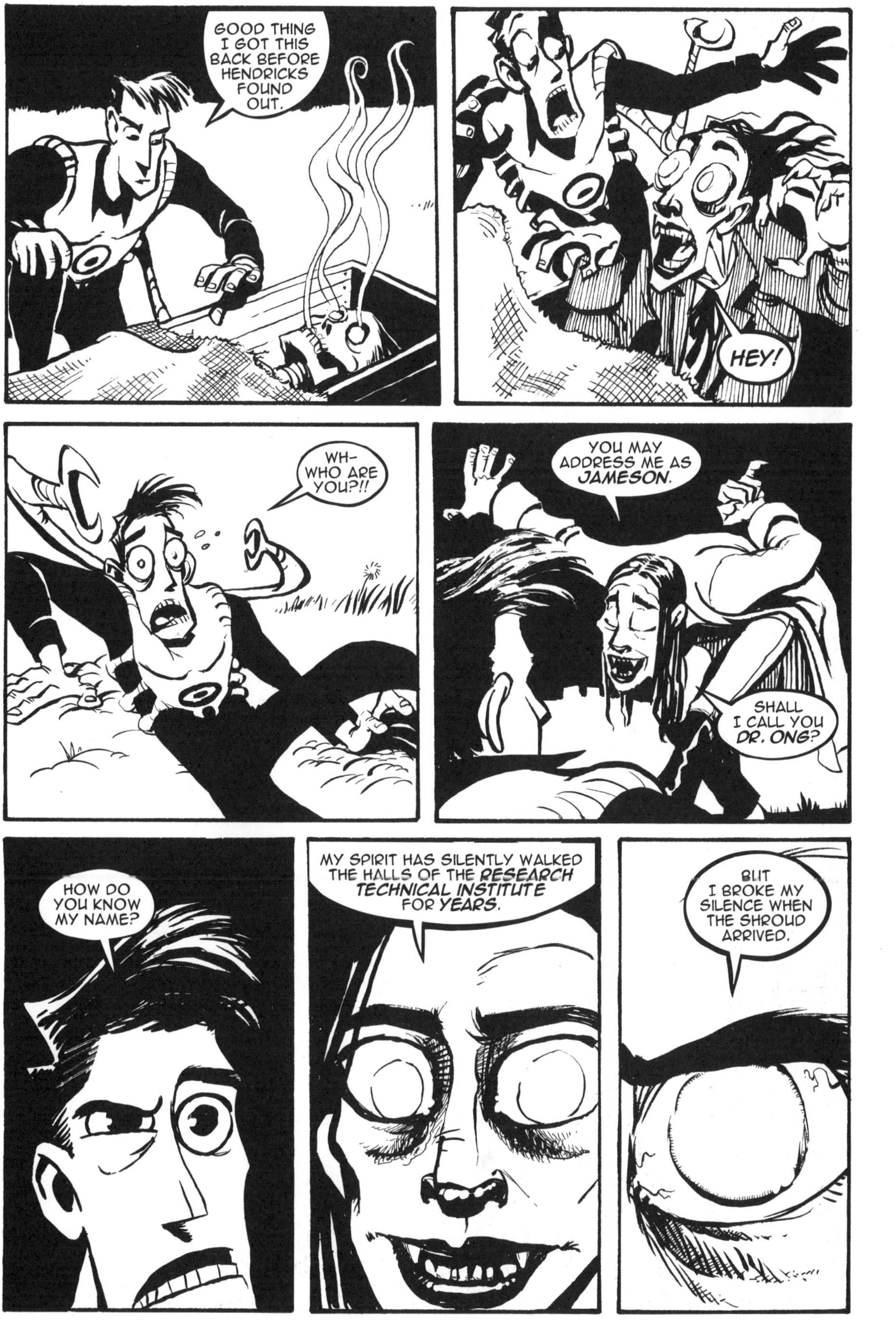
GOOD THING I GOT THIS BACK BEFORE HENDRICKS FOUND OUT.
HEY!
WH- WHO ARE YOU?!!
YOU MAY ADDRESS ME AS JAMESON.
SHALL I CALL YOU DR. ONG?
HOW DO YOU KNOW MY NAME?
MY SPIRIT HAS SILENTLY WALKED THE HALLS OF THE RESEARCH TECHNICAL INSTITUTE FOR YEARS.
BUT I BROKE MY SILENCE WHEN THE SHROUD ARRIVED.

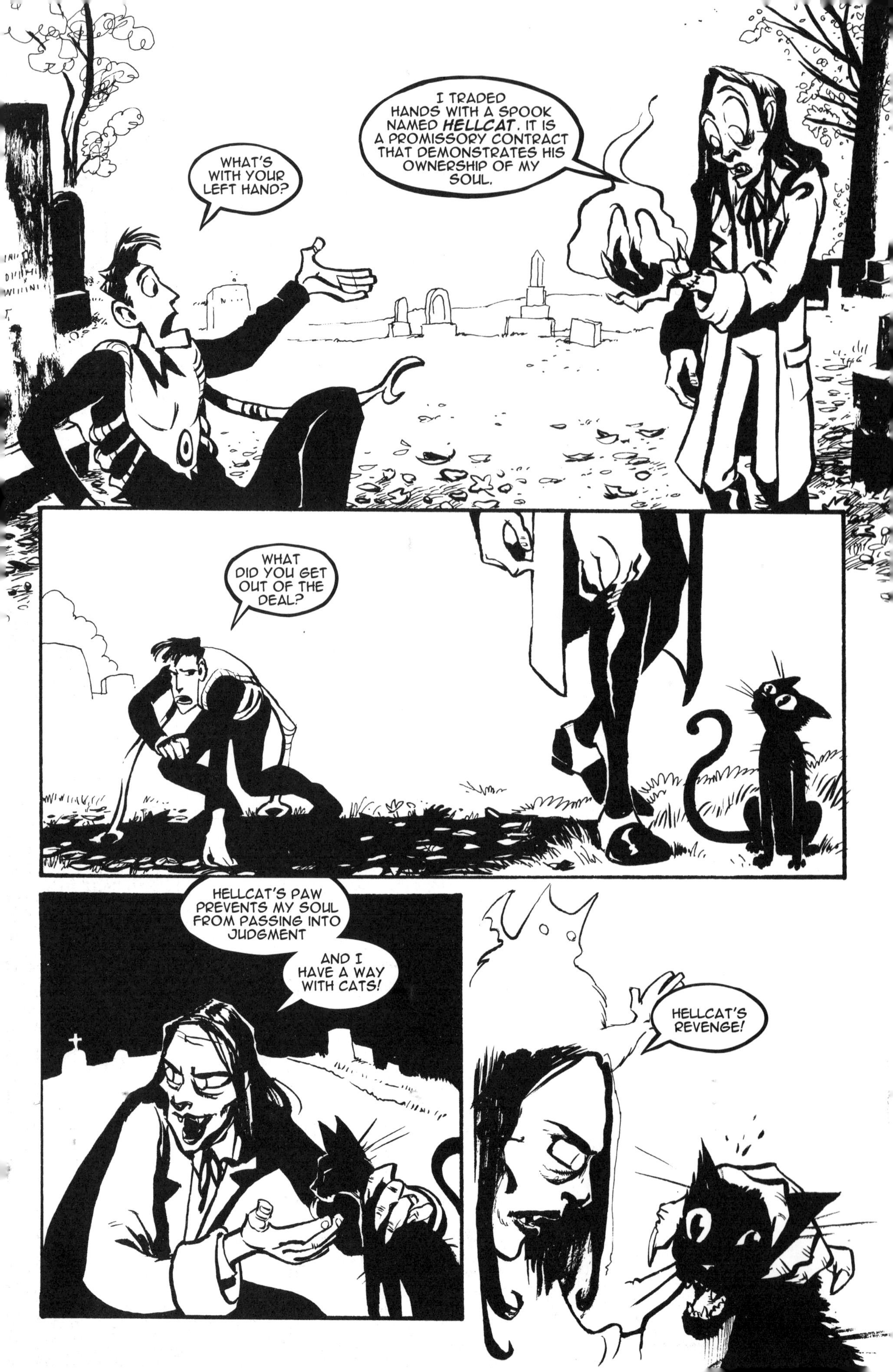
WHAT'S WITH YOUR LEFT HAND?
I TRADED HANDS WITH A SPOOK NAMED HELLCAT. IT IS A PROMISSORY CONTRACT THAT DEMONSTRATES HIS OWNERSHIP OF MY SOUL.
WHAT DID YOU GET OUT OF THE DEAL?
HELLCAT'S PAW PREVENTS MY SOUL FROM PASSING INTO JUDGMENT
AND I HAVE A WAY WITH CATS!
HELLCAT'S REVENGE!

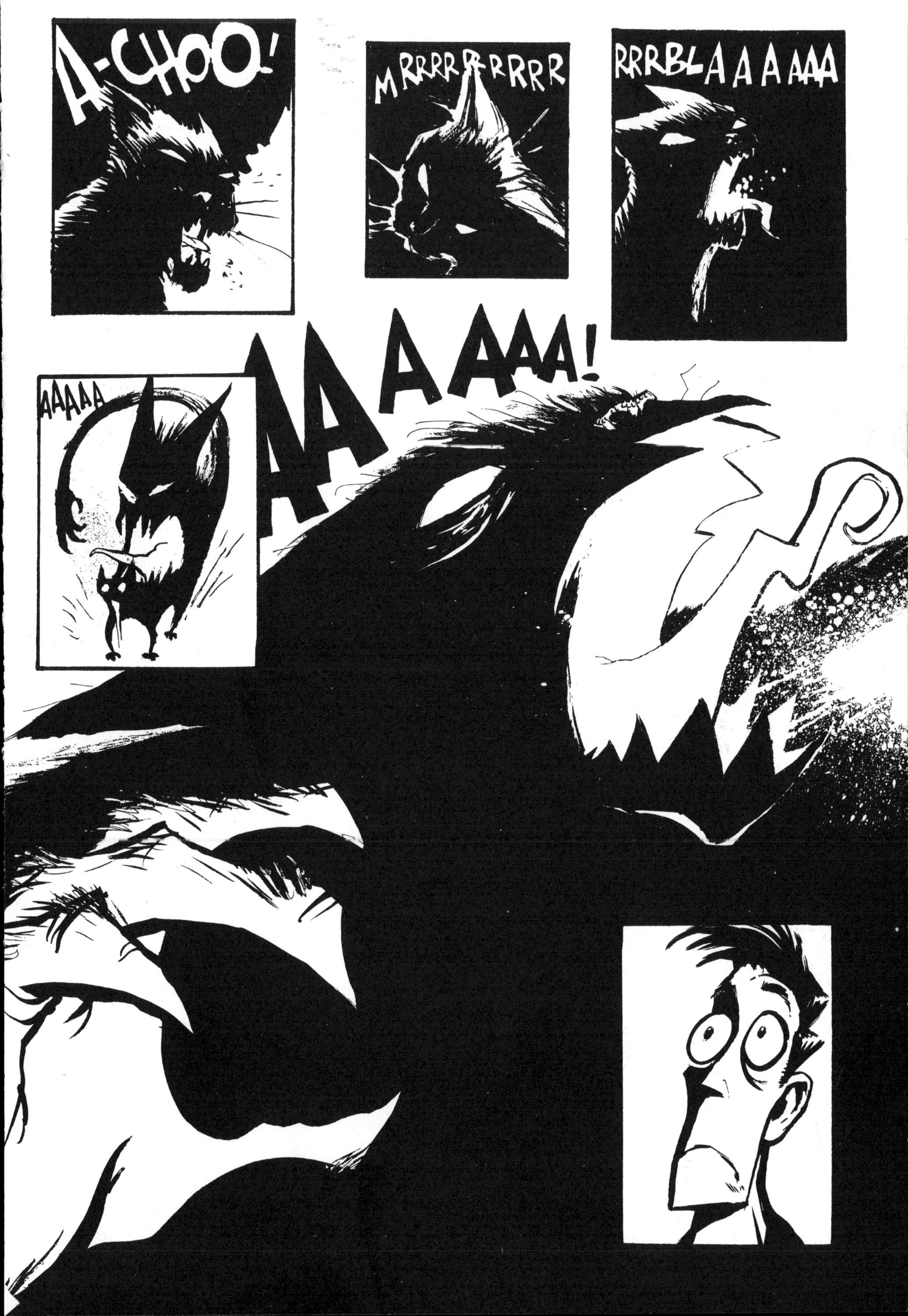
A-CHOO!
MRRRRRRRRRR
RRRBLA A A AAA
AAAAA
AA A AAA!

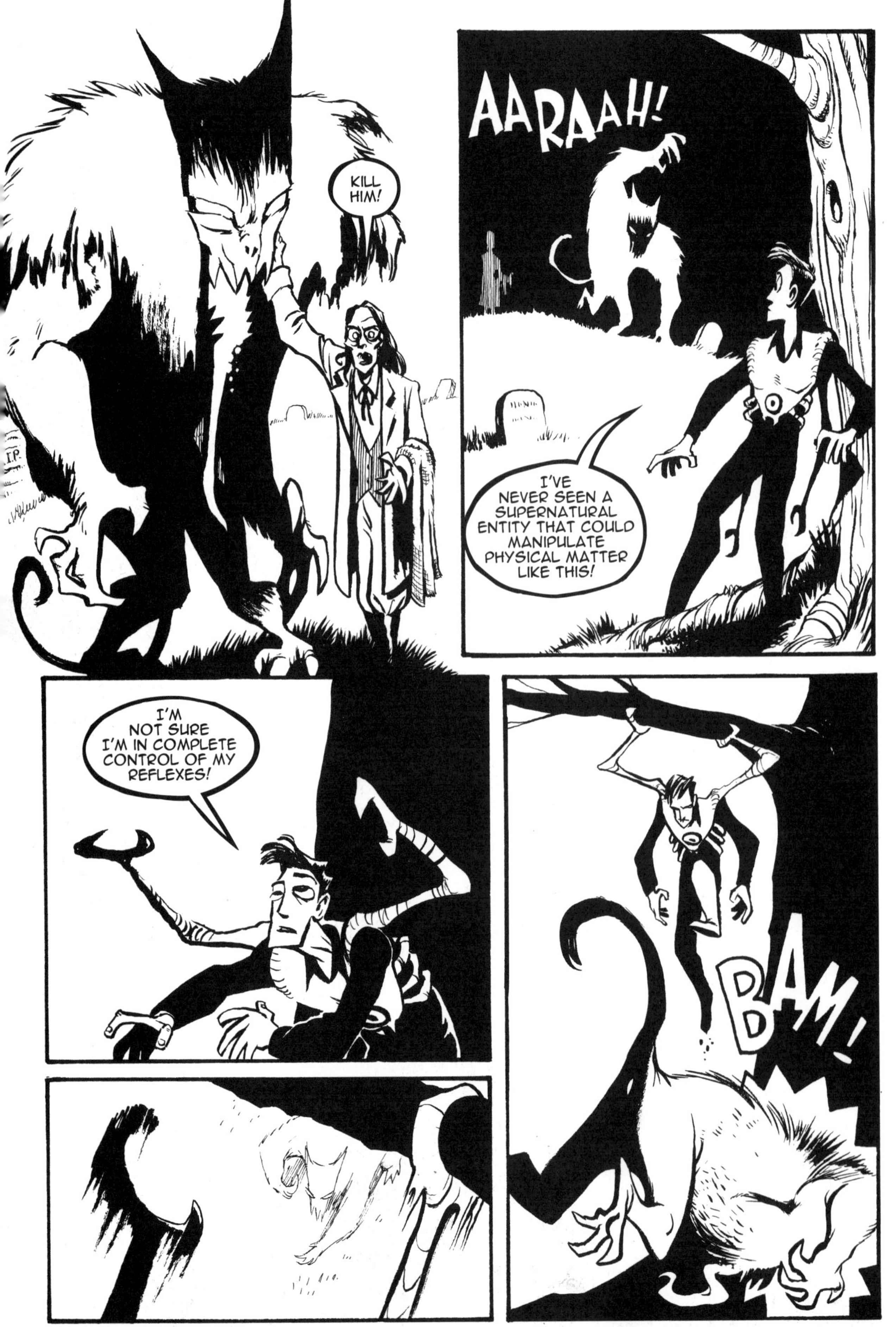
KILL HIM!
AARAAH!
I'VE NEVER SEEN A SUPERNATURAL ENTITY THAT COULD MANIPULATE PHYSICAL MATTER LIKE THIS!
I'M NOT SURE I'M IN COMPLETE CONTROL OF MY REFLEXES!
BAM!

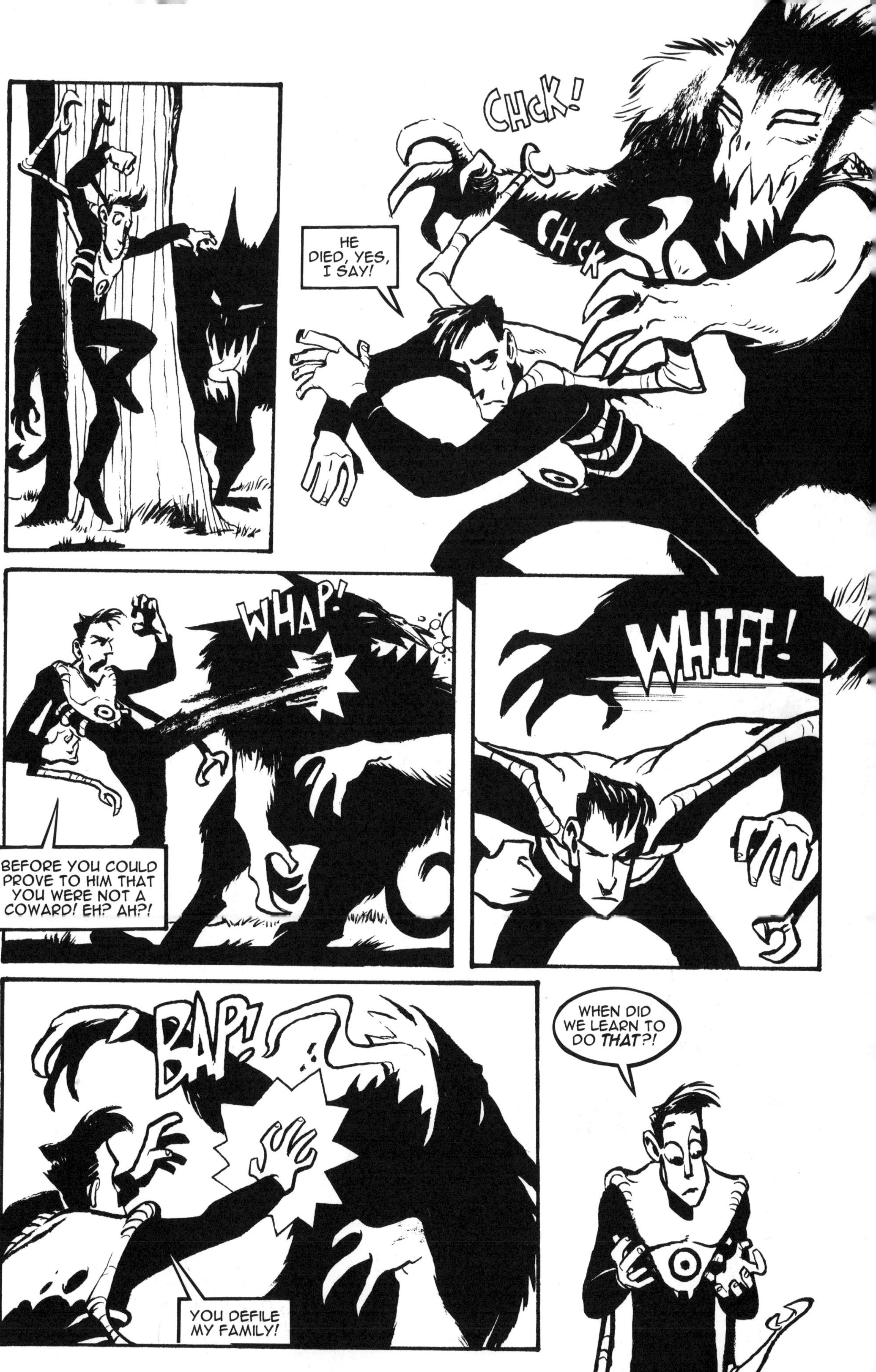
CHCK!
CH-CK
HE DIED, YES, I SAY!
WHAP!
BEFORE YOU COULD PROVE TO HIM THAT YOU WERE NOT A COWARD! EH? AH?!
WHIFF!
BAP!
YOU DEFILE MY FAMILY!
WHEN DID WE LEARN TO DO *THAT*?!

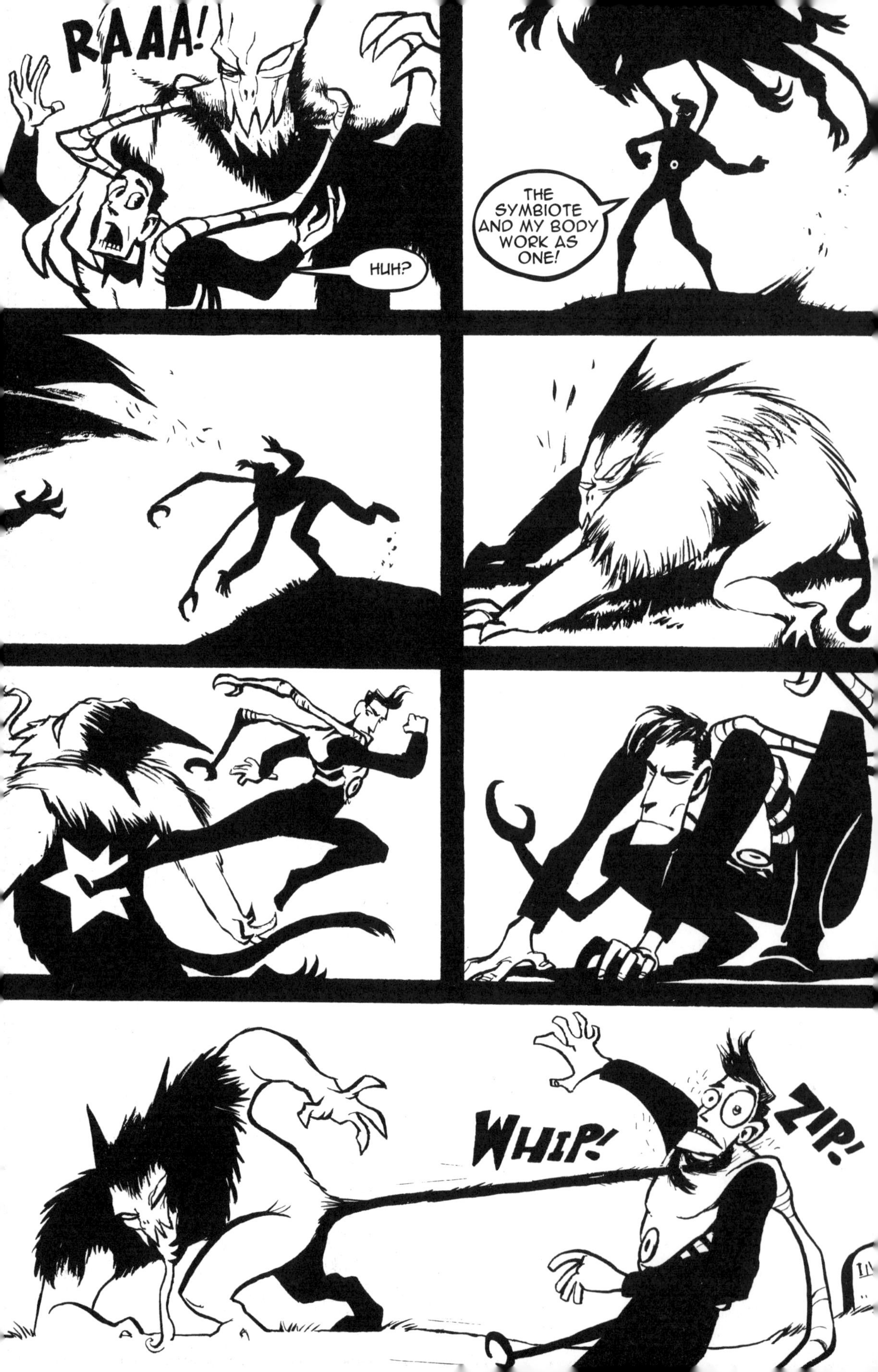
RAAA!
HUH?
THE SYMBIOTE AND MY BODY WORK AS ONE!
WHIP!
ZIP!

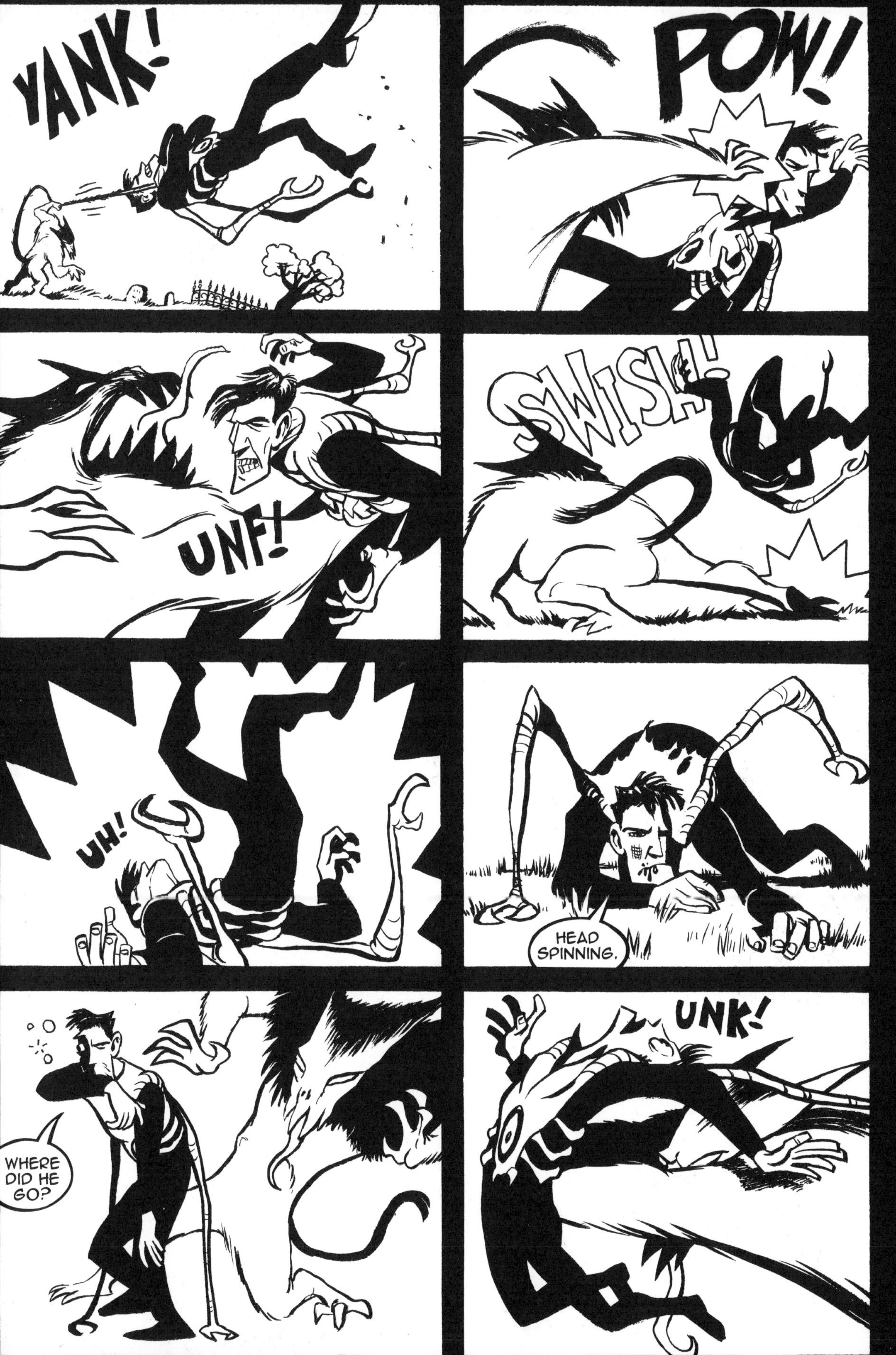
YANK!
POW!
UNF!
SWISH!
UH!
HEAD SPINNING.
WHERE DID HE GO?
UNK!

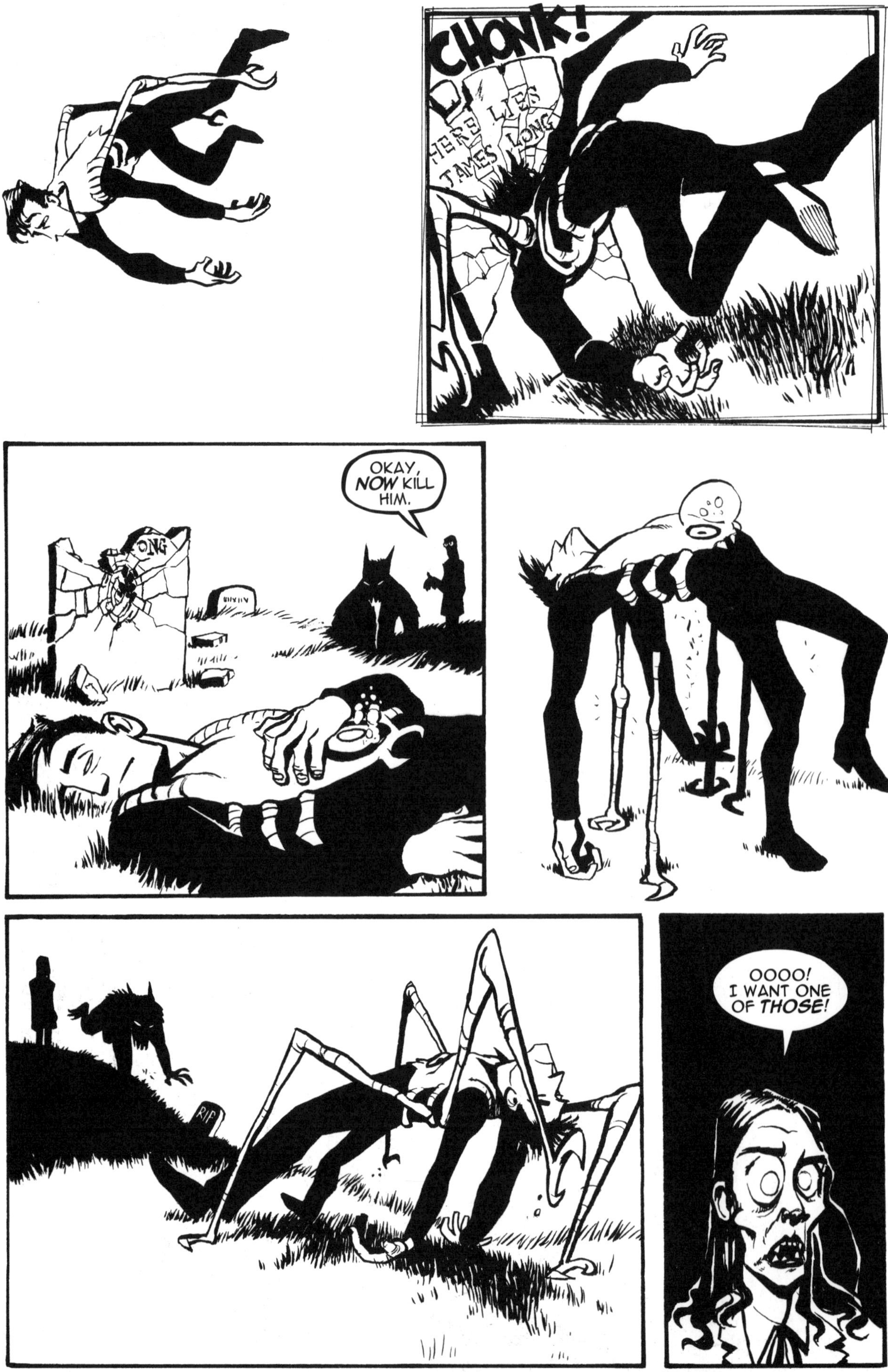
CHONK!
HERE LIES
JAMES LONG
OKAY, NOW KILL HIM.
RIP
OOOO! I WANT ONE OF THOSE!

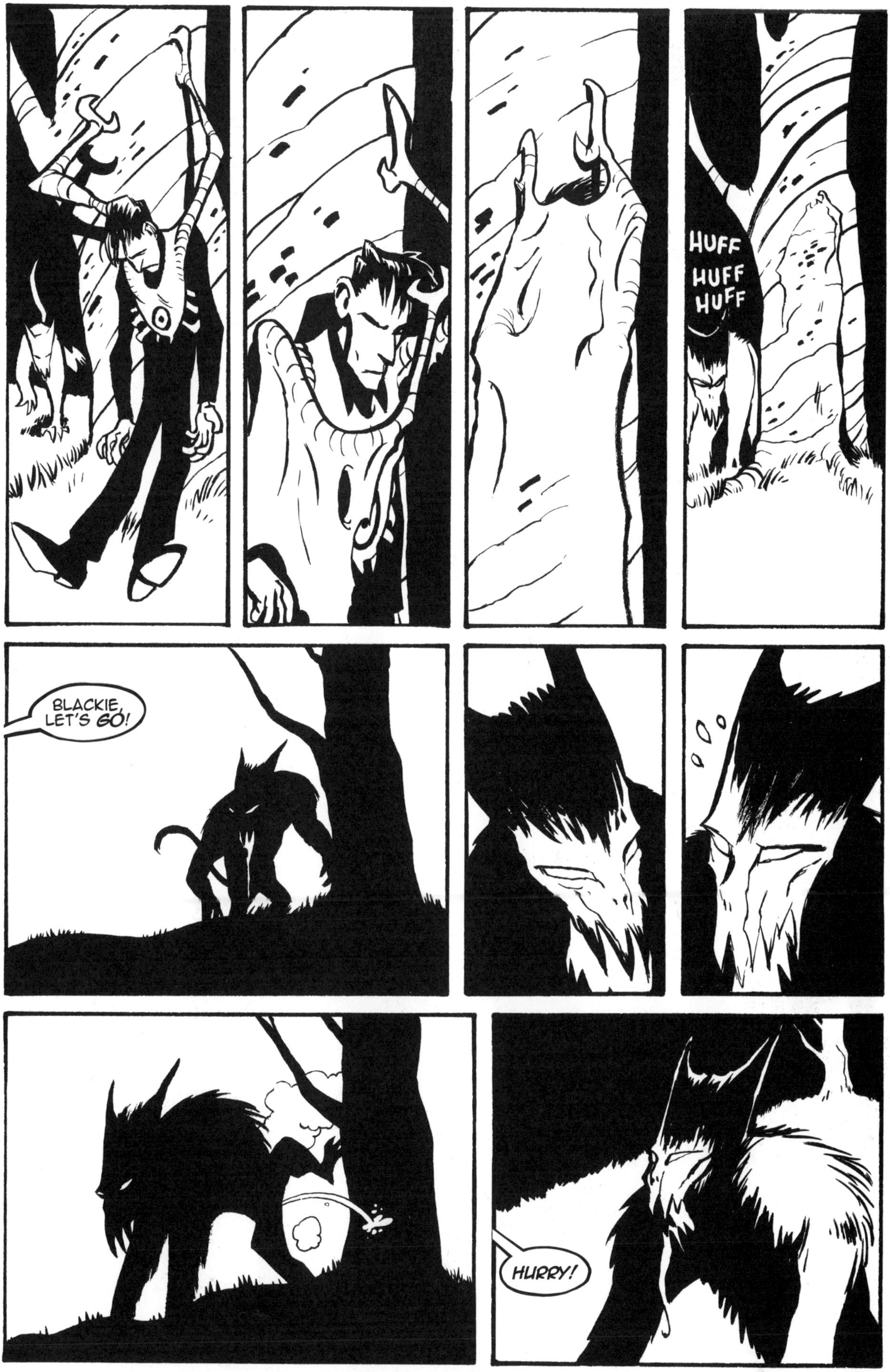
HUFF
HUFF
HUFF
BLACKIE, LET'S GO!
HURRY!

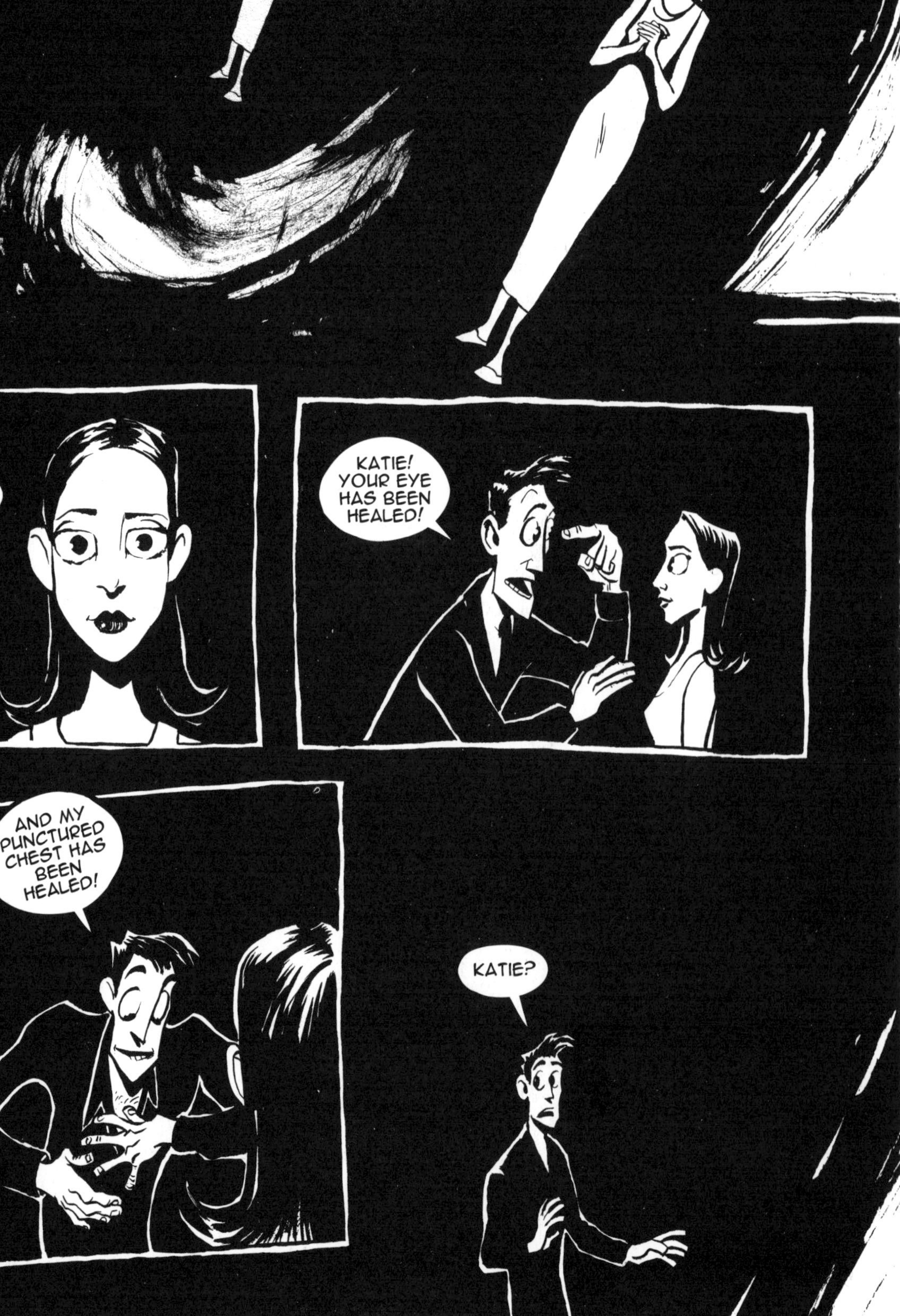
KATIE! YOUR EYE HAS BEEN HEALED!
AND MY PUNCTURED CHEST HAS BEEN HEALED!
KATIE?

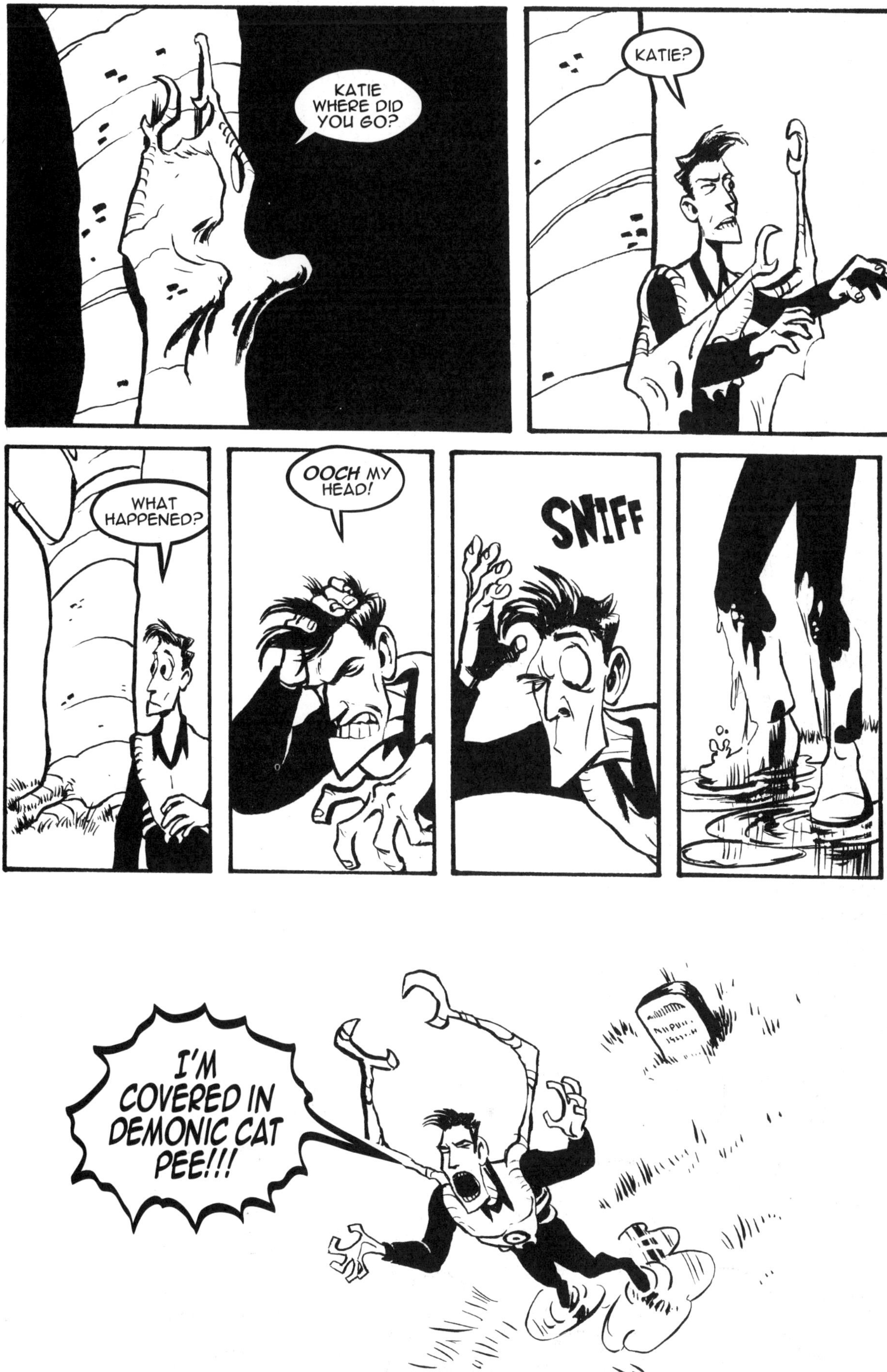
KATIE WHERE DID YOU GO?
KATIE?
WHAT HAPPENED?
OOCH MY HEAD!
SNIFF
I'M COVERED IN DEMONIC CAT PEE!!!

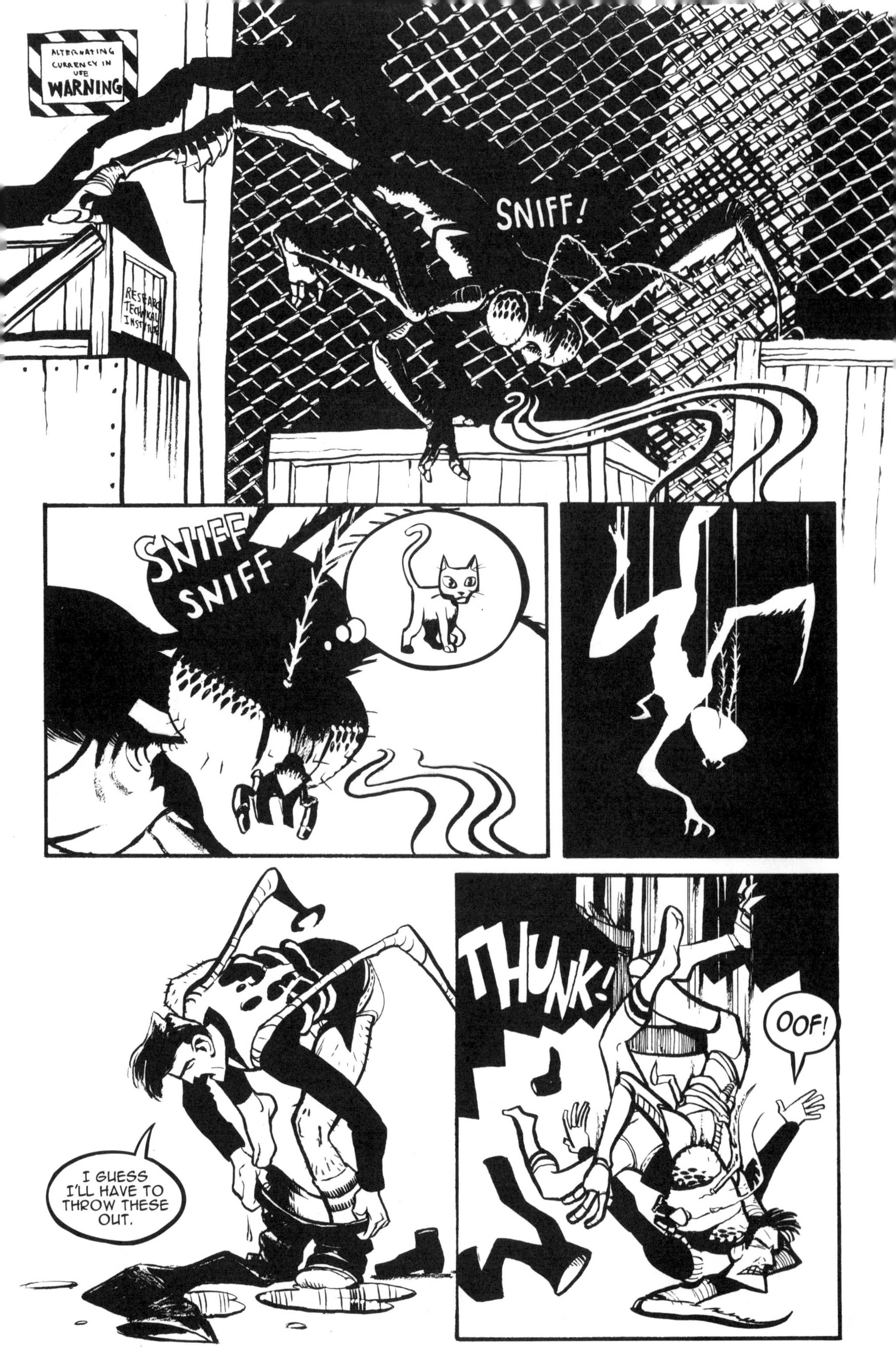
ALTERNATING CURRENCY IN USE
WARNING
SNIFF!
SNIFF SNIFF
I GUESS I'LL HAVE TO THROW THESE OUT.
THUNK!
OOF!

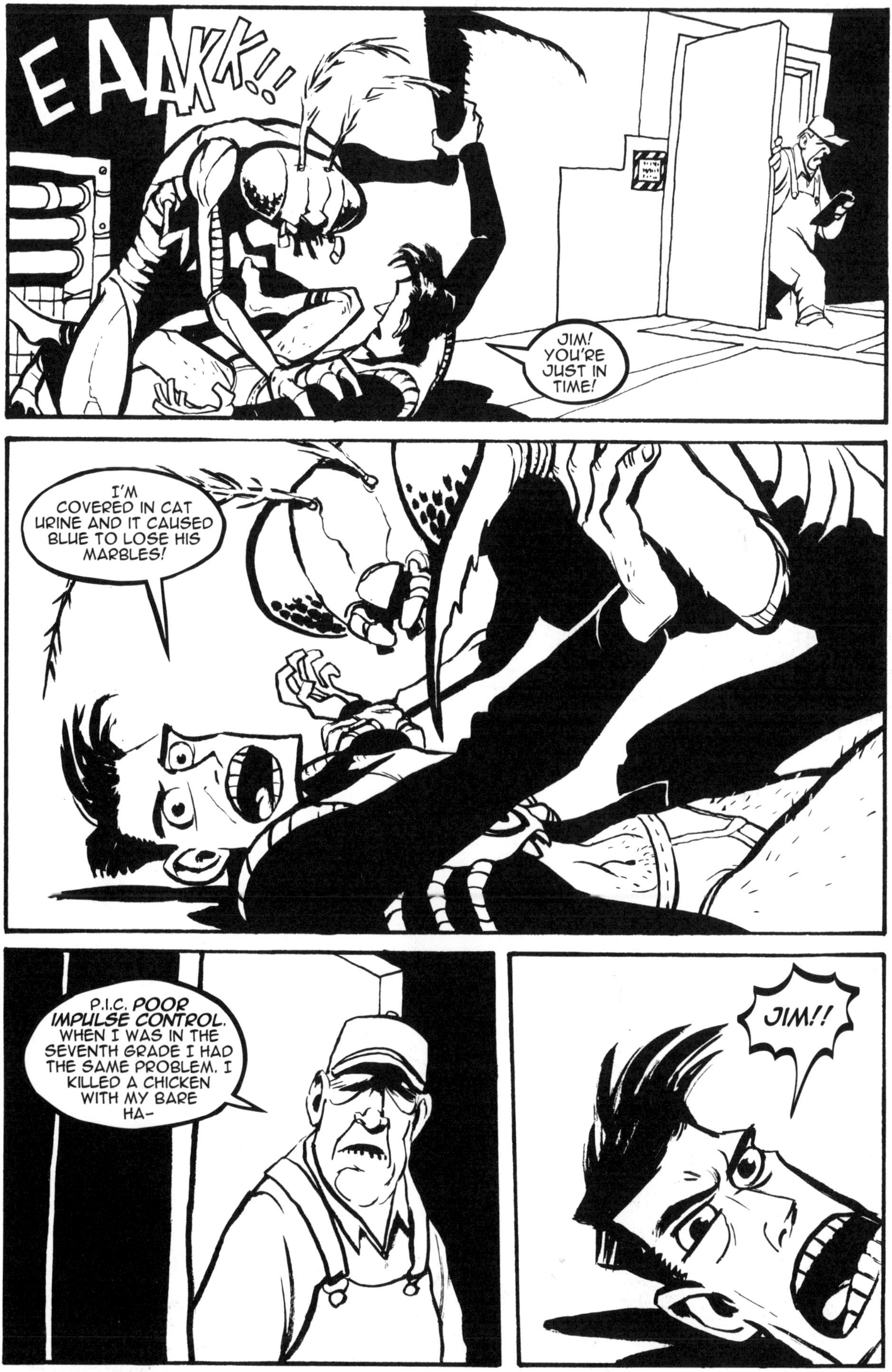
EAAKK!!
JIM! YOU'RE JUST IN TIME!
I'M COVERED IN CAT URINE AND IT CAUSED BLUE TO LOSE HIS MARBLES!
P.I.C. POOR IMPULSE CONTROL. WHEN I WAS IN THE SEVENTH GRADE I HAD THE SAME PROBLEM. I KILLED A CHICKEN WITH MY BARE HA-
JIM!!

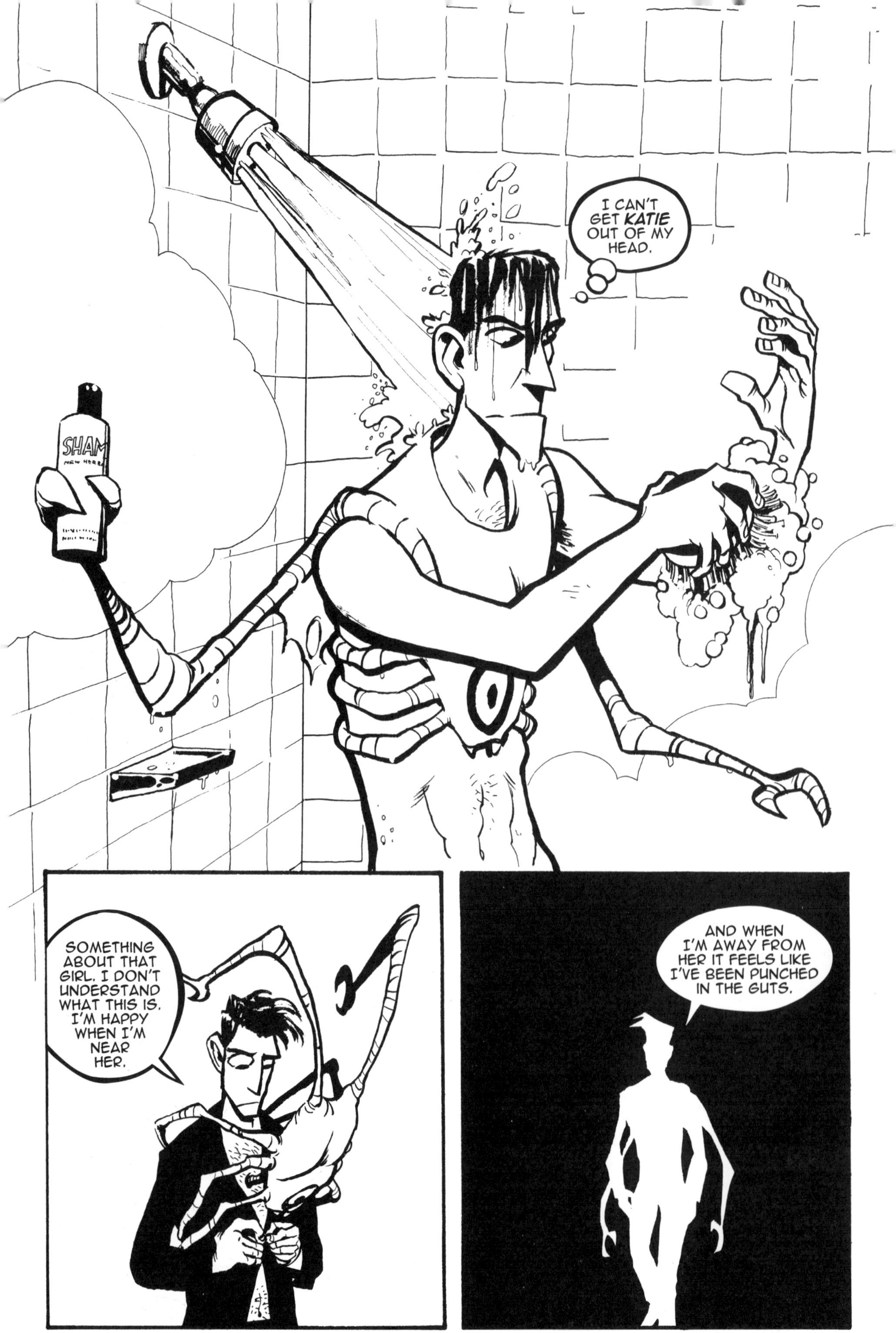

SHAM
I CAN'T GET KATIE OUT OF MY HEAD.
SOMETHING ABOUT THAT GIRL. I DON'T UNDERSTAND WHAT THIS IS. I'M HAPPY WHEN I'M NEAR HER.
AND WHEN I'M AWAY FROM HER IT FEELS LIKE I'VE BEEN PUNCHED IN THE GUTS.

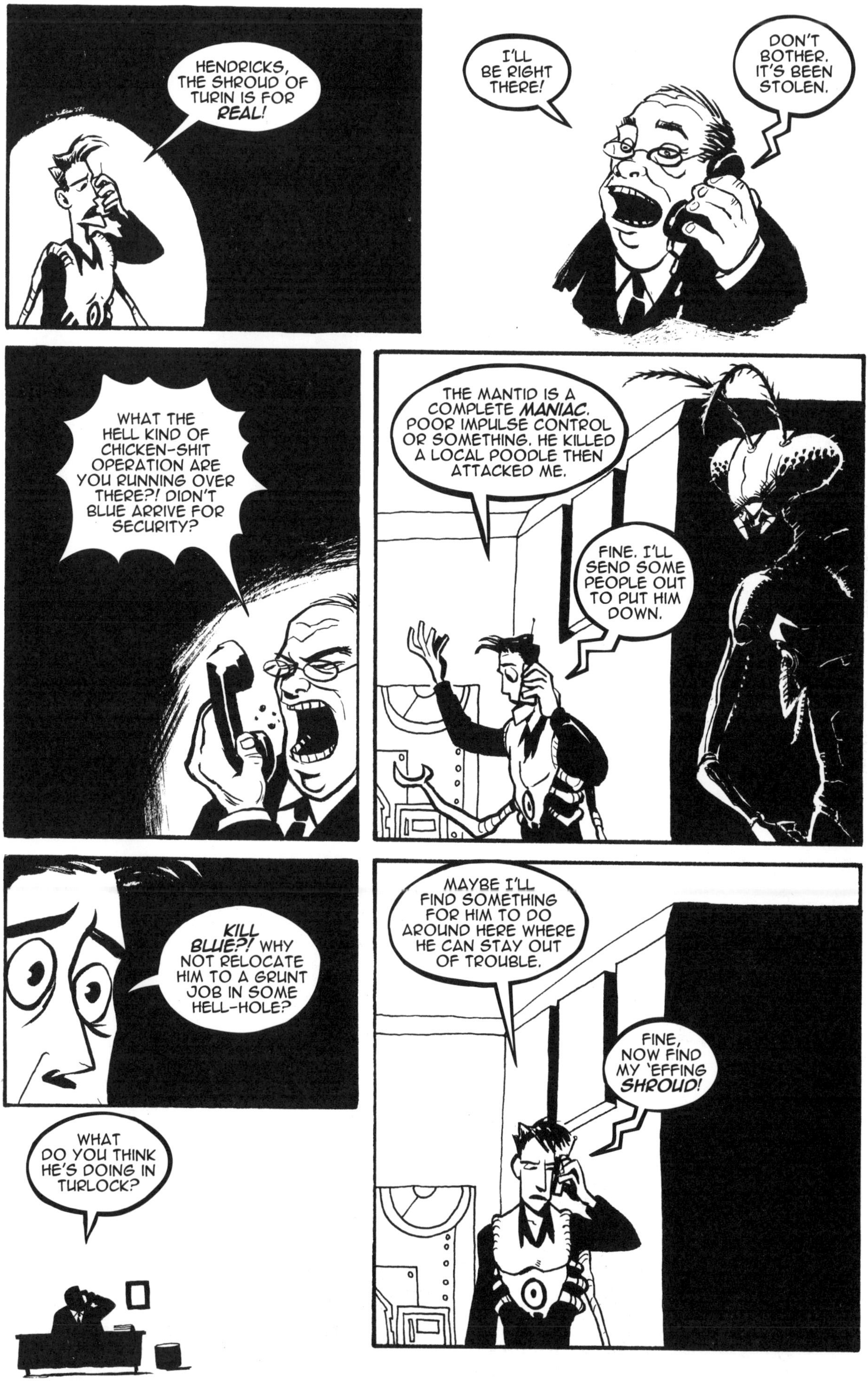
HENDRICKS, THE SHROUD OF TURIN IS FOR REAL!
I'LL BE RIGHT THERE!
DON'T BOTHER. IT'S BEEN STOLEN.
WHAT THE HELL KIND OF CHICKEN-SHIT OPERATION ARE YOU RUNNING OVER THERE?! DIDN'T BLUE ARRIVE FOR SECURITY?
THE MANTID IS A COMPLETE MANIAC. POOR IMPULSE CONTROL OR SOMETHING. HE KILLED A LOCAL POODLE THEN ATTACKED ME.
FINE. I'LL SEND SOME PEOPLE OUT TO PUT HIM DOWN.
KILL BLUE?! WHY NOT RELOCATE HIM TO A GRUNT JOB IN SOME HELL-HOLE?
WHAT DO YOU THINK HE'S DOING IN TURLOCK?
MAYBE I'LL FIND SOMETHING FOR HIM TO DO AROUND HERE WHERE HE CAN STAY OUT OF TROUBLE.
FINE, NOW FIND MY 'EFFING SHROUD!

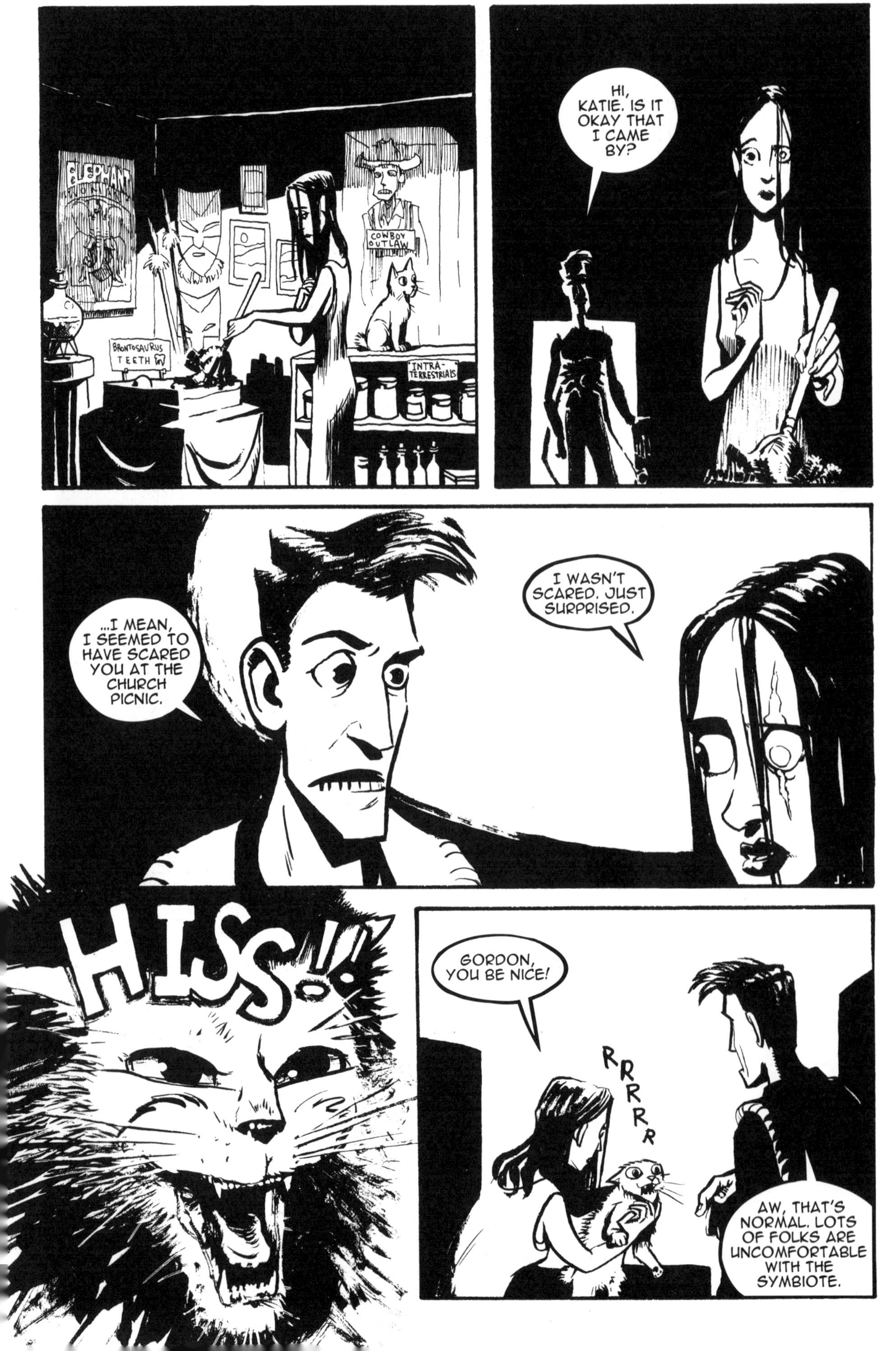
ELEPHANT
BRONTOSAURUS TEETH
COWBOY OUTLAW
INTRA-TERRESTRIALS
HI, KATIE. IS IT OKAY THAT I CAME BY?
...I MEAN, I SEEMED TO HAVE SCARED YOU AT THE CHURCH PICNIC.
I WASN'T SCARED. JUST SURPRISED.
HISS!!
GORDON, YOU BE NICE!
RRRRR
AW, THAT'S NORMAL. LOTS OF FOLKS ARE UNCOMFORTABLE WITH THE SYMBIOTE.

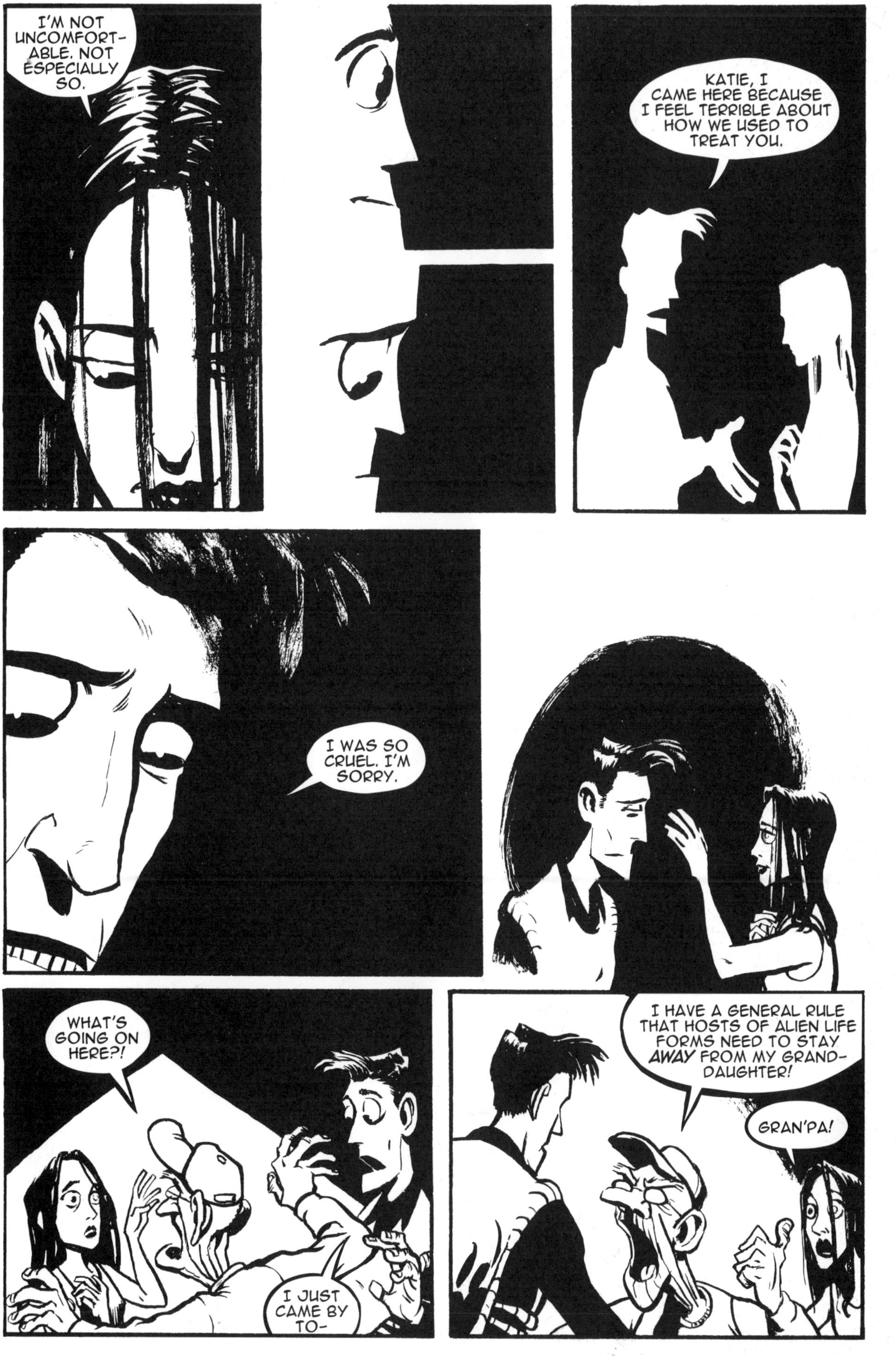
I'M NOT UNCOMFORTABLE. NOT ESPECIALLY SO.
KATIE, I CAME HERE BECAUSE I FEEL TERRIBLE ABOUT HOW WE USED TO TREAT YOU.
I WAS SO CRUEL. I'M SORRY.
WHAT'S GOING ON HERE?!
I JUST CAME BY TO-
I HAVE A GENERAL RULE THAT HOSTS OF ALIEN LIFE FORMS NEED TO STAY AWAY FROM MY GRAND-DAUGHTER!
GRAN'PA!

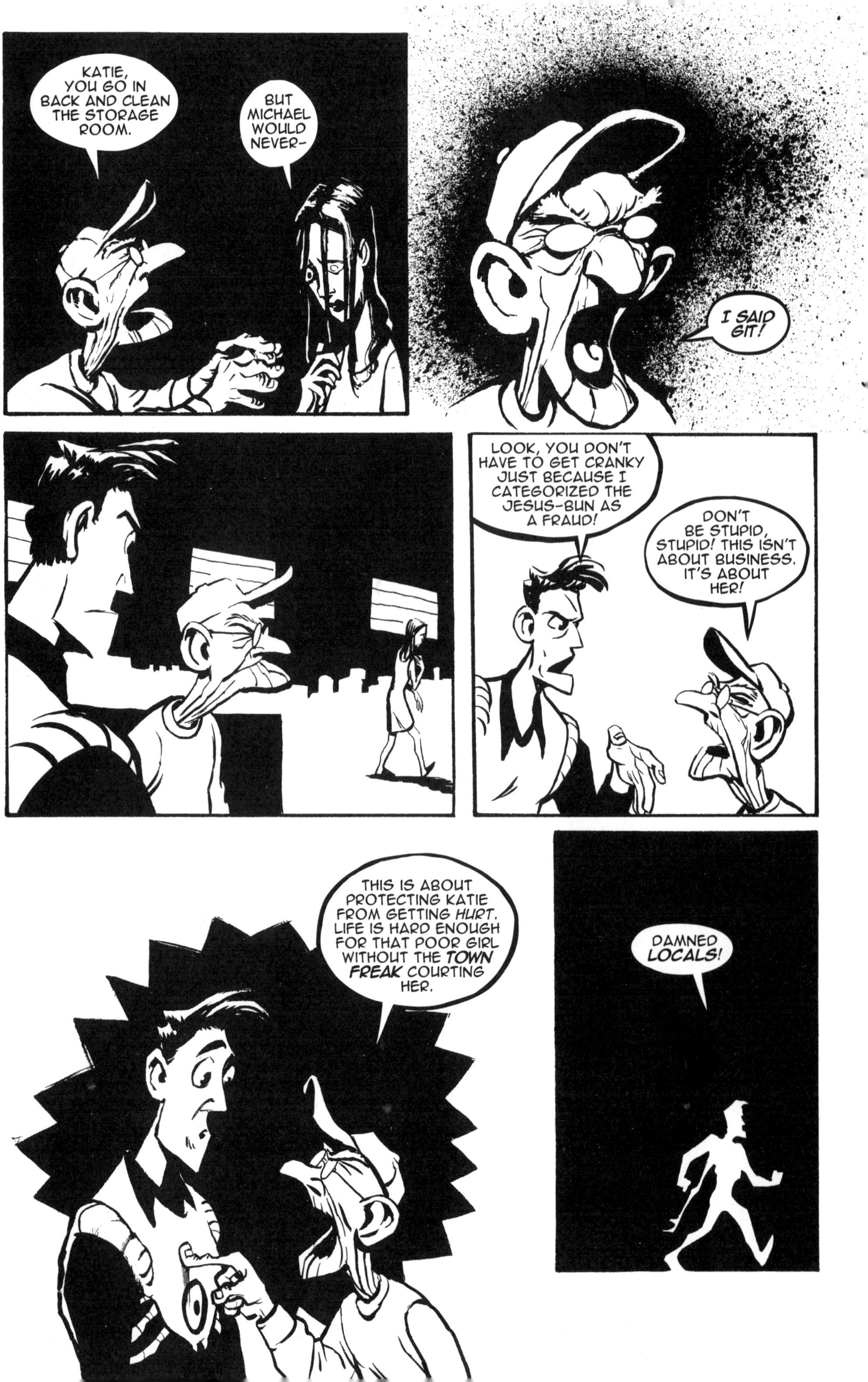
KATIE, YOU GO IN BACK AND CLEAN THE STORAGE ROOM.
BUT MICHAEL WOULD NEVER-
I SAID GIT!
LOOK, YOU DON'T HAVE TO GET CRANKY JUST BECAUSE I CATEGORIZED THE JESUS-BUN AS A FRAUD!
DON'T BE STUPID, STUPID! THIS ISN'T ABOUT BUSINESS. IT'S ABOUT HER!
THIS IS ABOUT PROTECTING KATIE FROM GETTING *HURT*. LIFE IS HARD ENOUGH FOR THAT POOR GIRL WITHOUT THE ***TOWN FREAK*** COURTING HER.
DAMNED ***LOCALS!***

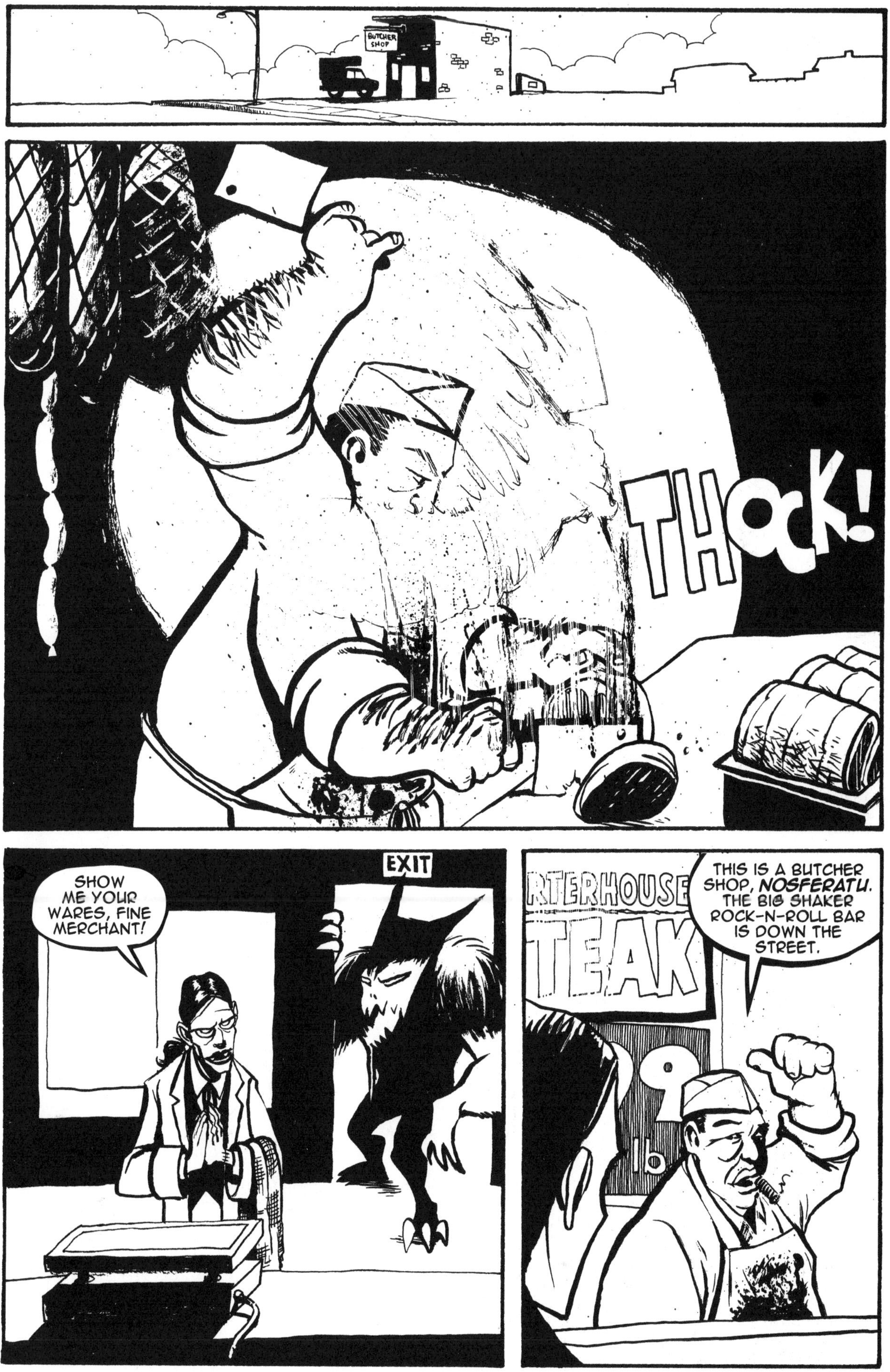
BUTCHER SHOP
THOCK!
EXIT
SHOW ME YOUR WARES, FINE MERCHANT!
RTERHOUSE
TEAK
9
lb
THIS IS A BUTCHER SHOP, *NOSFERATU*. THE BIG SHAKER ROCK-N-ROLL BAR IS DOWN THE STREET.

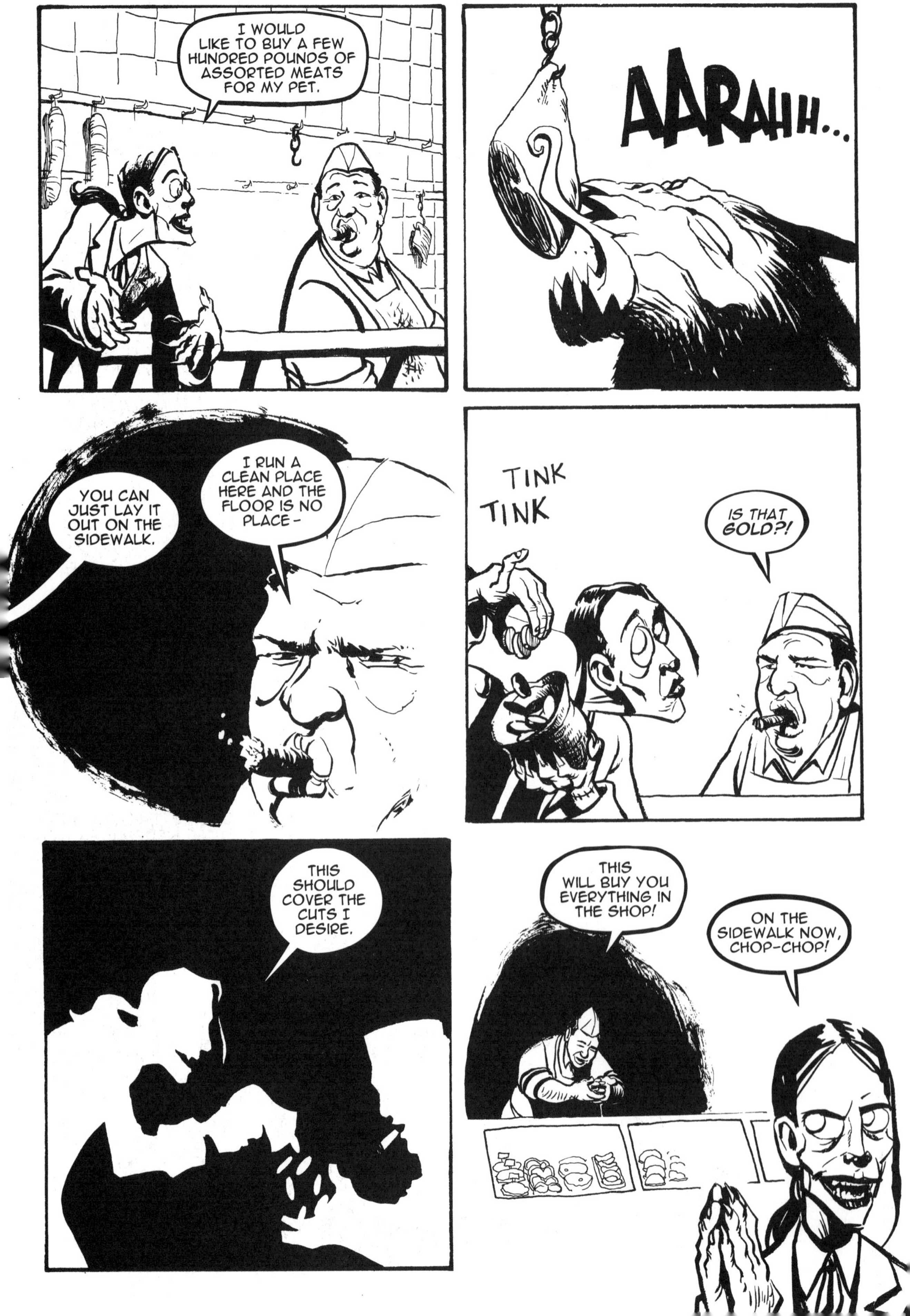
I WOULD LIKE TO BUY A FEW HUNDRED POUNDS OF ASSORTED MEATS FOR MY PET.
AARAHH...
YOU CAN JUST LAY IT OUT ON THE SIDEWALK.
I RUN A CLEAN PLACE HERE AND THE FLOOR IS NO PLACE-
TINK
TINK
IS THAT GOLD?!
THIS SHOULD COVER THE CUTS I DESIRE.
THIS WILL BUY YOU EVERYTHING IN THE SHOP!
ON THE SIDEWALK NOW, CHOP-CHOP!

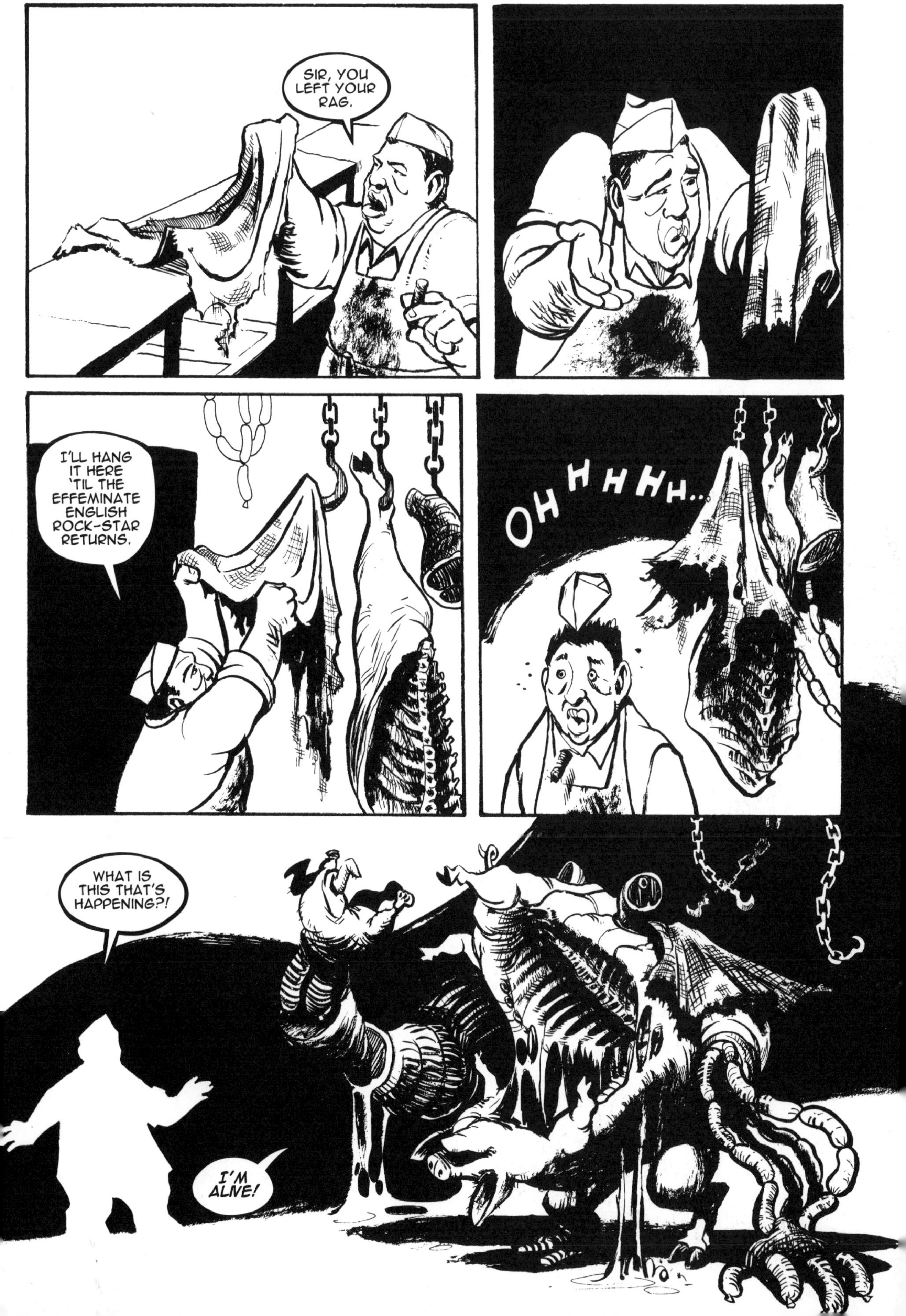

SIR, YOU LEFT YOUR RAG.
I'LL HANG IT HERE 'TIL THE EFFEMINATE ENGLISH ROCK-STAR RETURNS.
OHHHHHH...
WHAT IS THIS THAT'S HAPPENING?!
I'M ALIVE!

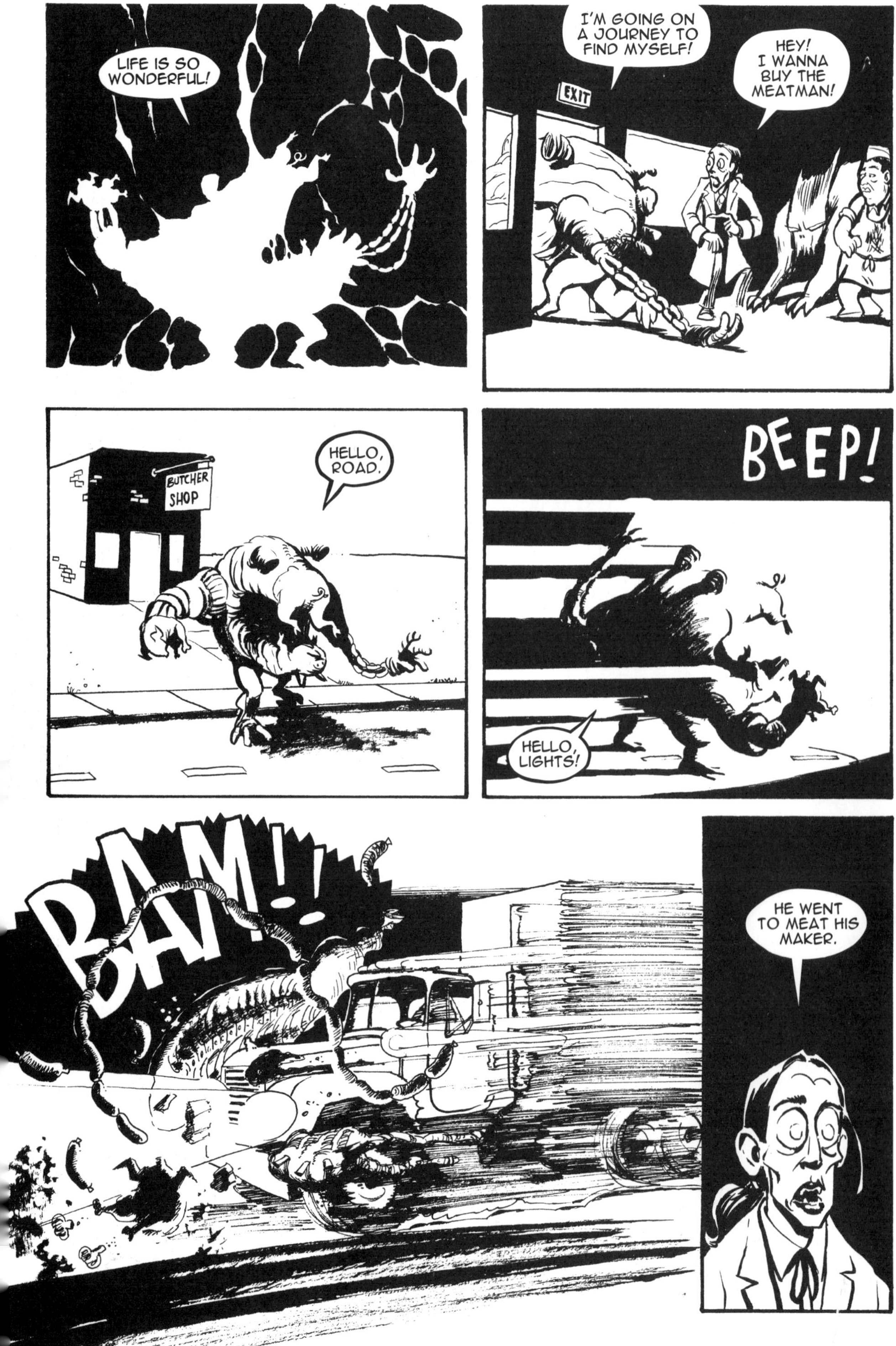
LIFE IS SO WONDERFUL!
I'M GOING ON A JOURNEY TO FIND MYSELF!
HEY! I WANNA BUY THE MEATMAN!
EXIT
BUTCHER SHOP
HELLO, ROAD.
BEEP!
HELLO, LIGHTS!
BAM!! BAM!!
HE WENT TO MEAT HIS MAKER.

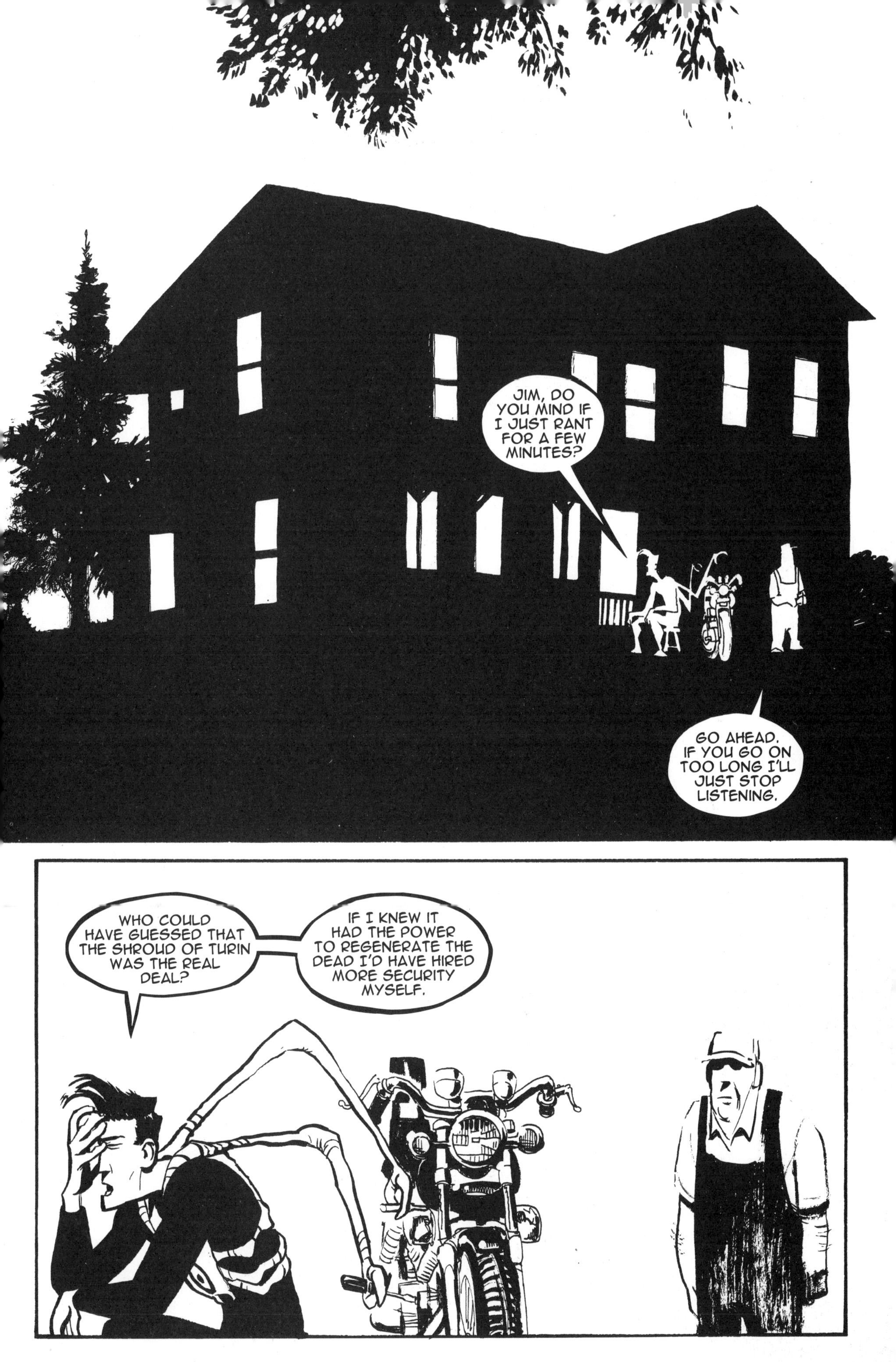
JIM, DO YOU MIND IF I JUST RANT FOR A FEW MINUTES?
GO AHEAD. IF YOU GO ON TOO LONG I'LL JUST STOP LISTENING.
WHO COULD HAVE GUESSED THAT THE SHROUD OF TURIN WAS THE REAL DEAL?
IF I KNEW IT HAD THE POWER TO REGENERATE THE DEAD I'D HAVE HIRED MORE SECURITY MYSELF.

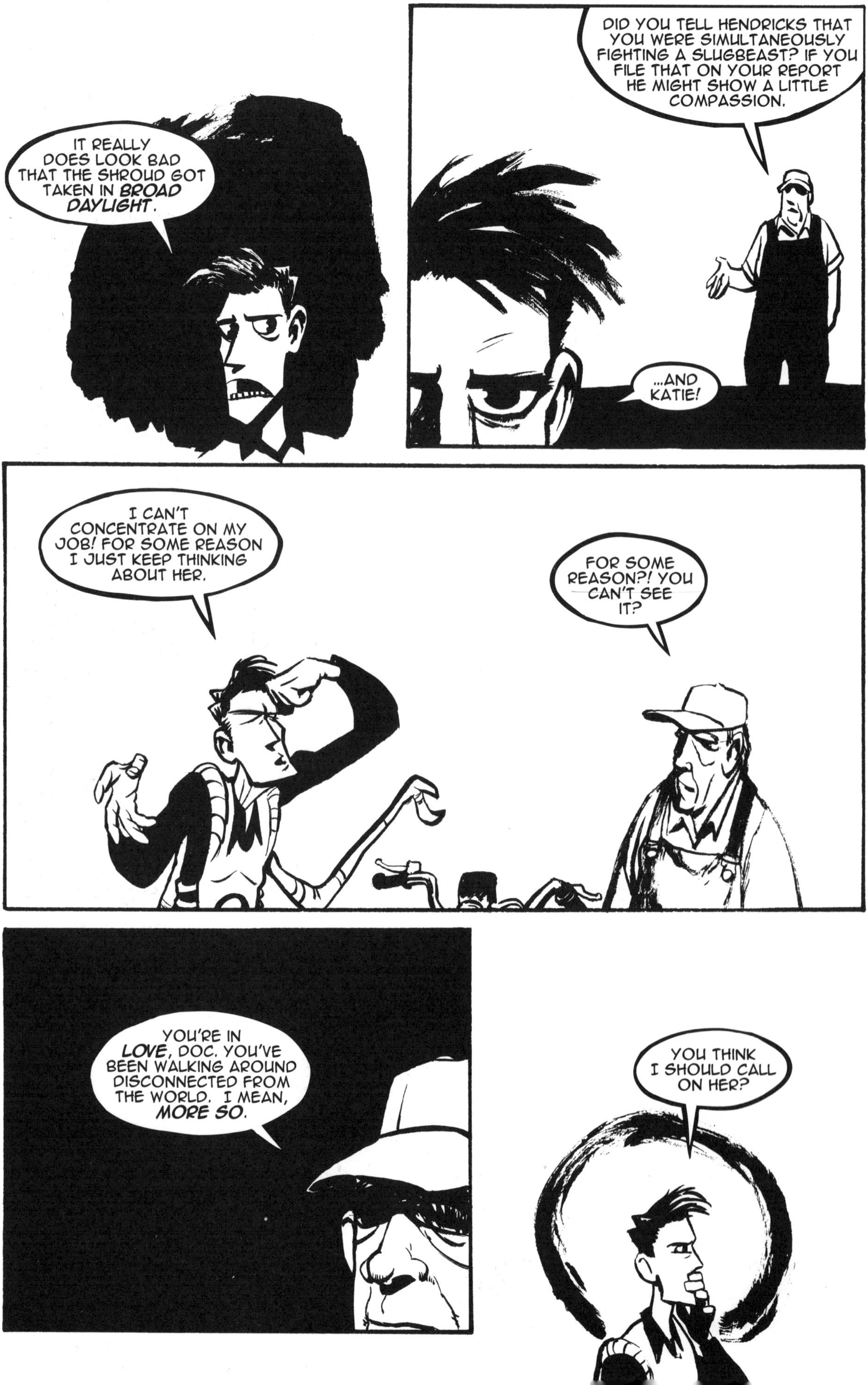
IT REALLY DOES LOOK BAD THAT THE SHROUD GOT TAKEN IN *BROAD DAYLIGHT*.
DID YOU TELL HENDRICKS THAT YOU WERE SIMULTANEOUSLY FIGHTING A SLUGBEAST? IF YOU FILE THAT ON YOUR REPORT HE MIGHT SHOW A LITTLE COMPASSION.
...AND KATIE!
I CAN'T CONCENTRATE ON MY JOB! FOR SOME REASON I JUST KEEP THINKING ABOUT HER.
FOR SOME REASON?! YOU CAN'T SEE IT?
YOU'RE IN *LOVE*, DOC. YOU'VE BEEN WALKING AROUND DISCONNECTED FROM THE WORLD. I MEAN, *MORE SO*.
YOU THINK I SHOULD CALL ON HER?

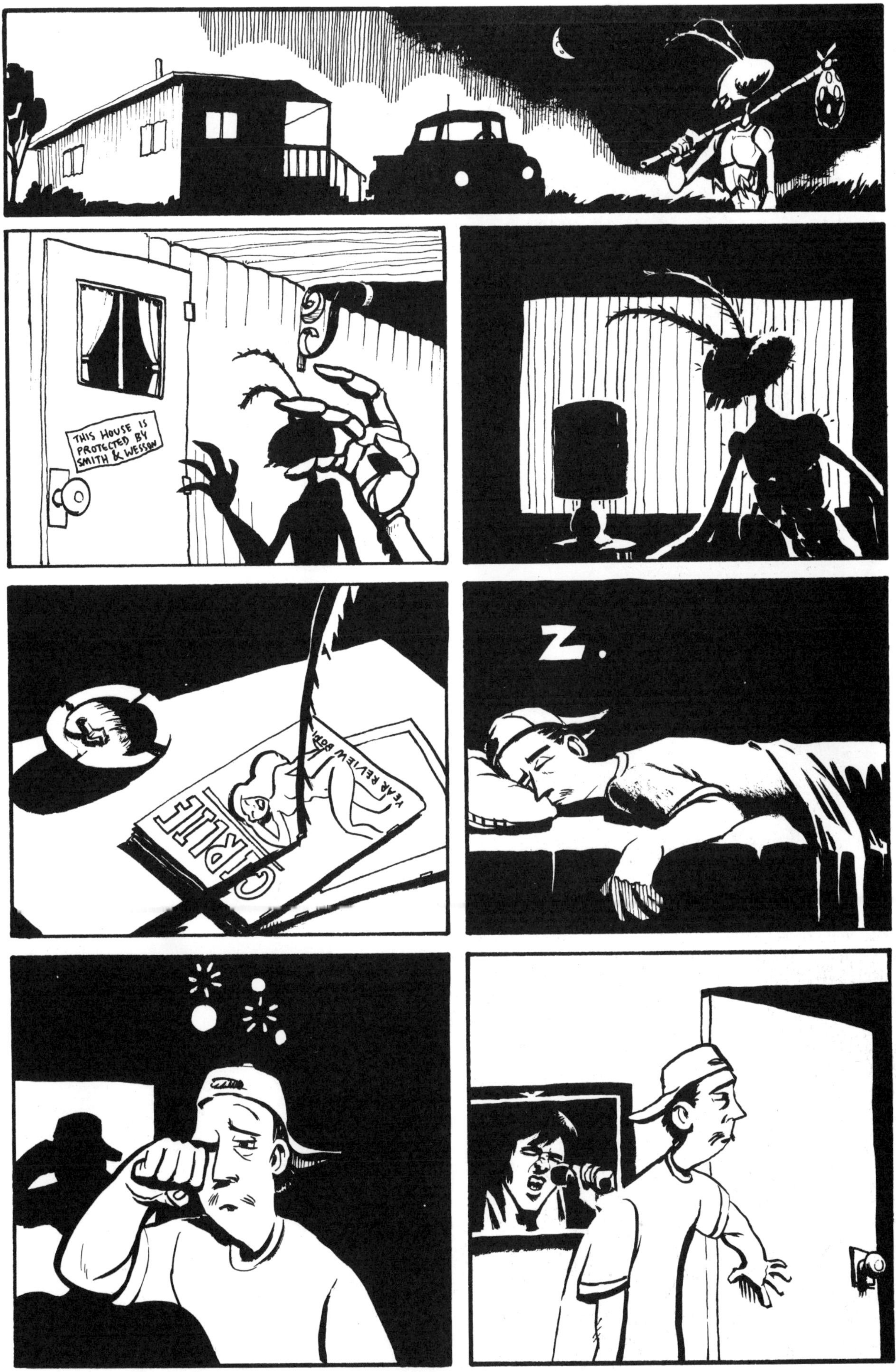
THIS HOUSE IS PROTECTED BY SMITH & WESSON
Z.

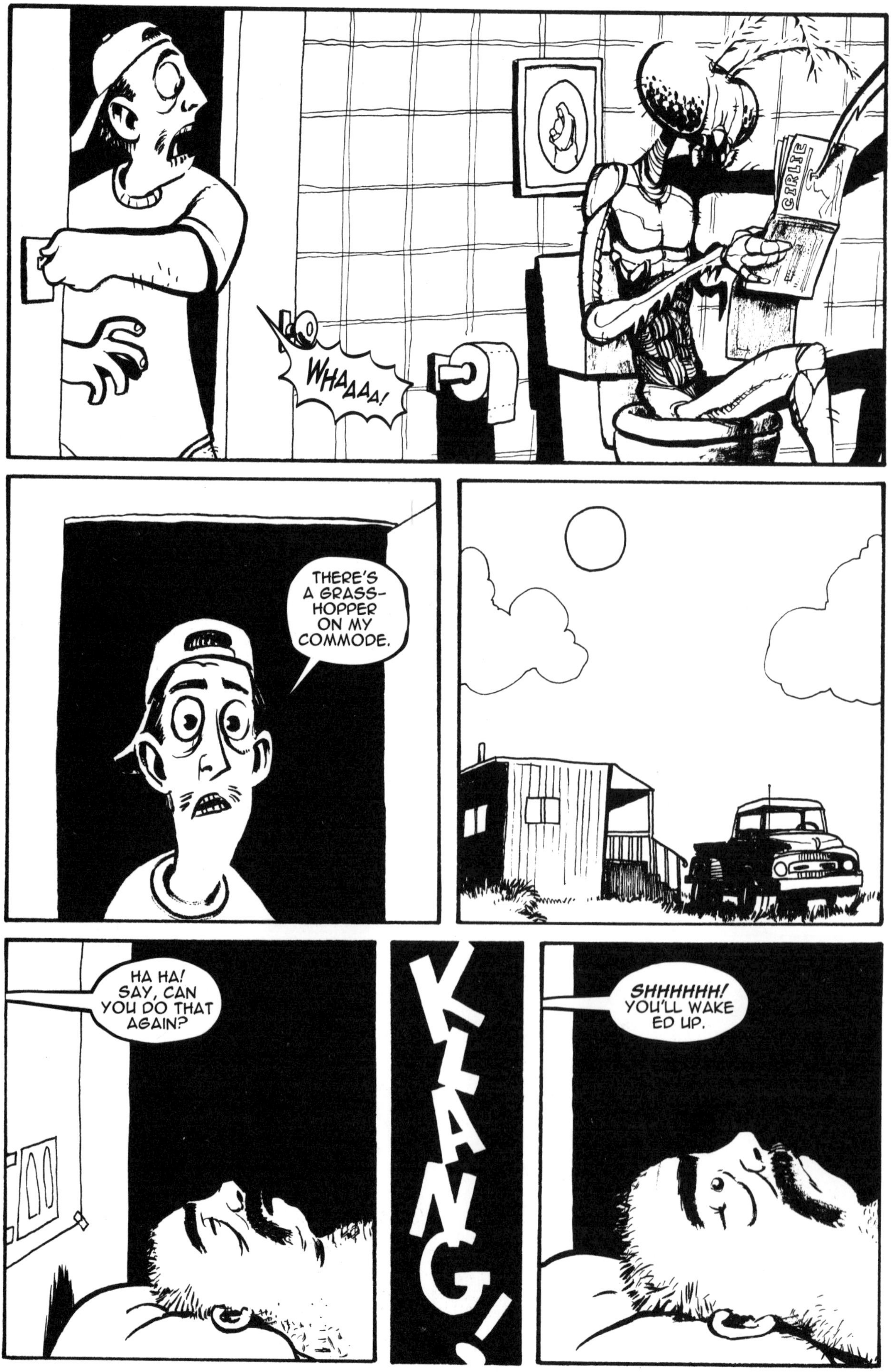
GIRLIE
WHAAAA!
THERE'S A GRASS-HOPPER ON MY COMMODE.
HA HA! SAY, CAN YOU DO THAT AGAIN?
KLANG!
SHHHHHH! YOU'LL WAKE ED UP.

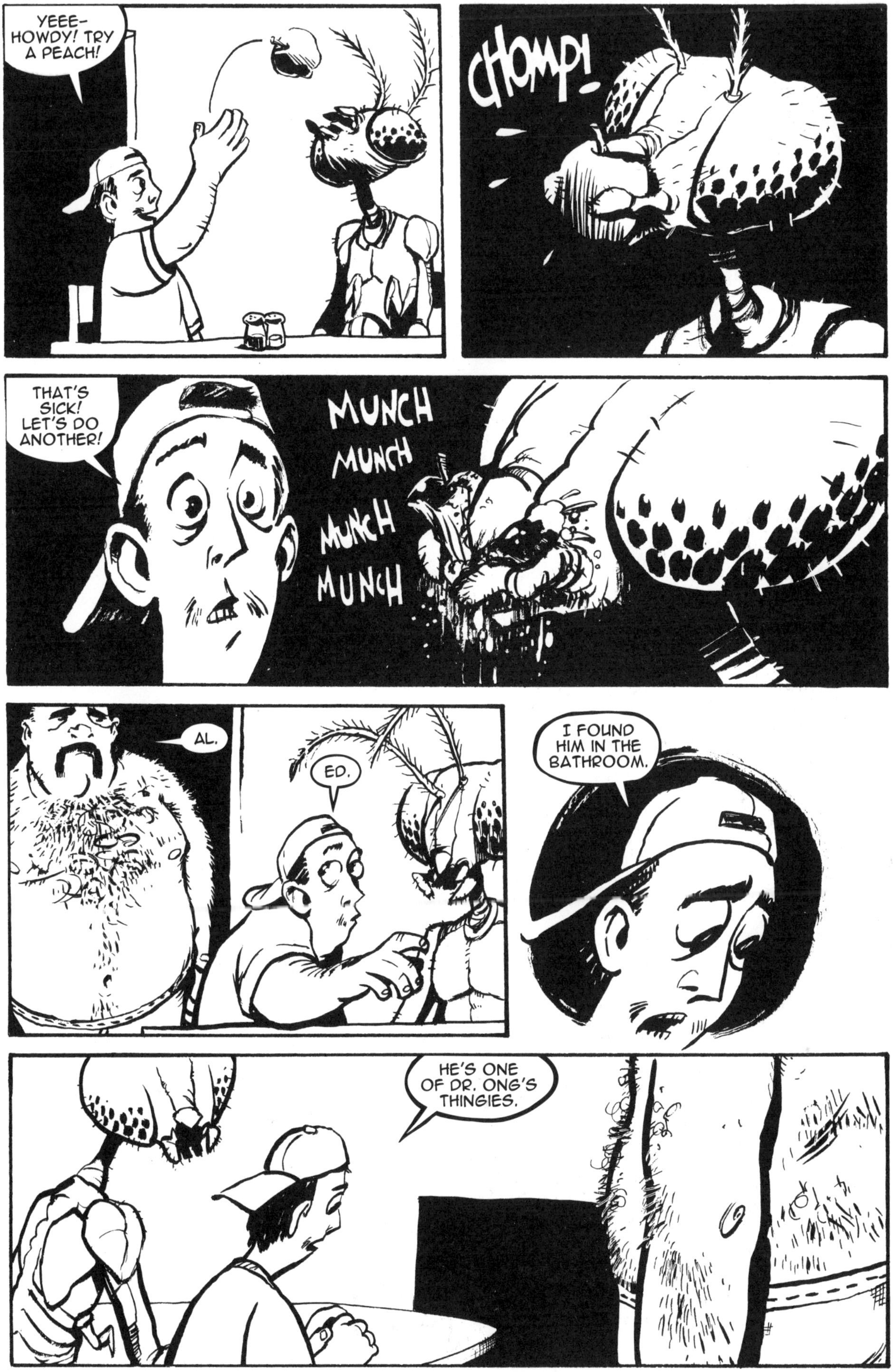
YEEE-HOWDY! TRY A PEACH!
CHOMP!
THAT'S SICK! LET'S DO ANOTHER!
MUNCH
MUNCH
MUNCH
MUNCH
AL.
ED.
I FOUND HIM IN THE BATHROOM.
HE'S ONE OF DR. ONG'S THINGIES.

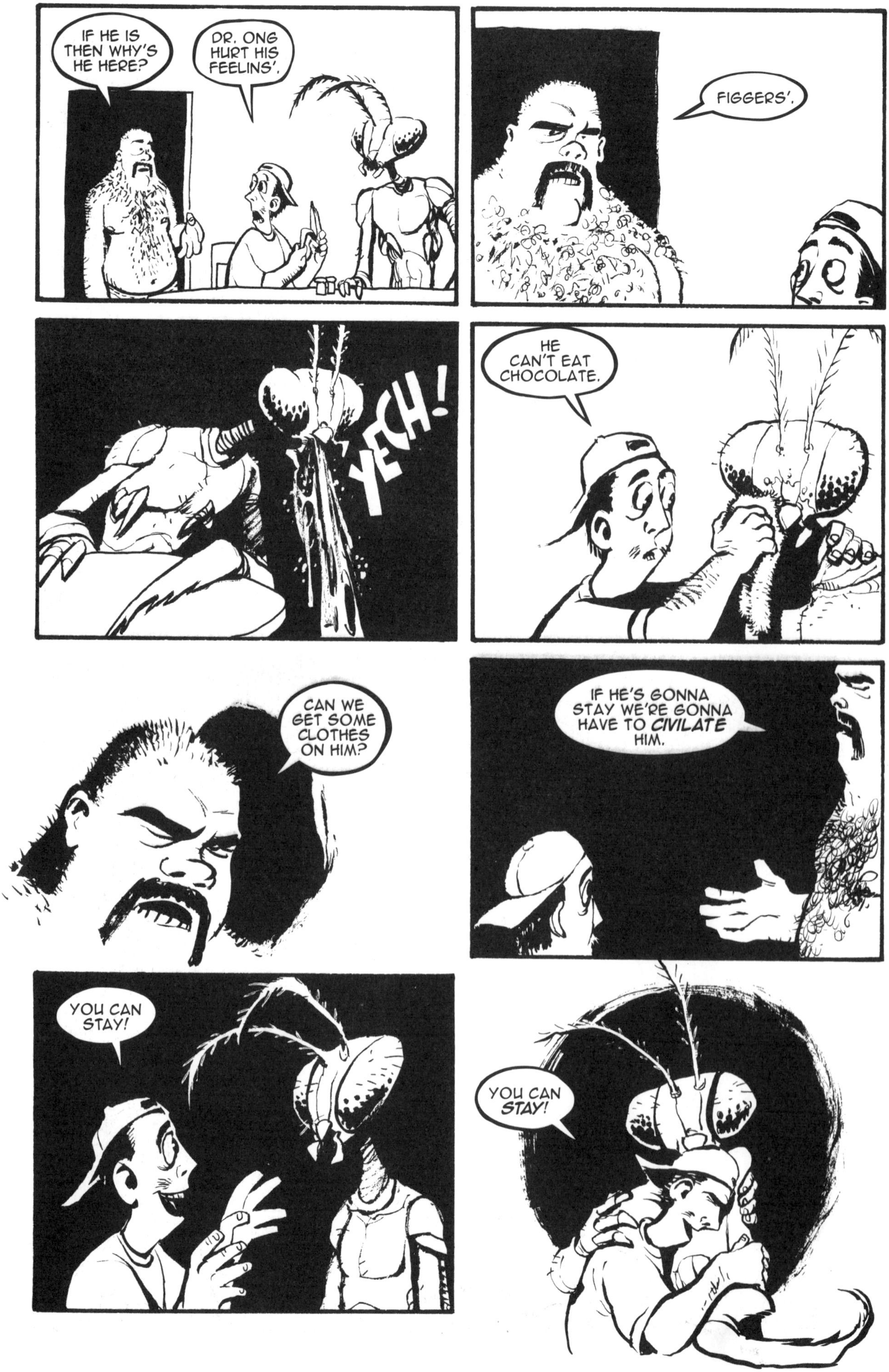
IF HE IS THEN WHY'S HE HERE?
DR. ONG HURT HIS FEELINS'.
FIGGERS'.
YECH!
HE CAN'T EAT CHOCOLATE.
CAN WE GET SOME CLOTHES ON HIM?
IF HE'S GONNA STAY WE'RE GONNA HAVE TO *CIVILATE* HIM.
YOU CAN STAY!
YOU CAN *STAY!*

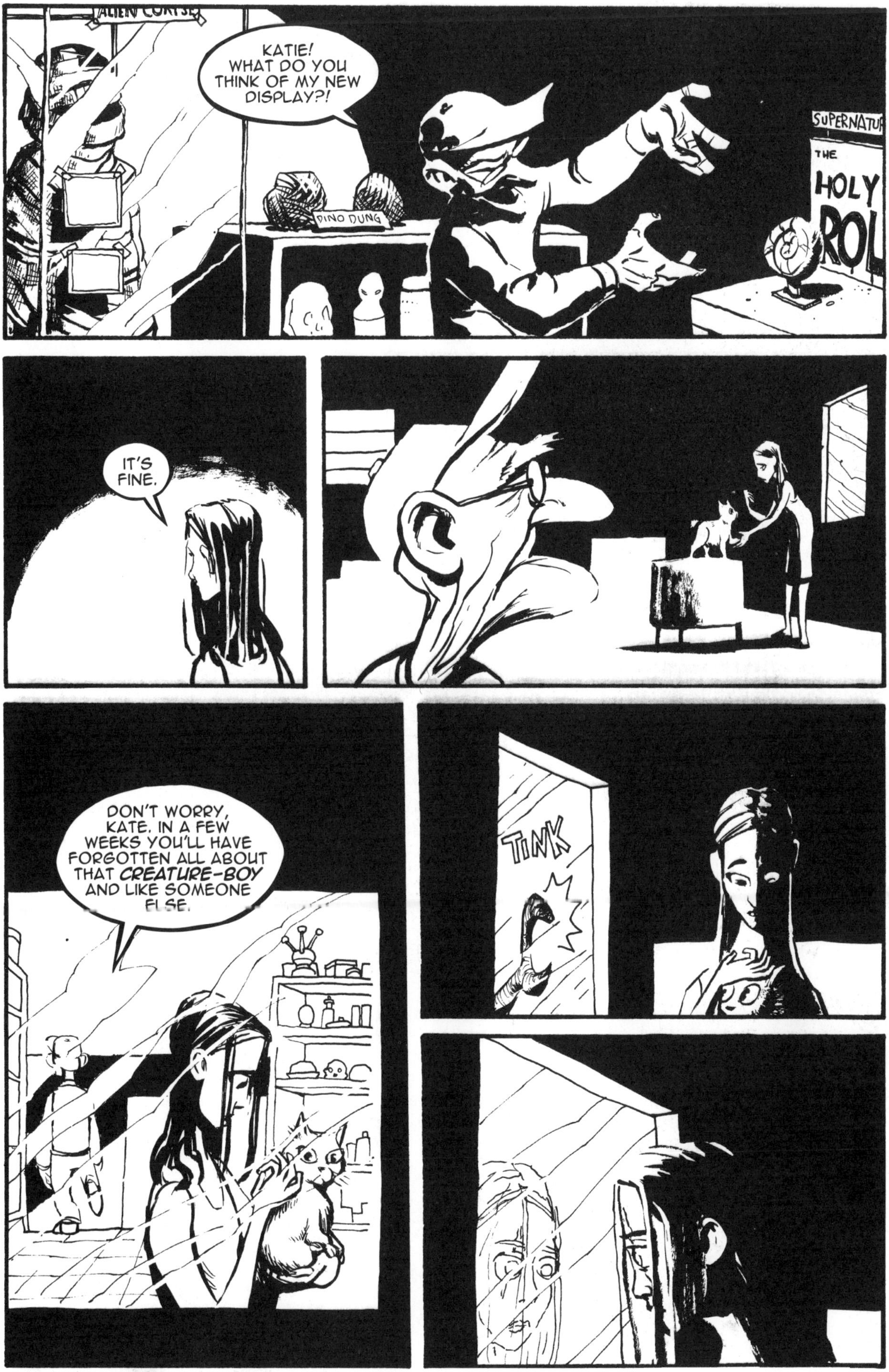
ALIEN CORPSE
KATIE! WHAT DO YOU THINK OF MY NEW DISPLAY?!
DINO DUNG
SUPERNATUR
THE HOLY ROL
IT'S FINE.
DON'T WORRY, KATE. IN A FEW WEEKS YOU'LL HAVE FORGOTTEN ALL ABOUT THAT CREATURE-BOY AND LIKE SOMEONE ELSE.
TINK

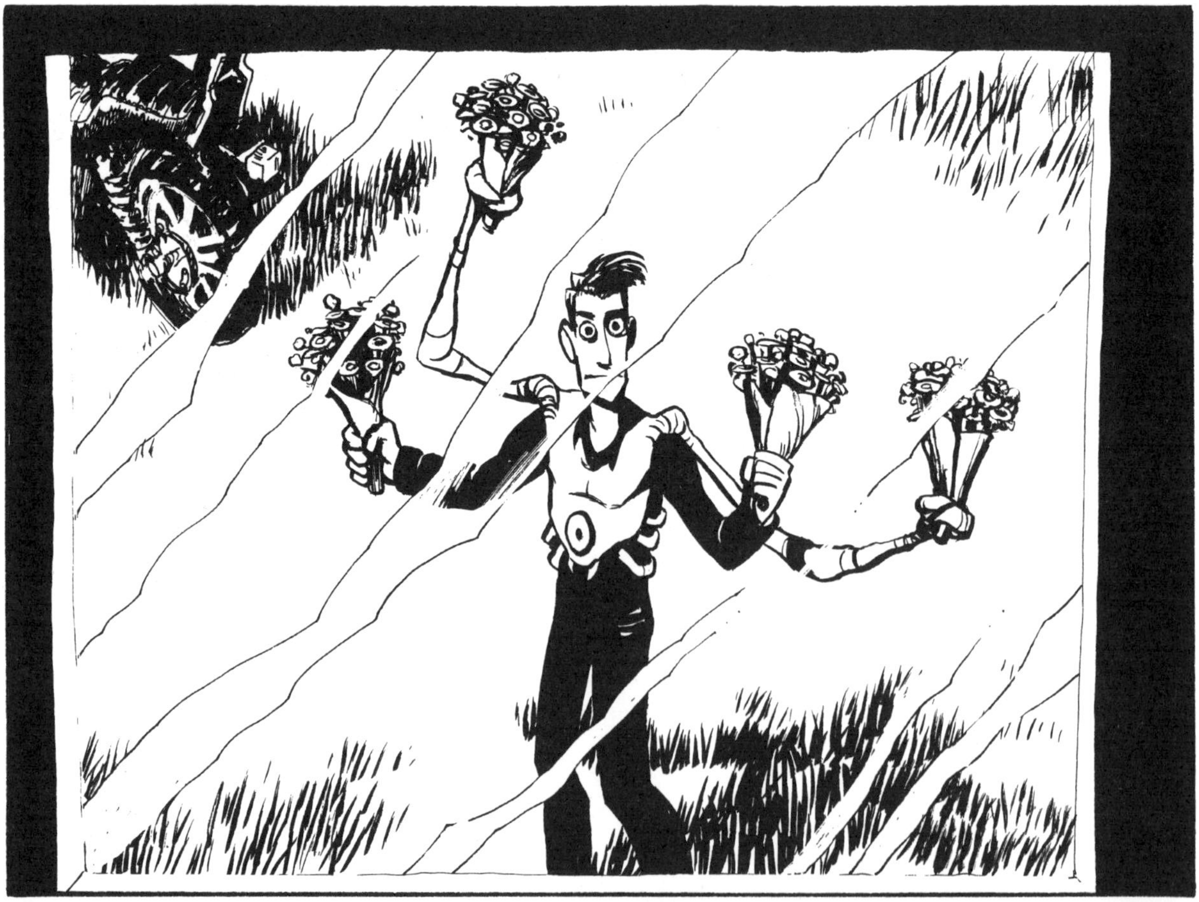
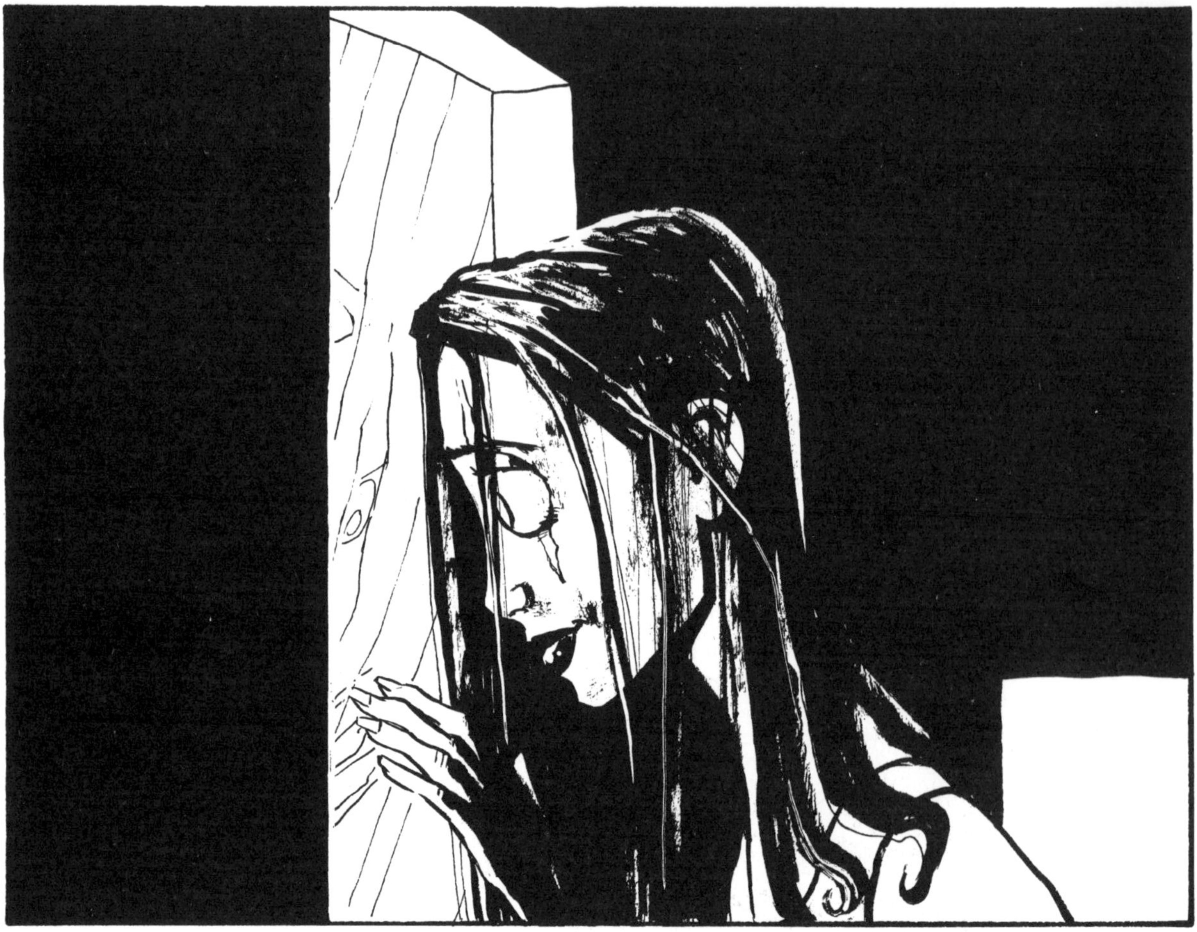

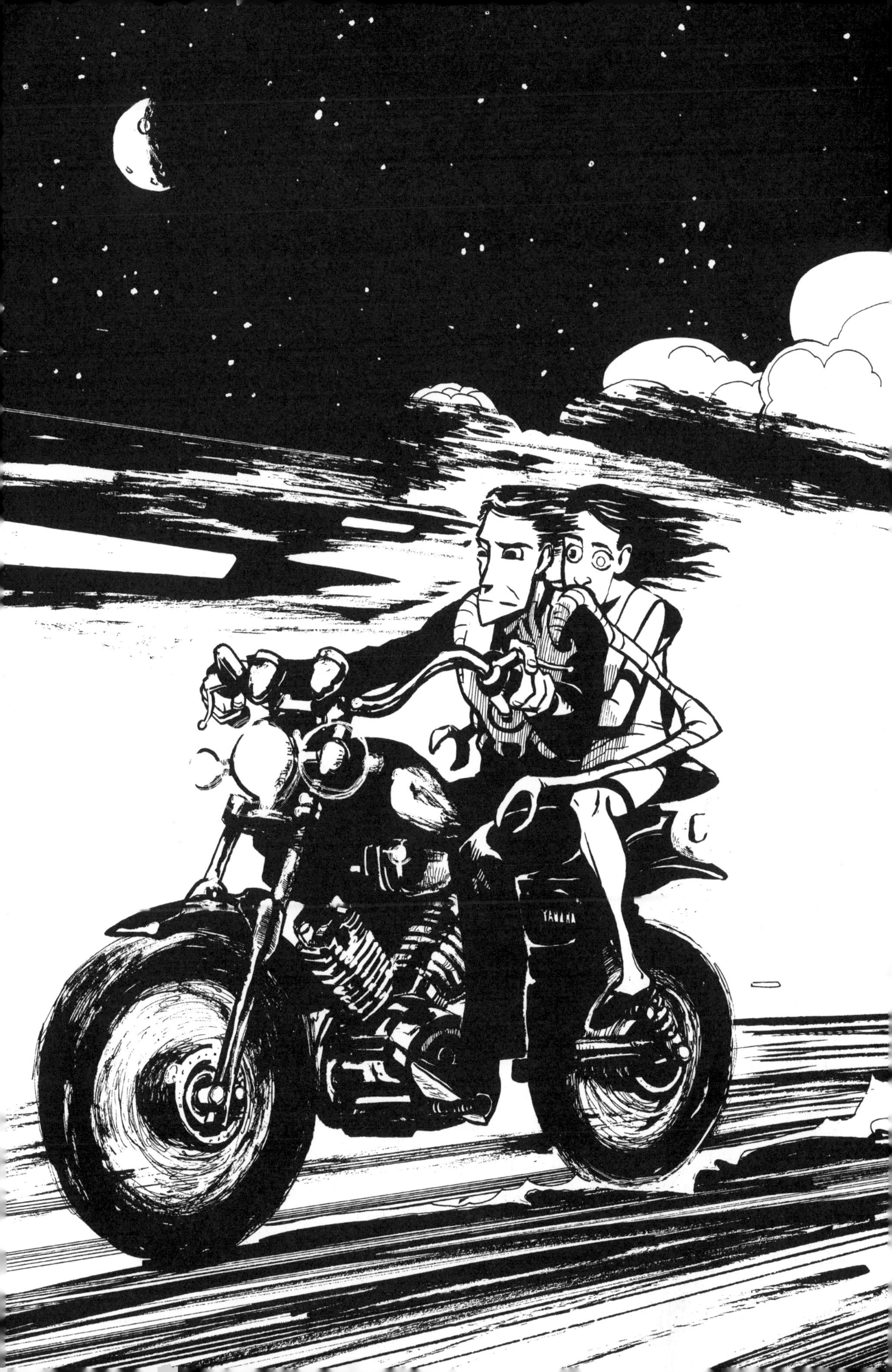
YAMAHA

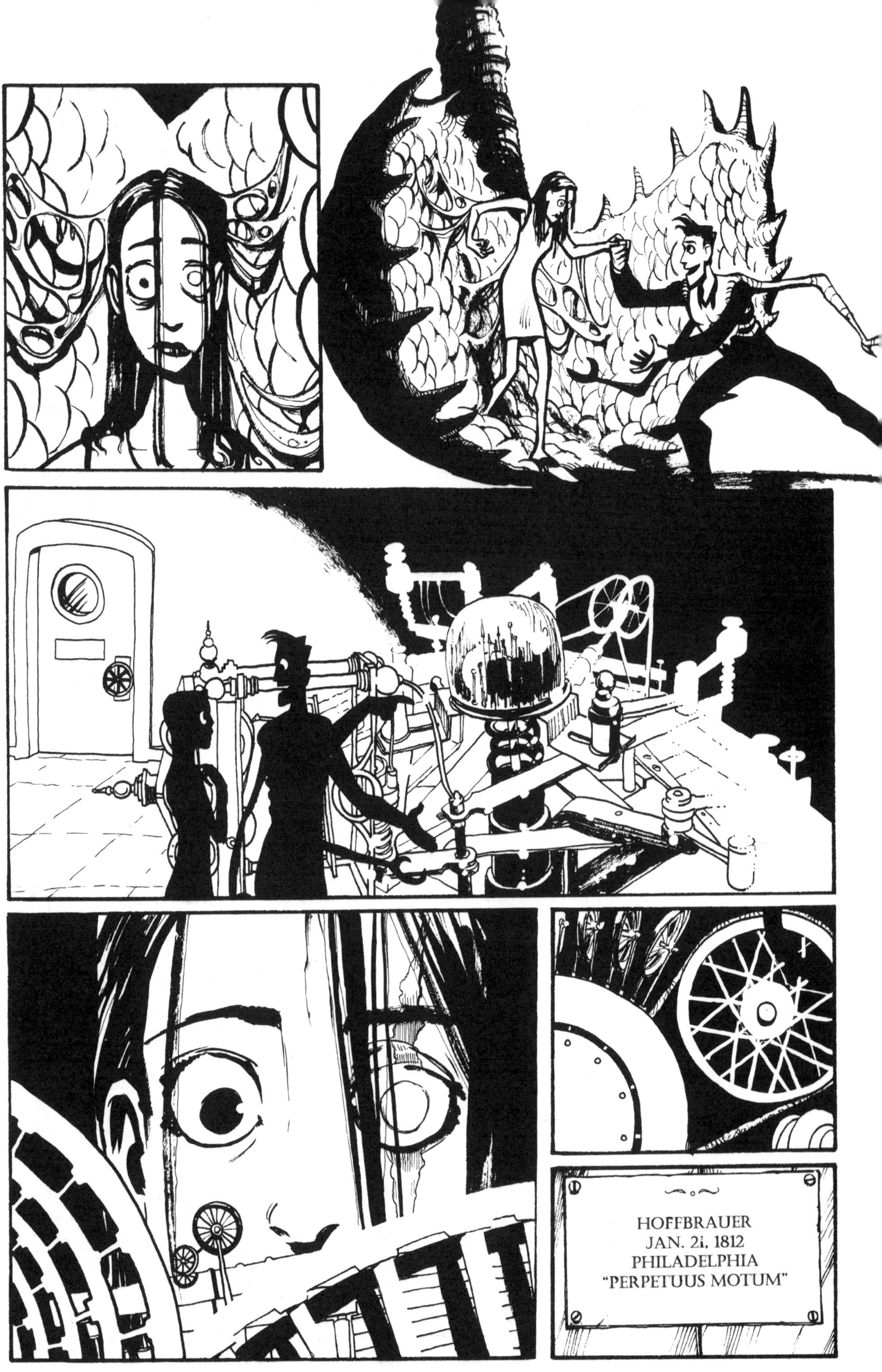
HOFFBRAUER
JAN. 2i, 1812
PHILADELPHIA
"PERPETUUS MOTUM"

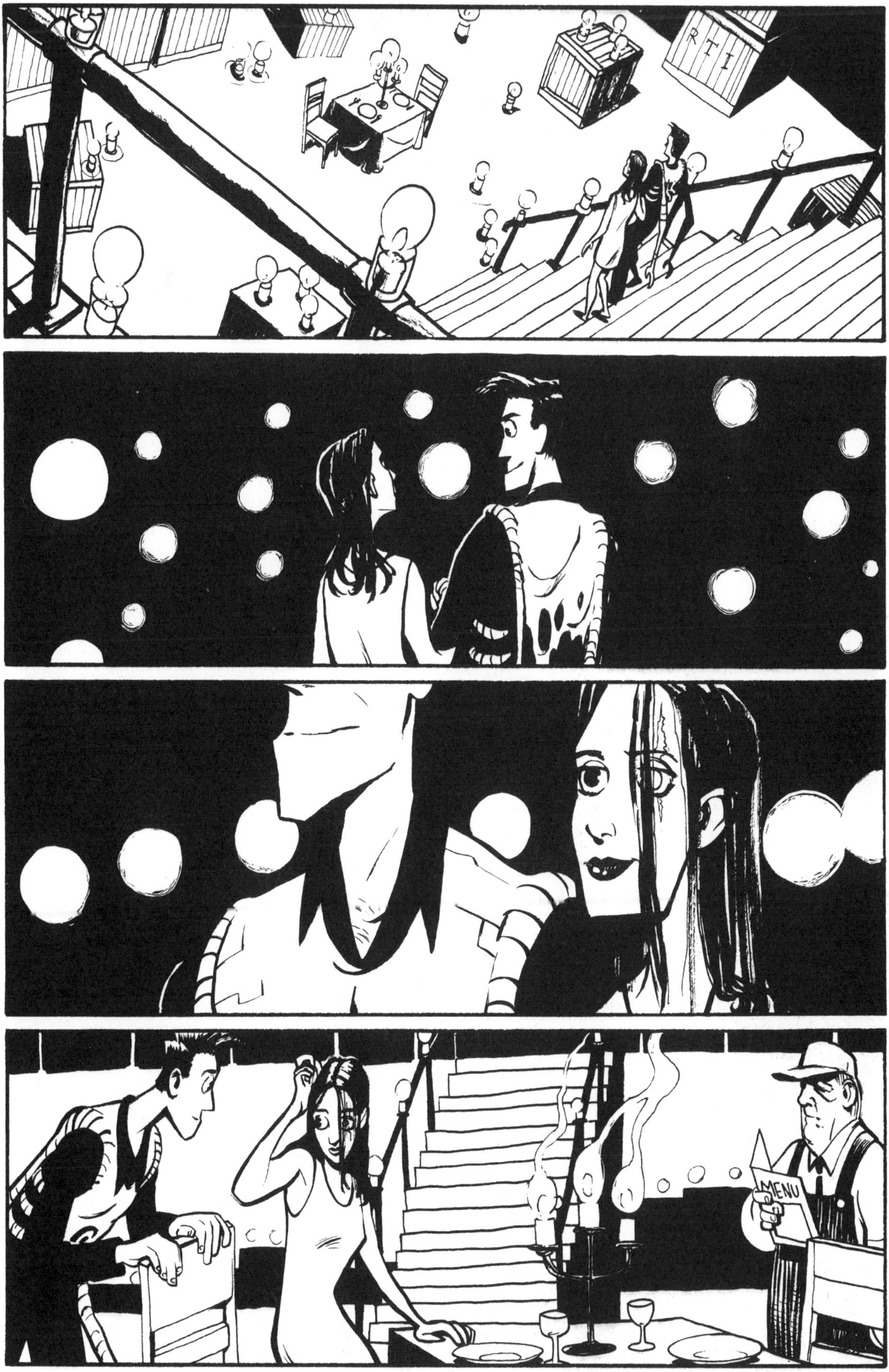
MENU

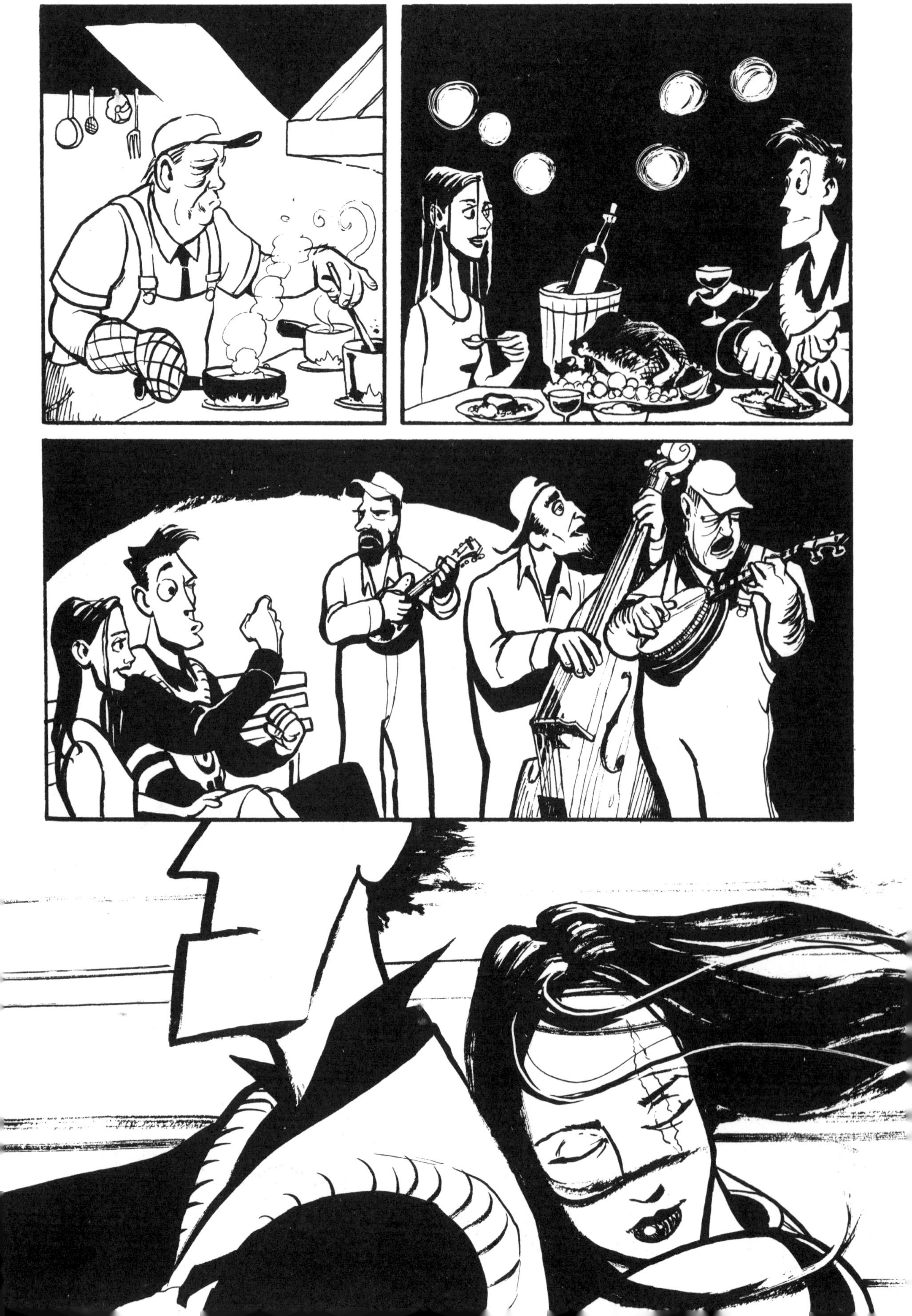

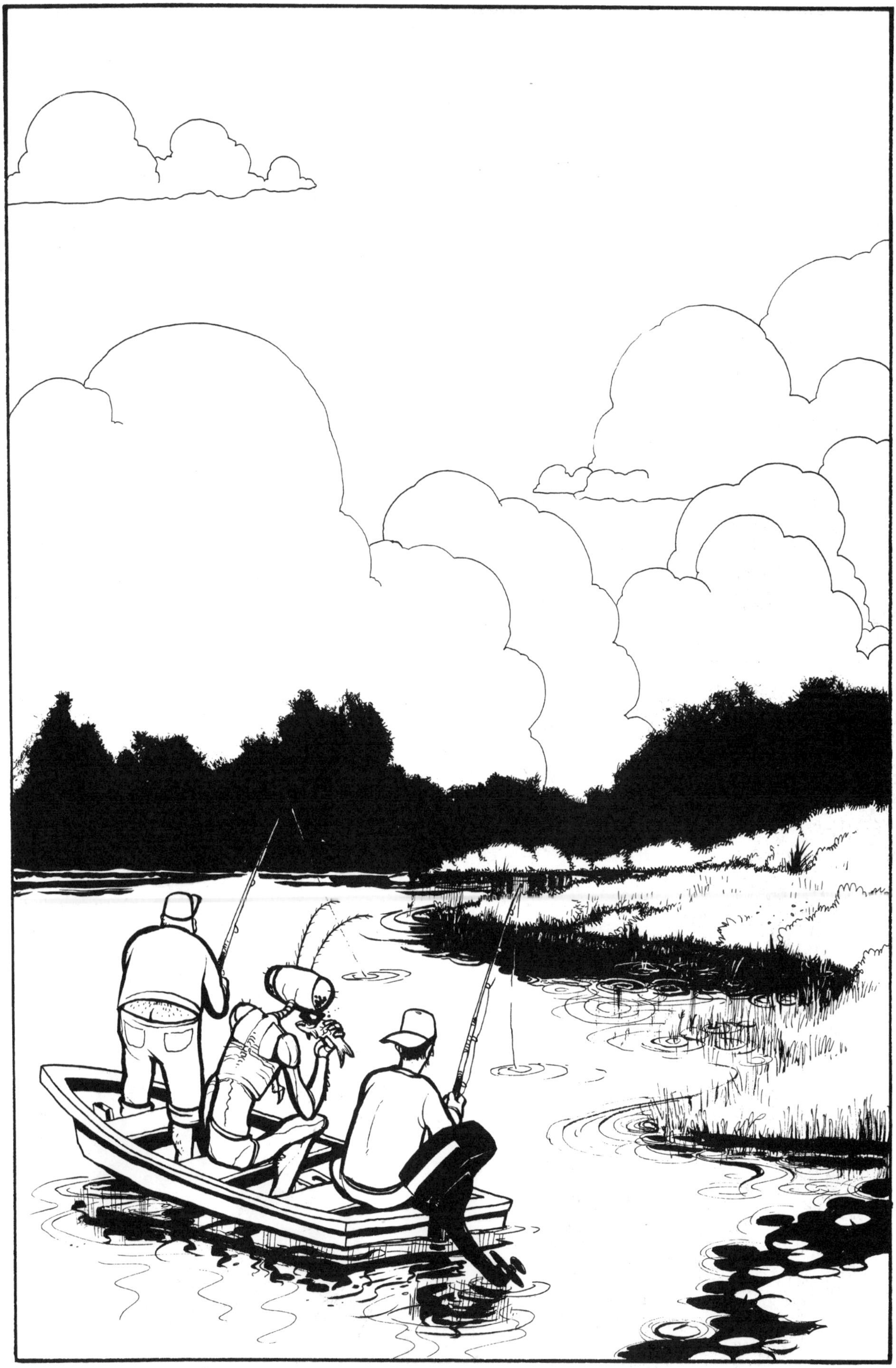

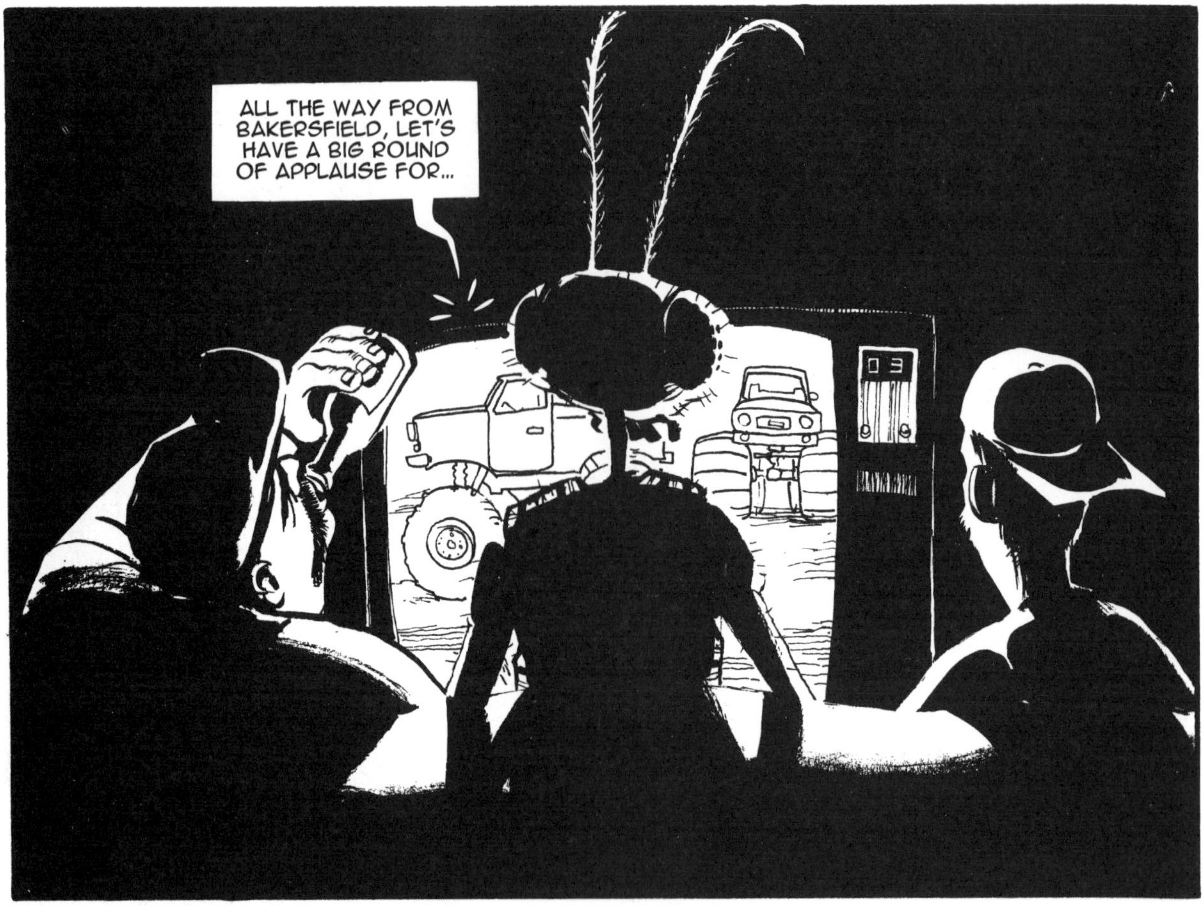
ALL THE WAY FROM BAKERSFIELD, LET'S HAVE A BIG ROUND OF APPLAUSE FOR...

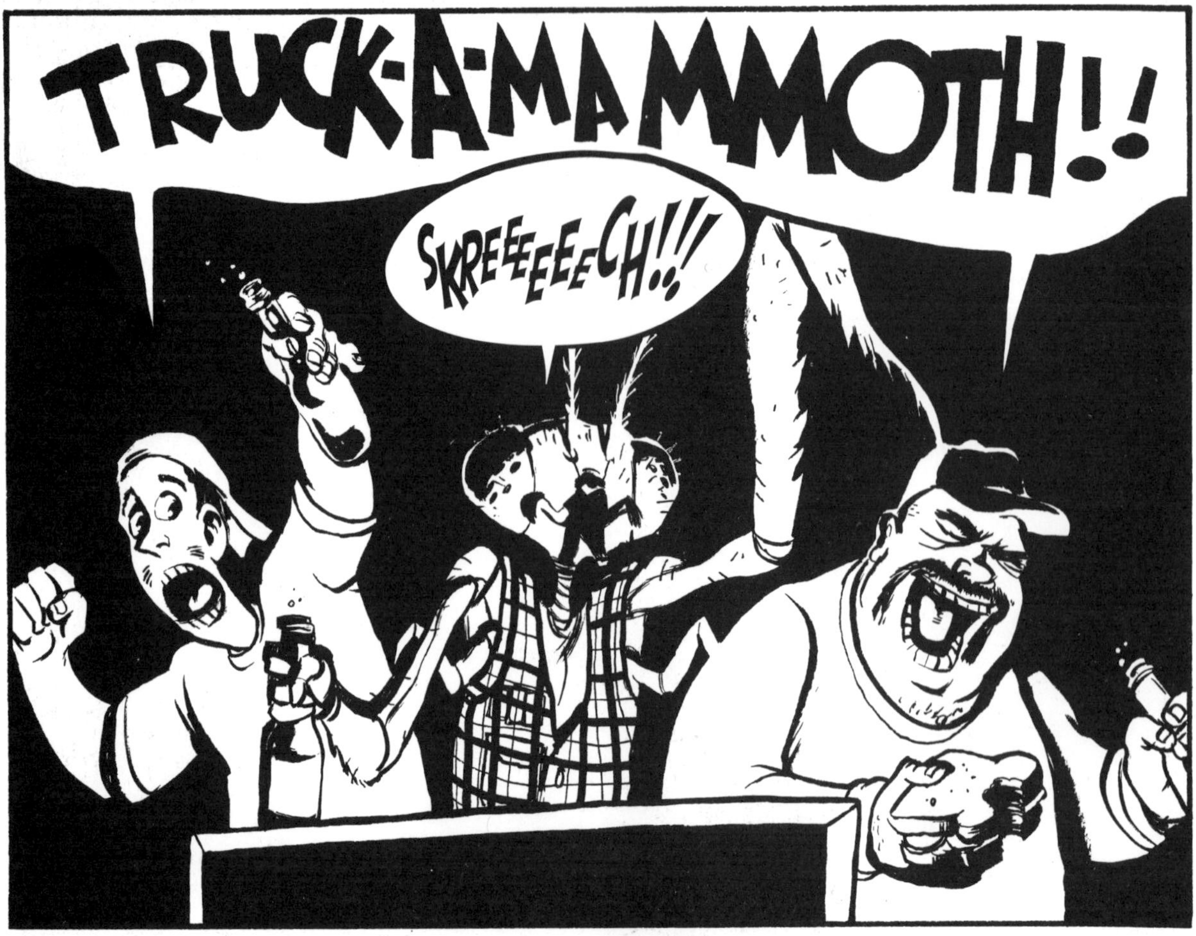
TRUCK-A-MAMMOTH!!
SKREEEEEEECH!!!

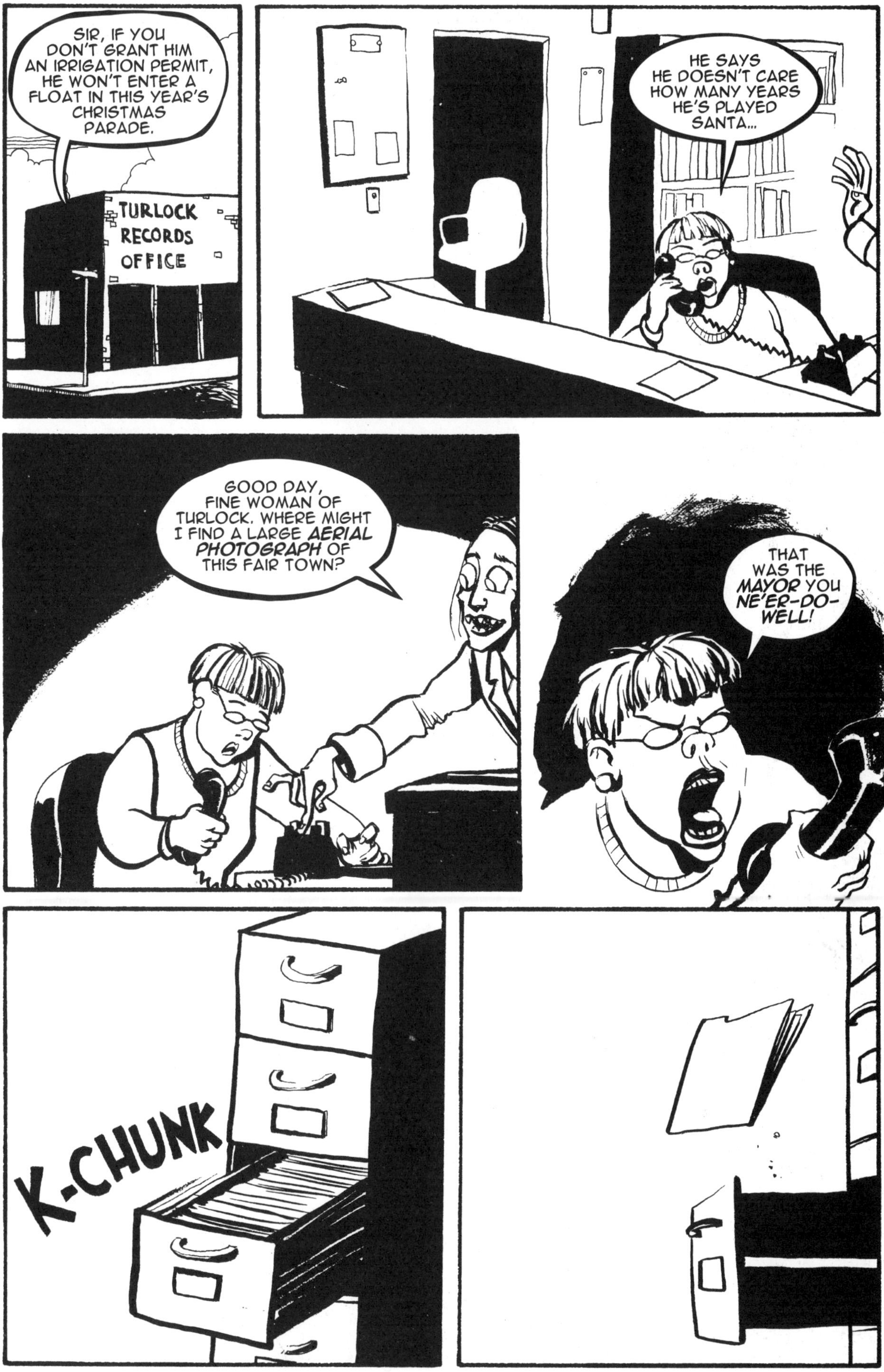
SIR, IF YOU DON'T GRANT HIM AN IRRIGATION PERMIT, HE WON'T ENTER A FLOAT IN THIS YEAR'S CHRISTMAS PARADE.
TURLOCK RECORDS OFFICE
HE SAYS HE DOESN'T CARE HOW MANY YEARS HE'S PLAYED SANTA...
GOOD DAY, FINE WOMAN OF TURLOCK. WHERE MIGHT I FIND A LARGE *AERIAL PHOTOGRAPH* OF THIS FAIR TOWN?
THAT WAS THE *MAYOR* YOU *NE'ER-DO-WELL!*
K-CHUNK

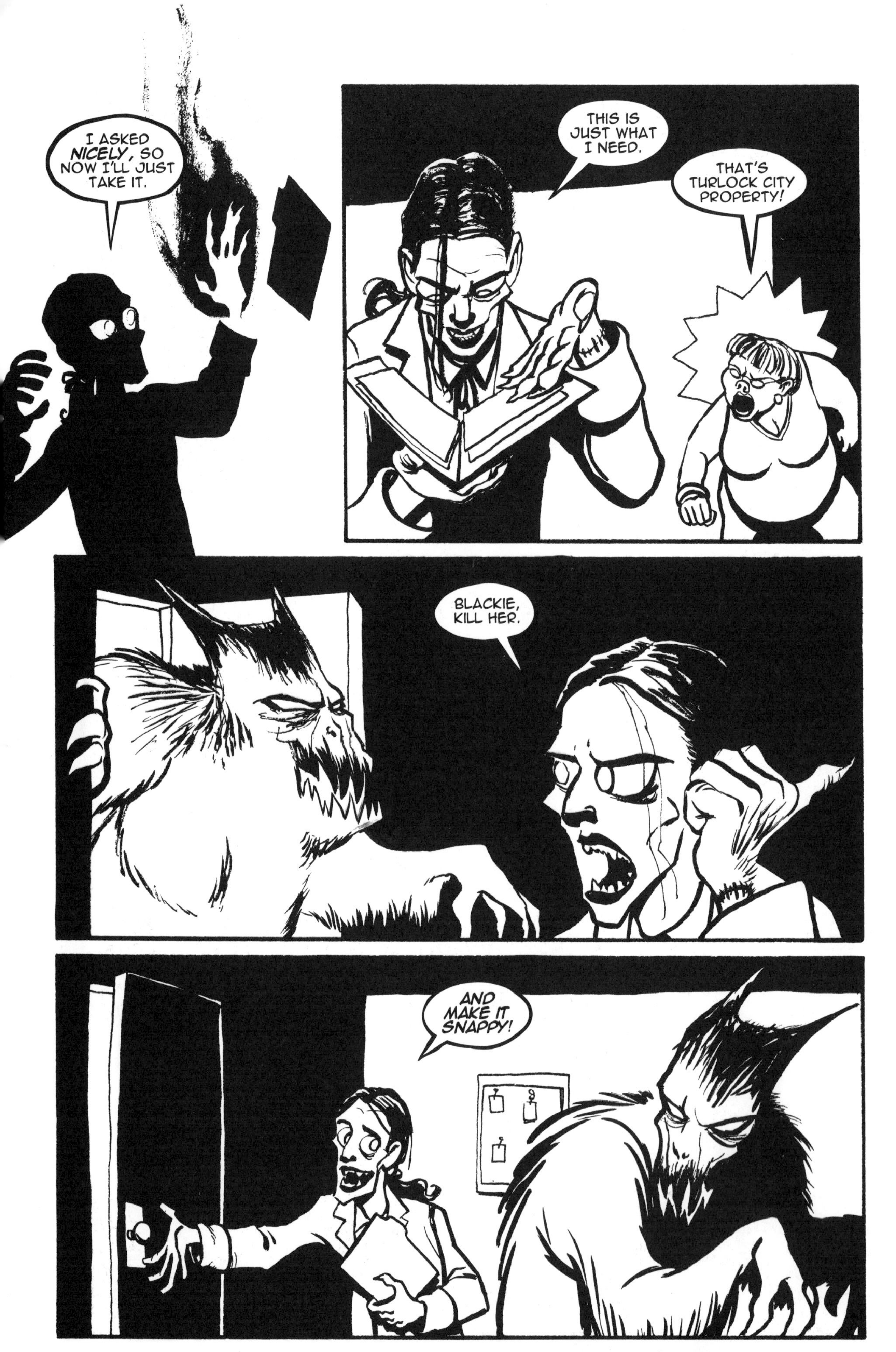
I ASKED NICELY, SO NOW I'LL JUST TAKE IT.
THIS IS JUST WHAT I NEED.
THAT'S TURLOCK CITY PROPERTY!
BLACKIE, KILL HER.
AND MAKE IT SNAPPY!

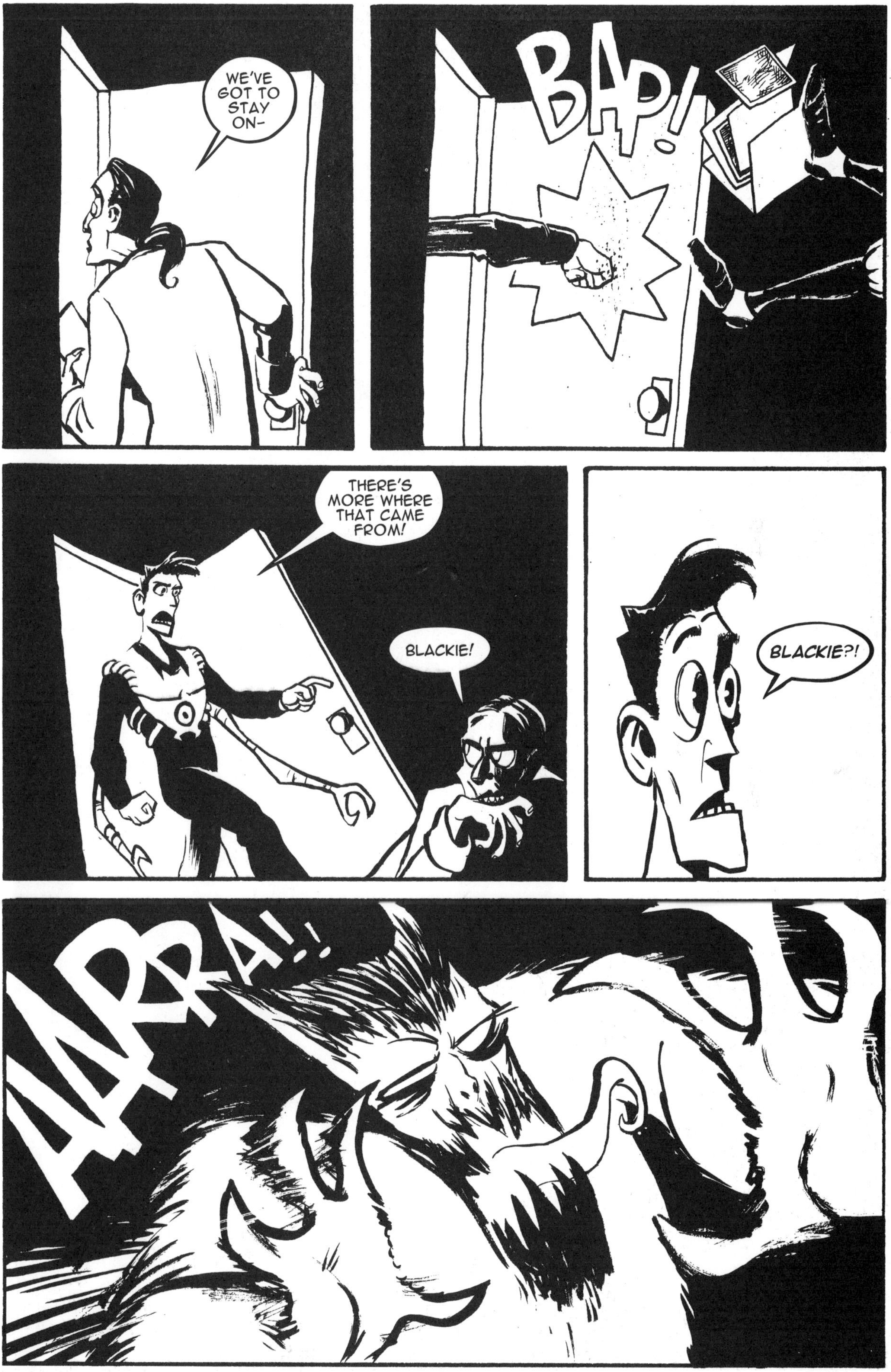
WE'VE GOT TO STAY ON-
BAP!
THERE'S MORE WHERE THAT CAME FROM!
BLACKIE!
BLACKIE?!
AARRA!!

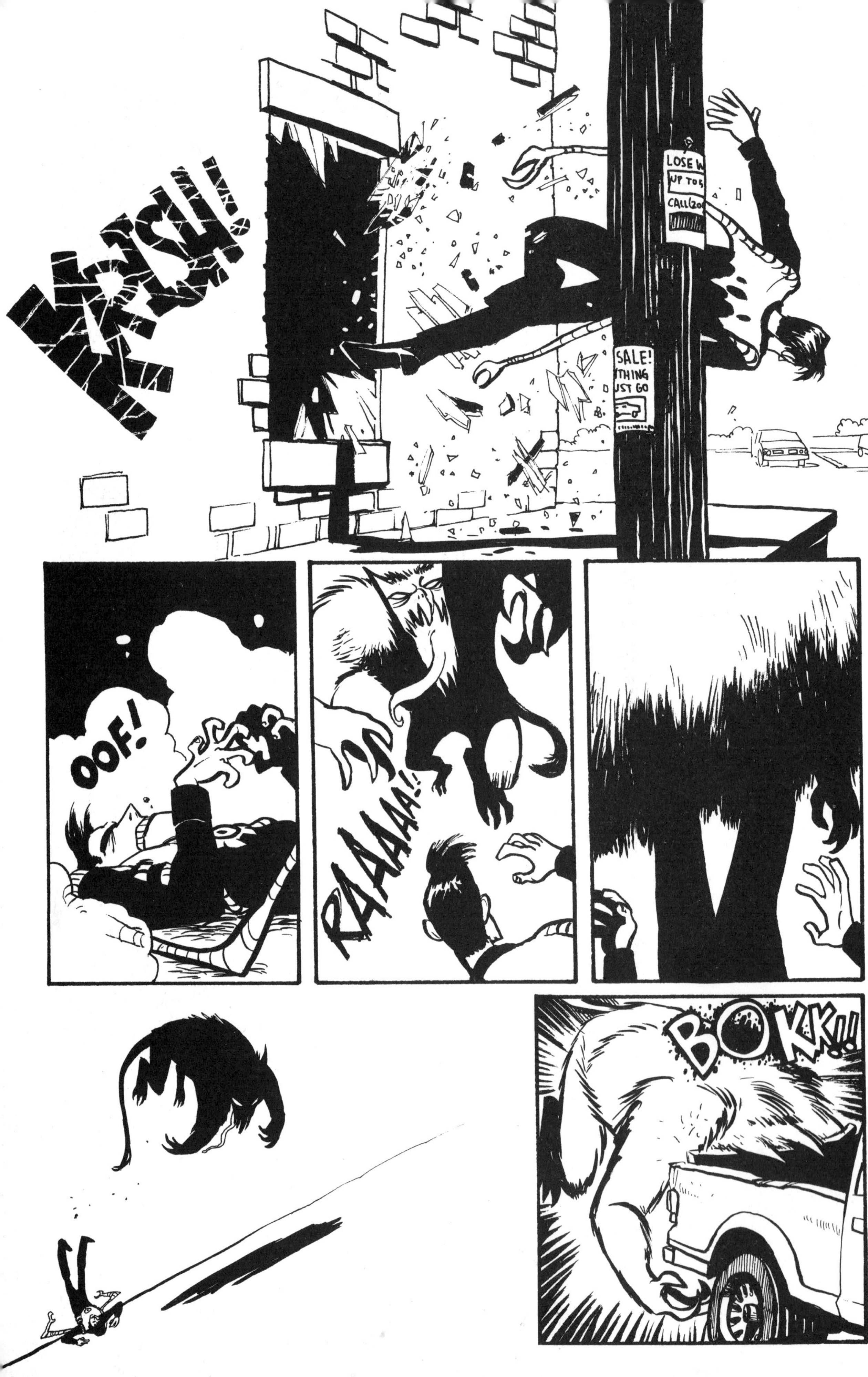
KRASH!
LOSE W
UP TO 5
CALL(20
SALE!
THING
UST GO
OOF!
RAAAAA!!
BOKK!!!

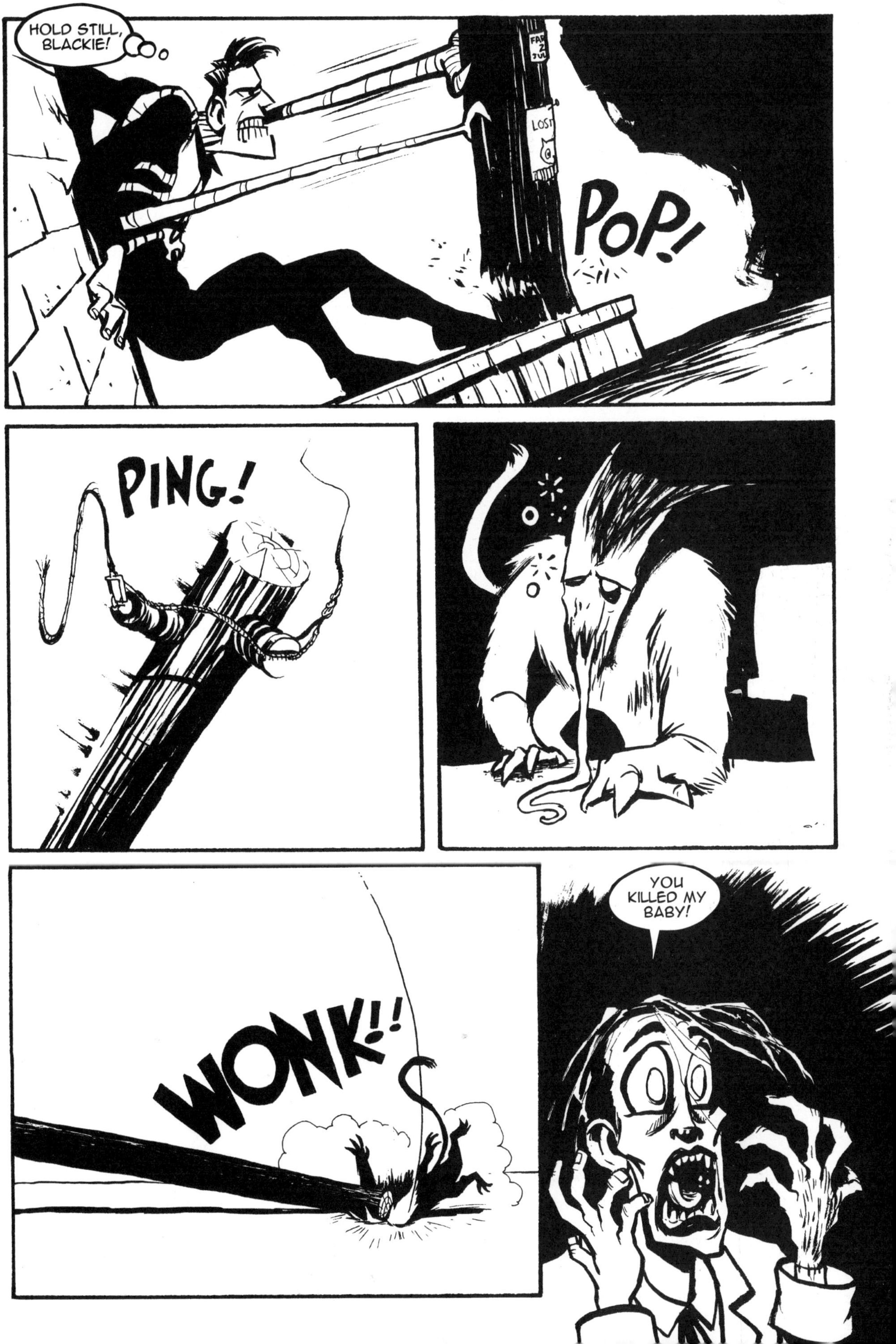
HOLD STILL, BLACKIE!
LOST
POP!
PING!
WONK!!
YOU KILLED MY BABY!

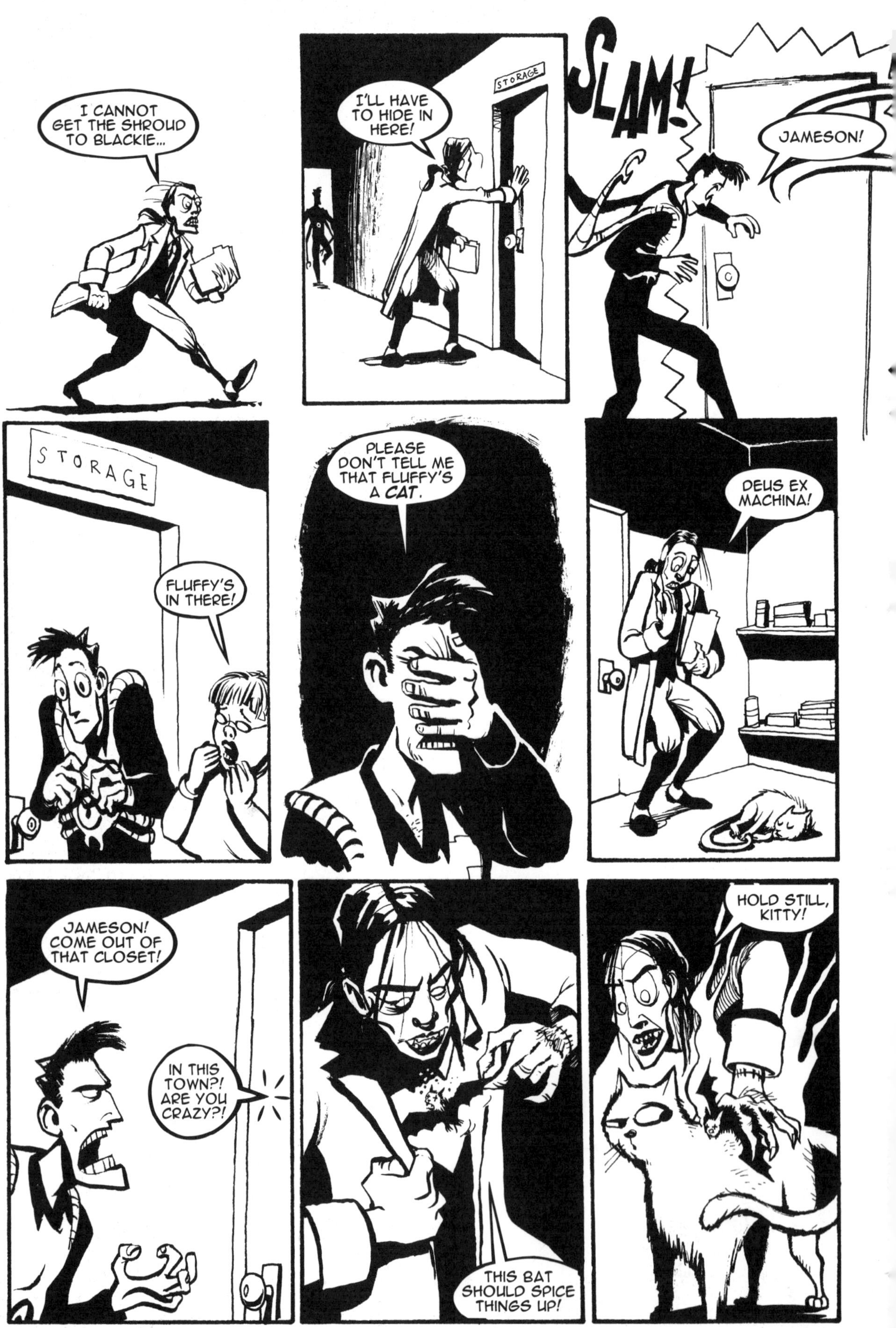
I CANNOT GET THE SHROUD TO BLACKIE...
STORAGE
I'LL HAVE TO HIDE IN HERE!
SLAM!
JAMESON!
STORAGE
FLUFFY'S IN THERE!
PLEASE DON'T TELL ME THAT FLUFFY'S A CAT.
DEUS EX MACHINA!
JAMESON! COME OUT OF THAT CLOSET!
IN THIS TOWN?! ARE YOU CRAZY?!
THIS BAT SHOULD SPICE THINGS UP!
HOLD STILL, KITTY!

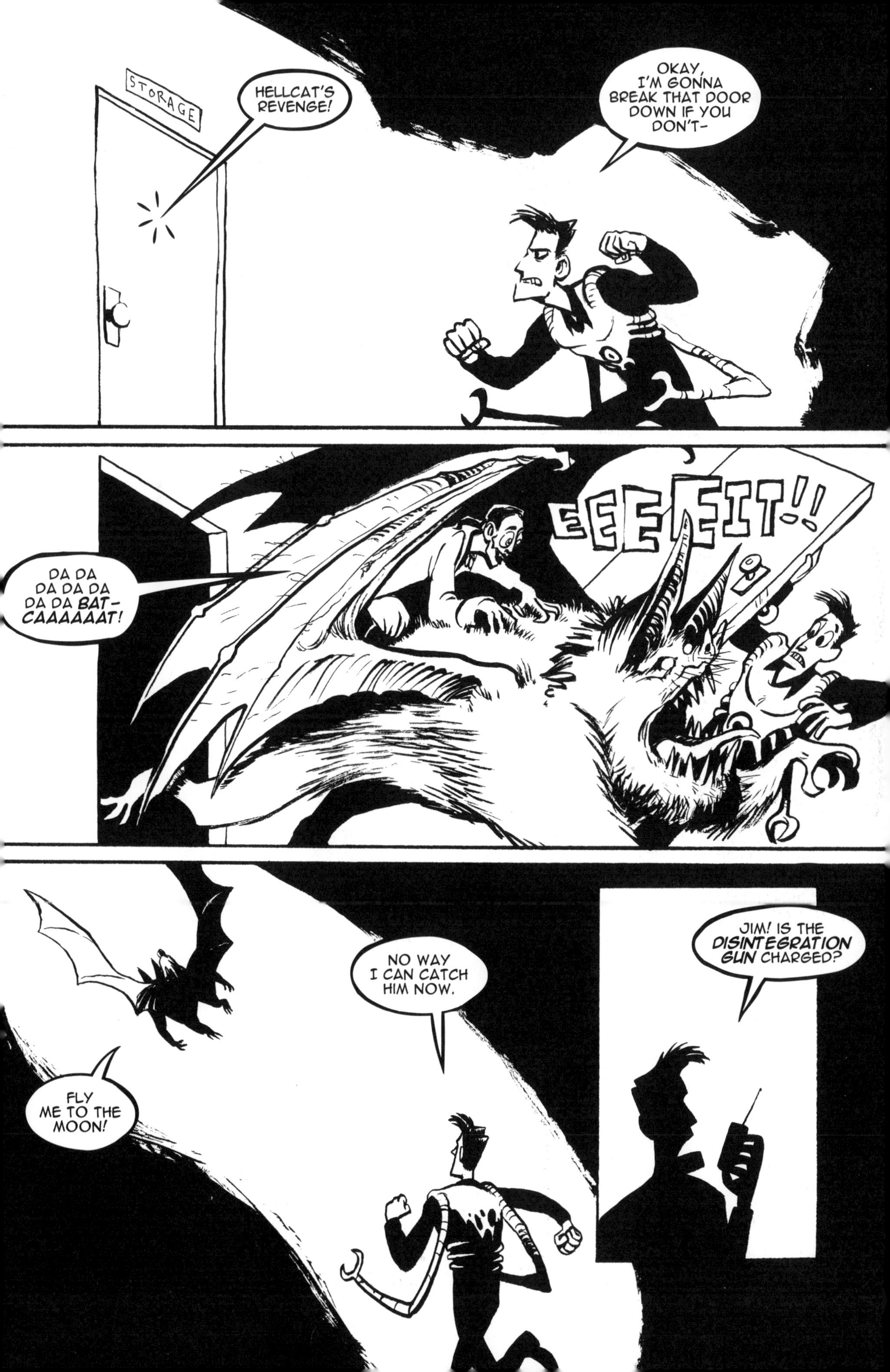
STORAGE
HELLCAT'S REVENGE!
OKAY, I'M GONNA BREAK THAT DOOR DOWN IF YOU DON'T-
EEEEIT-!!
DA DA DA DA DA DA DA BAT-CAAAAAAAT!
FLY ME TO THE MOON!
NO WAY I CAN CATCH HIM NOW.
JIM! IS THE DISINTEGRATION GUN CHARGED?

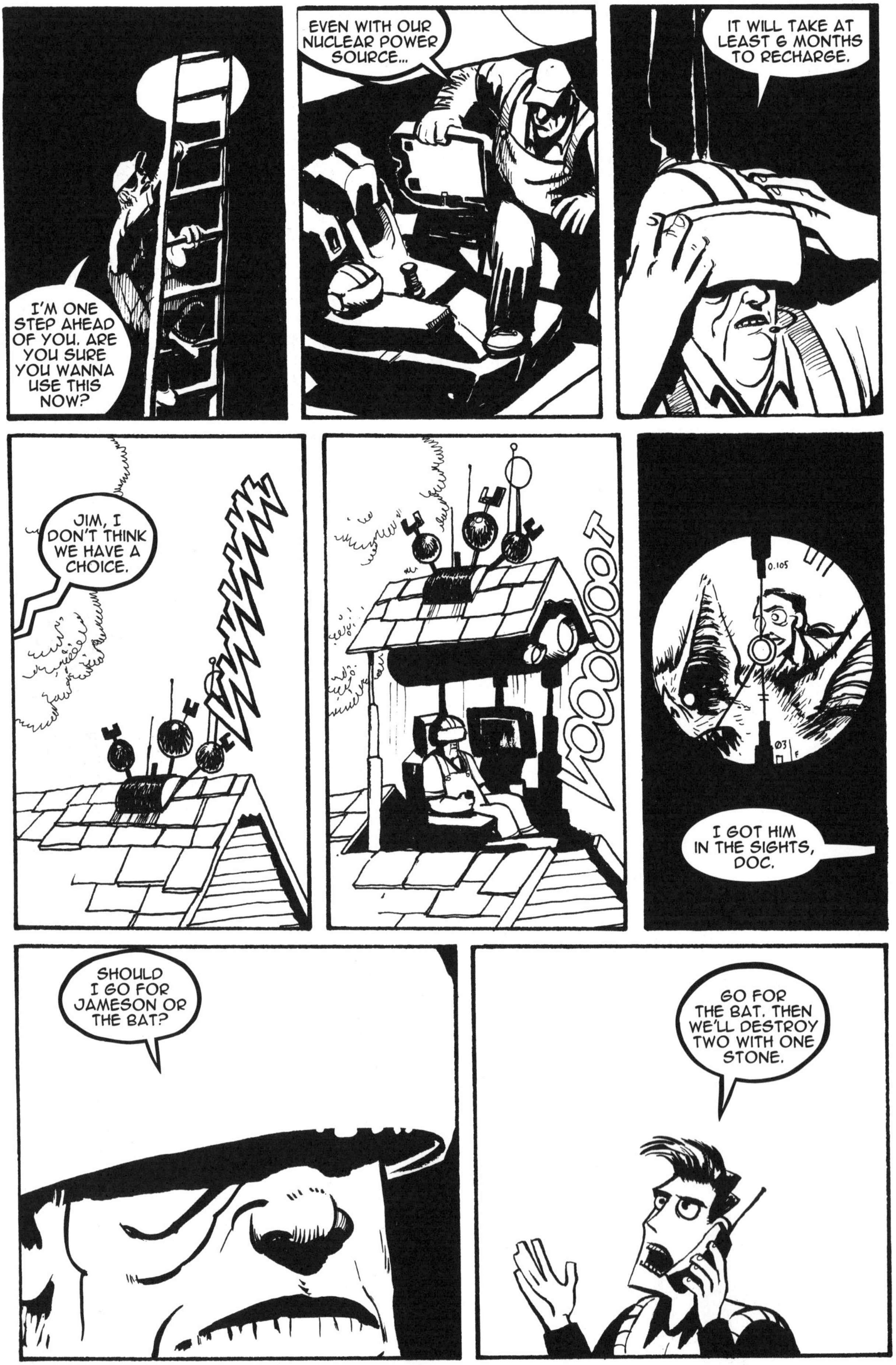
I'M ONE STEP AHEAD OF YOU. ARE YOU SURE YOU WANNA USE THIS NOW?
EVEN WITH OUR NUCLEAR POWER SOURCE...
IT WILL TAKE AT LEAST 6 MONTHS TO RECHARGE.
JIM, I DON'T THINK WE HAVE A CHOICE.
WWWWWW
VOOOOOOOT
I GOT HIM IN THE SIGHTS, DOC.
SHOULD I GO FOR JAMESON OR THE BAT?
GO FOR THE BAT. THEN WE'LL DESTROY TWO WITH ONE STONE.

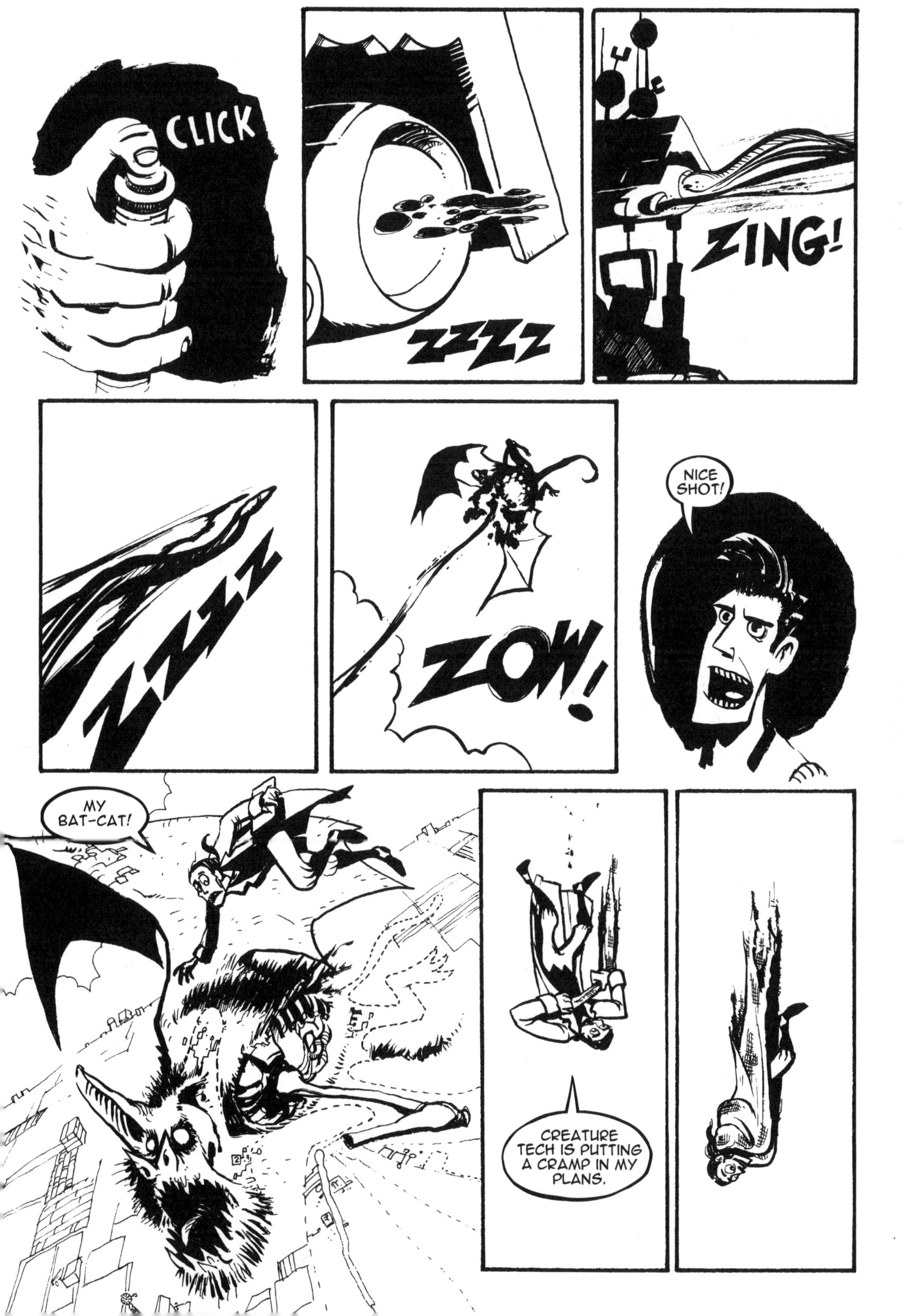
CLICK
ZZZZ
ZING!
ZZZZ
ZOW!
NICE SHOT!
MY BAT-CAT!
CREATURE TECH IS PUTTING A CRAMP IN MY PLANS.

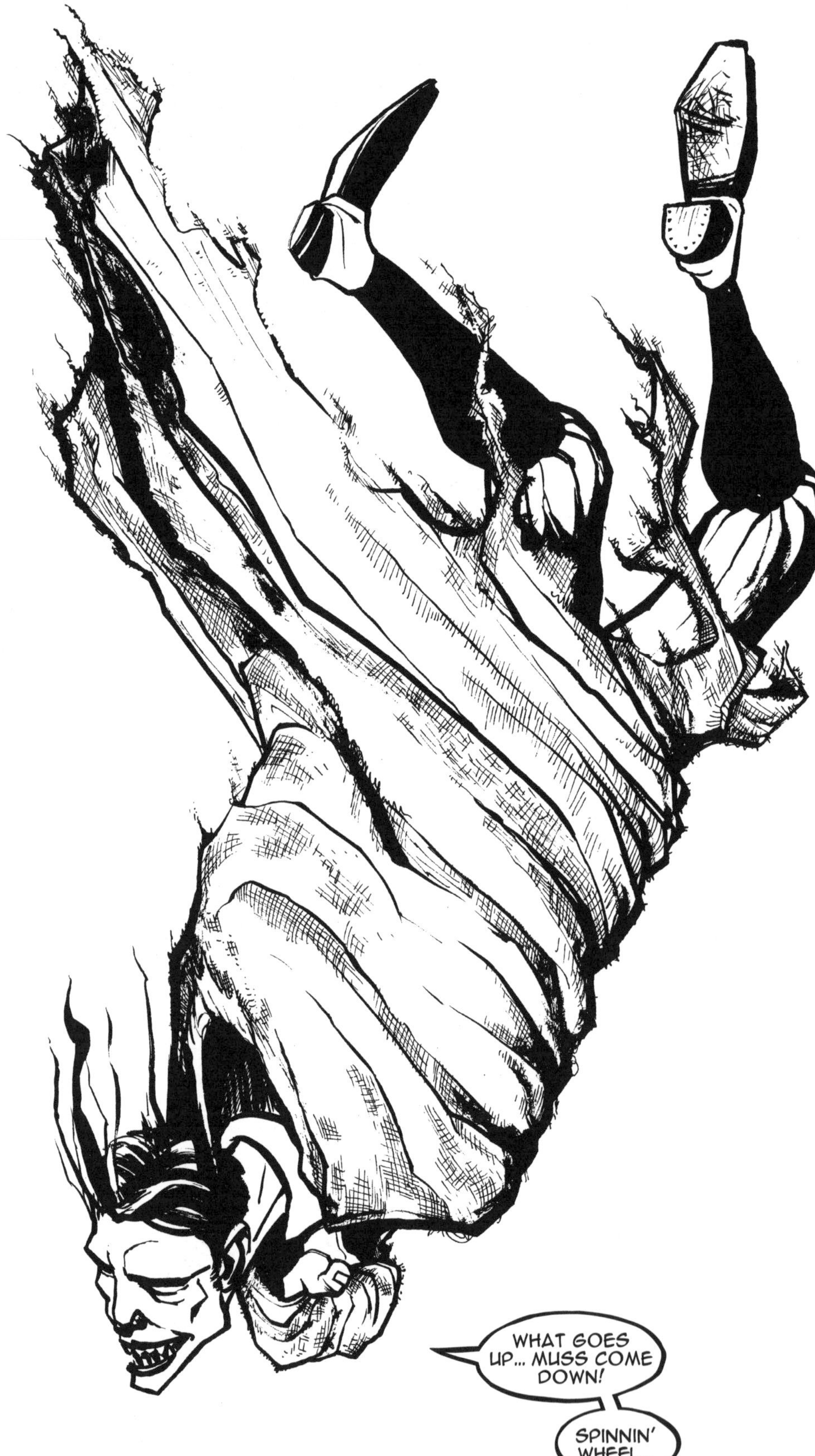
WHAT GOES UP... MUSS COME DOWN!
SPINNIN' WHEEL...

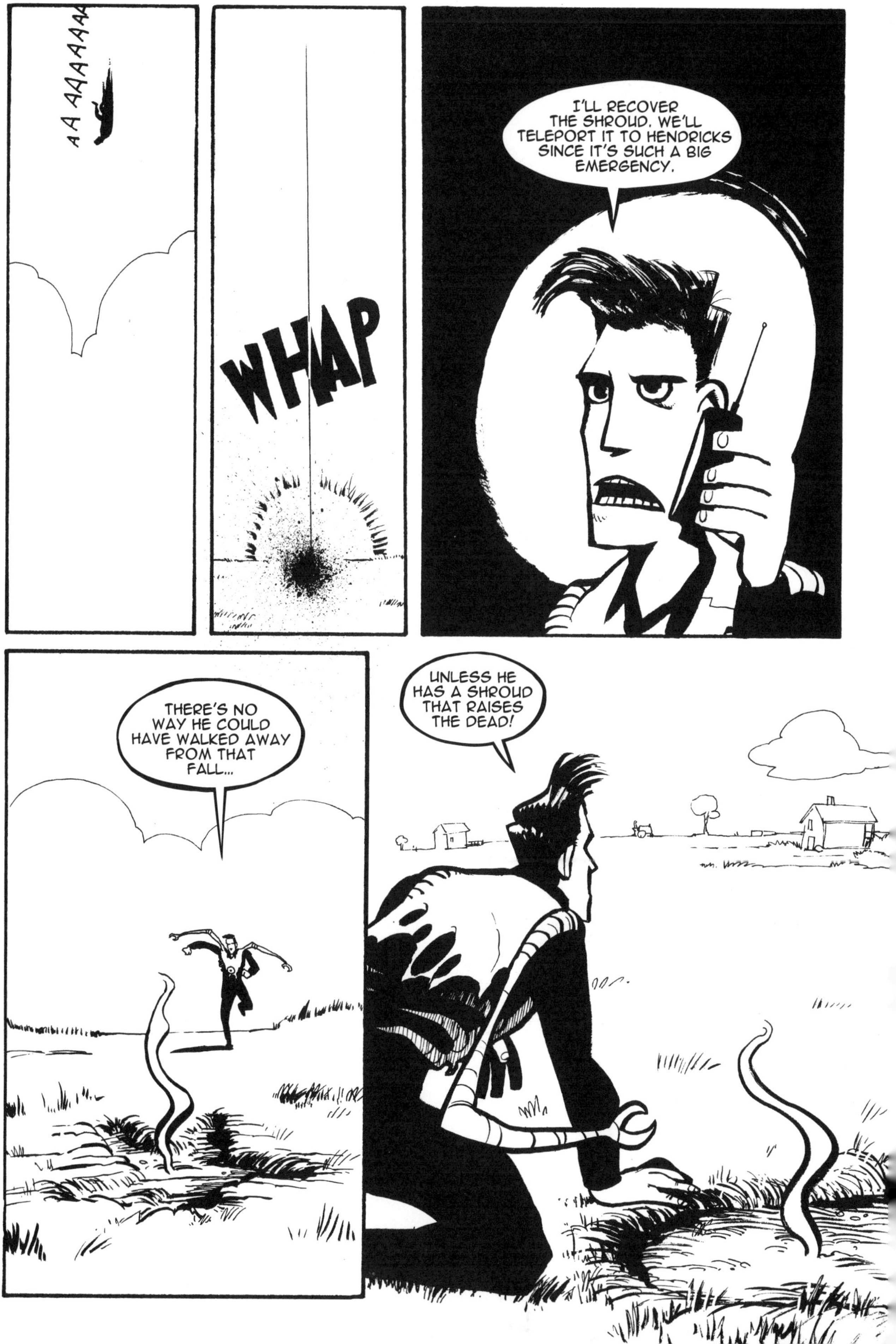

AAAAAAAAA
WHAP
I'LL RECOVER THE SHROUD. WE'LL TELEPORT IT TO HENDRICKS SINCE IT'S SUCH A BIG EMERGENCY.
THERE'S NO WAY HE COULD HAVE WALKED AWAY FROM THAT FALL...
UNLESS HE HAS A SHROUD THAT RAISES THE DEAD!

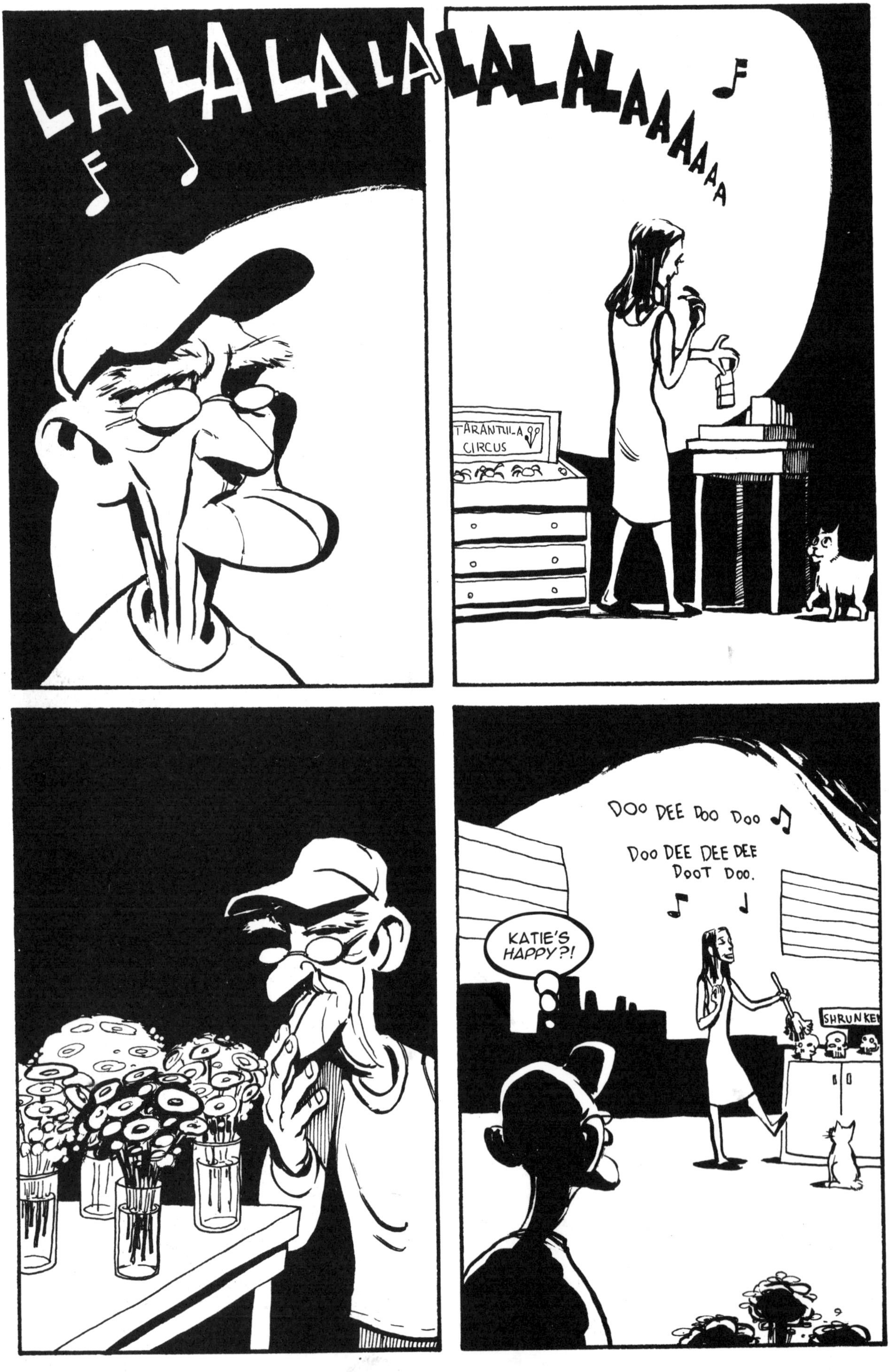

LA LA LA LA LA LA LA LAAAAAAAA
TARANTULA CIRCUS
DOO DEE DOO DOO
DOO DEE DEE DEE DOOT DOO.
KATIE'S HAPPY?!
SHRUNKEN

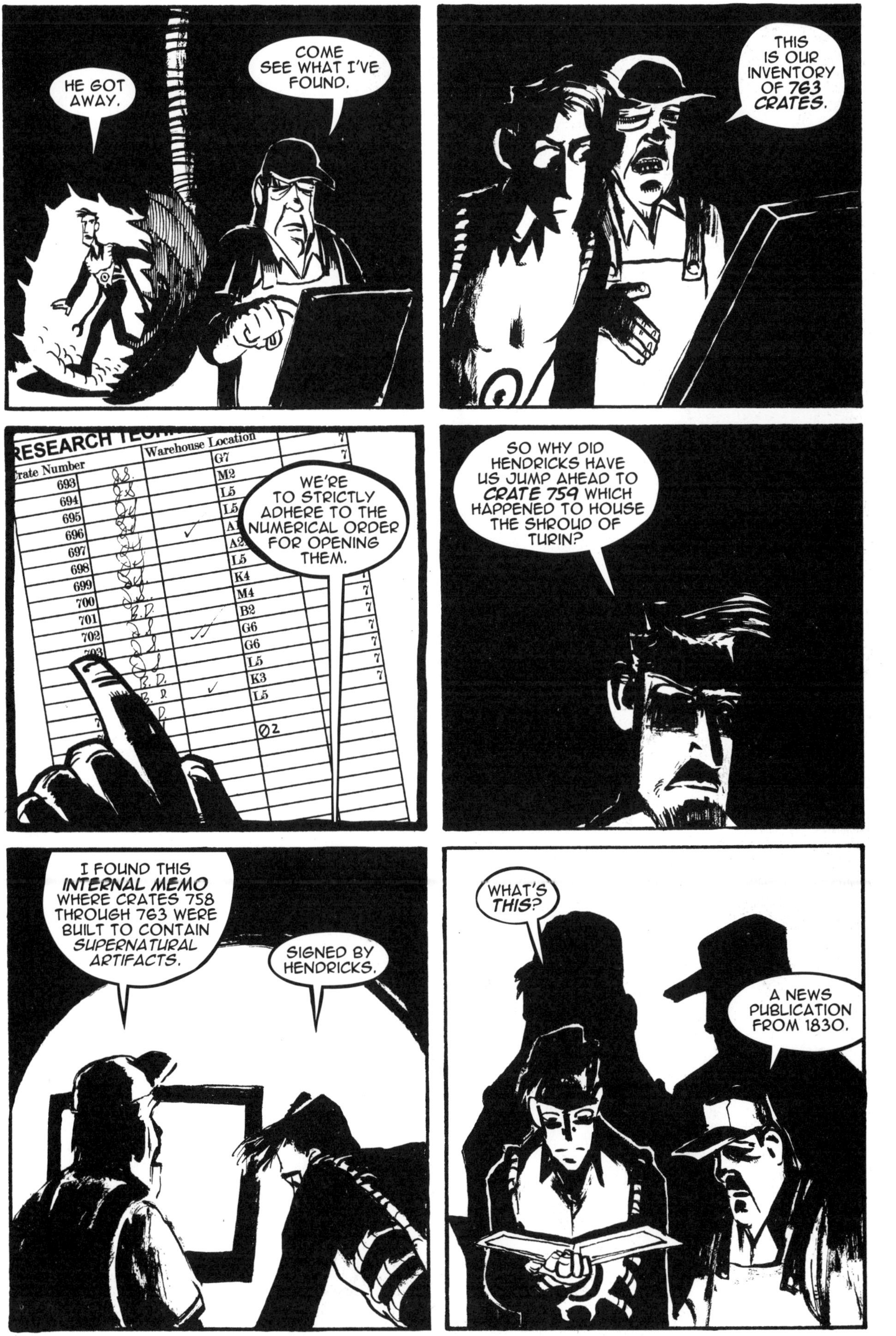
HE GOT AWAY.
COME SEE WHAT I'VE FOUND.
THIS IS OUR INVENTORY OF 763 CRATES.
RESEARCH TECH
Warehouse Location
Crate Number
WE'RE TO STRICTLY ADHERE TO THE NUMERICAL ORDER FOR OPENING THEM.
SO WHY DID HENDRICKS HAVE US JUMP AHEAD TO CRATE 759 WHICH HAPPENED TO HOUSE THE SHROUD OF TURIN?
I FOUND THIS INTERNAL MEMO WHERE CRATES 758 THROUGH 763 WERE BUILT TO CONTAIN SUPERNATURAL ARTIFACTS.
SIGNED BY HENDRICKS.
WHAT'S THIS?
A NEWS PUBLICATION FROM 1830.

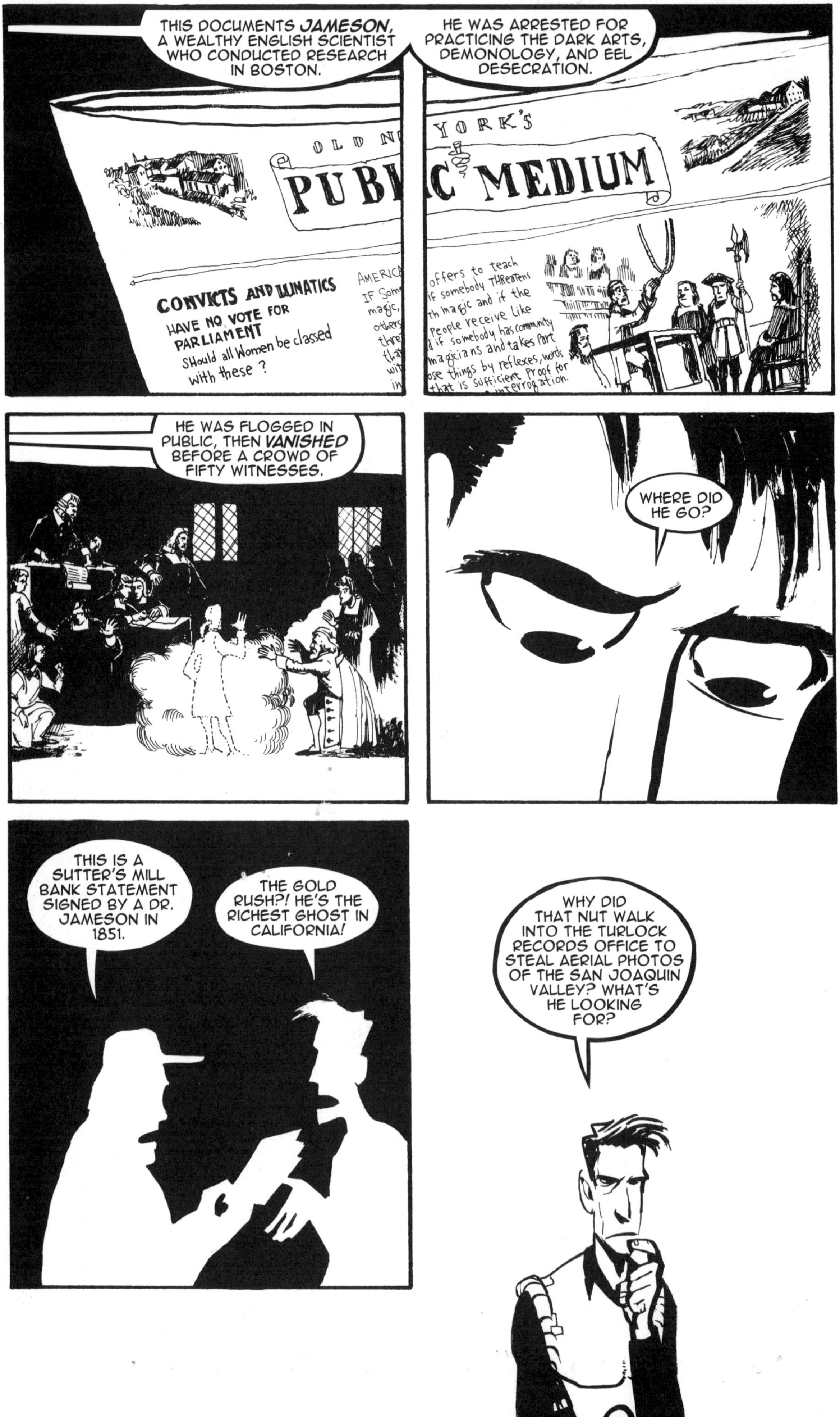
THIS DOCUMENTS JAMESON, A WEALTHY ENGLISH SCIENTIST WHO CONDUCTED RESEARCH IN BOSTON.
HE WAS ARRESTED FOR PRACTICING THE DARK ARTS, DEMONOLOGY, AND EEL DESECRATION.
YORK'S
MEDIUM
CONVICTS AND LUNATICS
HAVE NO VOTE FOR PARLIAMENT
SHould all Women be classed with these ?
offers to teach
if somebody THREatens
th magic and if the
People receive like
d if somebody has community
magicians and takes part
ose things by reflexes, words
that is sufficient Proof for
interrogation.
HE WAS FLOGGED IN PUBLIC, THEN VANISHED BEFORE A CROWD OF FIFTY WITNESSES.
WHERE DID HE GO?
THIS IS A SUTTER'S MILL BANK STATEMENT SIGNED BY A DR. JAMESON IN 1851.
THE GOLD RUSH?! HE'S THE RICHEST GHOST IN CALIFORNIA!
WHY DID THAT NUT WALK INTO THE TURLOCK RECORDS OFFICE TO STEAL AERIAL PHOTOS OF THE SAN JOAQUIN VALLEY? WHAT'S HE LOOKING FOR?

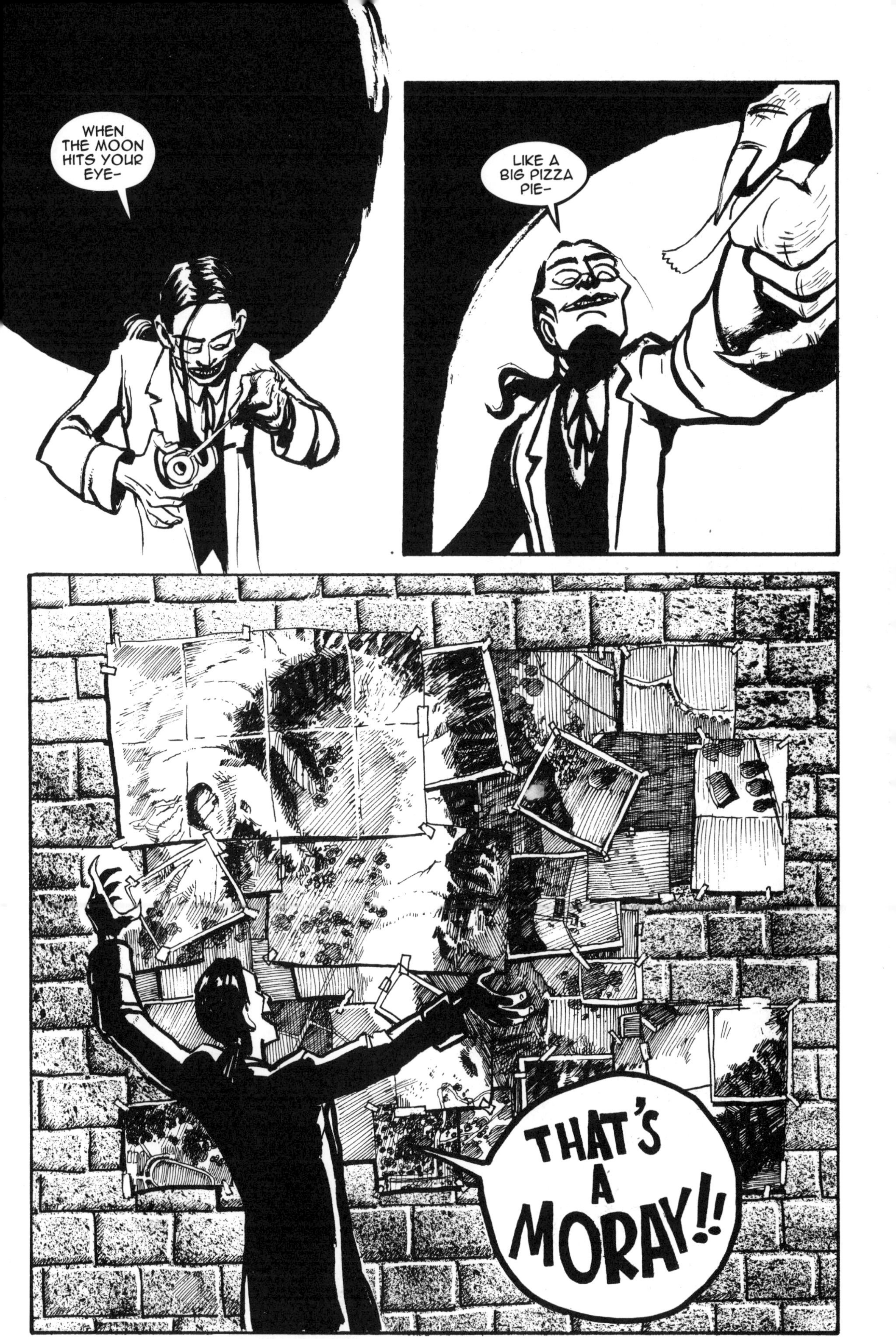
WHEN THE MOON HITS YOUR EYE-
LIKE A BIG PIZZA PIE-
THAT'S A MORAY!!

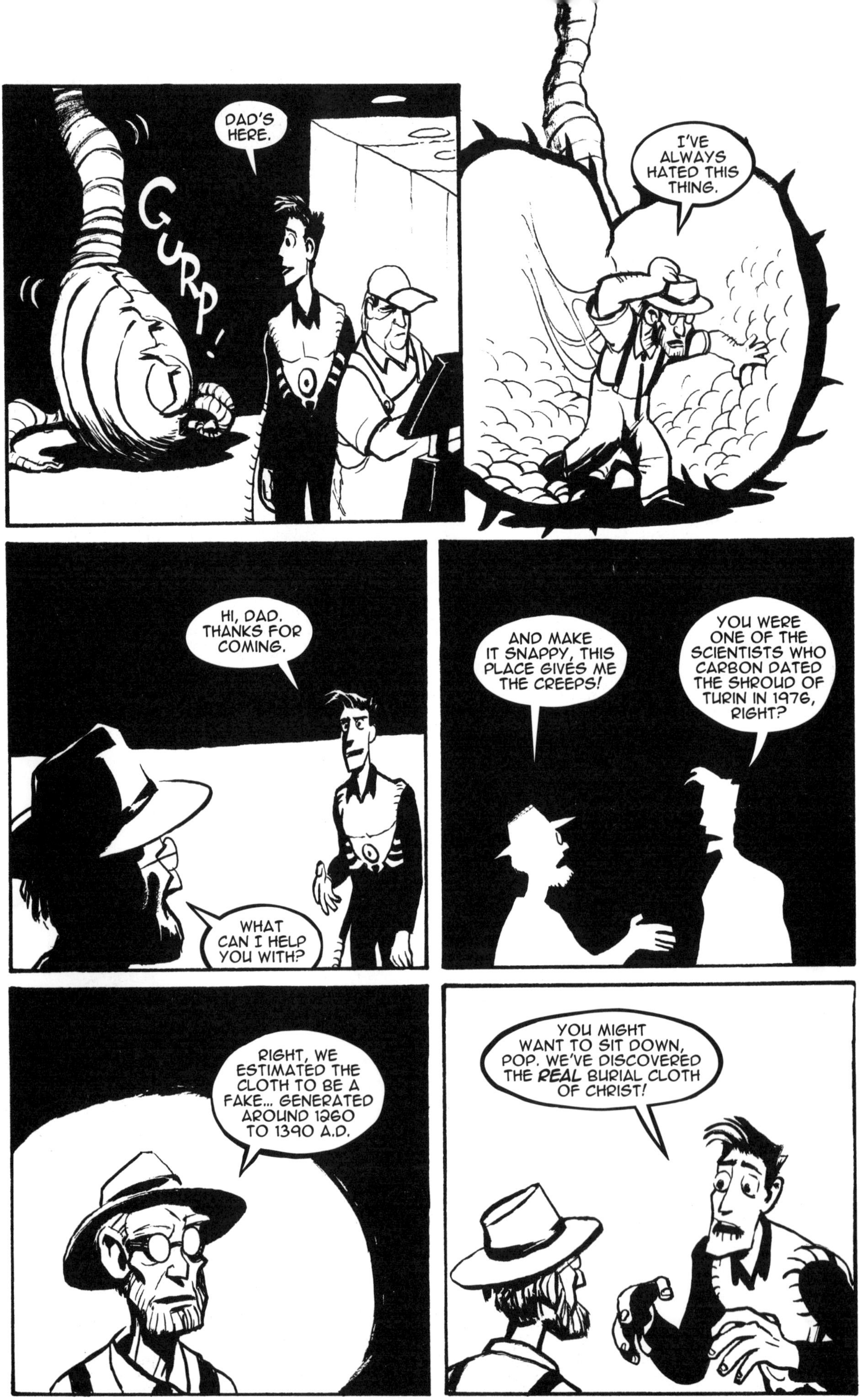
DAD'S HERE.
GURP!
I'VE ALWAYS HATED THIS THING.
HI, DAD. THANKS FOR COMING.
WHAT CAN I HELP YOU WITH?
AND MAKE IT SNAPPY, THIS PLACE GIVES ME THE CREEPS!
YOU WERE ONE OF THE SCIENTISTS WHO CARBON DATED THE SHROUD OF TURIN IN 1976, RIGHT?
RIGHT, WE ESTIMATED THE CLOTH TO BE A FAKE... GENERATED AROUND 1260 TO 1390 A.D.
YOU MIGHT WANT TO SIT DOWN, POP. WE'VE DISCOVERED THE *REAL* BURIAL CLOTH OF CHRIST!

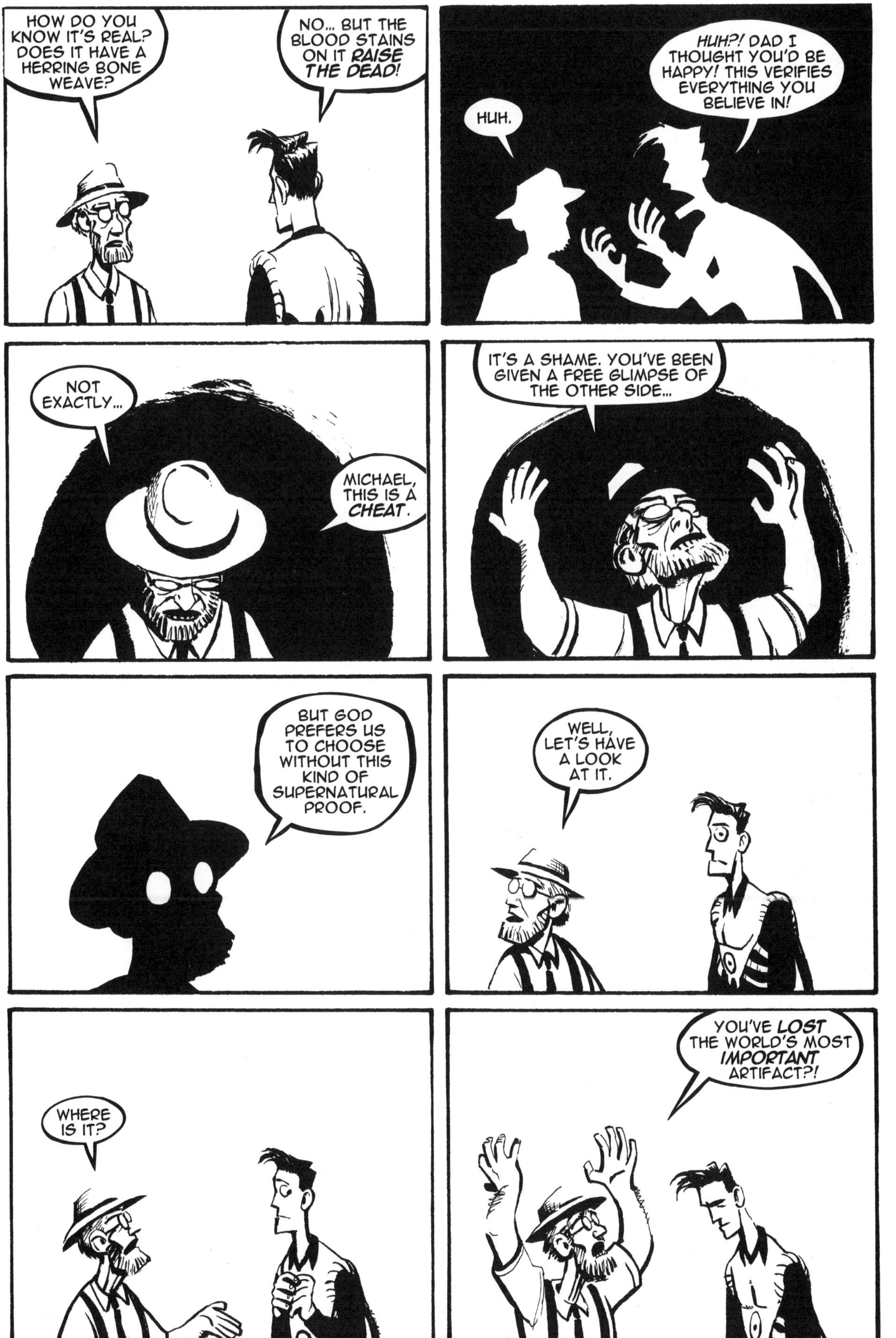
HOW DO YOU KNOW IT'S REAL? DOES IT HAVE A HERRING BONE WEAVE?
NO... BUT THE BLOOD STAINS ON IT *RAISE THE DEAD!*
HUH.
HUH?! DAD I THOUGHT YOU'D BE HAPPY! THIS VERIFIES EVERYTHING YOU BELIEVE IN!
NOT EXACTLY...
MICHAEL, THIS IS A *CHEAT*.
IT'S A SHAME. YOU'VE BEEN GIVEN A FREE GLIMPSE OF THE OTHER SIDE...
BUT GOD PREFERS US TO CHOOSE WITHOUT THIS KIND OF SUPERNATURAL PROOF.
WELL, LET'S HAVE A LOOK AT IT.
WHERE IS IT?
YOU'VE *LOST* THE WORLD'S MOST *IMPORTANT* ARTIFACT?!

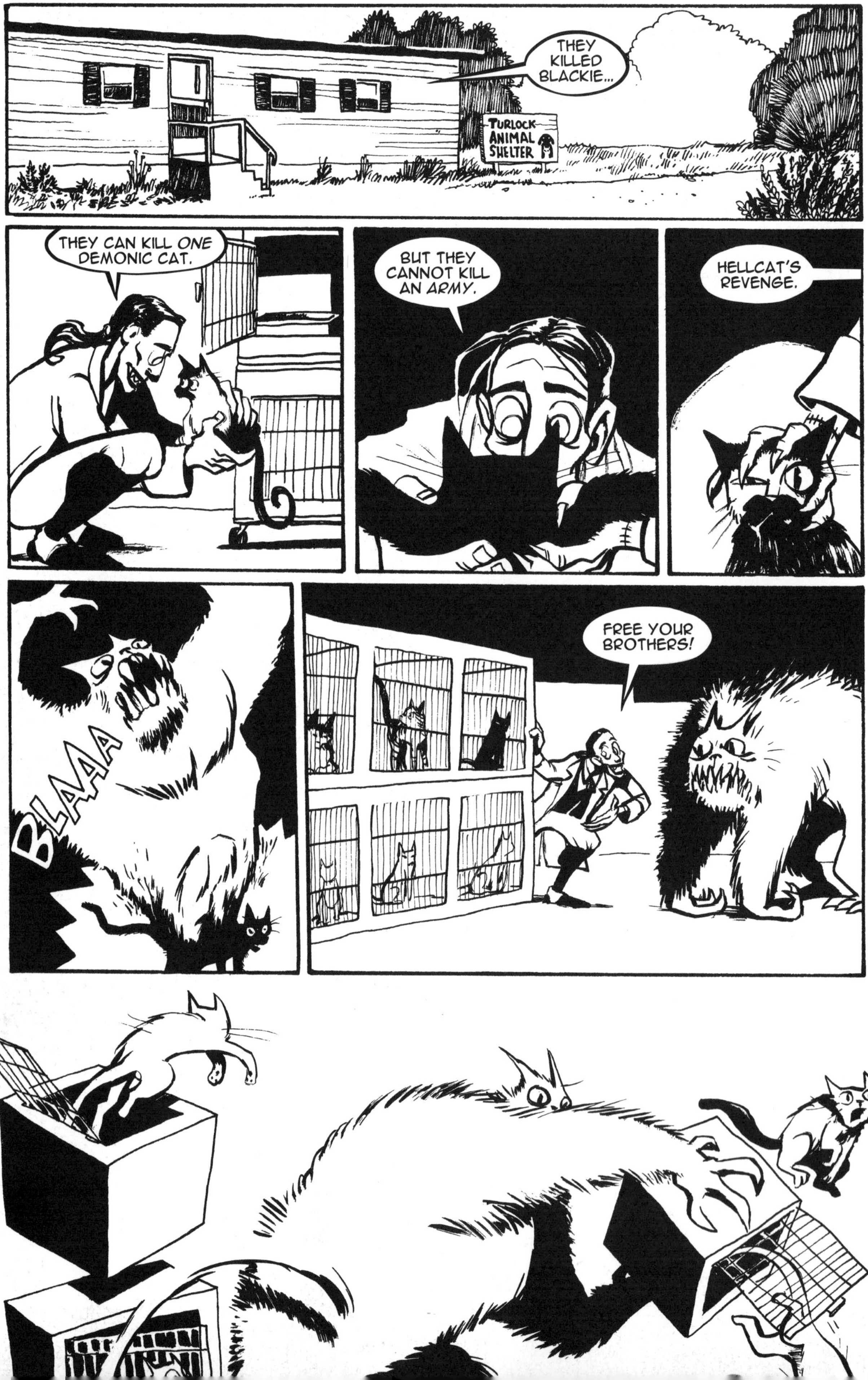
THEY KILLED BLACKIE...
TURLOCK ANIMAL SHELTER
THEY CAN KILL ONE DEMONIC CAT.
BUT THEY CANNOT KILL AN ARMY.
HELLCAT'S REVENGE.
BLAAAA
FREE YOUR BROTHERS!

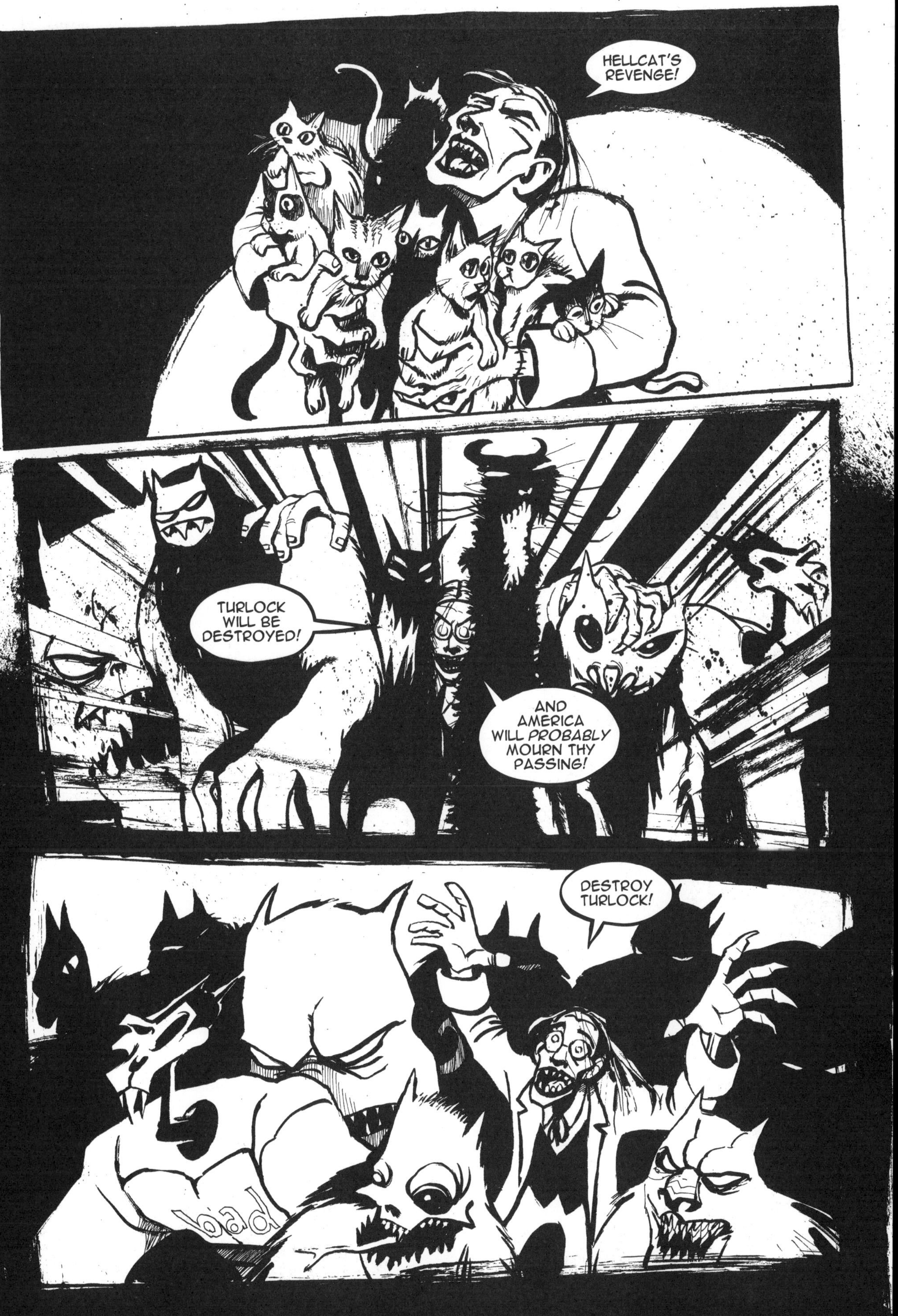
HELLCAT'S REVENGE!
TURLOCK WILL BE DESTROYED!
AND AMERICA WILL *PROBABLY* MOURN THY PASSING!
DESTROY TURLOCK!

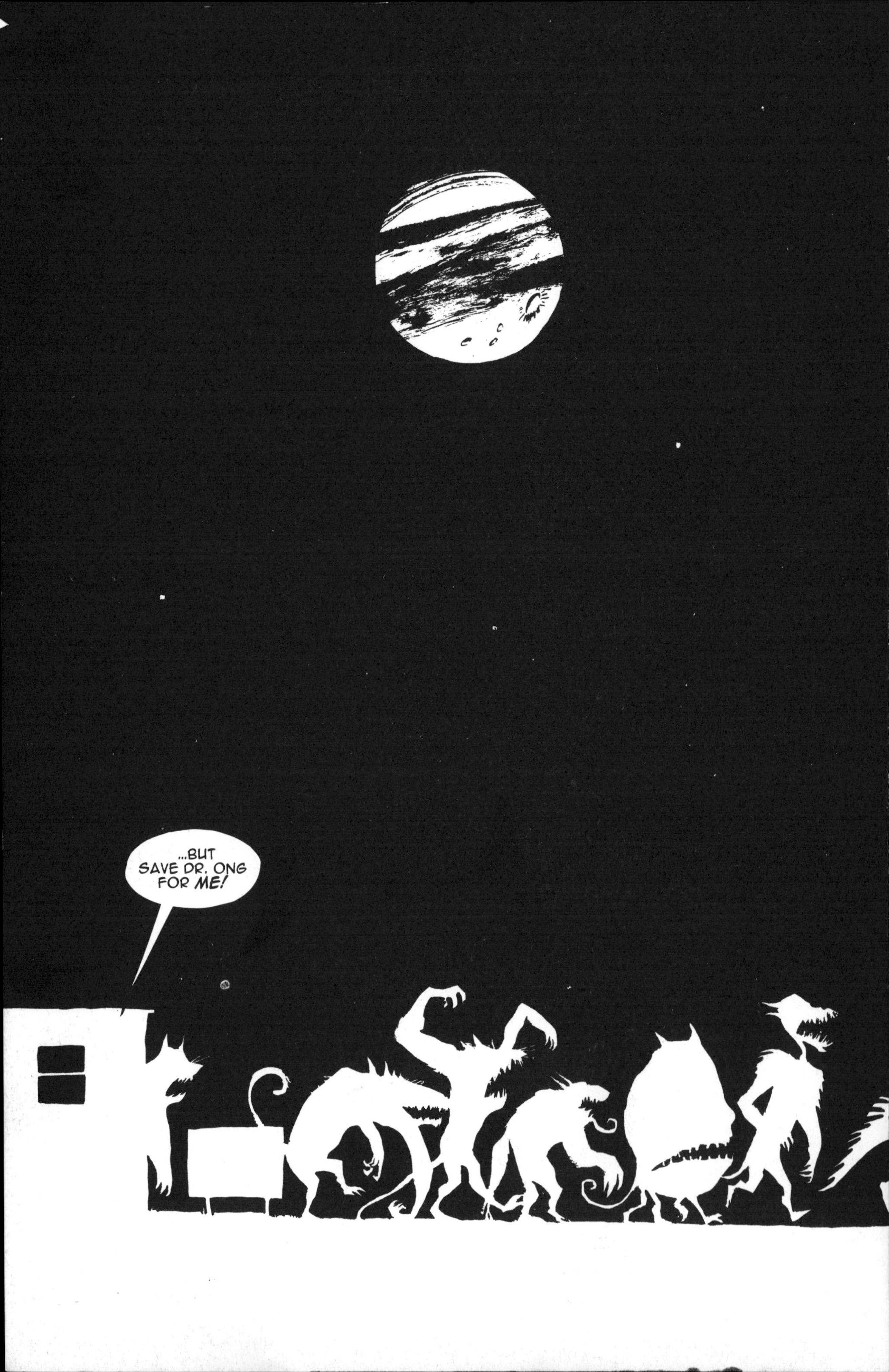
...BUT SAVE DR. ONG FOR ME!

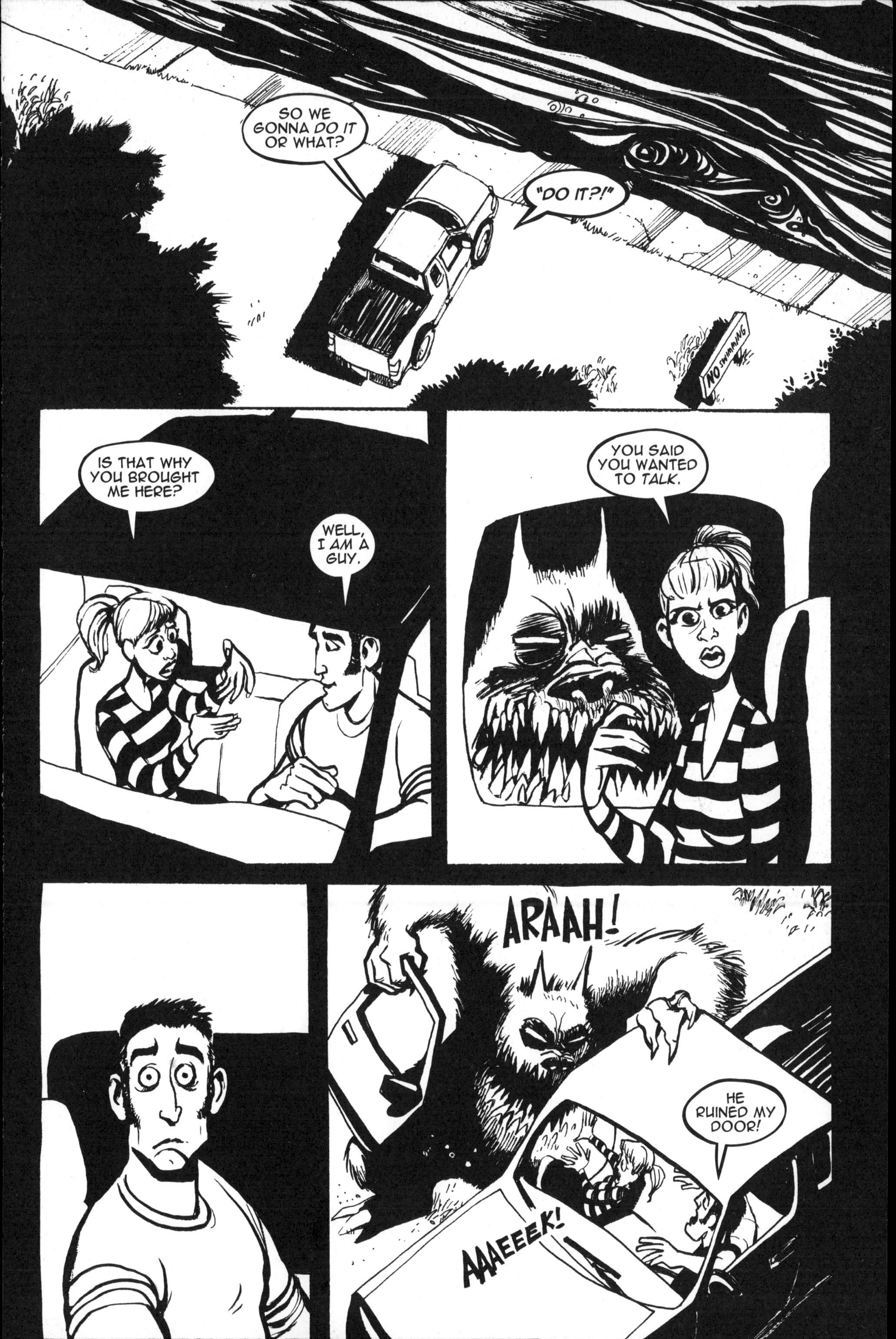
SO WE GONNA DO IT OR WHAT?
"DO IT?!"
IS THAT WHY YOU BROUGHT ME HERE?
WELL, I AM A GUY.
YOU SAID YOU WANTED TO TALK.
ARAAH!
HE RUINED MY DOOR!
AAAEEEK!

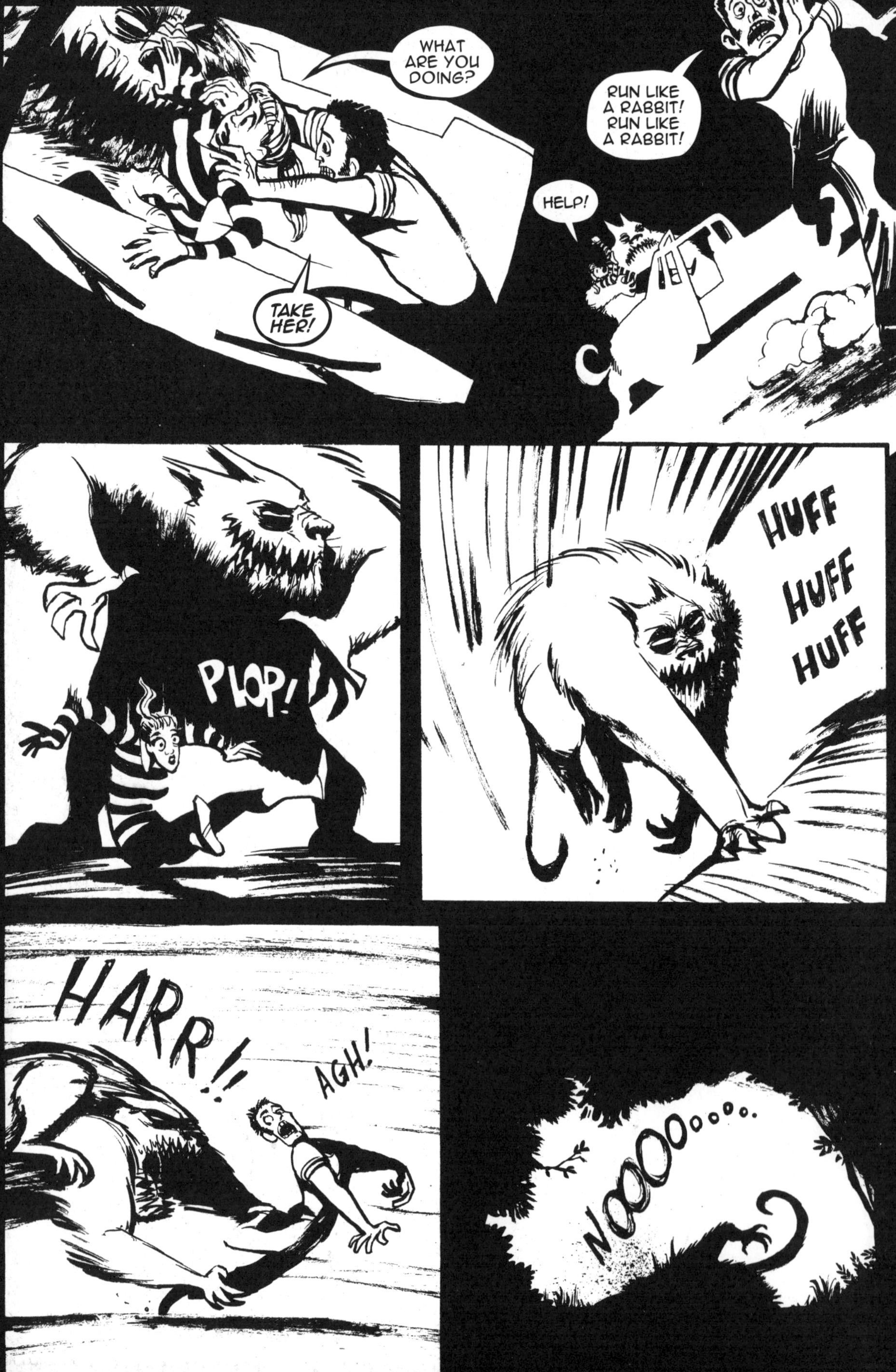
WHAT ARE YOU DOING?
TAKE HER!
RUN LIKE A RABBIT! RUN LIKE A RABBIT!
HELP!
PLOP!
HUFF HUFF HUFF
HARR!!!
AGH!
NOOOOooooo.

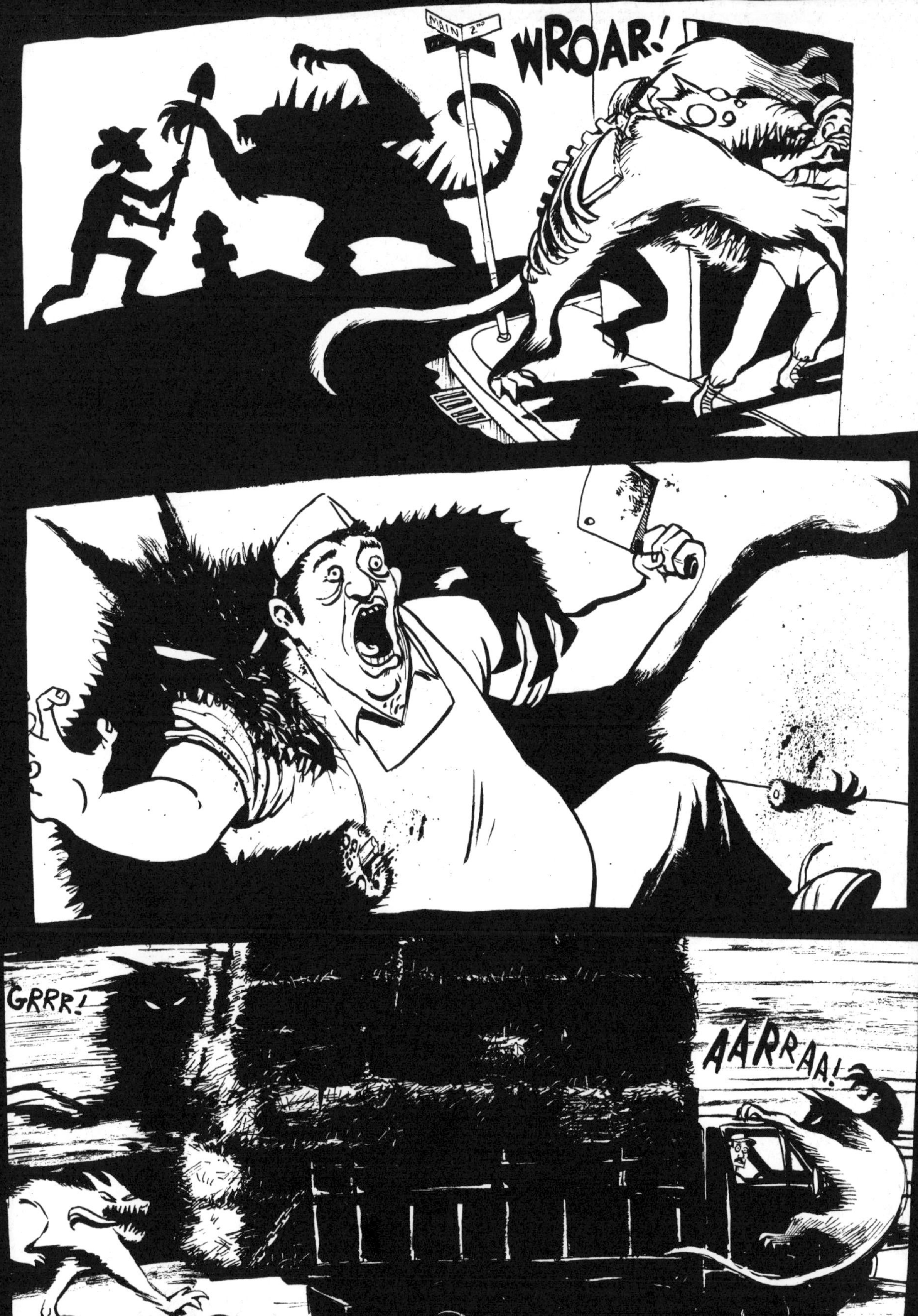
MAIN
2ND
WROAR!
GRRR!
AARRAA!

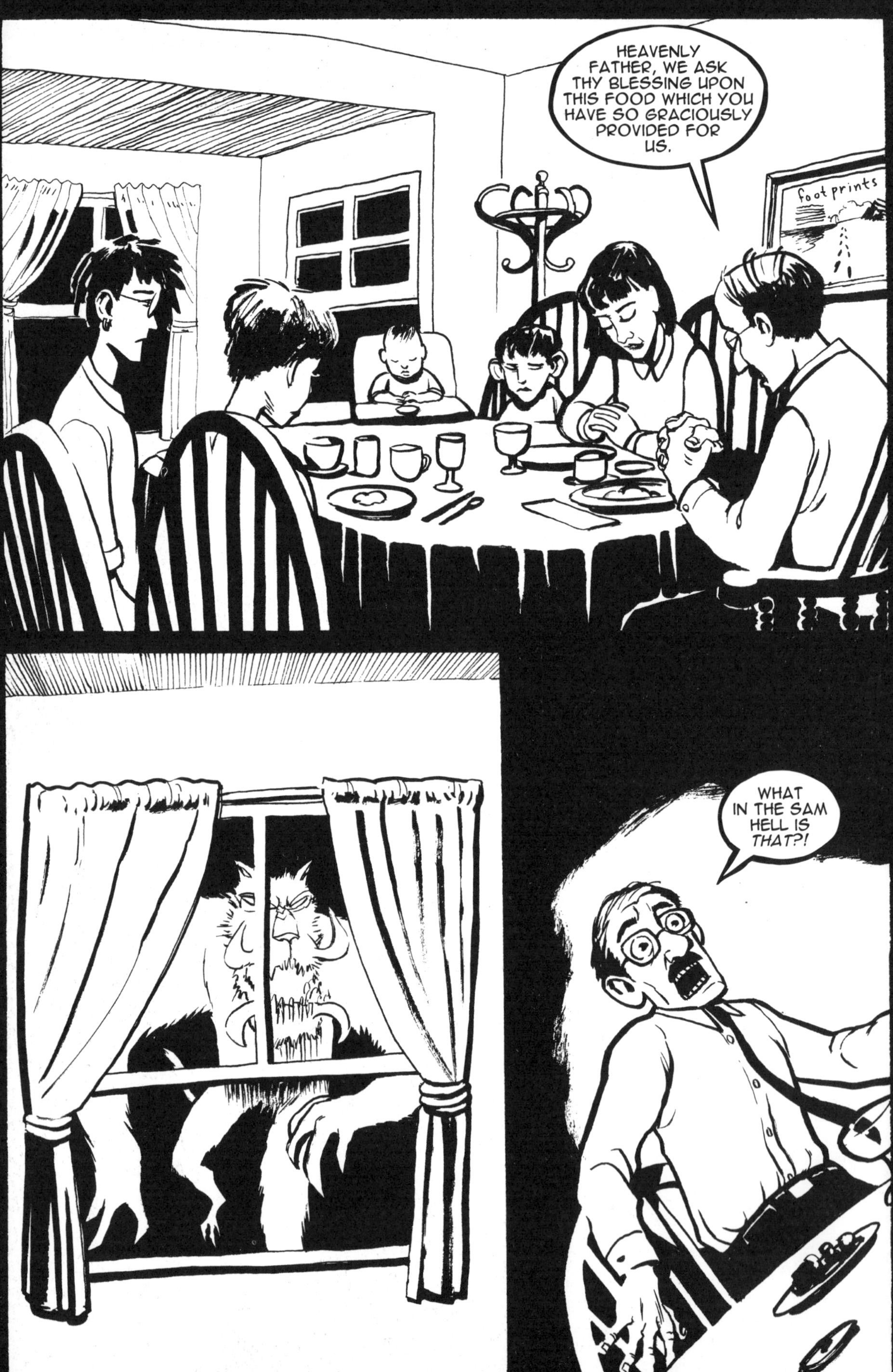
HEAVENLY FATHER, WE ASK THY BLESSING UPON THIS FOOD WHICH YOU HAVE SO GRACIOUSLY PROVIDED FOR US.
foot prints
WHAT IN THE SAM HELL IS *THAT?!*

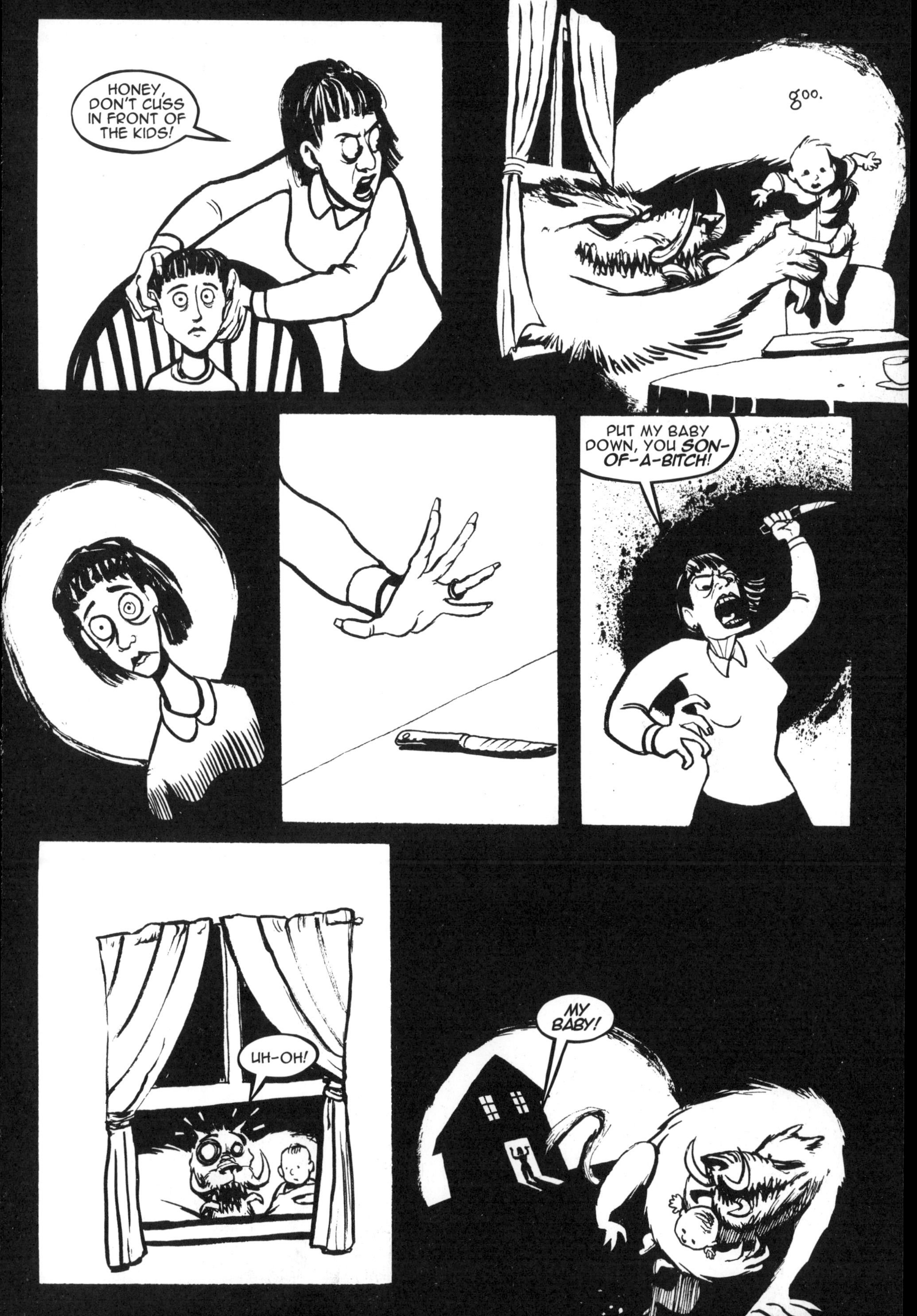
HONEY, DON'T CUSS IN FRONT OF THE KIDS!
goo.
PUT MY BABY DOWN, YOU SON-OF-A-BITCH!
UH-OH!
MY BABY!

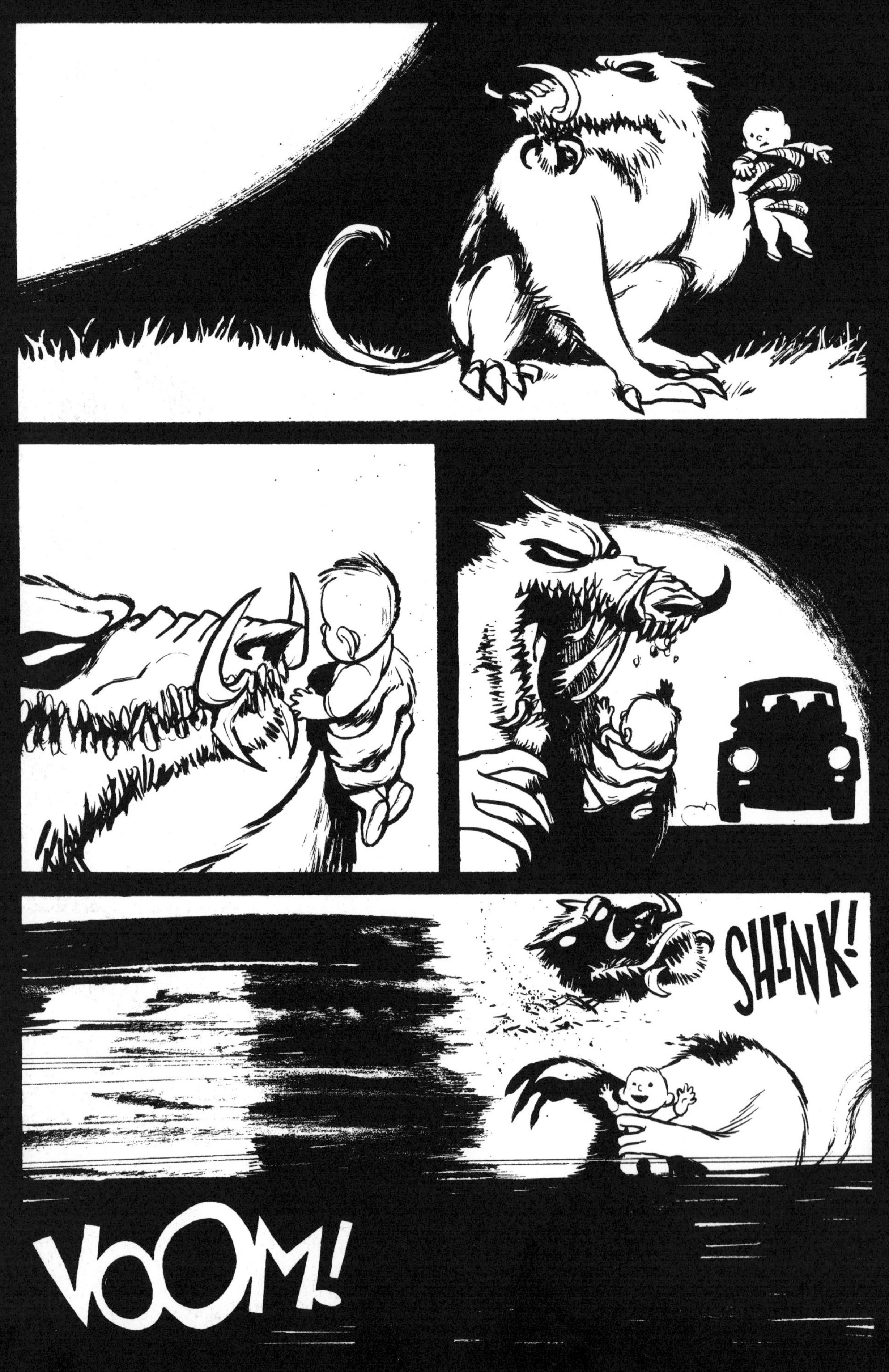
SHINK!
VOOM!

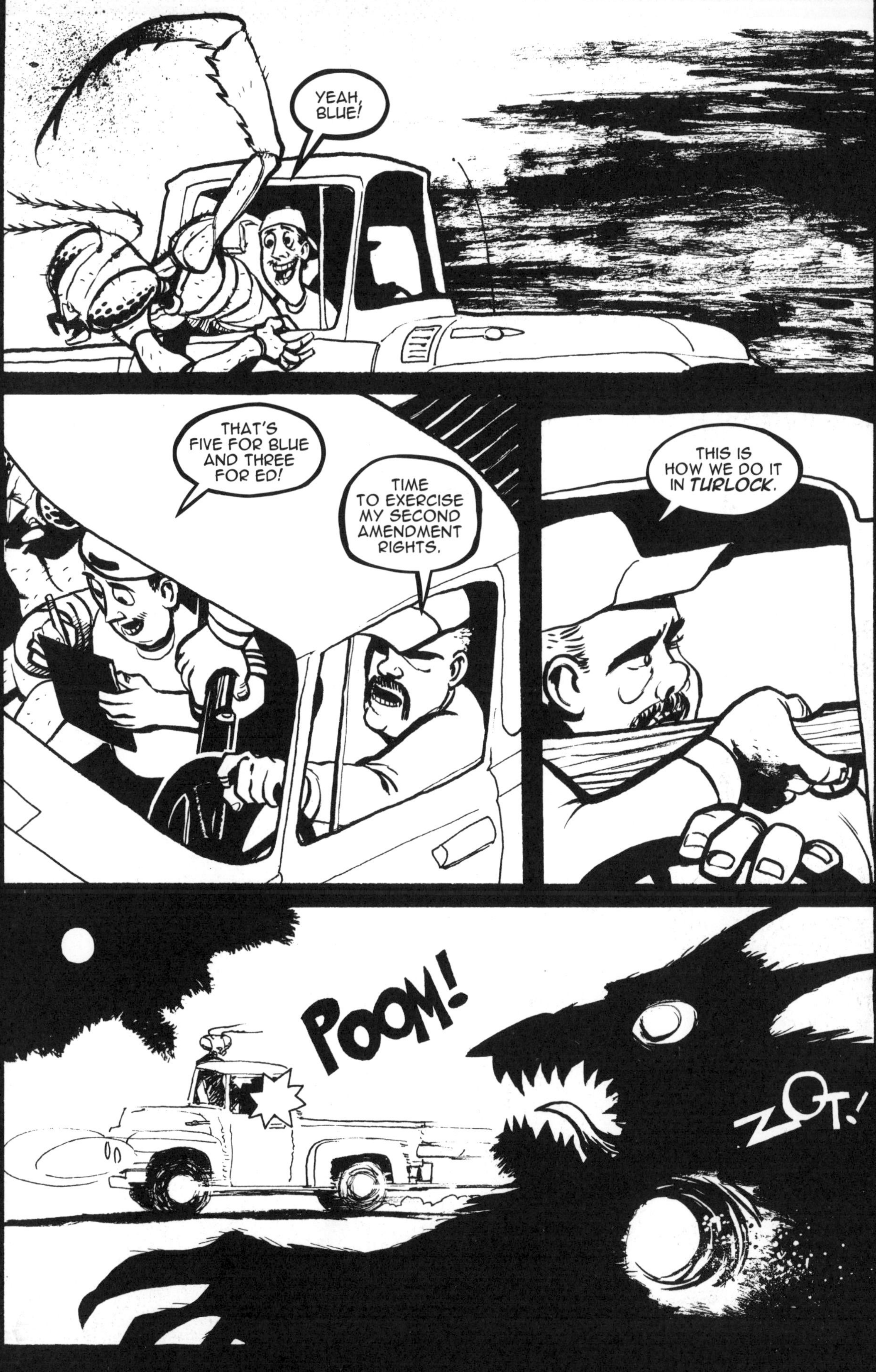
YEAH, BLUE!
THAT'S FIVE FOR BLUE AND THREE FOR ED!
TIME TO EXERCISE MY SECOND AMENDMENT RIGHTS.
THIS IS HOW WE DO IT IN *TURLOCK*.
POOM!
ZOT!

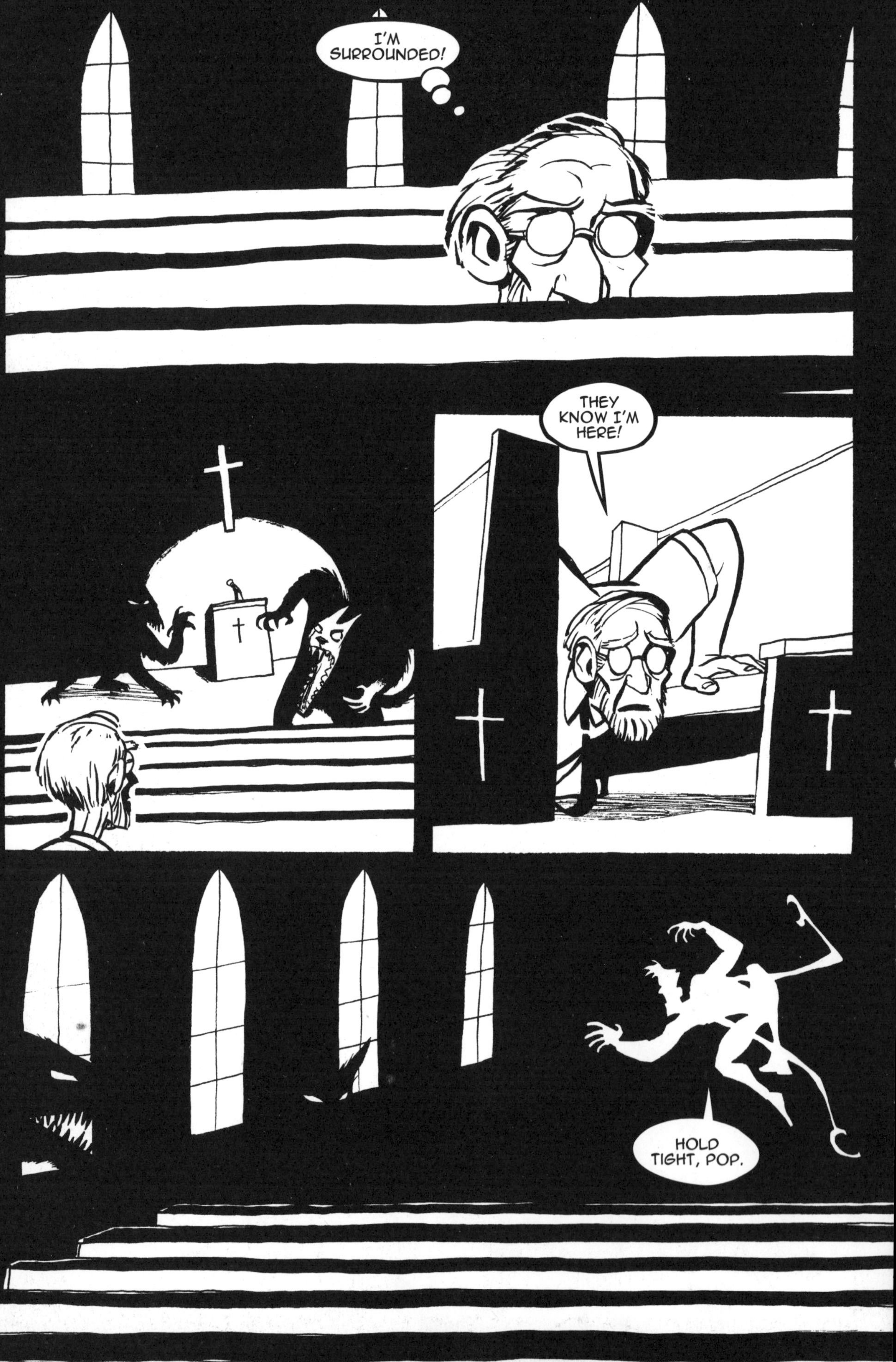
I'M SURROUNDED!
THEY KNOW I'M HERE!
HOLD TIGHT, POP.

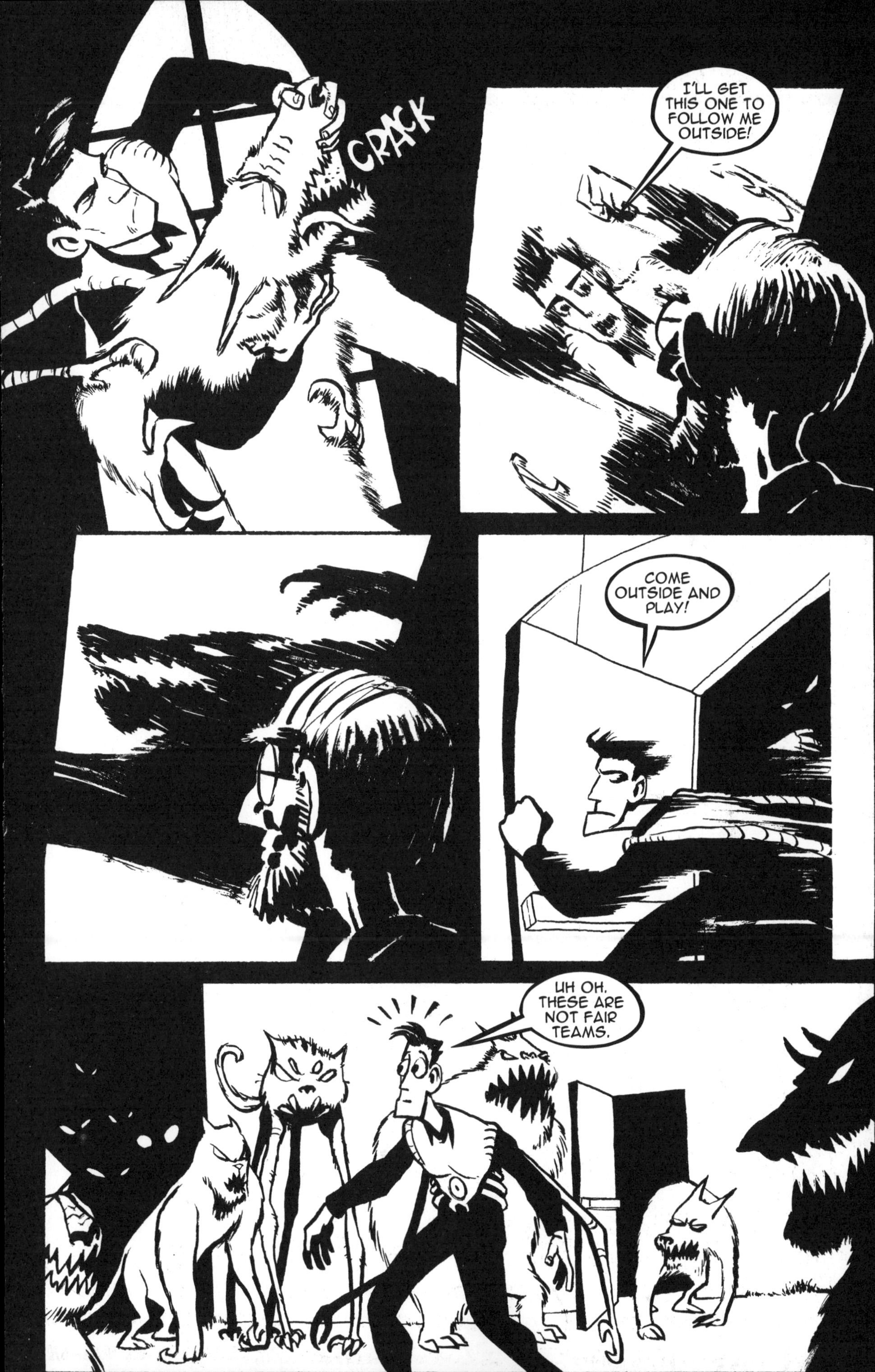
CRACK
I'LL GET THIS ONE TO FOLLOW ME OUTSIDE!
COME OUTSIDE AND PLAY!
UH OH. THESE ARE NOT FAIR TEAMS.

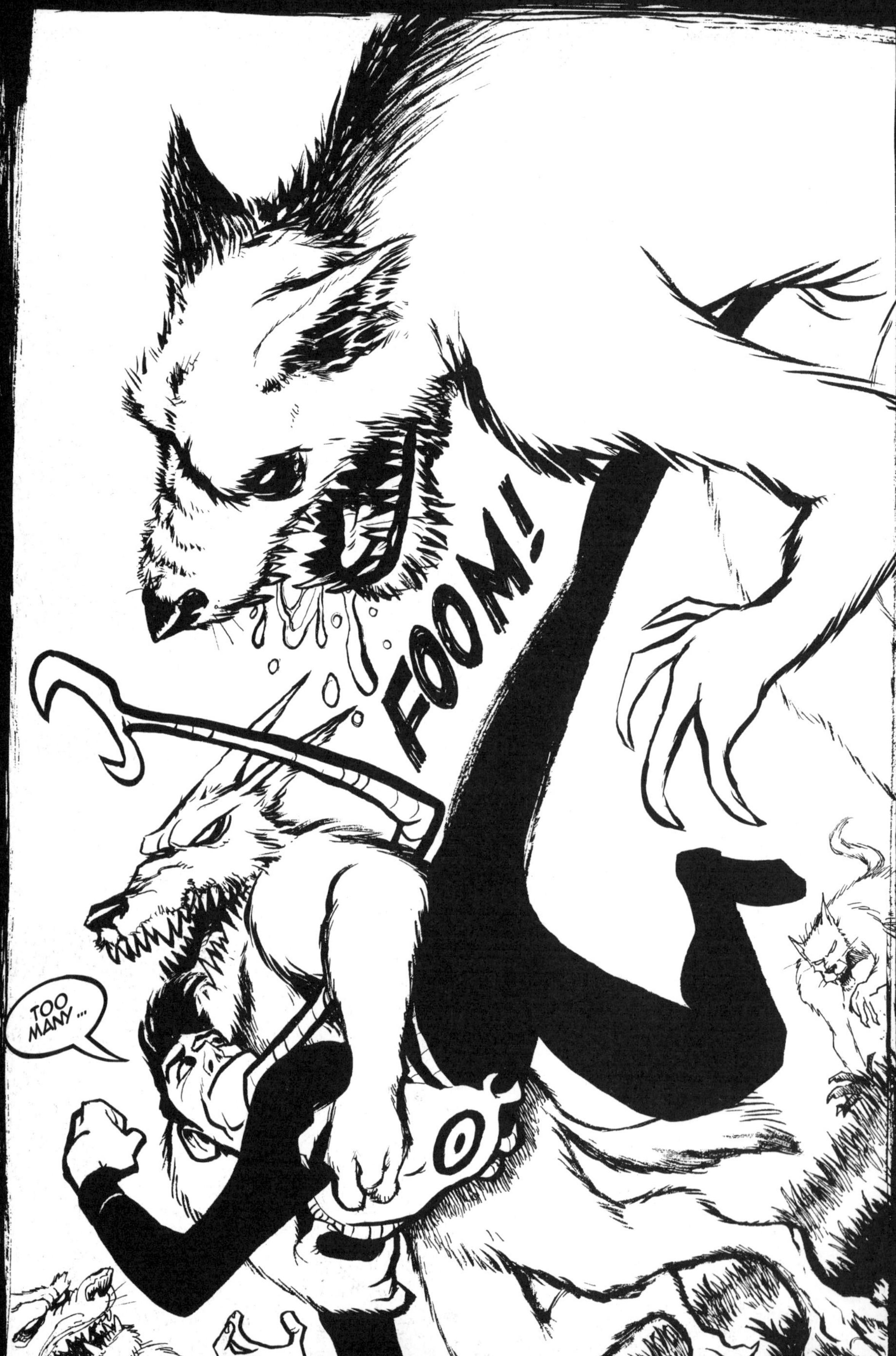
FOOM!!
TOO MANY...

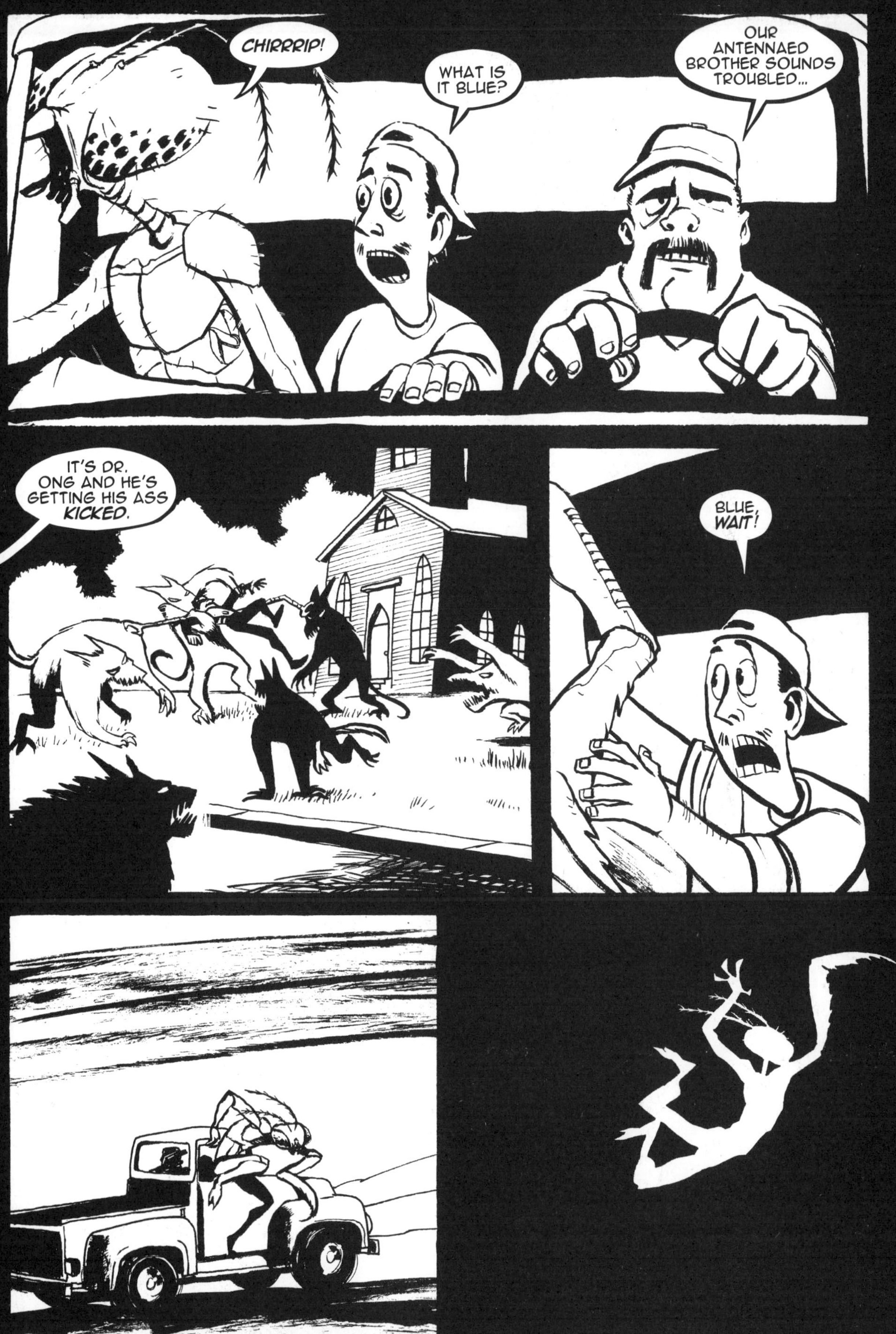
CHIRRRIP!
WHAT IS IT BLUE?
OUR ANTENNAED BROTHER SOUNDS TROUBLED...
IT'S DR. ONG AND HE'S GETTING HIS ASS KICKED.
BLUE, WAIT!

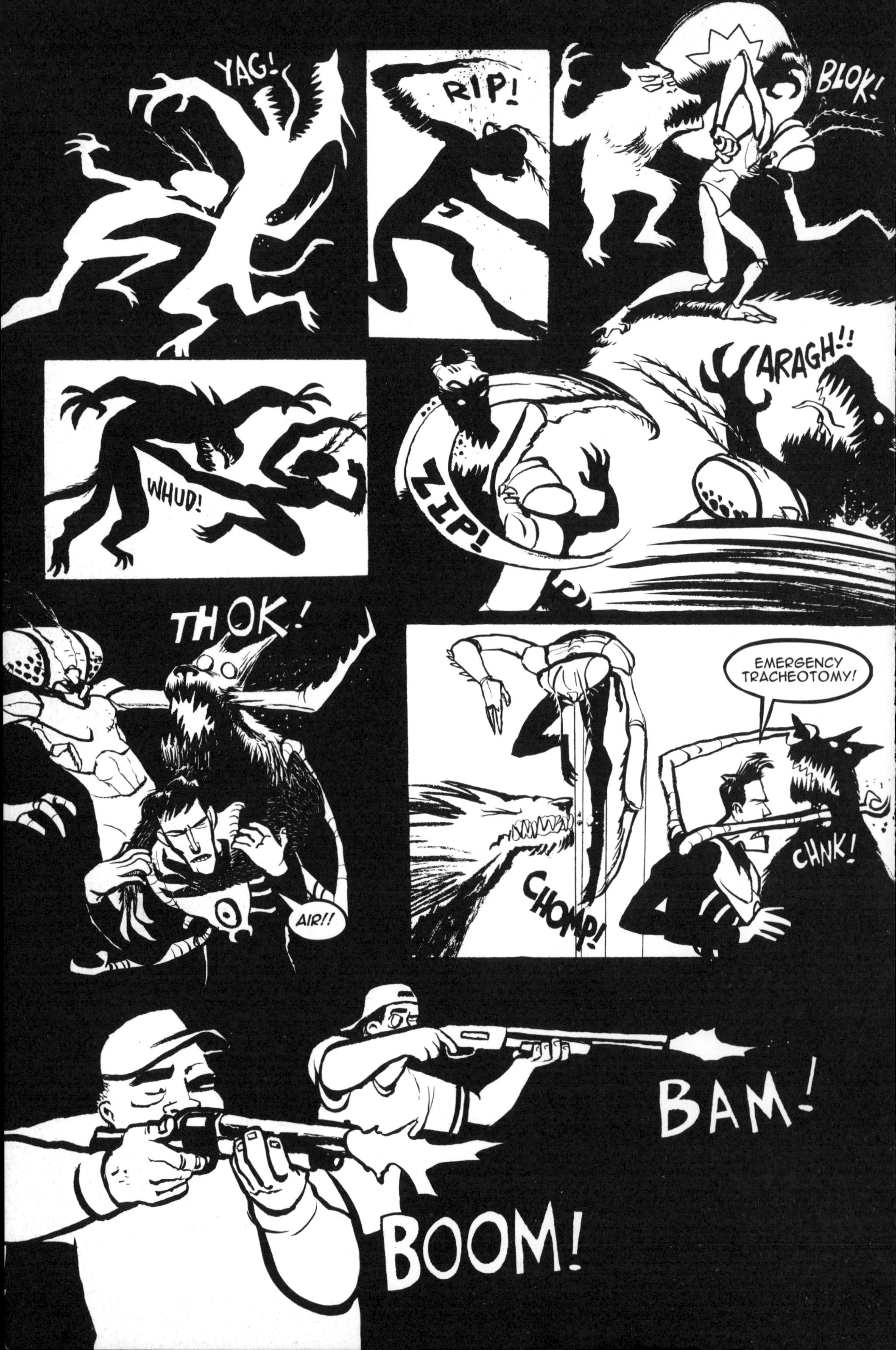
YAG!
RIP!
BLOK!
WHUD!
ZIP!
ARAGH!!
THOK!
AIR!!
EMERGENCY TRACHEOTOMY!
CHNK!
CHOMP!
BAM!
BOOM!

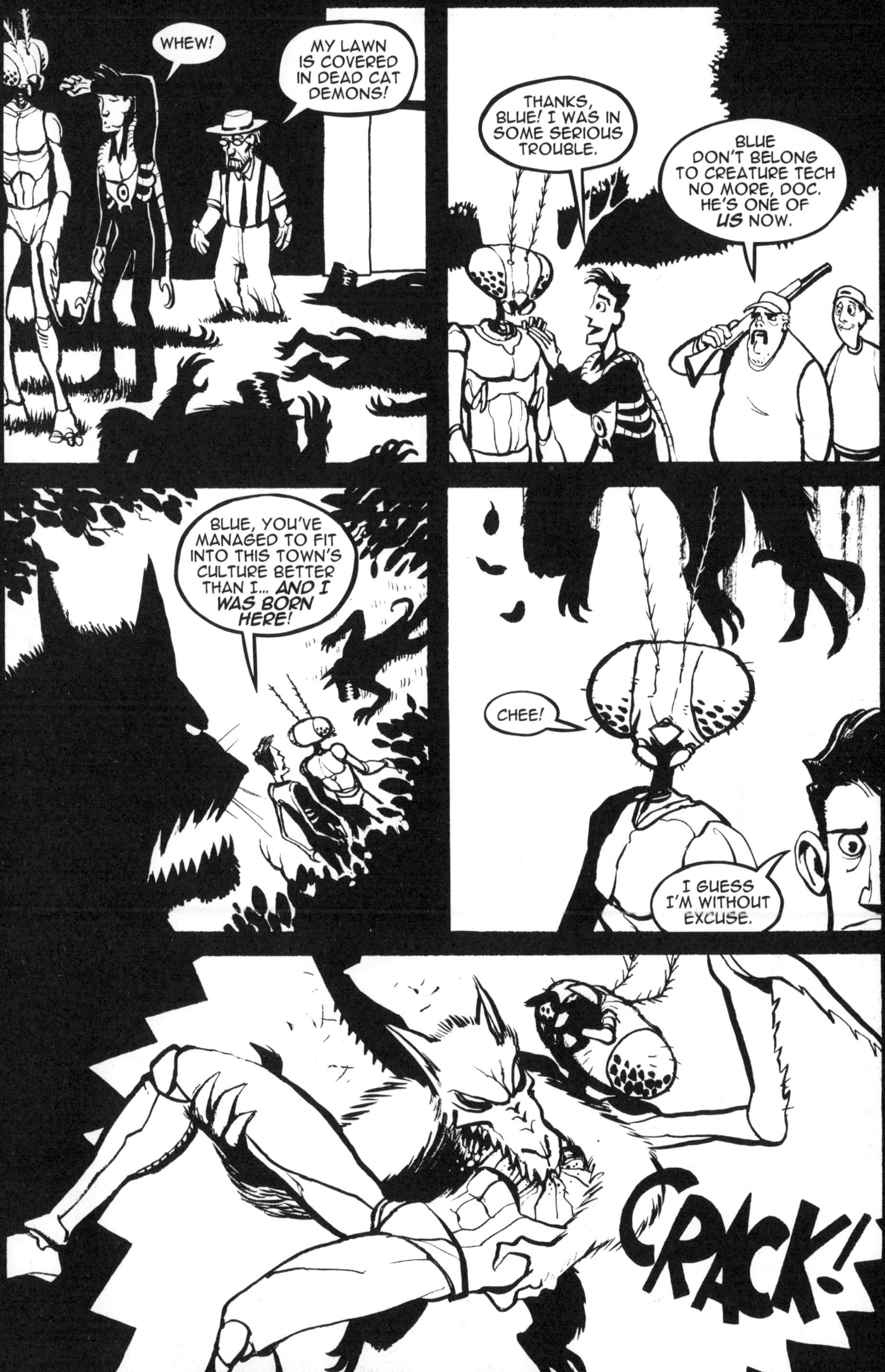
WHEW!
MY LAWN IS COVERED IN DEAD CAT DEMONS!
THANKS, BLUE! I WAS IN SOME SERIOUS TROUBLE.
BLUE DON'T BELONG TO CREATURE TECH NO MORE, DOC. HE'S ONE OF *US* NOW.
BLUE, YOU'VE MANAGED TO FIT INTO THIS TOWN'S CULTURE BETTER THAN I... ***AND I WAS BORN HERE!***
CHEE!
I GUESS I'M WITHOUT EXCUSE.
CRACK!

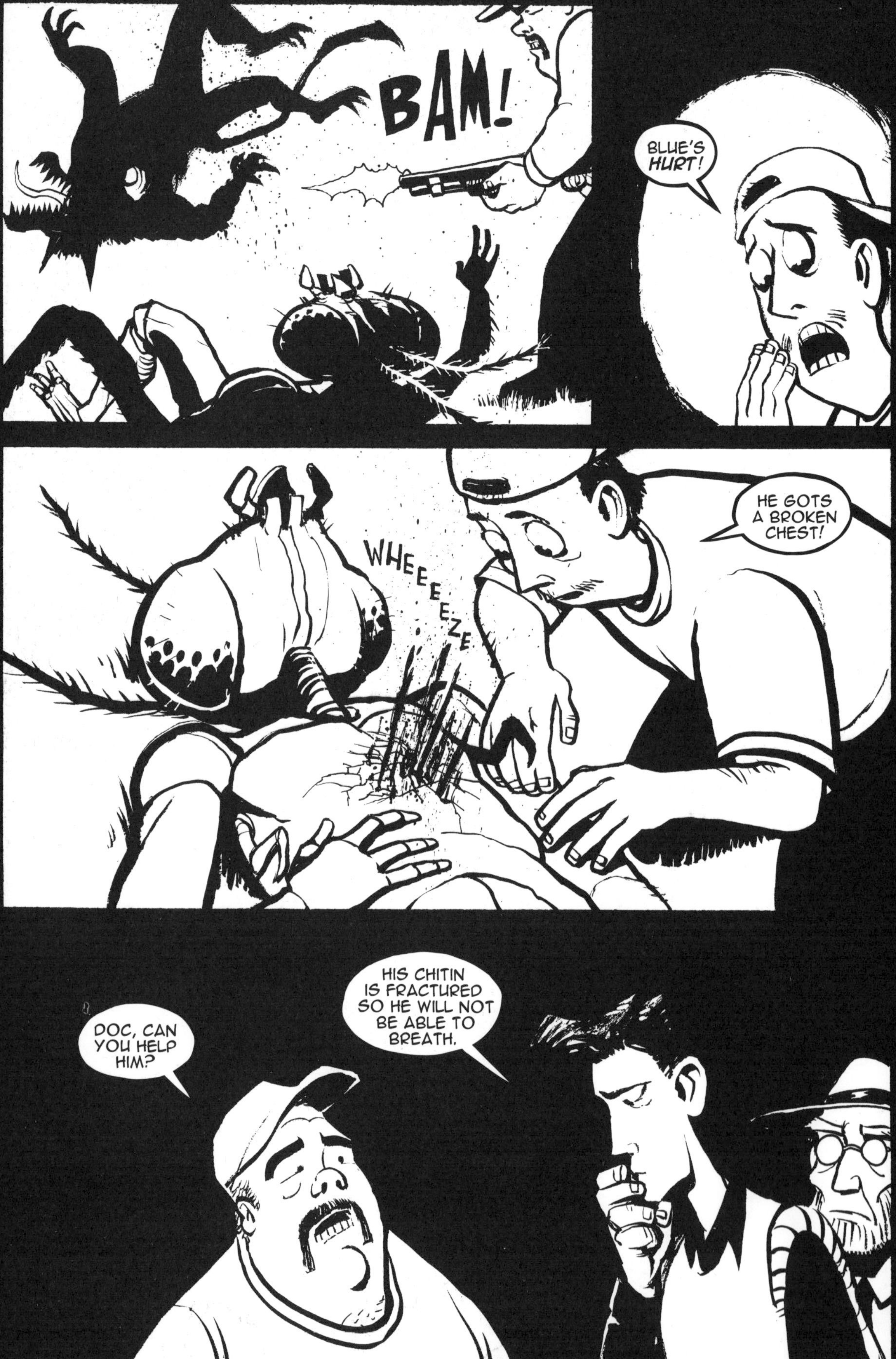

BAM!
BLUE'S HURT!
HE GOTS A BROKEN CHEST!
WHEEEEEZE
DOC, CAN YOU HELP HIM?
HIS CHITIN IS FRACTURED SO HE WILL NOT BE ABLE TO BREATH.

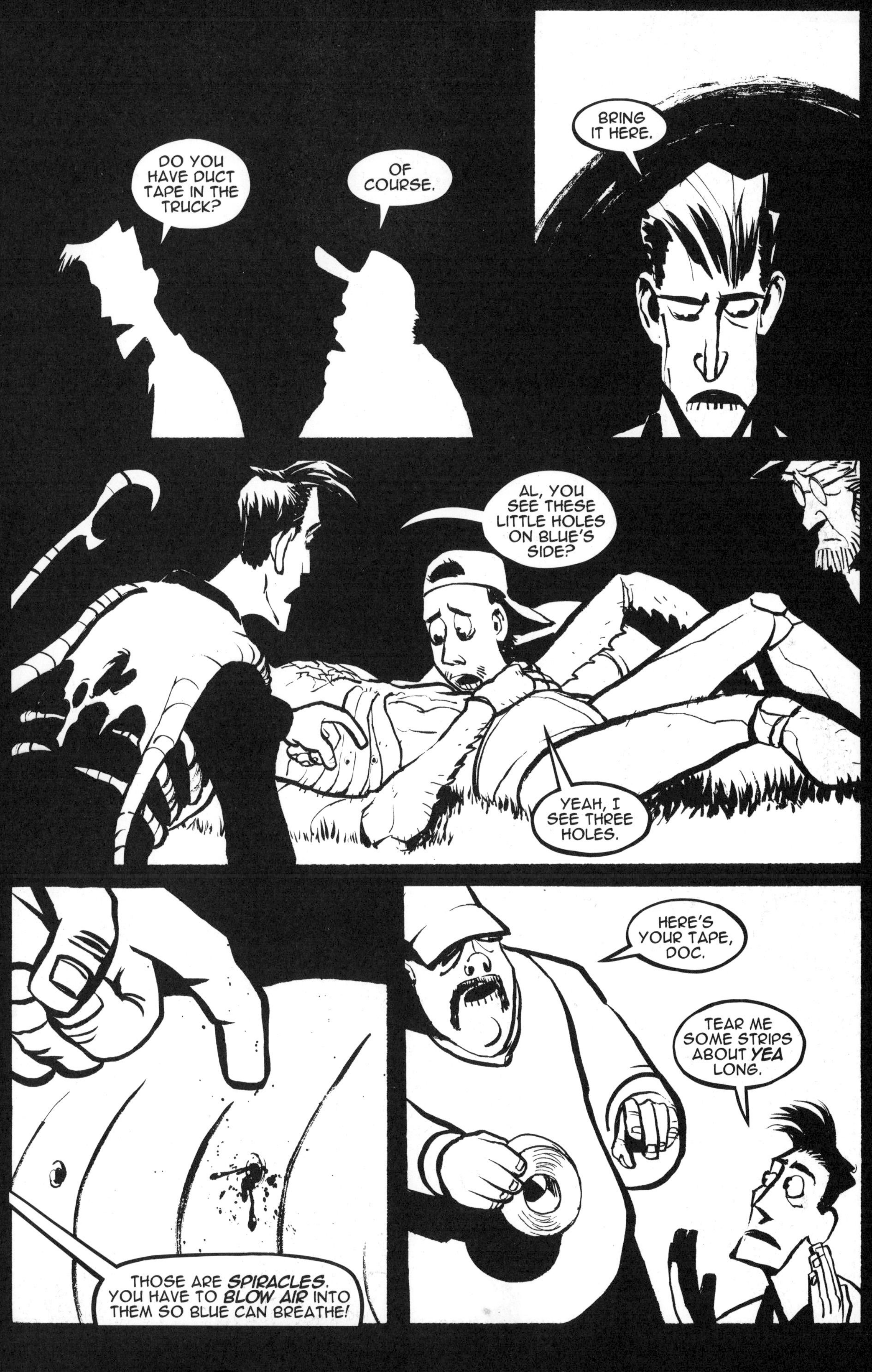
DO YOU HAVE DUCT TAPE IN THE TRUCK?
OF COURSE.
BRING IT HERE.
AL, YOU SEE THESE LITTLE HOLES ON BLUE'S SIDE?
YEAH, I SEE THREE HOLES.
THOSE ARE SPIRACLES. YOU HAVE TO BLOW AIR INTO THEM SO BLUE CAN BREATHE!
HERE'S YOUR TAPE, DOC.
TEAR ME SOME STRIPS ABOUT YEA LONG.

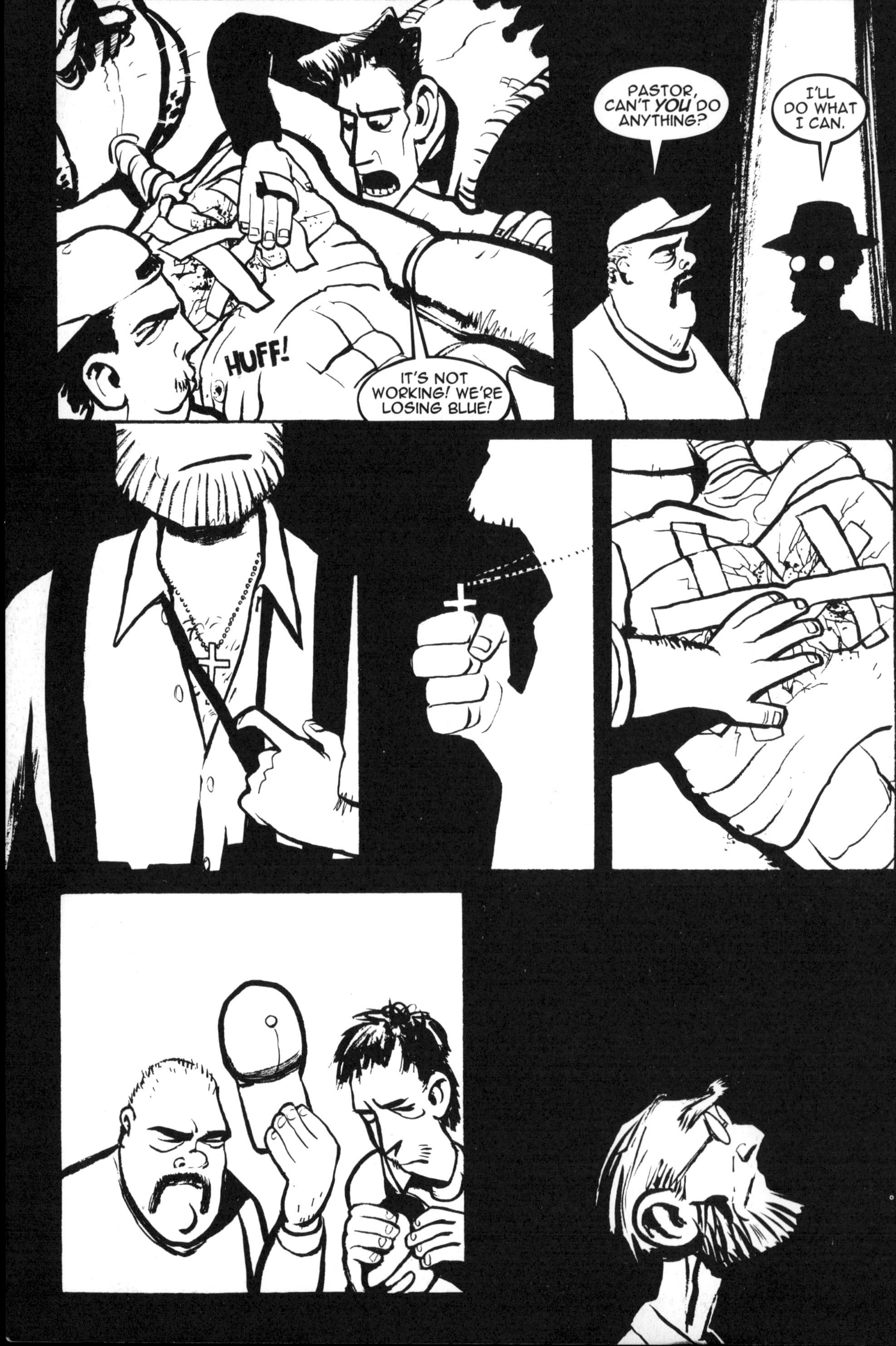
HUFF!
IT'S NOT WORKING! WE'RE LOSING BLUE!
PASTOR, CAN'T YOU DO ANYTHING?
I'LL DO WHAT I CAN.

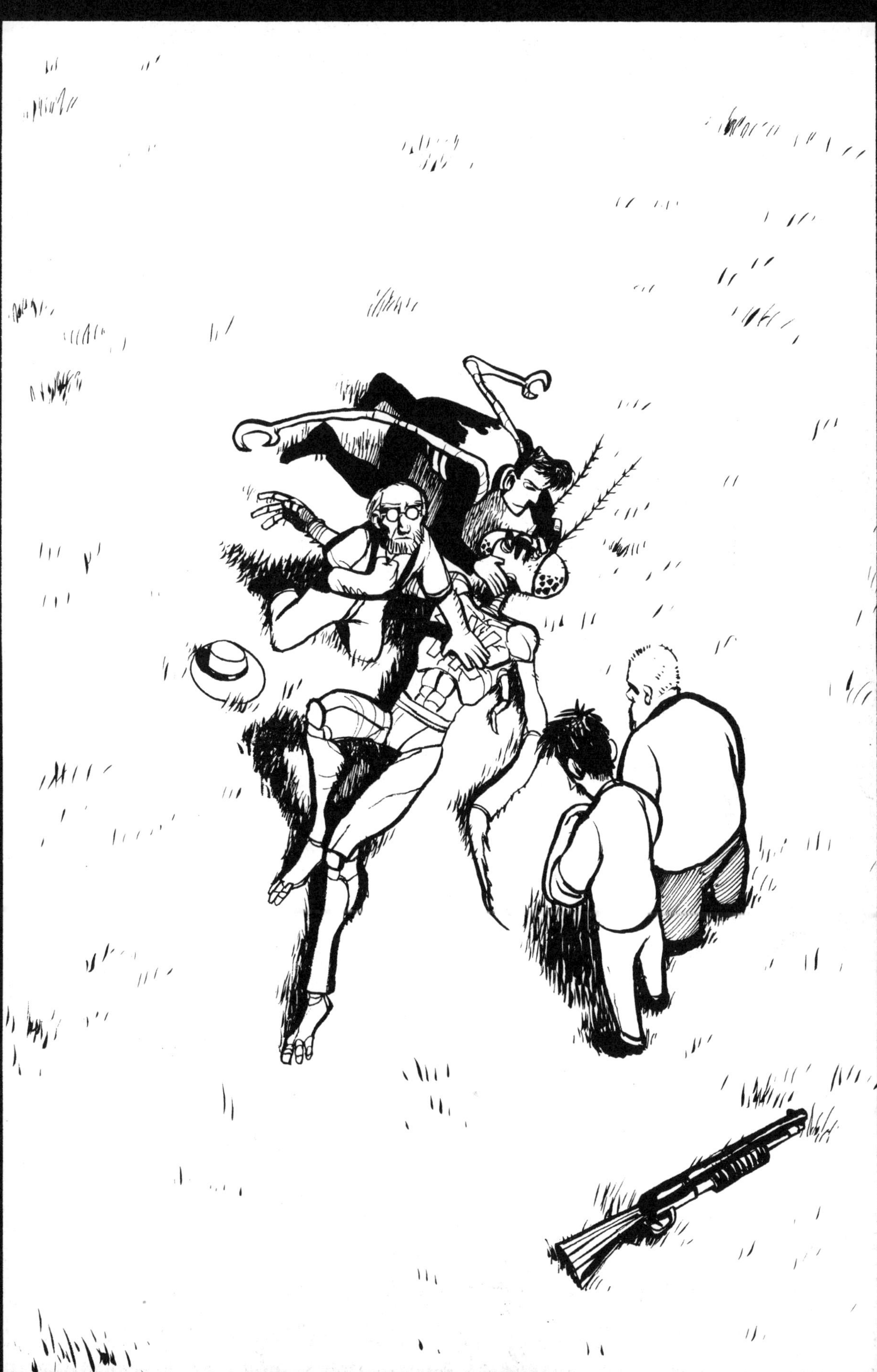

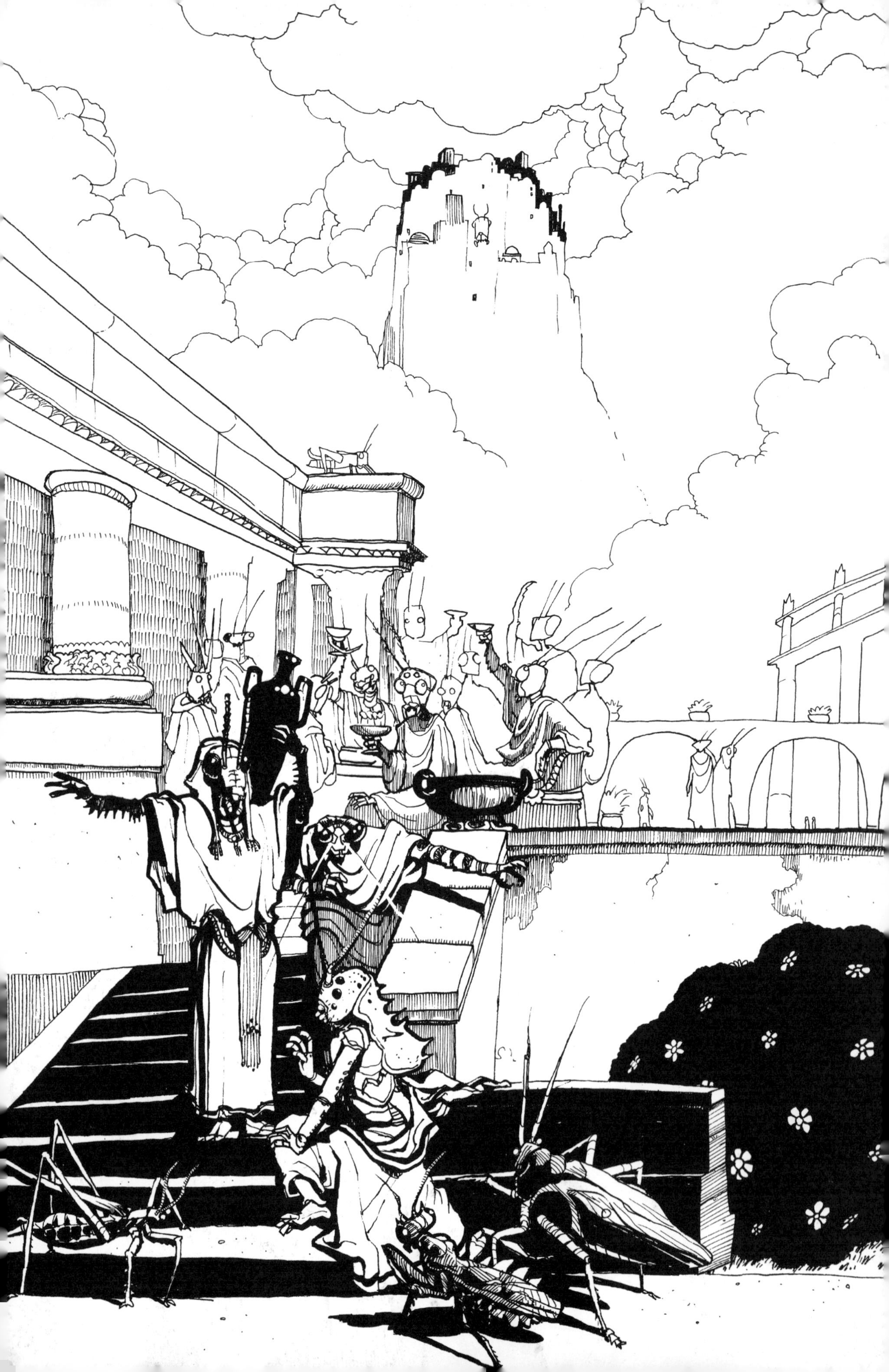

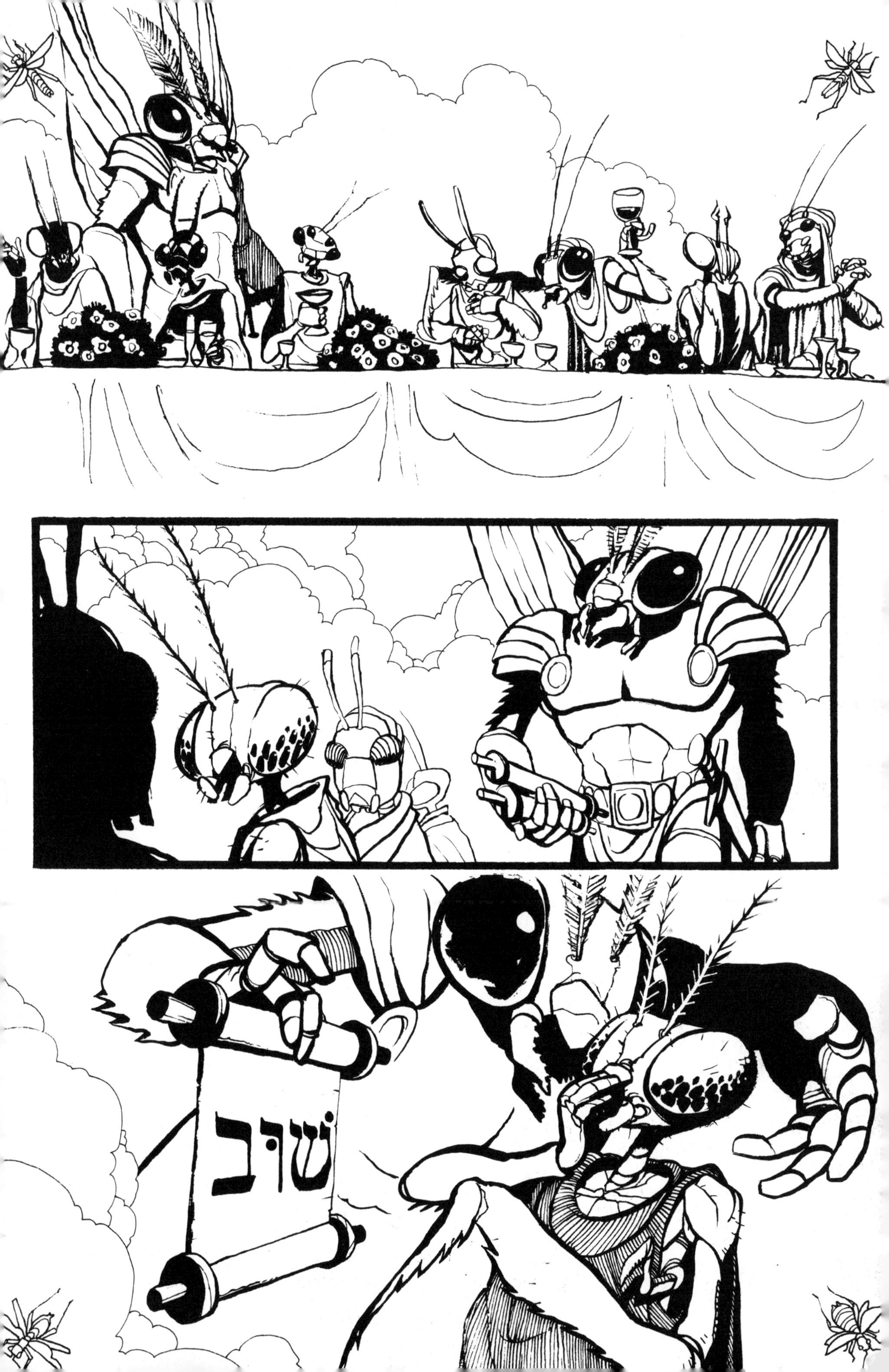
שׁוּב

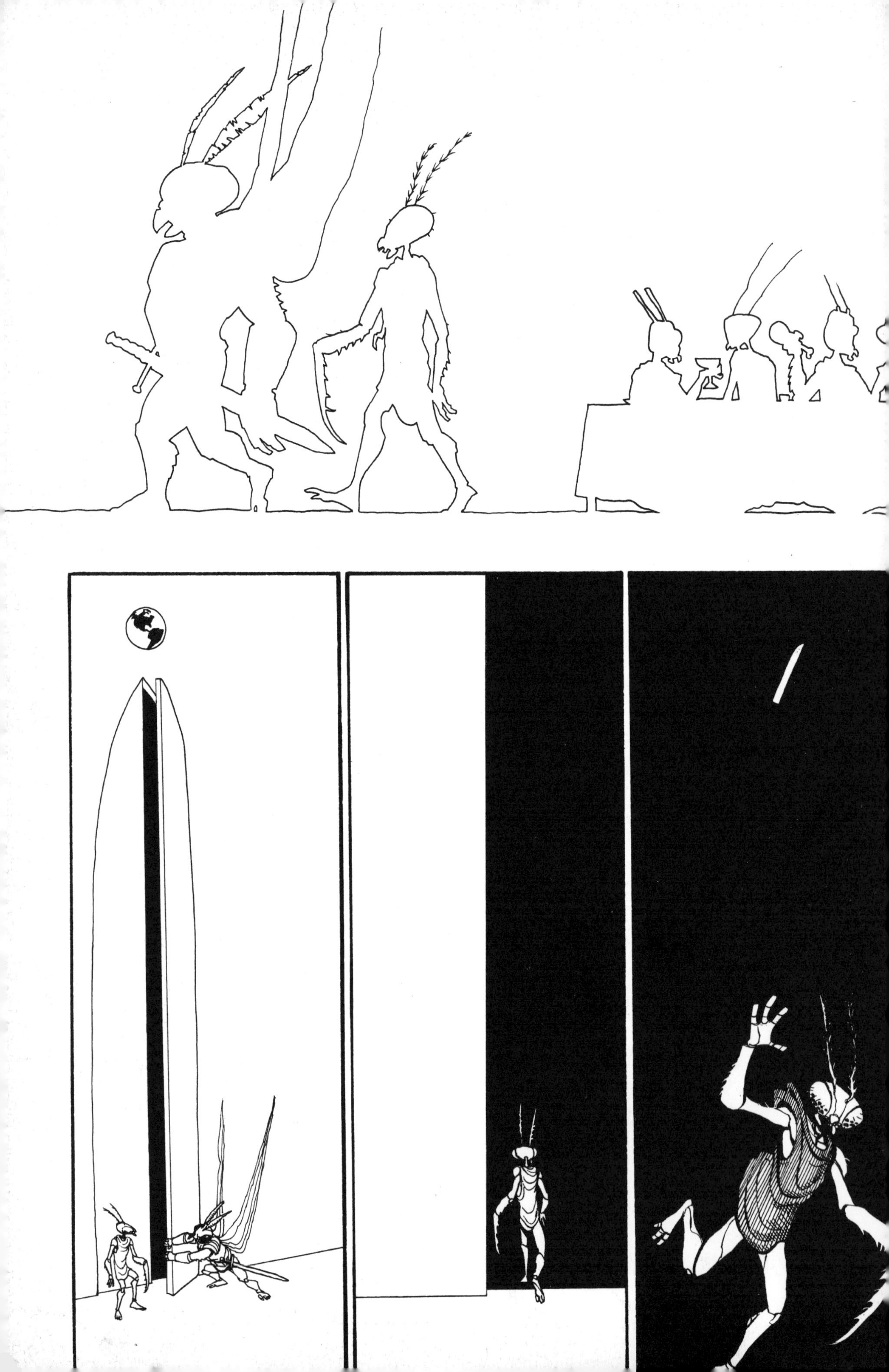

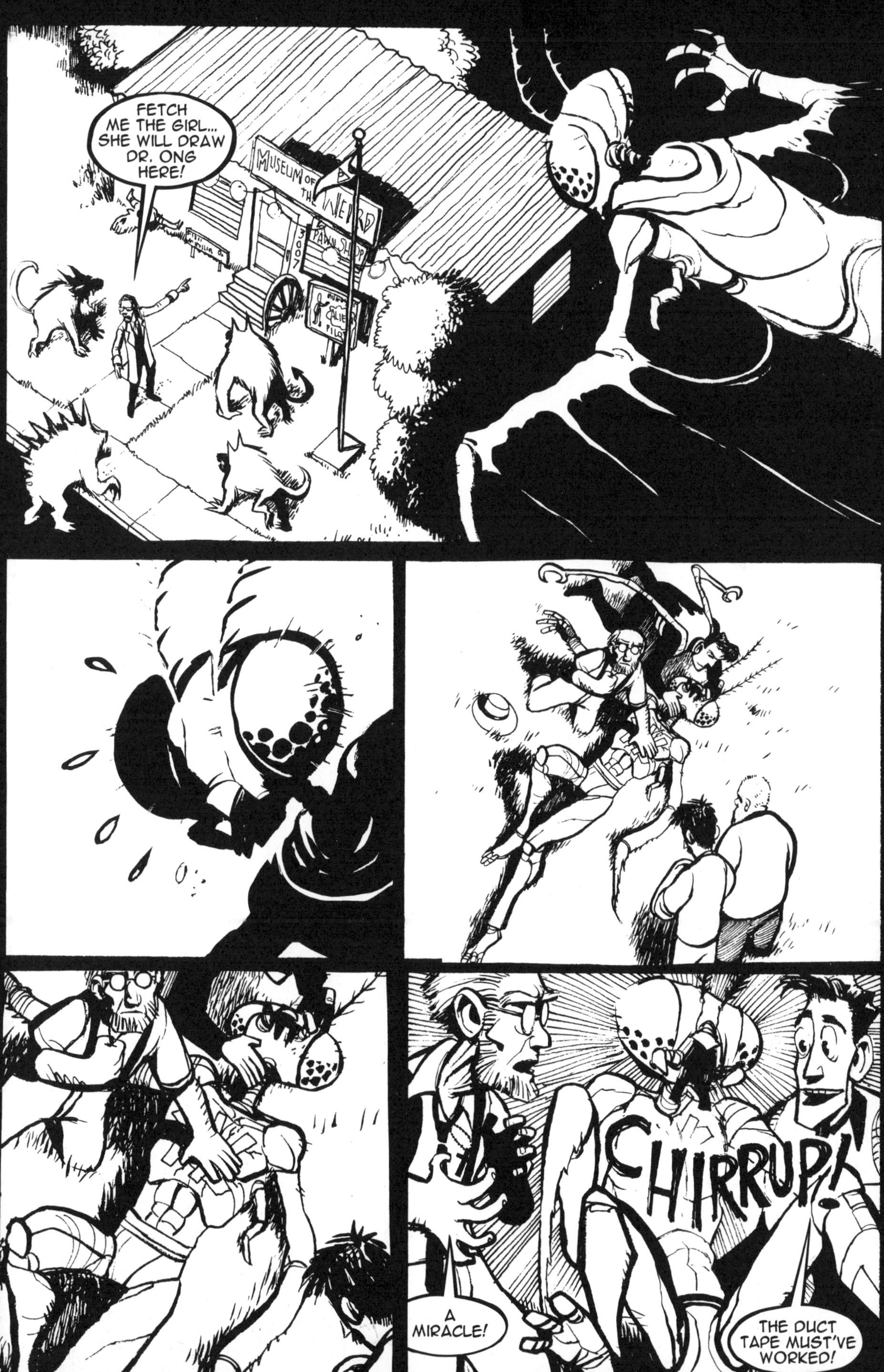
FETCH ME THE GIRL... SHE WILL DRAW DR. ONG HERE!
MUSEUM OF THE WEIRD
PAWN SHOP
3007
CHIRRUP!
A MIRACLE!
THE DUCT TAPE MUST'VE WORKED!

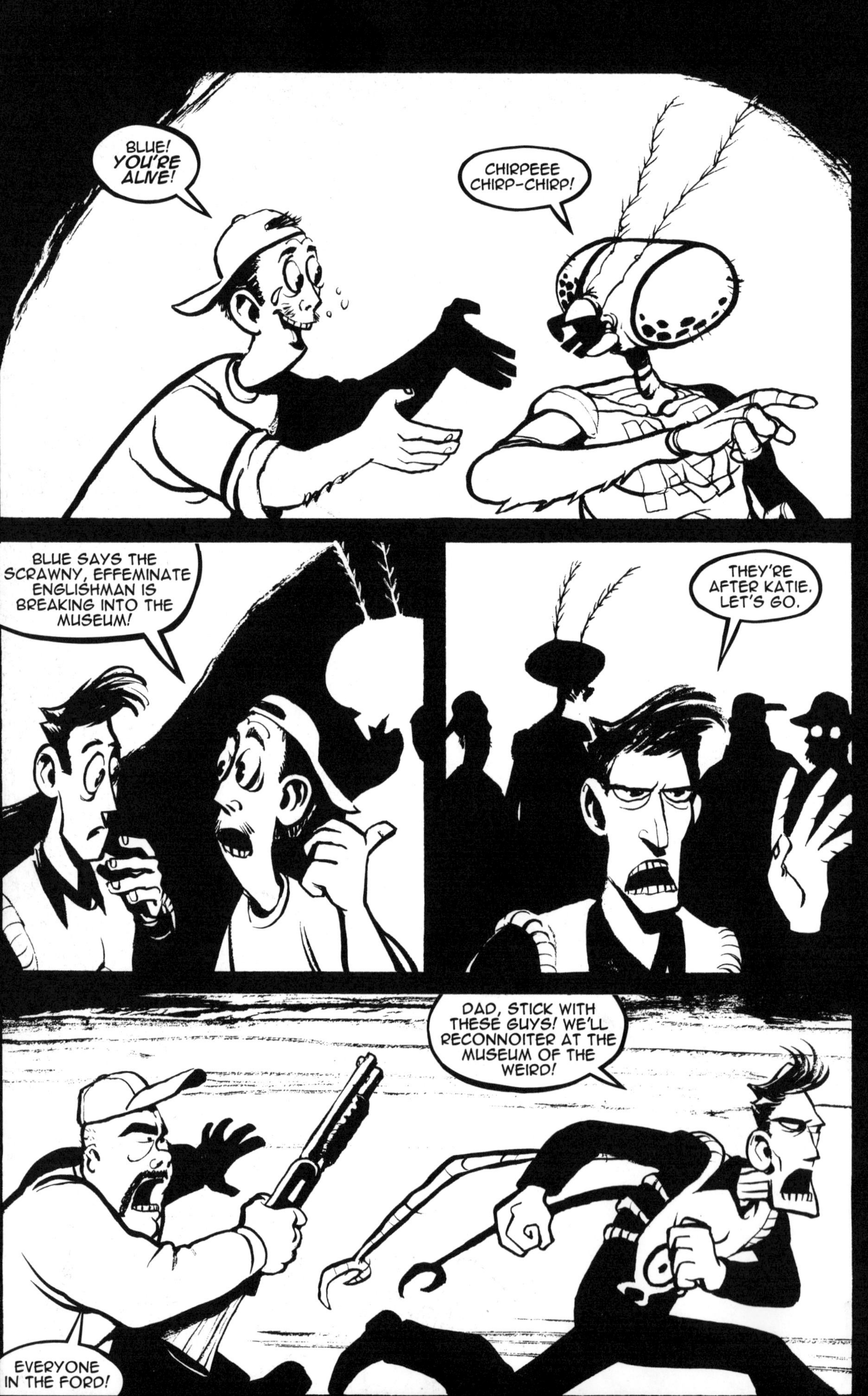
BLUE! YOU'RE ALIVE!
CHIRPEEE CHIRP-CHIRP!
BLUE SAYS THE SCRAWNY, EFFEMINATE ENGLISHMAN IS BREAKING INTO THE MUSEUM!
THEY'RE AFTER KATIE. LET'S GO.
DAD, STICK WITH THESE GUYS! WE'LL RECONNOITER AT THE MUSEUM OF THE WEIRD!
EVERYONE IN THE FORD!

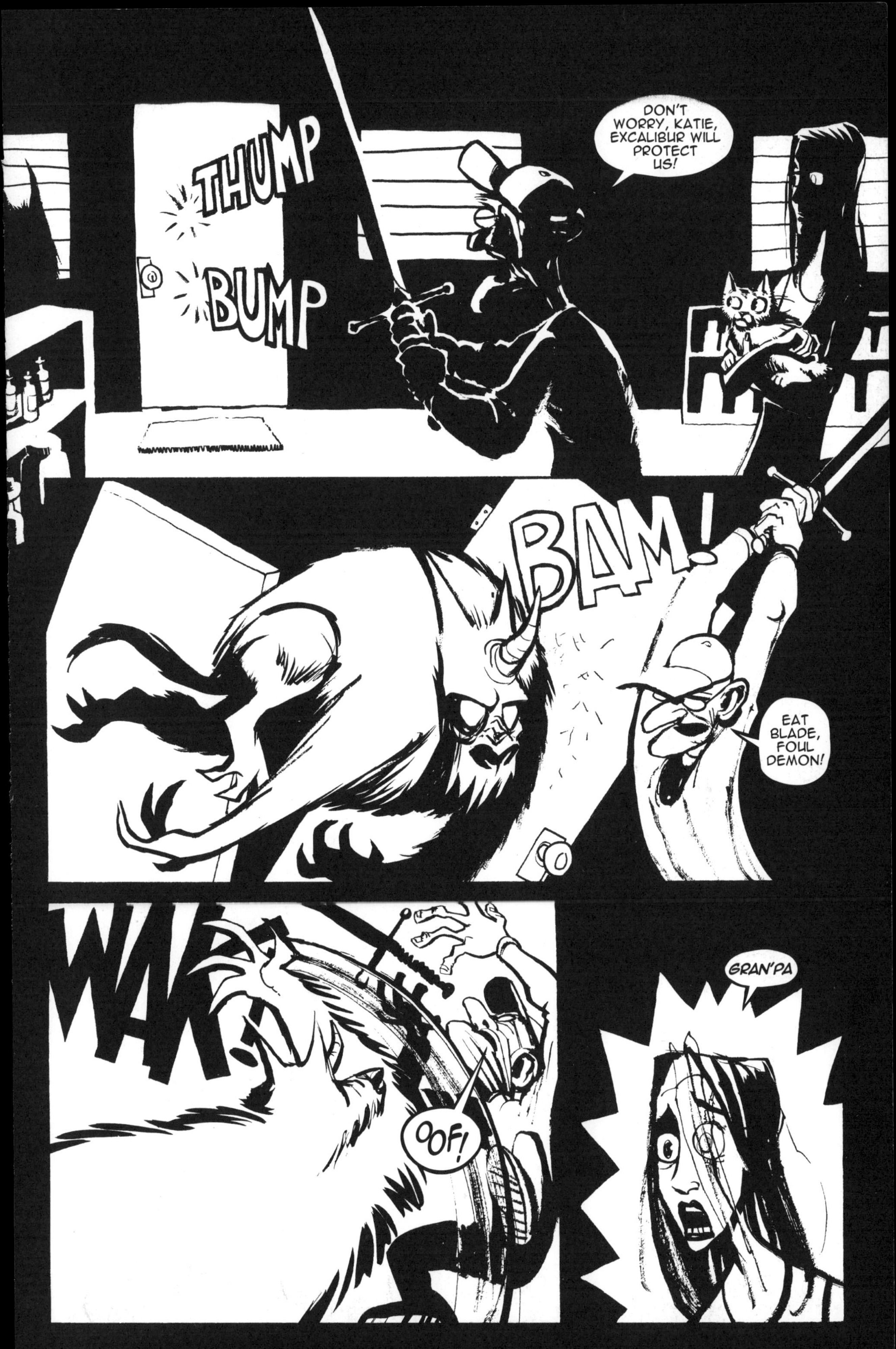
THUMP
BUMP
DON'T WORRY, KATIE, EXCALIBUR WILL PROTECT US!
BAM!
EAT BLADE, FOUL DEMON!
OOF!
GRAN'PA

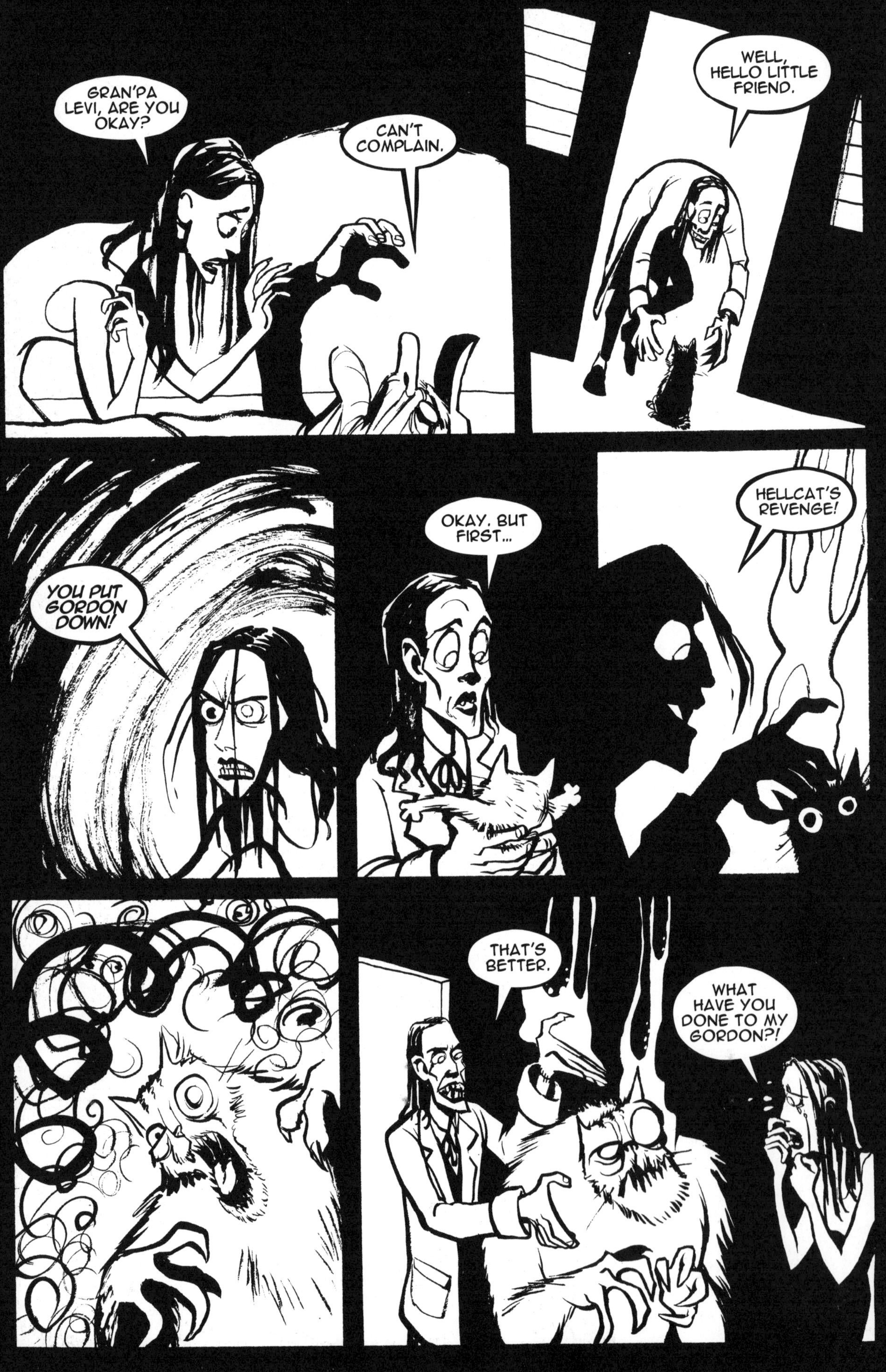
GRAN'PA LEVI, ARE YOU OKAY?
CAN'T COMPLAIN.
WELL, HELLO LITTLE FRIEND.
YOU PUT GORDON DOWN!
OKAY. BUT FIRST...
HELLCAT'S REVENGE!
THAT'S BETTER.
WHAT HAVE YOU DONE TO MY GORDON?!

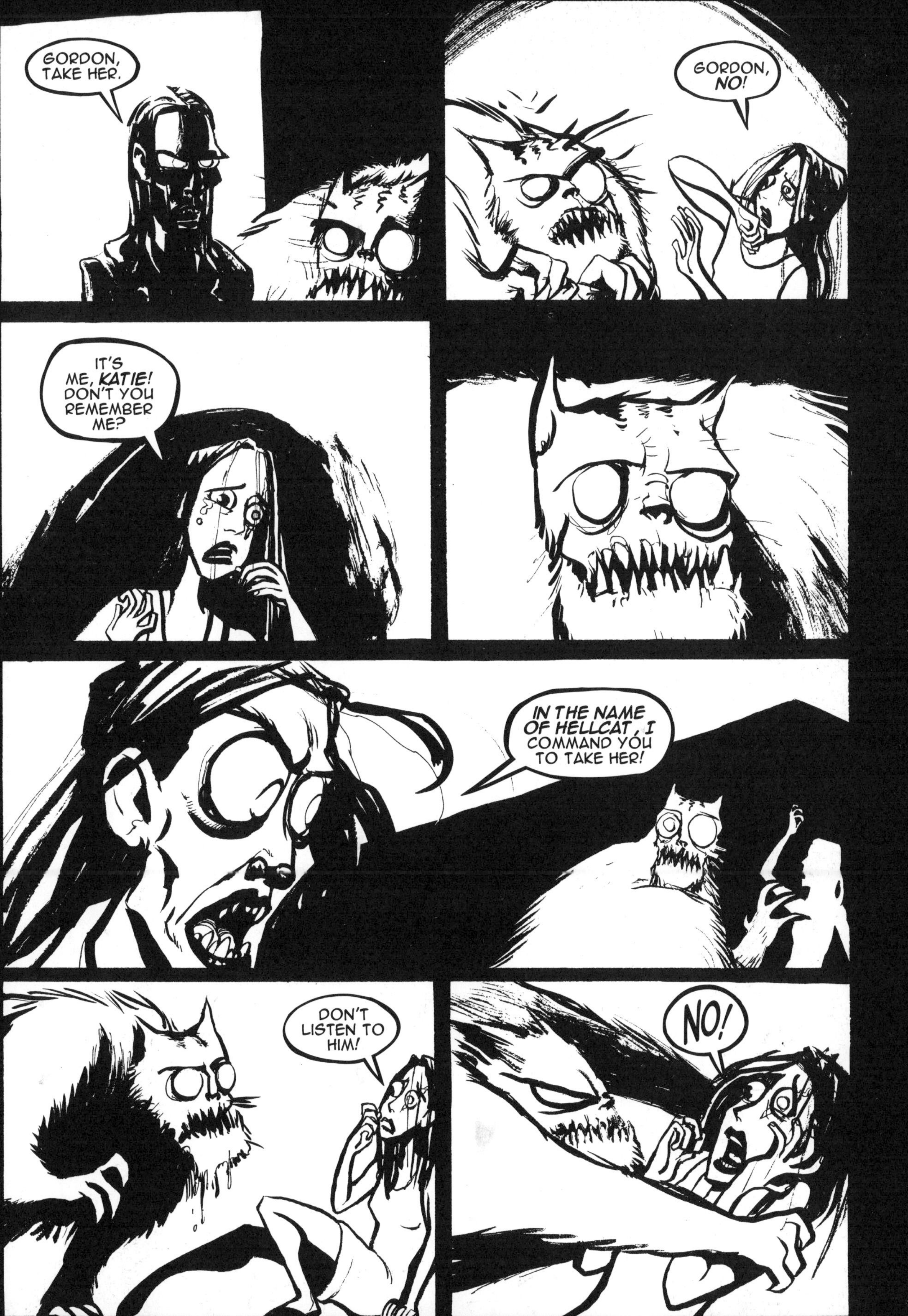
GORDON, TAKE HER.
GORDON, NO!
IT'S ME, KATIE! DON'T YOU REMEMBER ME?
IN THE NAME OF HELLCAT, I COMMAND YOU TO TAKE HER!
DON'T LISTEN TO HIM!
NO!

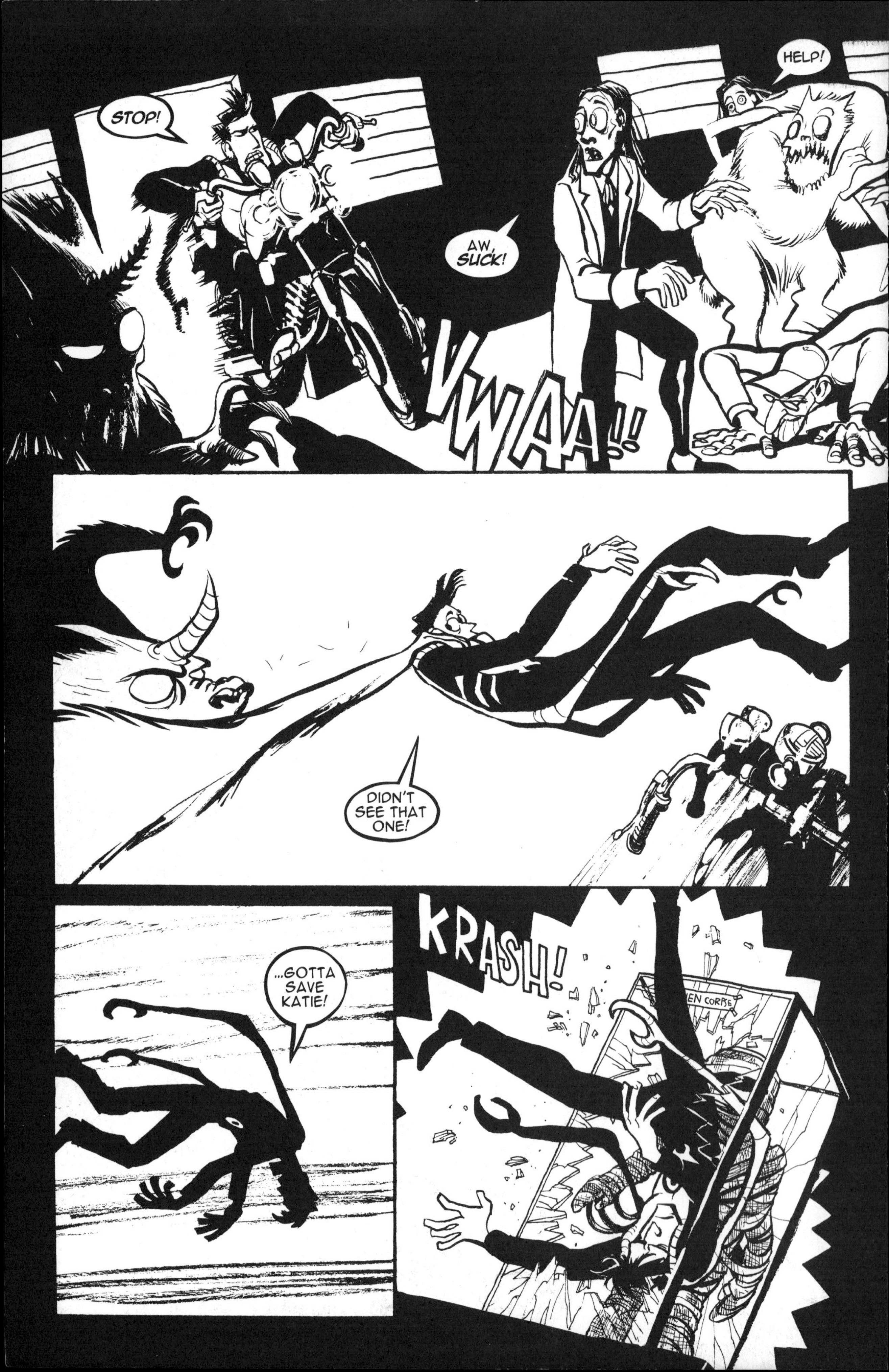
STOP!
AW, SUCK!
HELP!
VWAA!!
DIDN'T SEE THAT ONE!
...GOTTA SAVE KATIE!
KRASH!

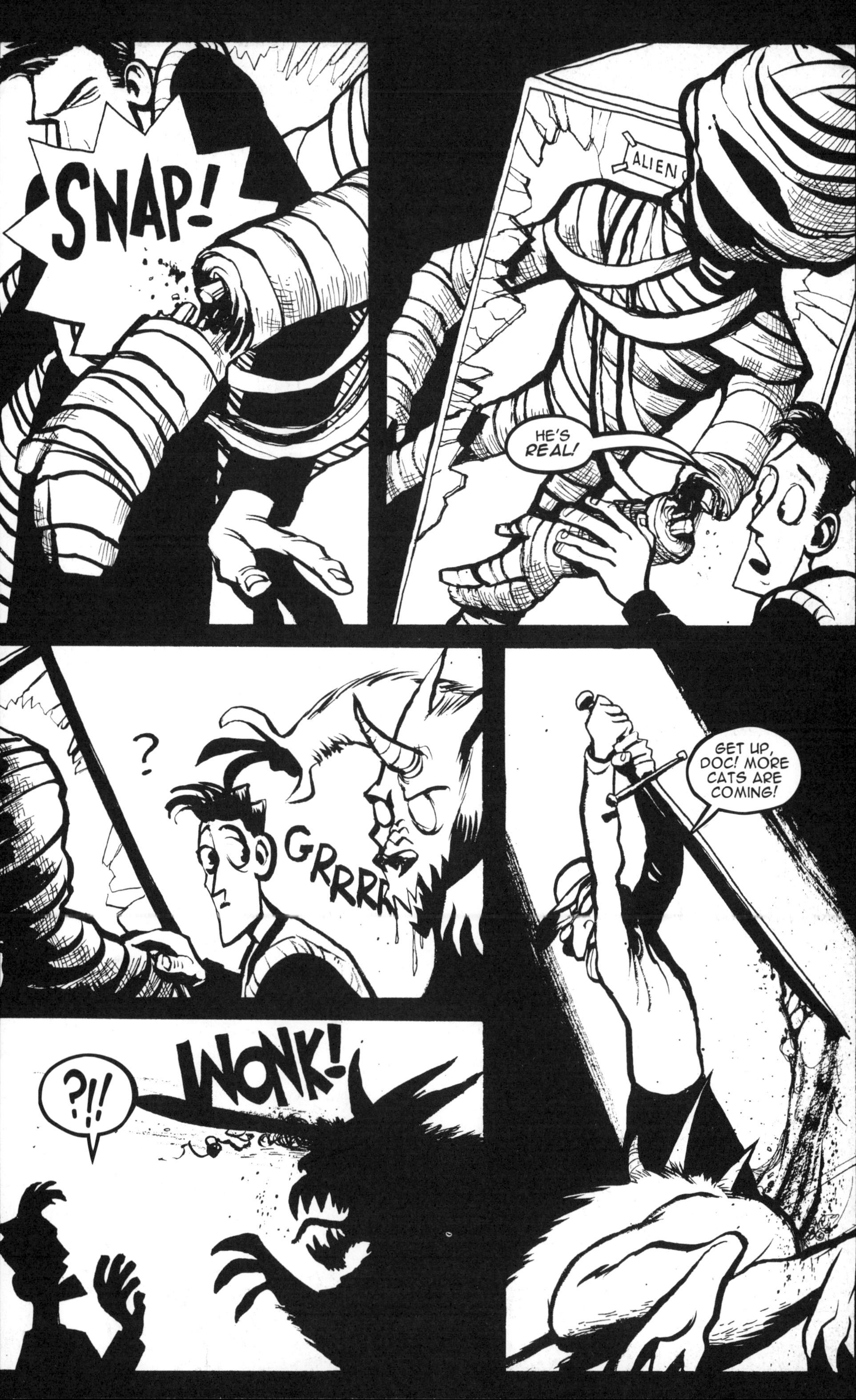
SNAP!
ALIEN
HE'S REAL!
?
GRRRRR
GET UP, DOC! MORE CATS ARE COMING!
WONK!
?!!

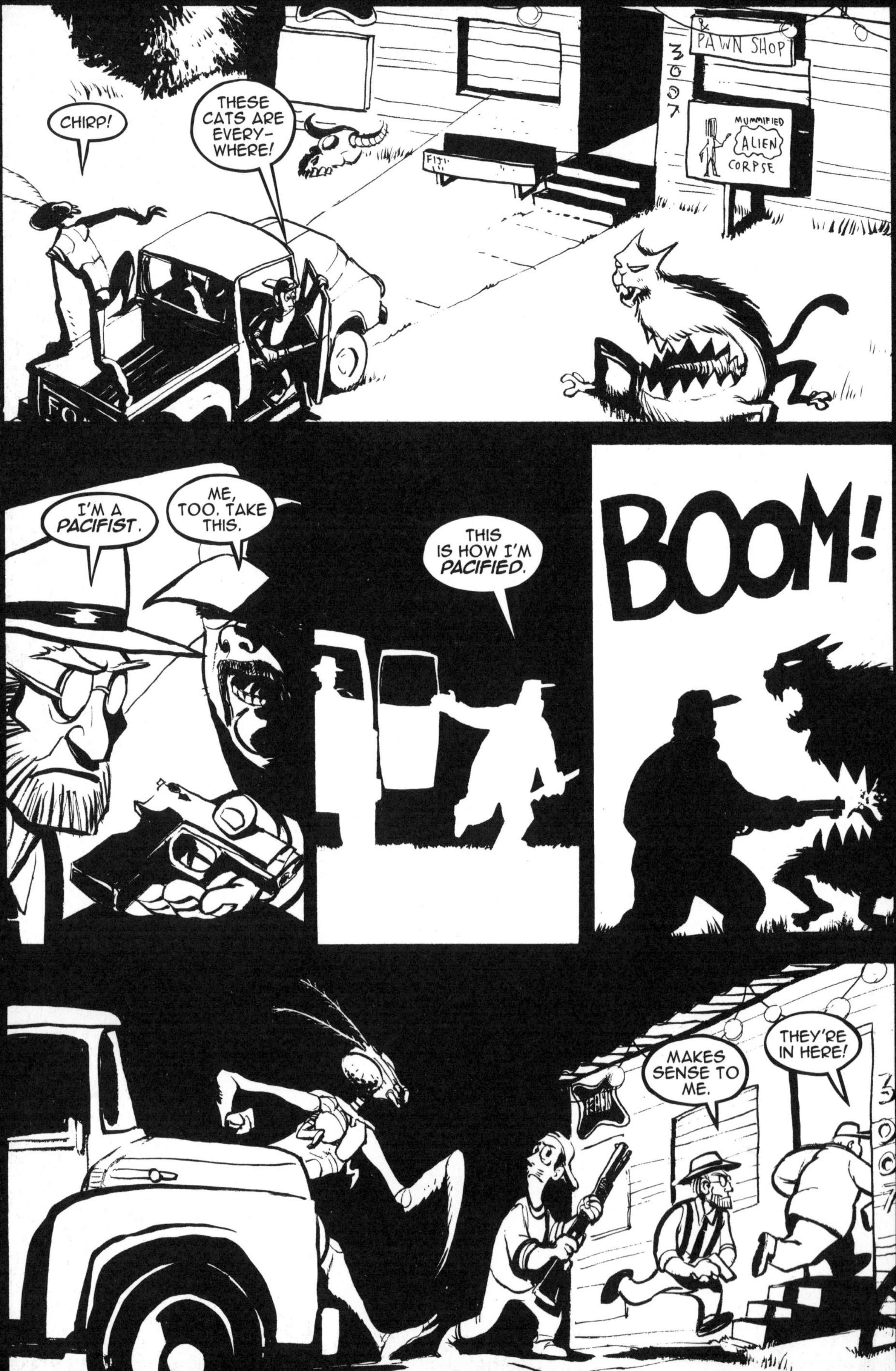

PAWN SHOP
3007
MUMMIFIED
ALIEN
CORPSE
FIJI
CHIRP!
THESE CATS ARE EVERY-WHERE!
I'M A *PACIFIST*.
ME, TOO. TAKE THIS.
THIS IS HOW I'M *PACIFIED*.
BOOM!
MAKES SENSE TO ME.
THEY'RE IN HERE!

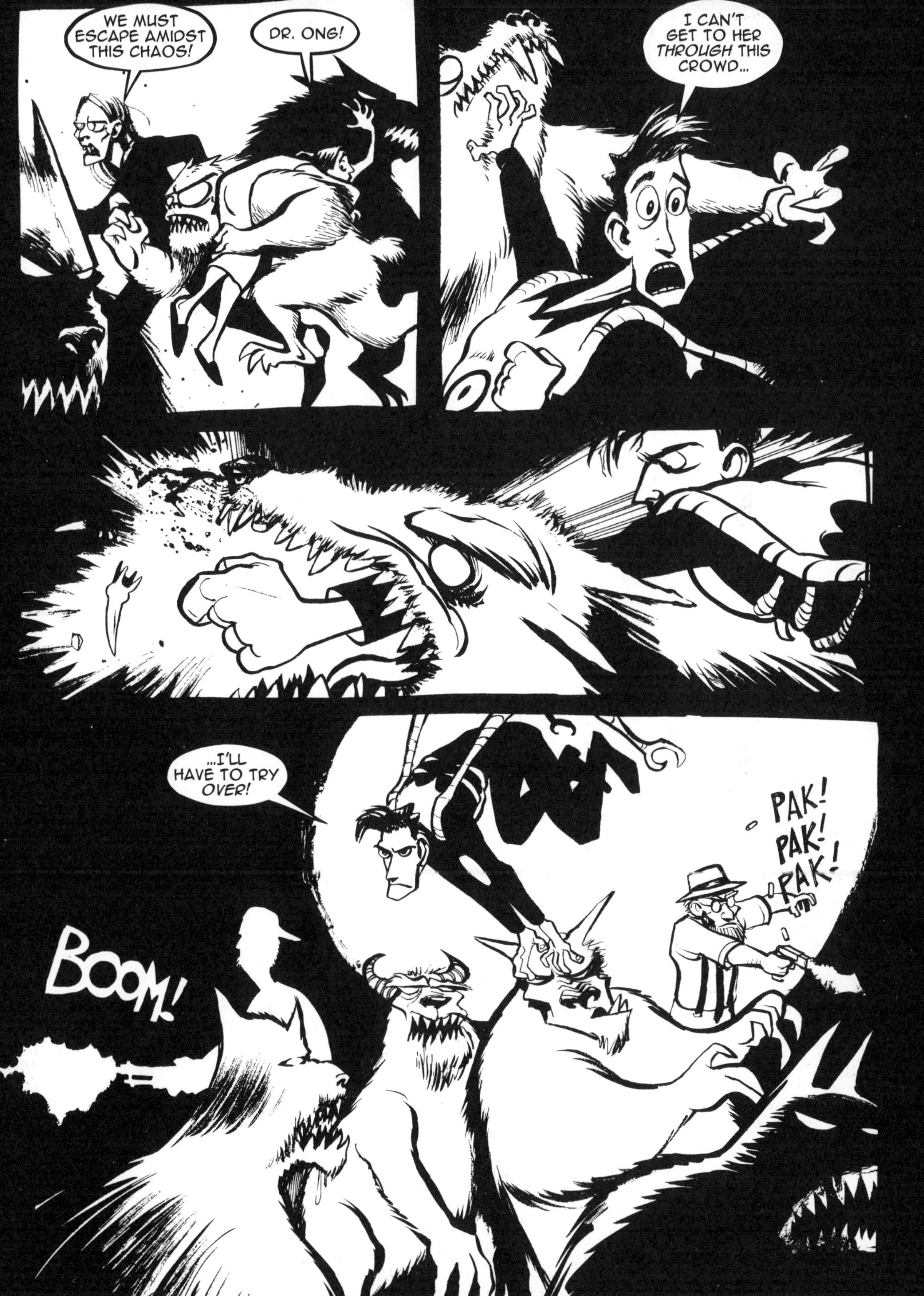
WE MUST ESCAPE AMIDST THIS CHAOS!
DR. ONG!
I CAN'T GET TO HER *THROUGH* THIS CROWD...
...I'LL HAVE TO TRY *OVER*!
PAK! PAK! PAK!
BOOM!

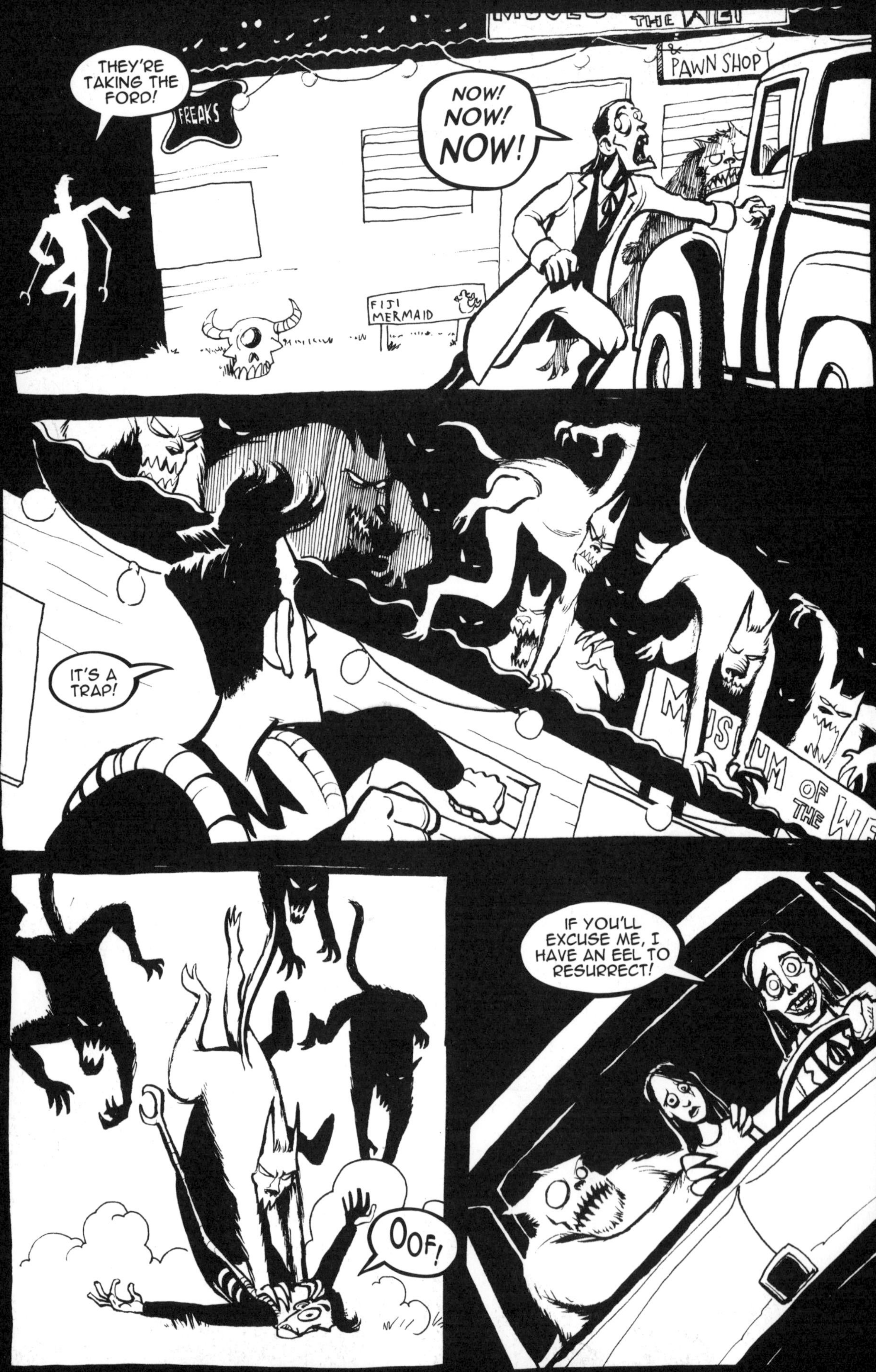
THEY'RE TAKING THE FORD!
FREAKS
PAWN SHOP
NOW! NOW! NOW!
FIJI MERMAID
IT'S A TRAP!
MUSEUM OF THE
IF YOU'LL EXCUSE ME, I HAVE AN EEL TO RESURRECT!
OOF!

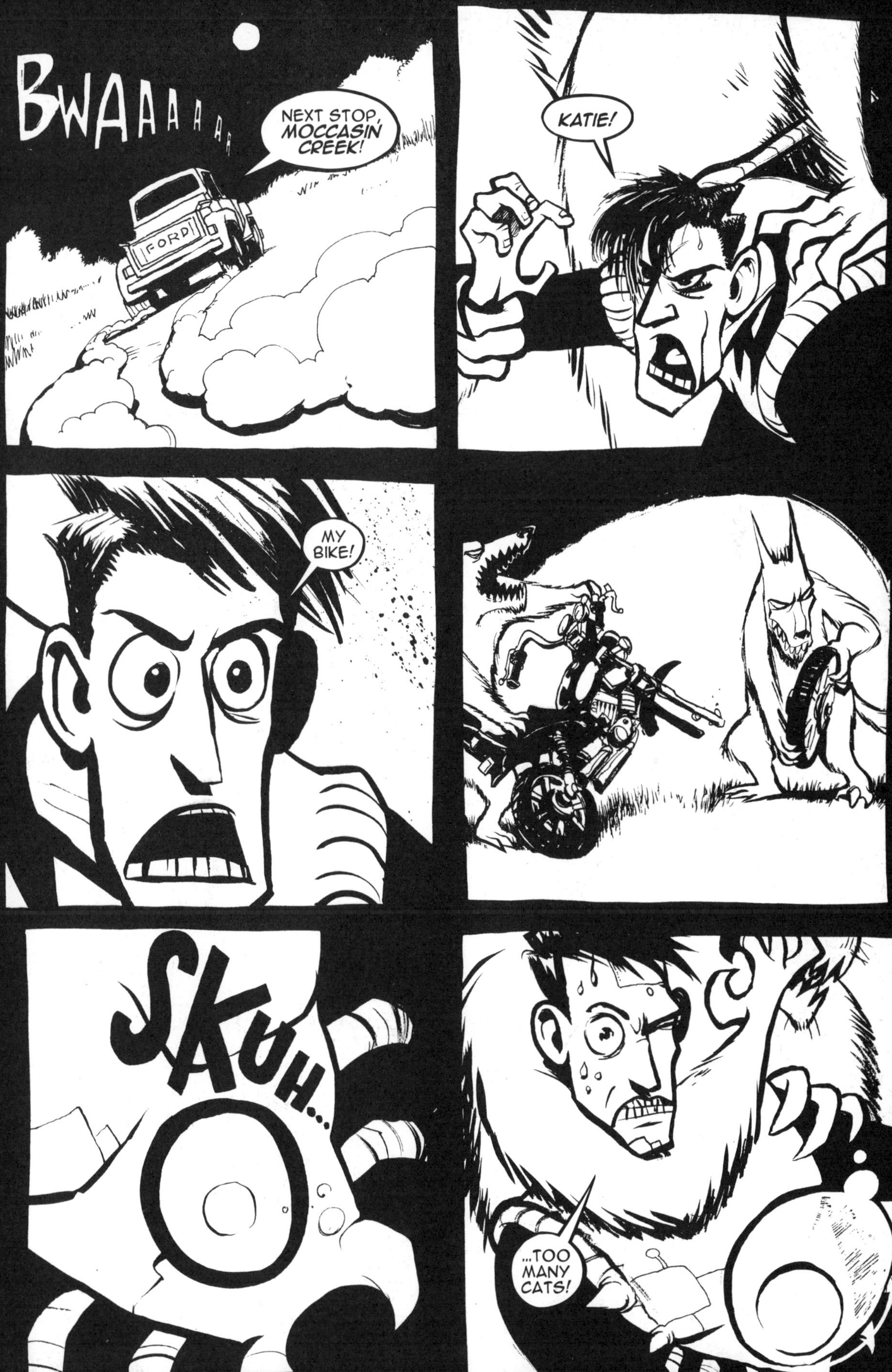
BWAAAAAA
NEXT STOP, MOCCASIN CREEK!
FORD
KATIE!
MY BIKE!
SKUH...
...TOO MANY CATS!

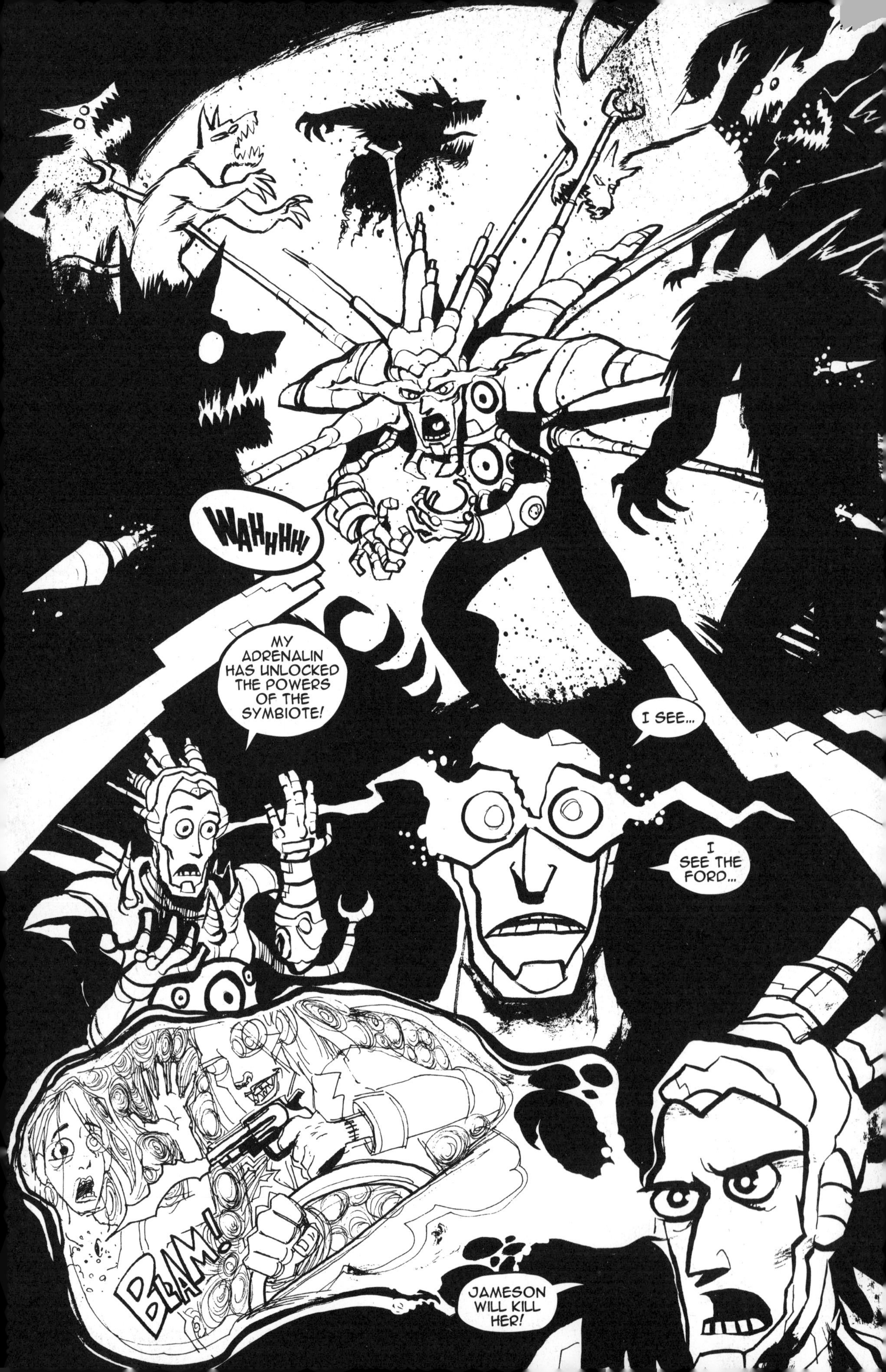
WAHHHH!
MY ADRENALIN HAS UNLOCKED THE POWERS OF THE SYMBIOTE!
I SEE...
I SEE THE FORD...
BLAM!
JAMESON WILL KILL HER!

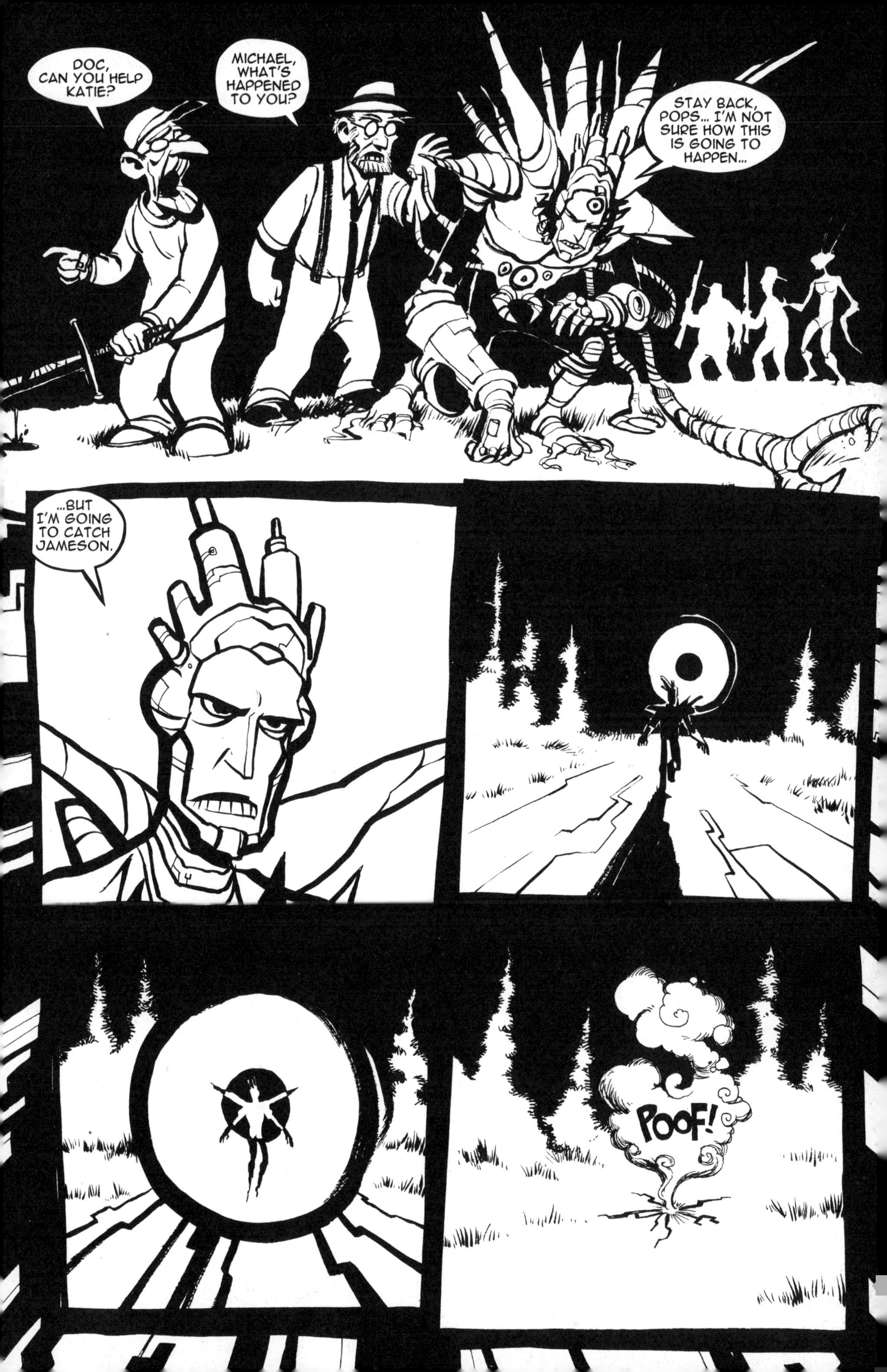
DOC, CAN YOU HELP KATIE?
MICHAEL, WHAT'S HAPPENED TO YOU?
STAY BACK, POPS... I'M NOT SURE HOW THIS IS GOING TO HAPPEN...
...BUT I'M GOING TO CATCH JAMESON.
POOF!

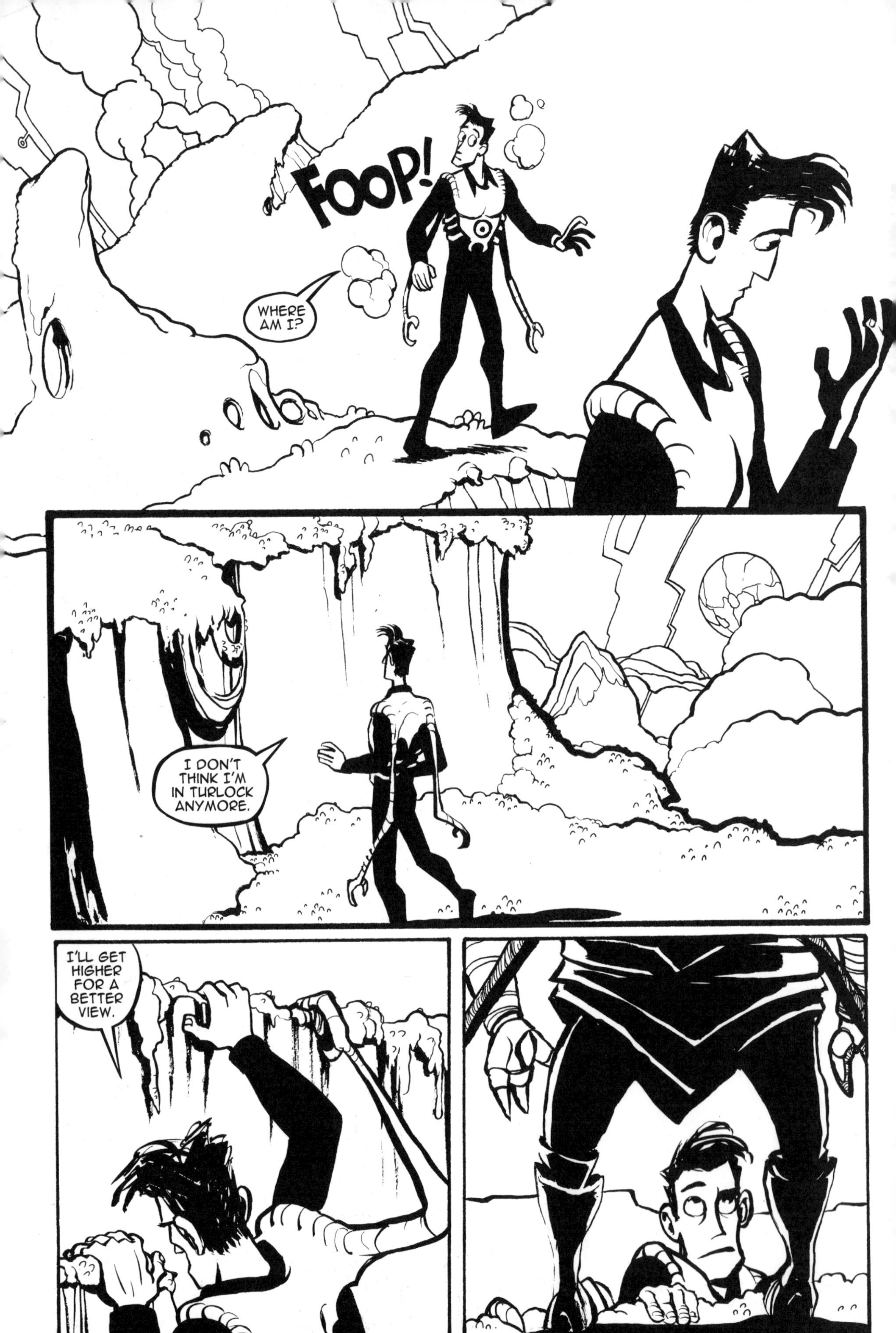
FOOP!
WHERE AM I?
I DON'T THINK I'M IN TURLOCK ANYMORE.
I'LL GET HIGHER FOR A BETTER VIEW.

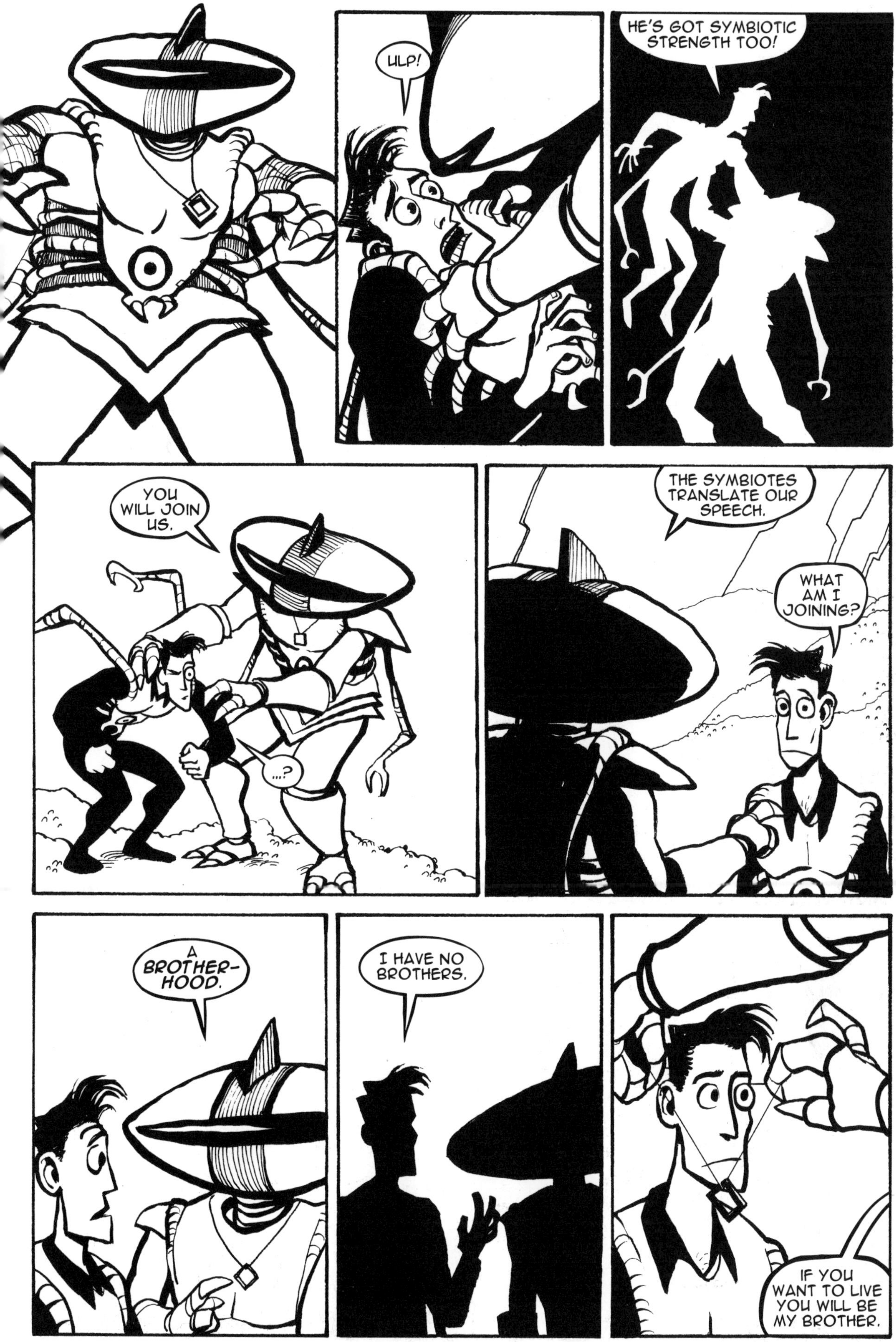
ULP!
HE'S GOT SYMBIOTIC STRENGTH TOO!
YOU WILL JOIN US.
...?
THE SYMBIOTES TRANSLATE OUR SPEECH.
WHAT AM I JOINING?
A BROTHER-HOOD.
I HAVE NO BROTHERS.
IF YOU WANT TO LIVE YOU WILL BE MY BROTHER.

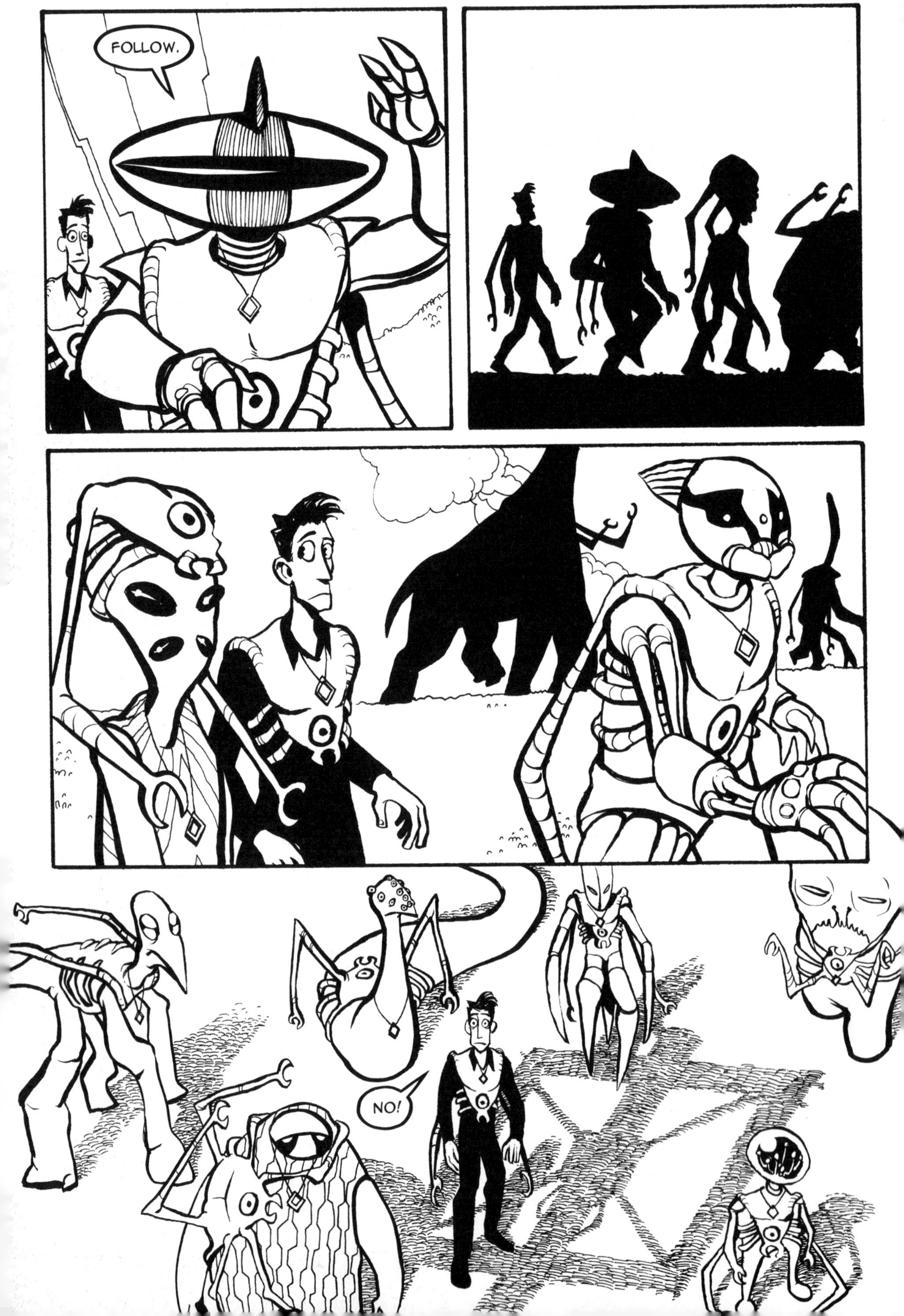
FOLLOW.
NO!

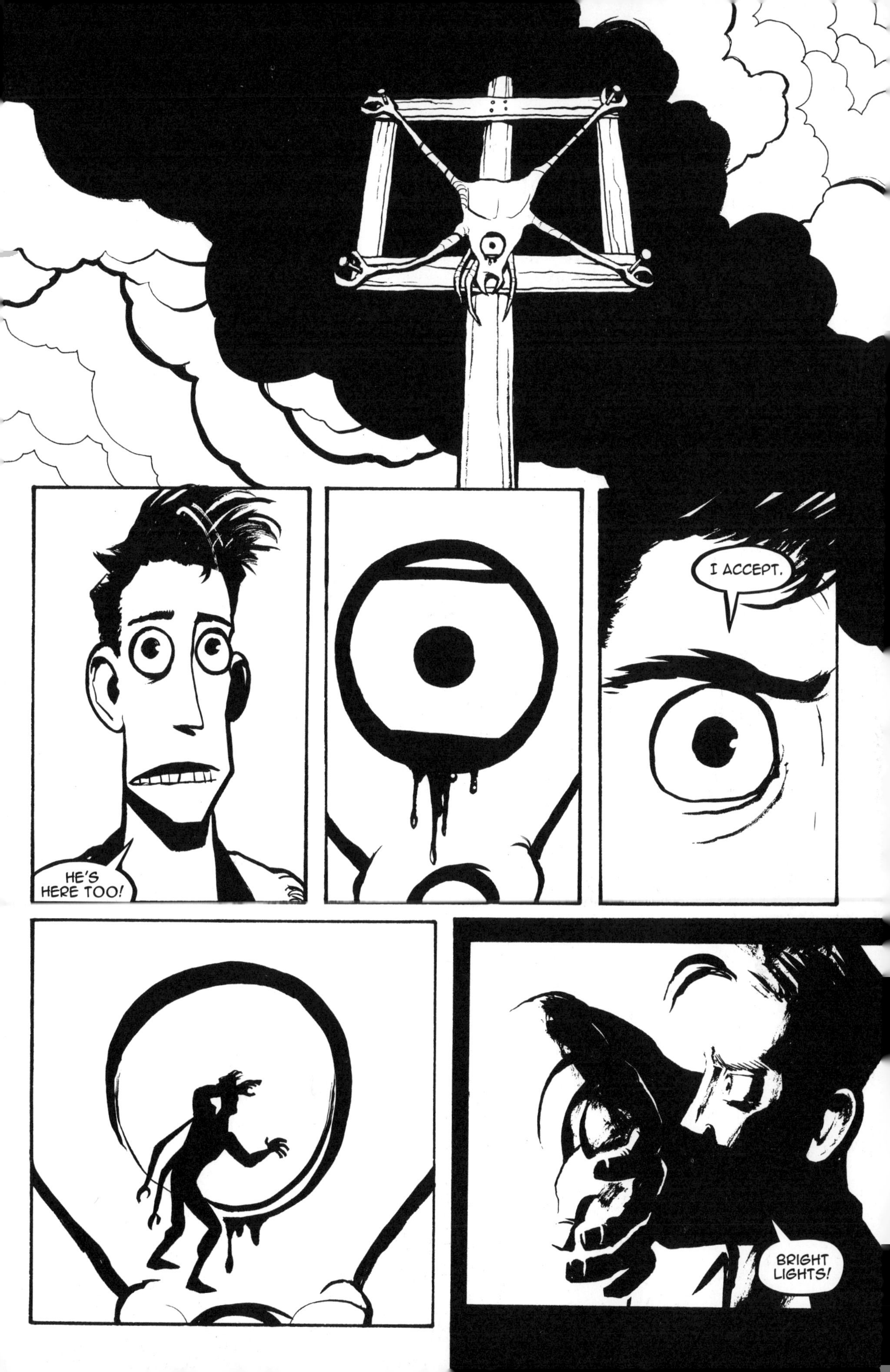
HE'S HERE TOO!
I ACCEPT.
BRIGHT LIGHTS!

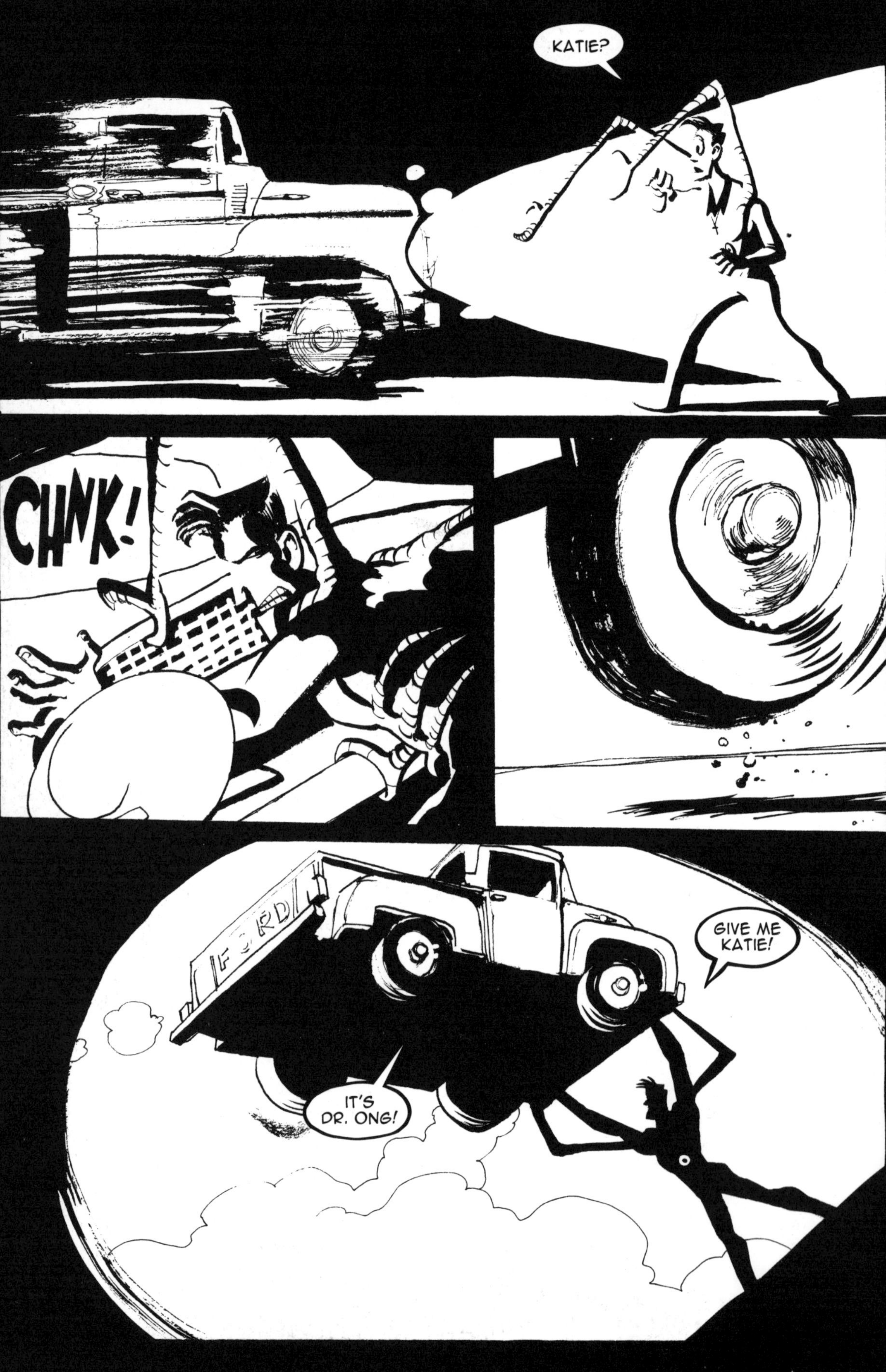
KATIE?
CHNK!
GIVE ME KATIE!
IT'S DR. ONG!

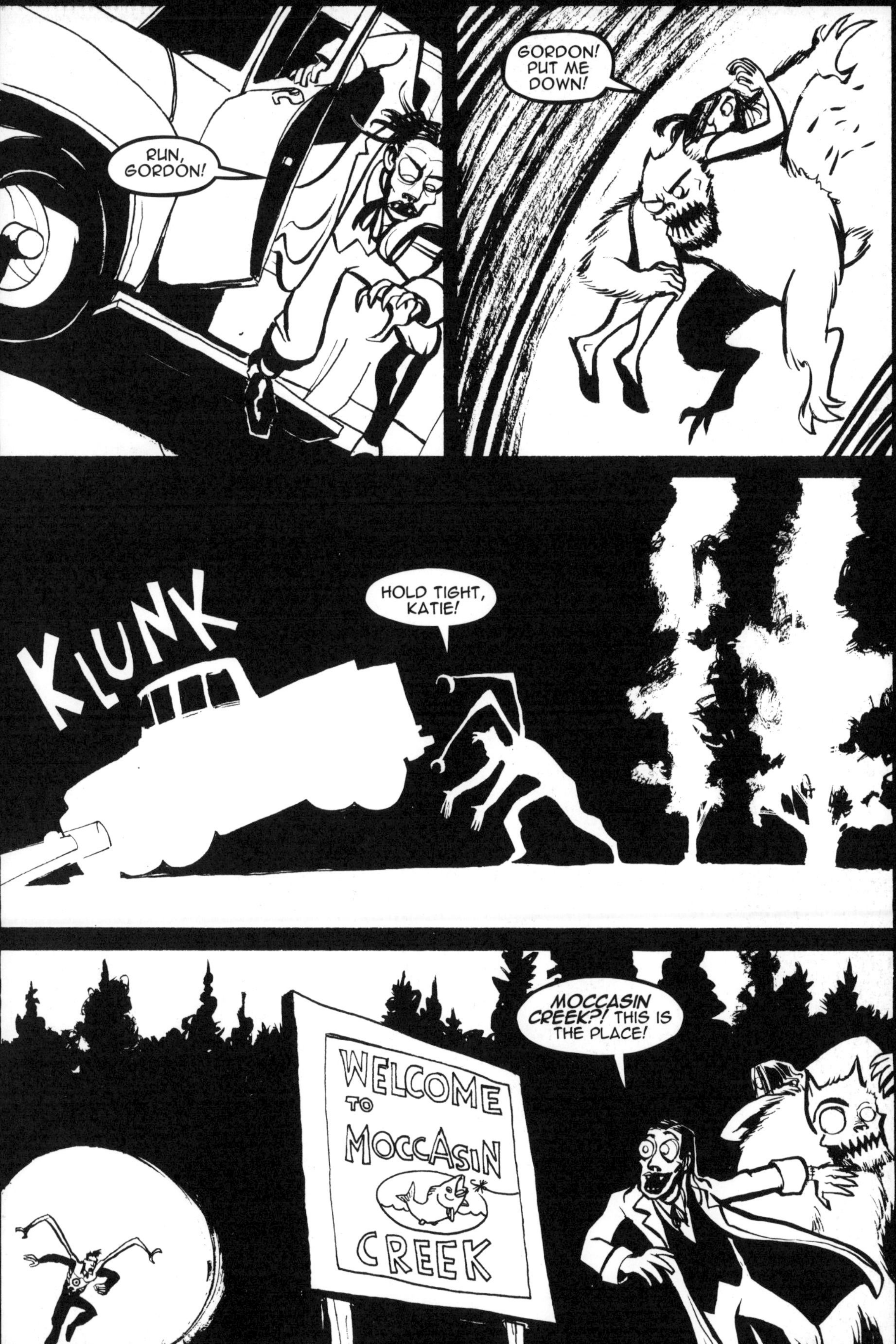
RUN, GORDON!
GORDON! PUT ME DOWN!
KLUNK
HOLD TIGHT, KATIE!
WELCOME TO MOCCASIN CREEK
MOCCASIN CREEK?! THIS IS THE PLACE!

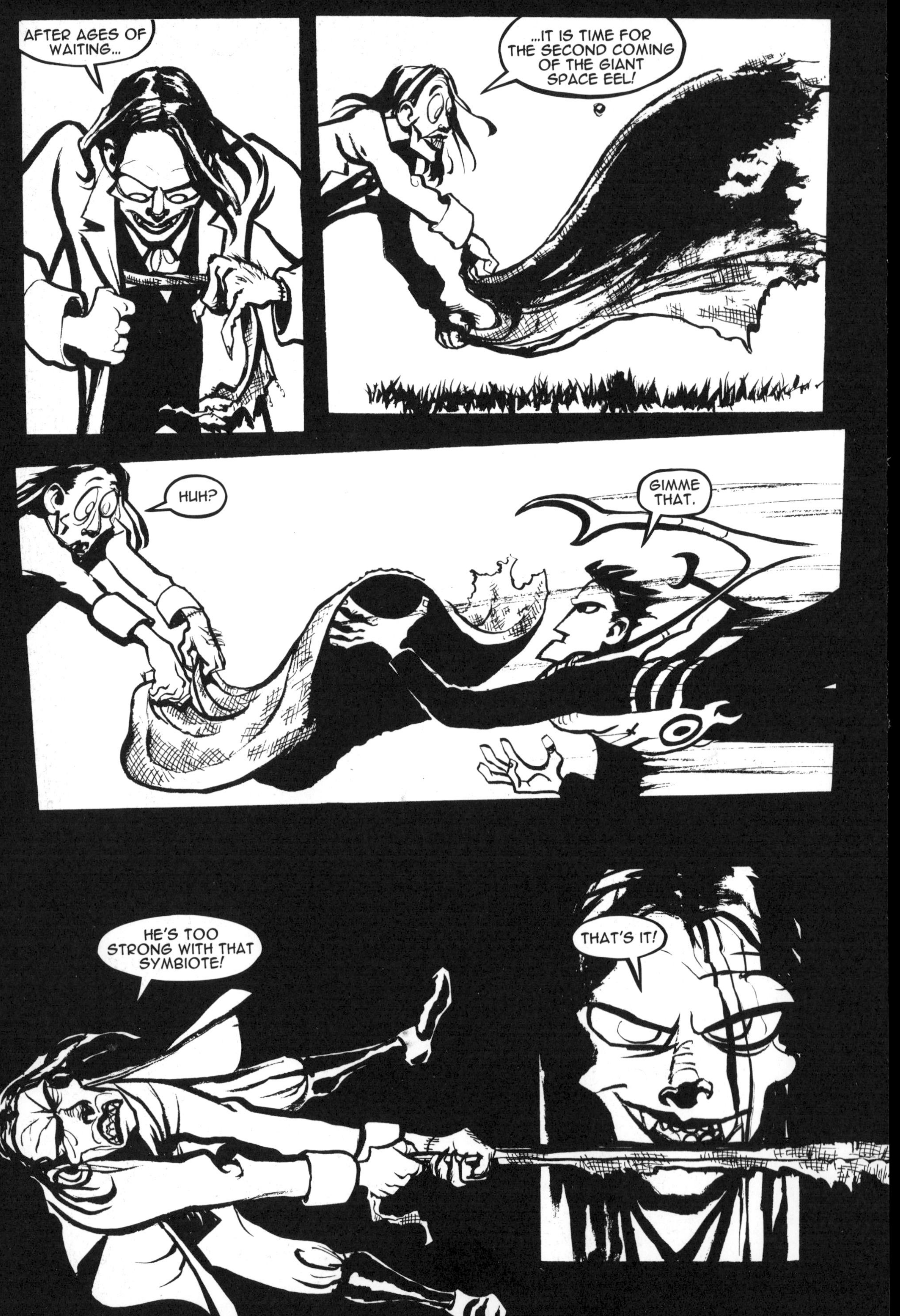
AFTER AGES OF WAITING...
...IT IS TIME FOR THE SECOND COMING OF THE GIANT SPACE EEL!
HUH?
GIMME THAT.
HE'S TOO STRONG WITH THAT SYMBIOTE!
THAT'S IT!

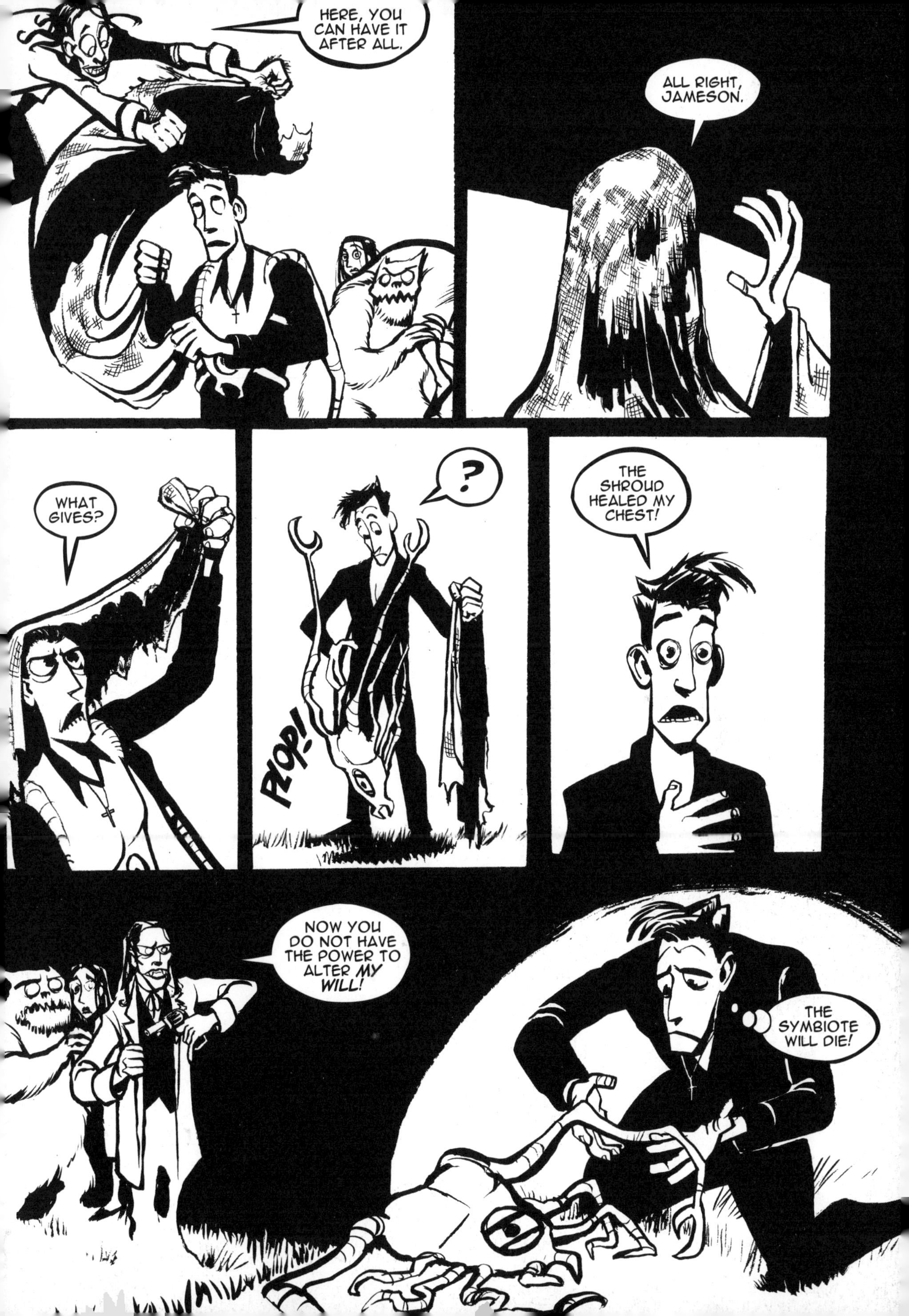
HERE, YOU CAN HAVE IT AFTER ALL.
ALL RIGHT, JAMESON.
WHAT GIVES?
?
PLOP!
THE SHROUD HEALED MY CHEST!
NOW YOU DO NOT HAVE THE POWER TO ALTER MY WILL!
THE SYMBIOTE WILL DIE!

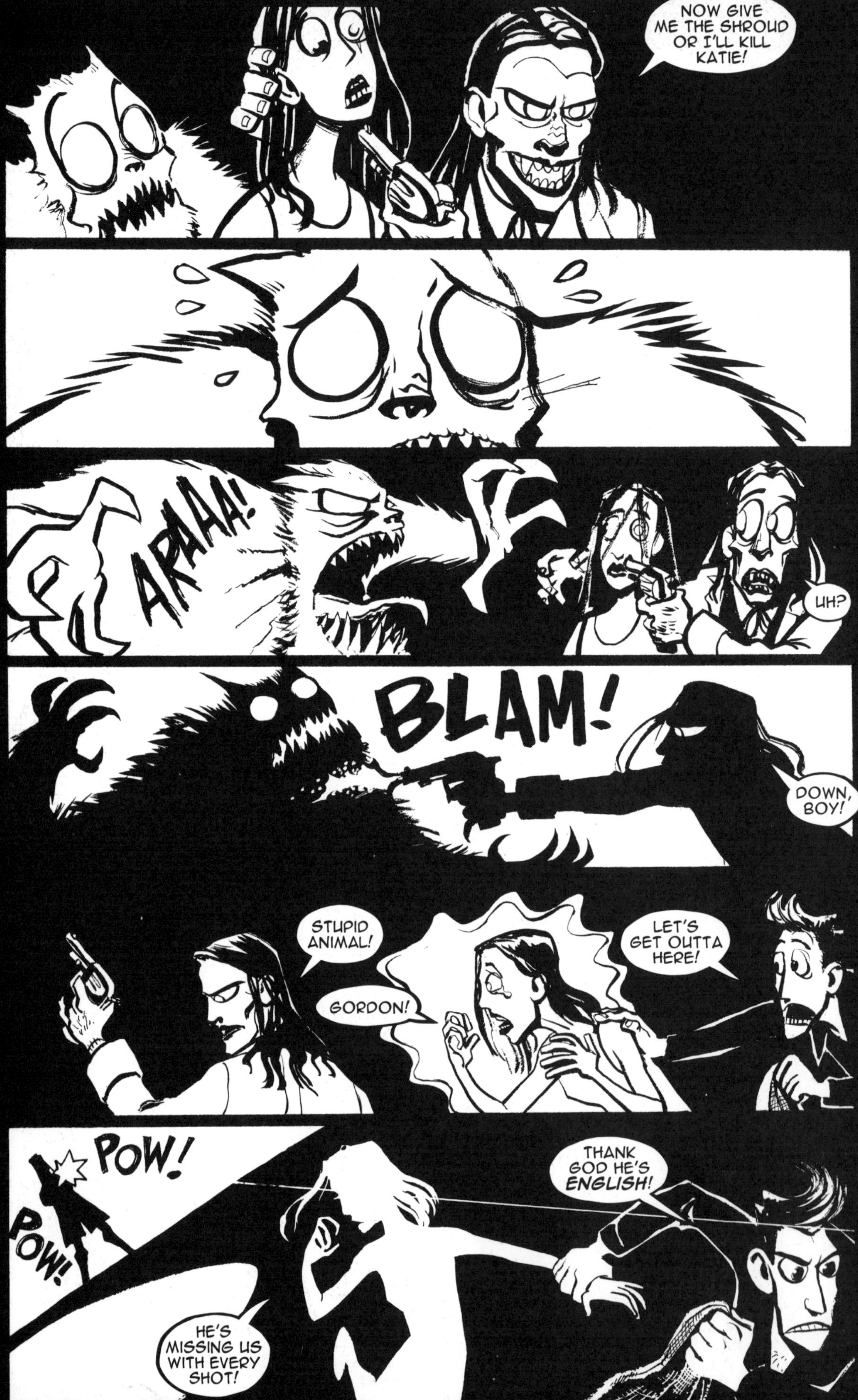
NOW GIVE ME THE SHROUD OR I'LL KILL KATIE!
ARAAA!
UH?
BLAM!
DOWN, BOY!
STUPID ANIMAL!
GORDON!
LET'S GET OUTTA HERE!
POW!
POW!
THANK GOD HE'S ENGLISH!
HE'S MISSING US WITH EVERY SHOT!

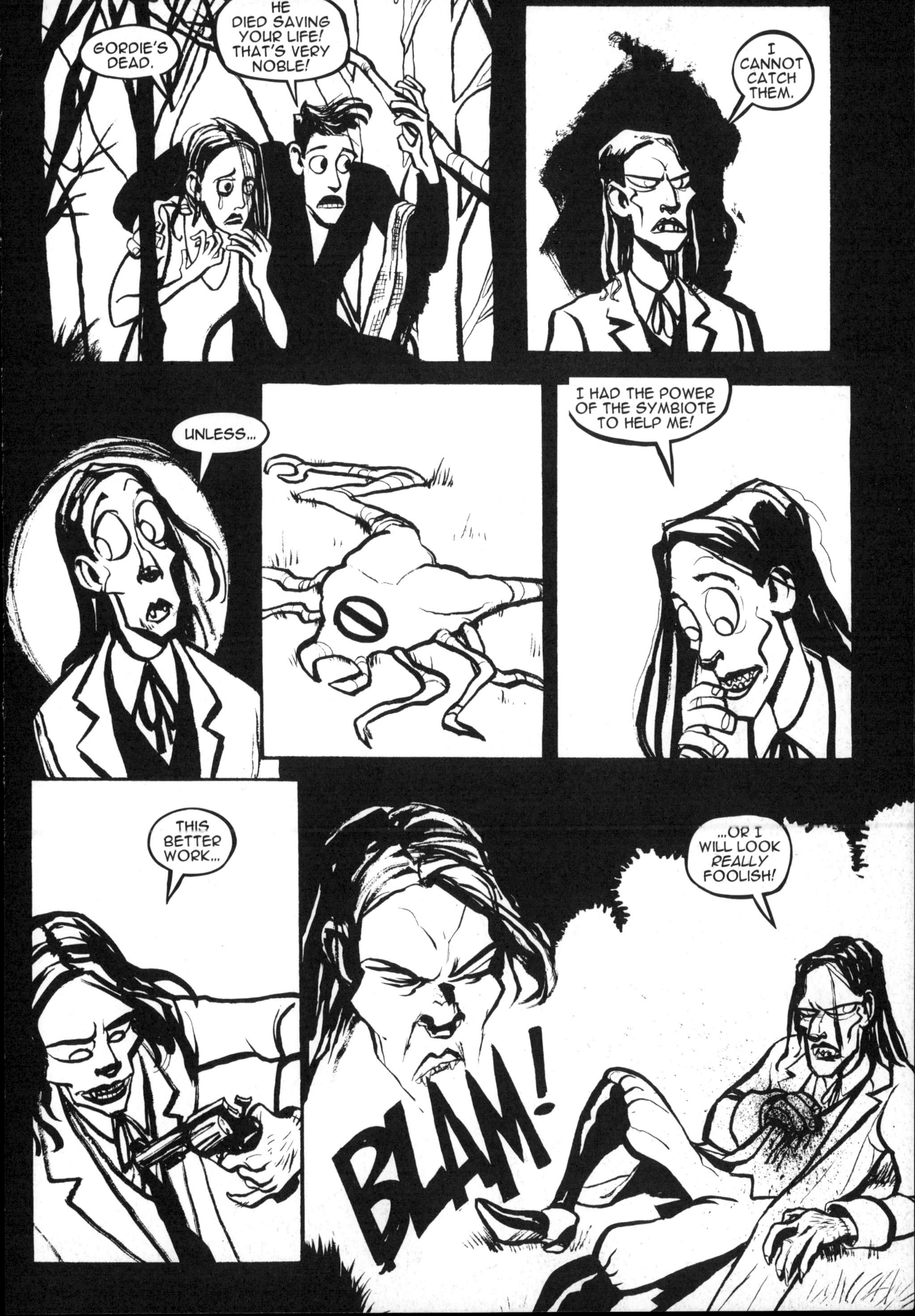
GORDIE'S DEAD.
HE DIED SAVING YOUR LIFE! THAT'S VERY NOBLE!
I CANNOT CATCH THEM.
UNLESS...
I HAD THE POWER OF THE SYMBIOTE TO HELP ME!
THIS BETTER WORK...
...OR I WILL LOOK REALLY FOOLISH!
BLAM!

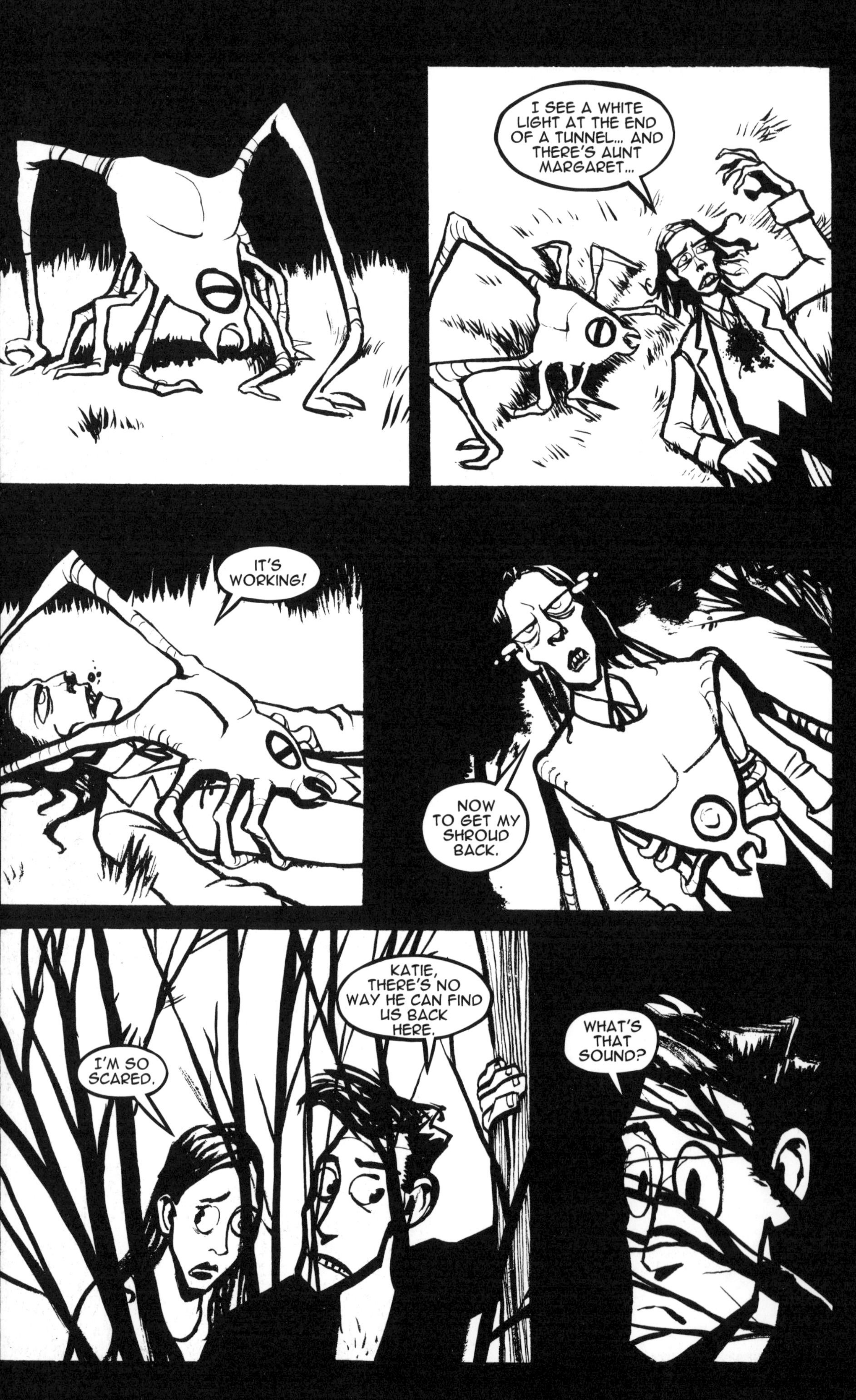
I SEE A WHITE LIGHT AT THE END OF A TUNNEL... AND THERE'S AUNT MARGARET...
IT'S WORKING!
NOW TO GET MY SHROUD BACK.
I'M SO SCARED.
KATIE, THERE'S NO WAY HE CAN FIND US BACK HERE.
WHAT'S THAT SOUND?

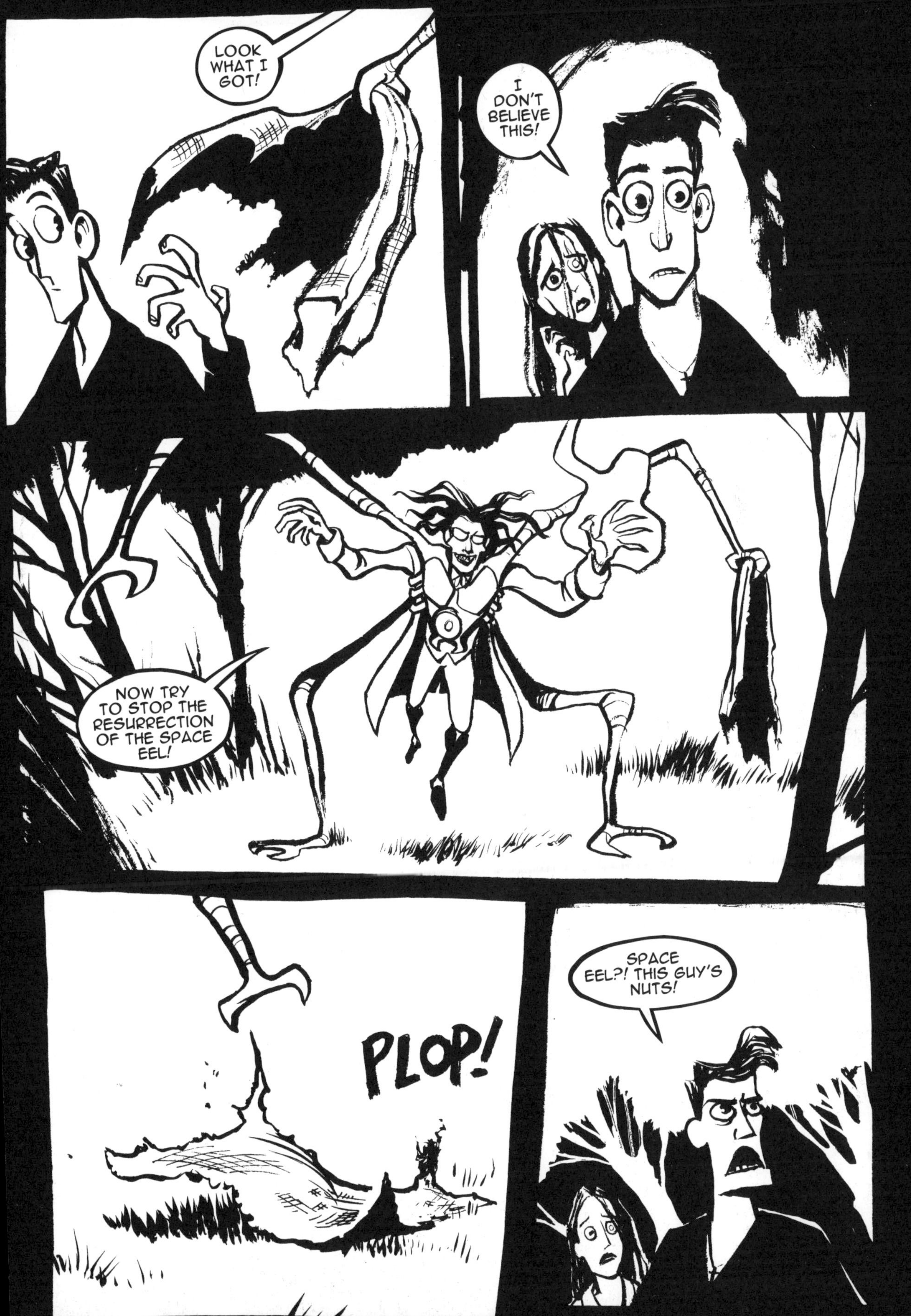
LOOK WHAT I GOT!
I DON'T BELIEVE THIS!
NOW TRY TO STOP THE RESURRECTION OF THE SPACE EEL!
PLOP!
SPACE EEL?! THIS GUY'S NUTS!

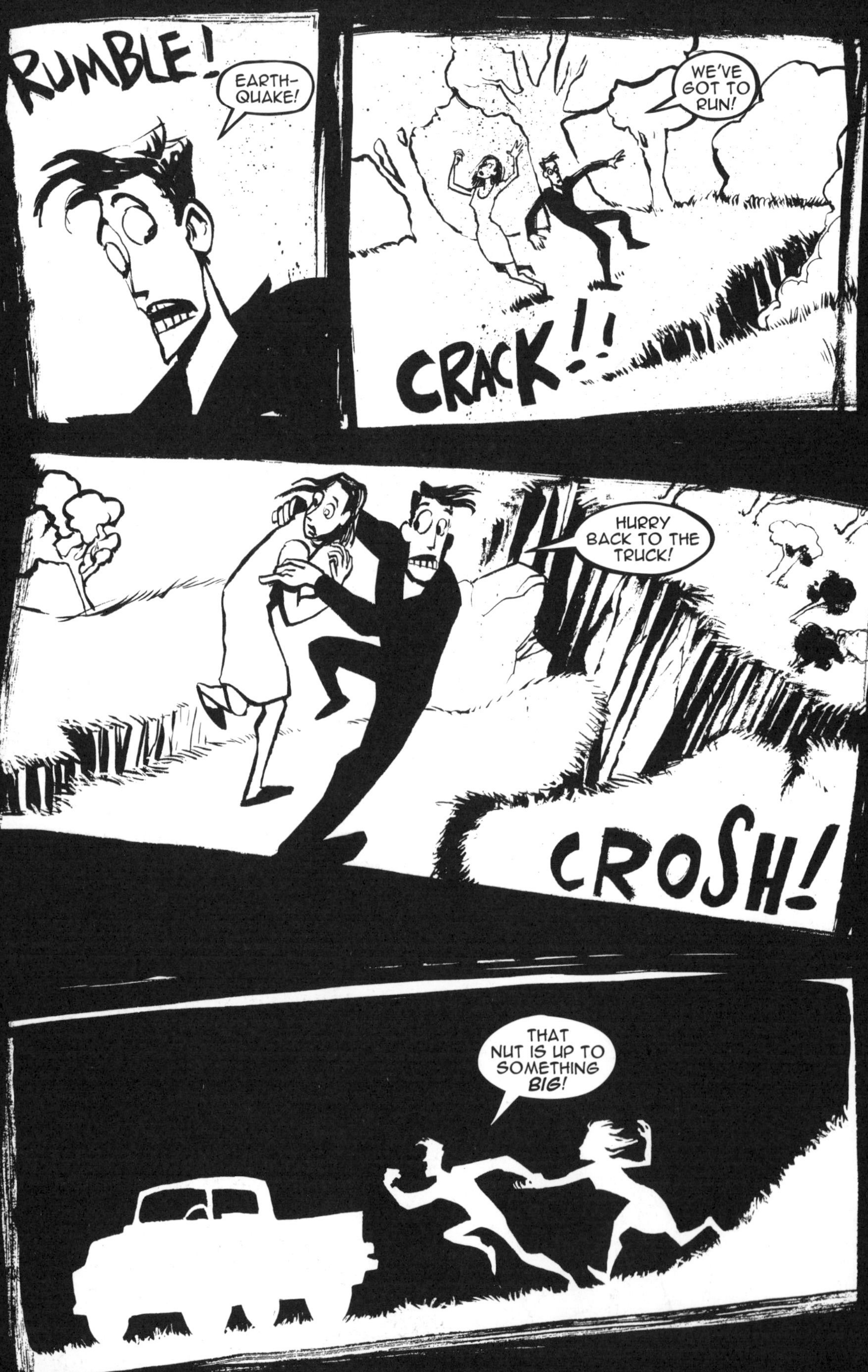
RUMBLE!
EARTH-QUAKE!
WE'VE GOT TO RUN!
CRACK!!
HURRY BACK TO THE TRUCK!
CROSH!
THAT NUT IS UP TO SOMETHING *BIG*!

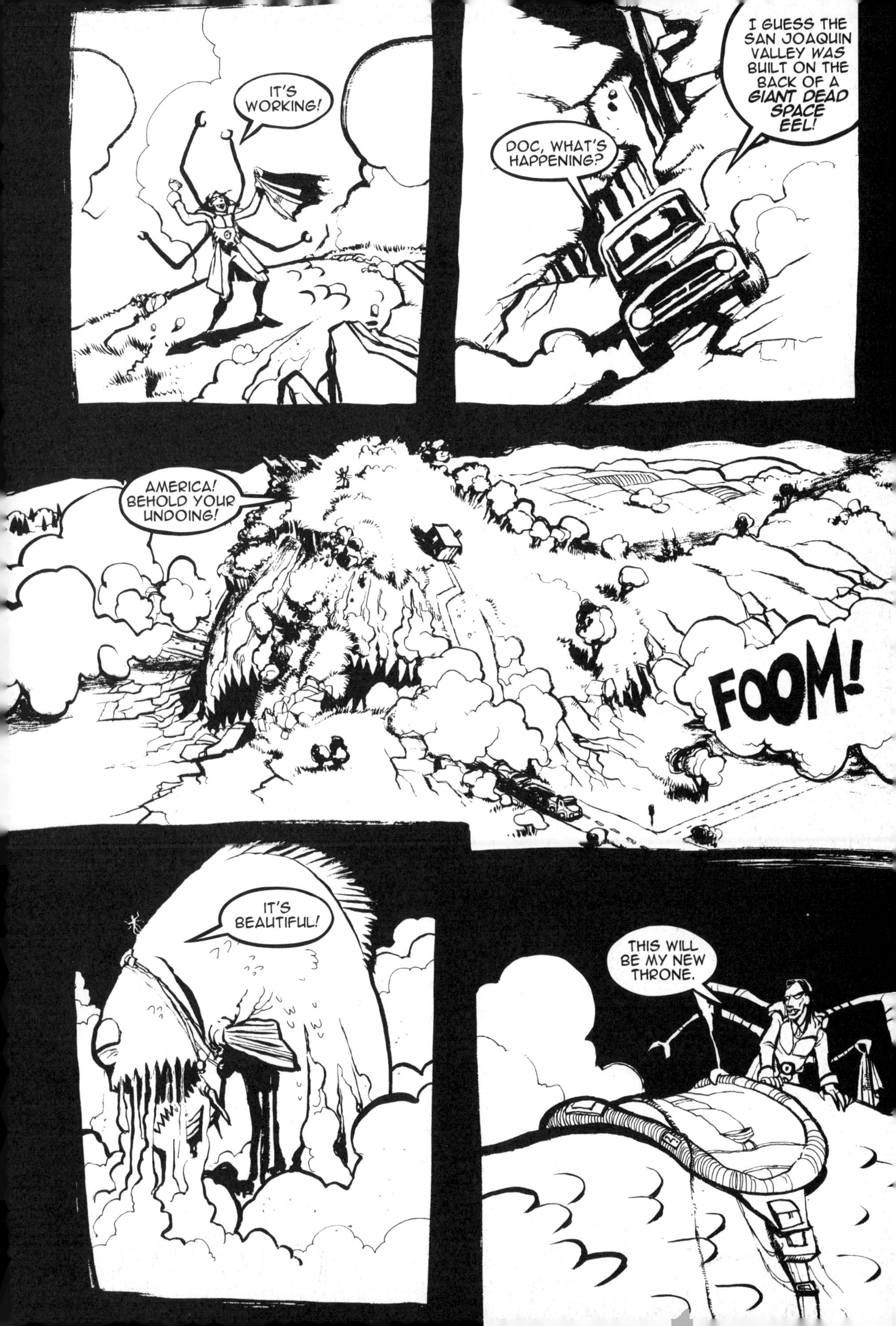
IT'S WORKING!
DOC, WHAT'S HAPPENING?
I GUESS THE SAN JOAQUIN VALLEY WAS BUILT ON THE BACK OF A GIANT DEAD SPACE EEL!
AMERICA! BEHOLD YOUR UNDOING!
FOOM!
IT'S BEAUTIFUL!
THIS WILL BE MY NEW THRONE.

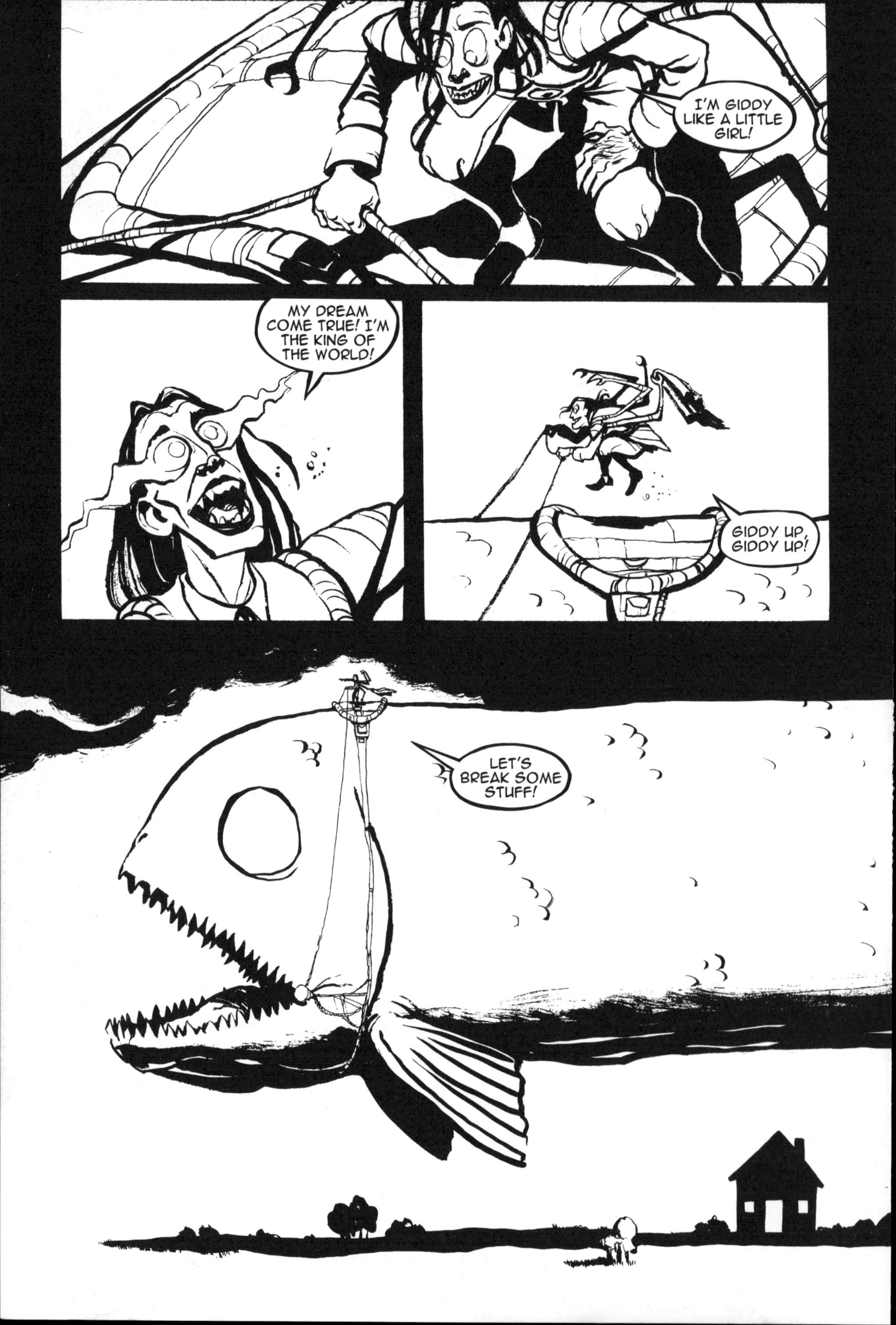
I'M GIDDY LIKE A LITTLE GIRL!
MY DREAM COME TRUE! I'M THE KING OF THE WORLD!
GIDDY UP, GIDDY UP!
LET'S BREAK SOME STUFF!

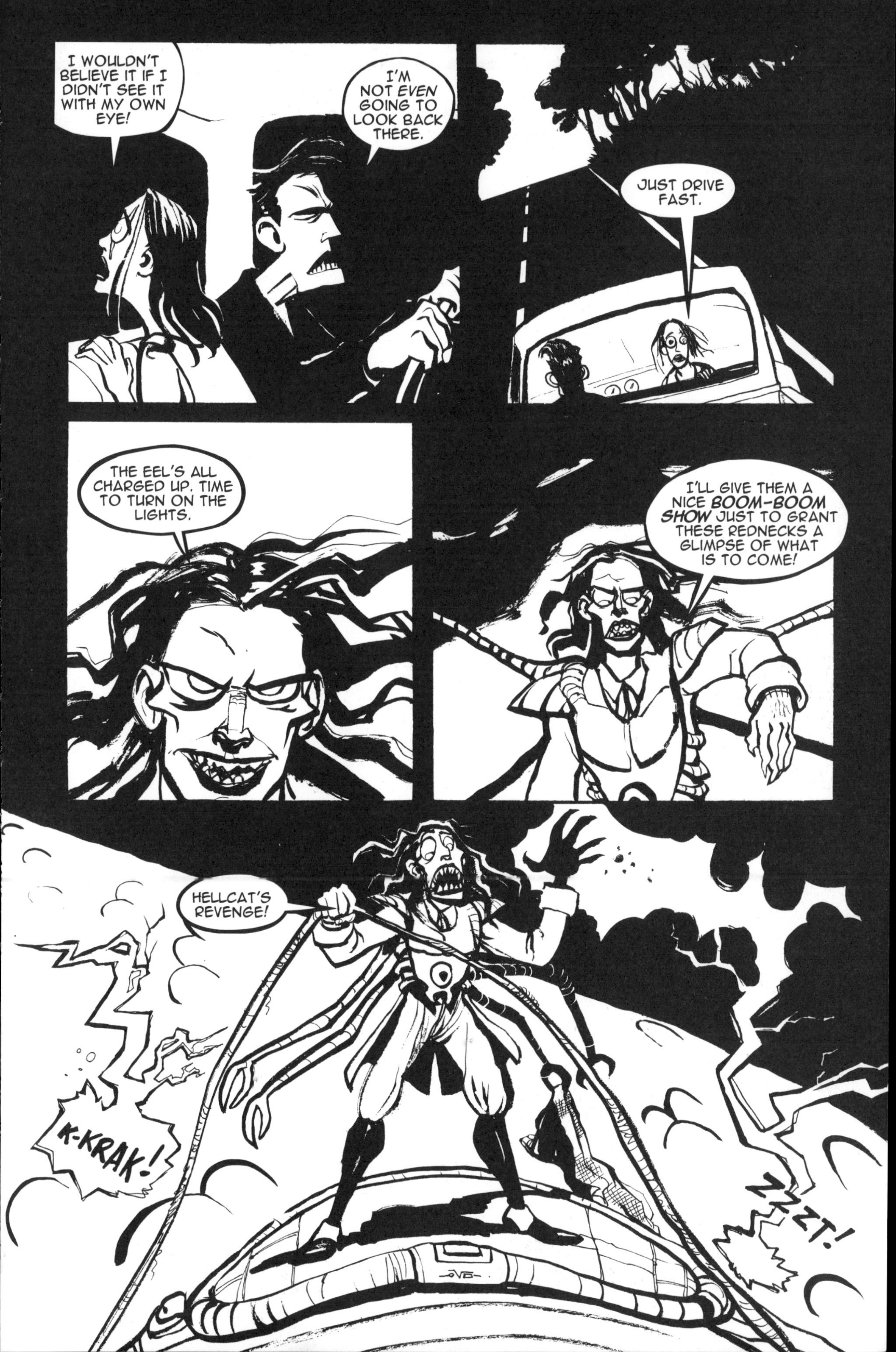
I WOULDN'T BELIEVE IT IF I DIDN'T SEE IT WITH MY OWN EYE!
I'M NOT *EVEN* GOING TO LOOK BACK THERE.
JUST DRIVE FAST.
THE EEL'S ALL CHARGED UP. TIME TO TURN ON THE LIGHTS.
I'LL GIVE THEM A NICE ***BOOM-BOOM SHOW*** JUST TO GRANT THESE REDNECKS A GLIMPSE OF WHAT IS TO COME!
HELLCAT'S REVENGE!
K-KRAK!
ZZZT!

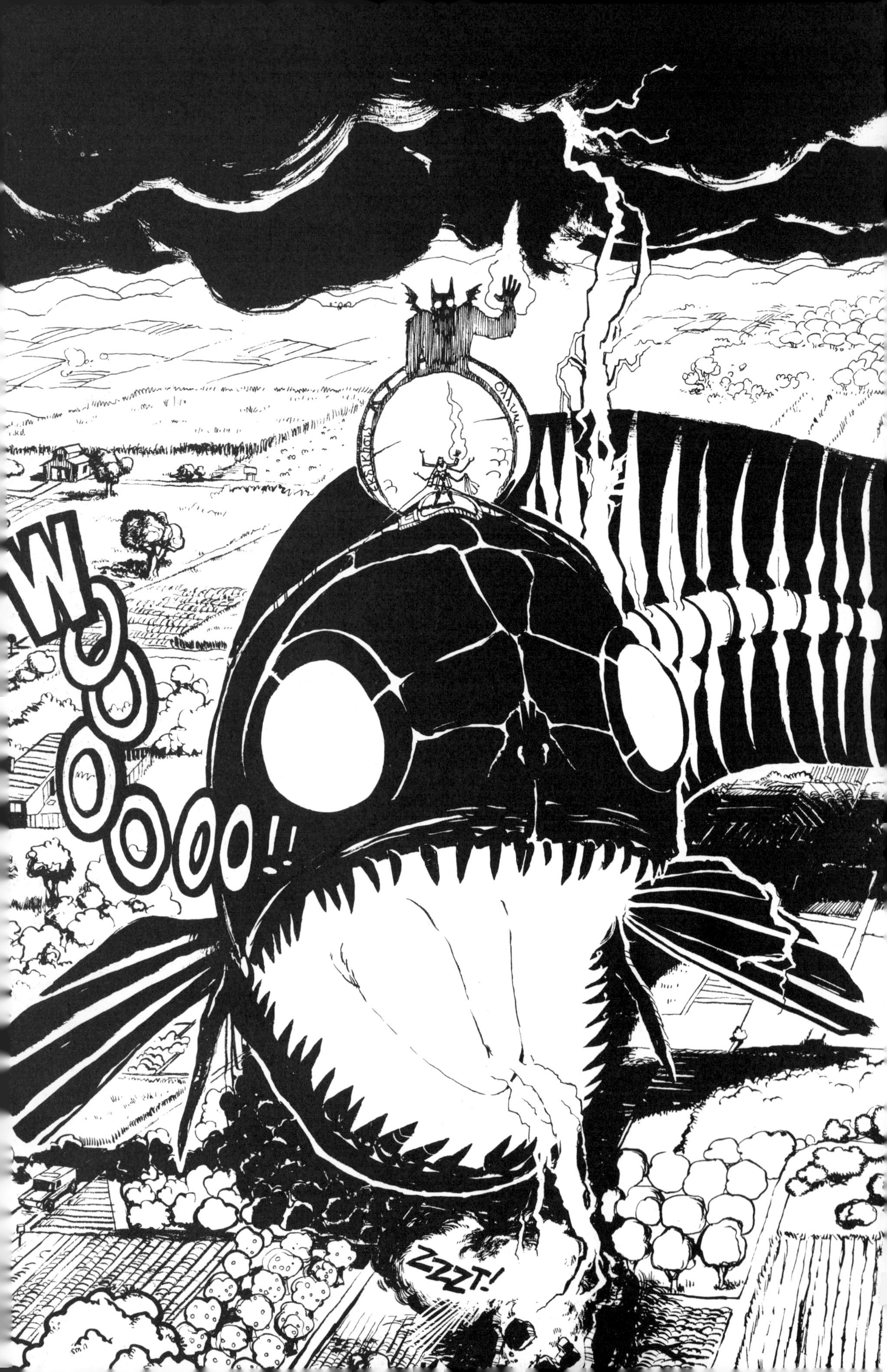
WOOOOOO!!
ZZZT!

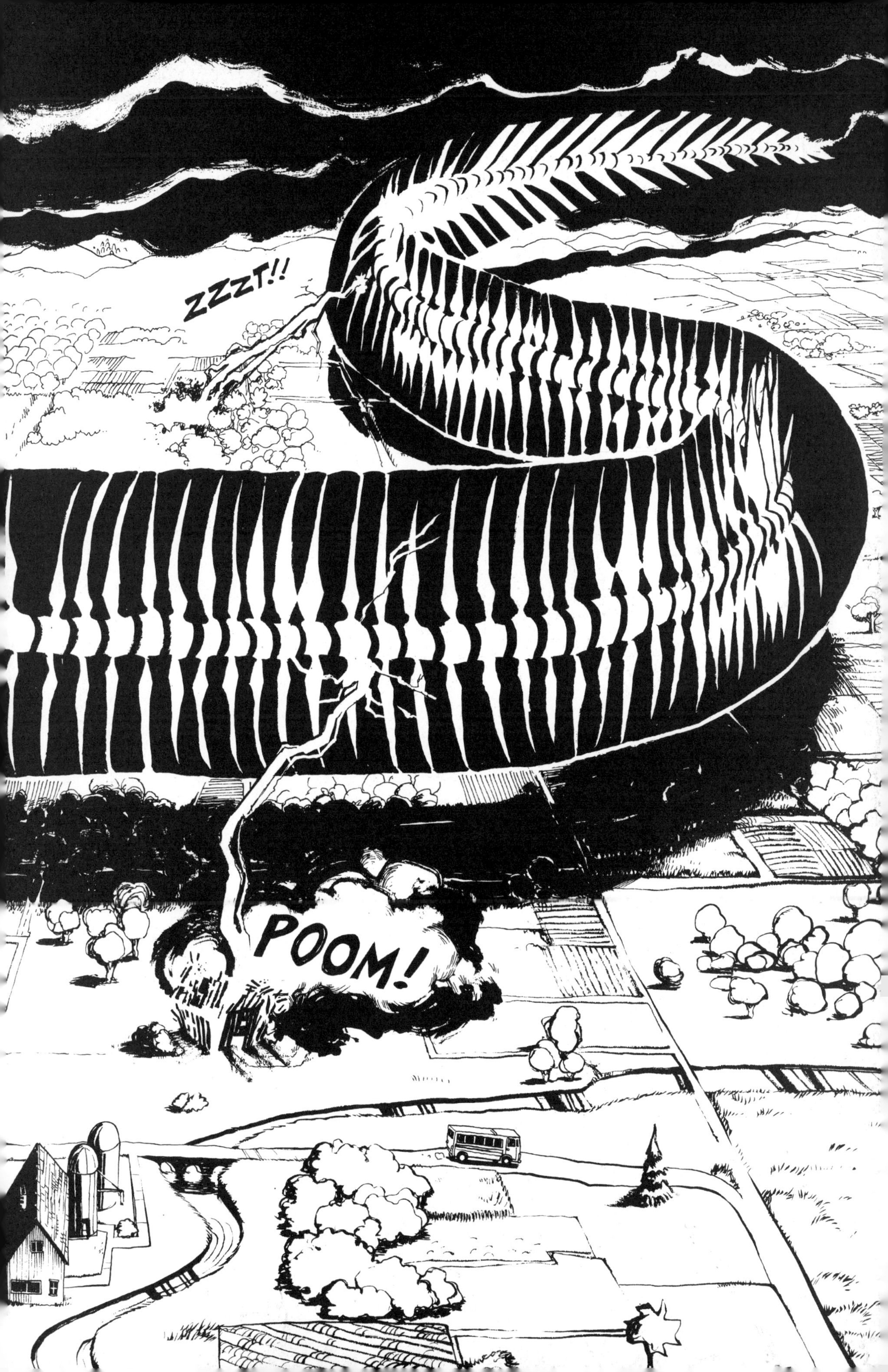
ZZZT!!
POOM!

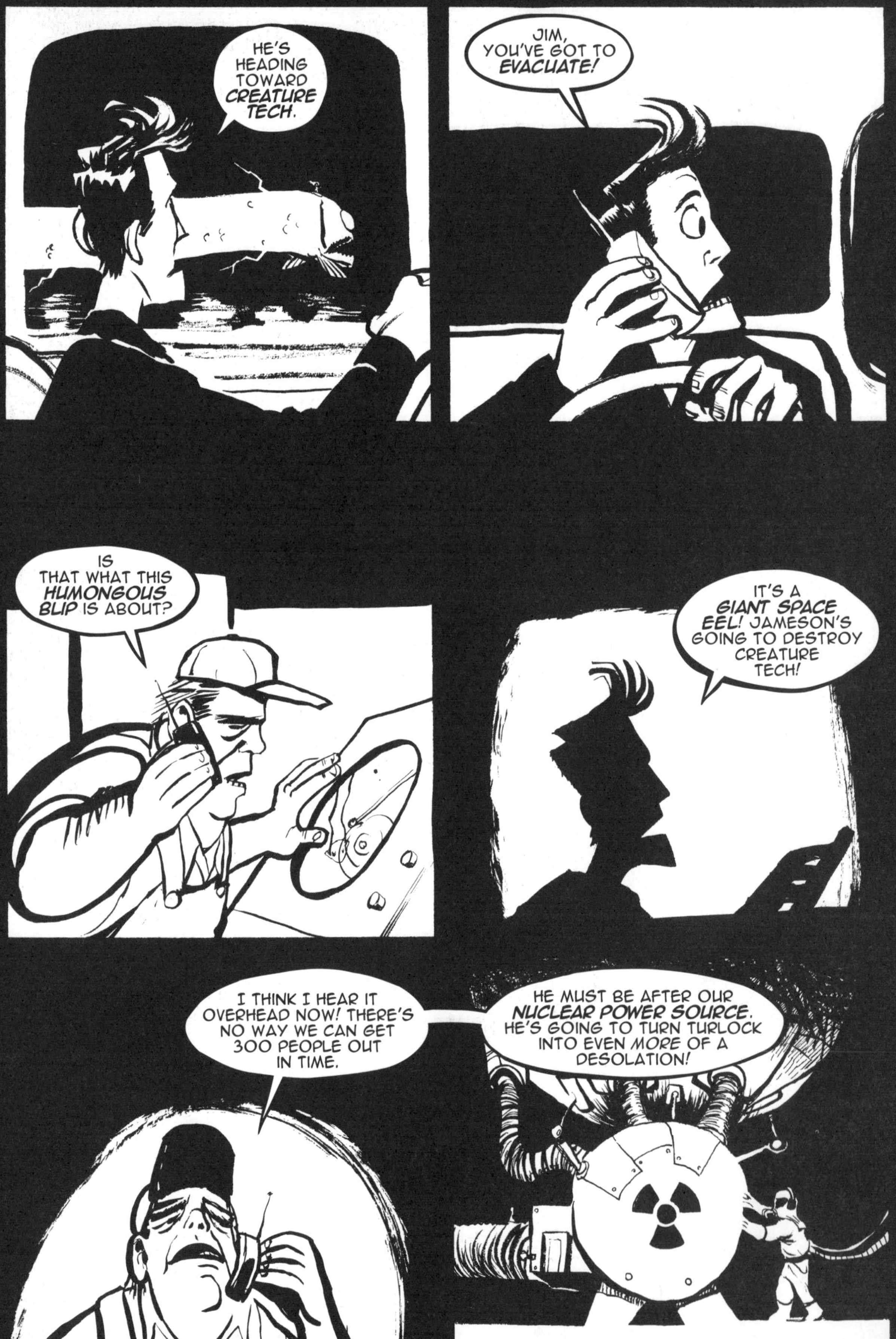
HE'S HEADING TOWARD CREATURE TECH.
JIM, YOU'VE GOT TO EVACUATE!
IS THAT WHAT THIS HUMONGOUS BLIP IS ABOUT?
IT'S A GIANT SPACE EEL! JAMESON'S GOING TO DESTROY CREATURE TECH!
I THINK I HEAR IT OVERHEAD NOW! THERE'S NO WAY WE CAN GET 300 PEOPLE OUT IN TIME.
HE MUST BE AFTER OUR NUCLEAR POWER SOURCE. HE'S GOING TO TURN TURLOCK INTO EVEN MORE OF A DESOLATION!

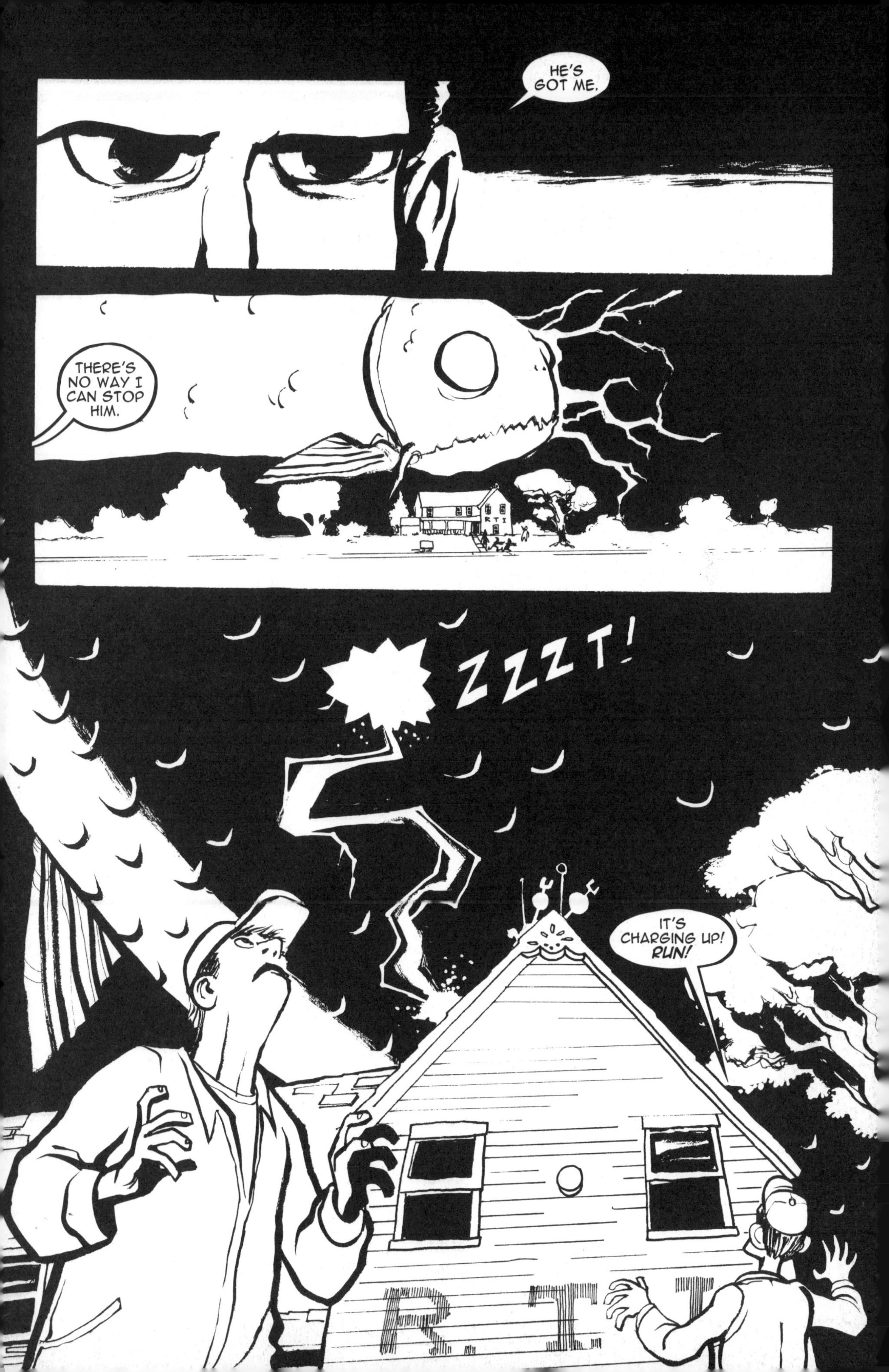
HE'S GOT ME.
THERE'S NO WAY I CAN STOP HIM.
ZZZT!
IT'S CHARGING UP! *RUN!*
R T I

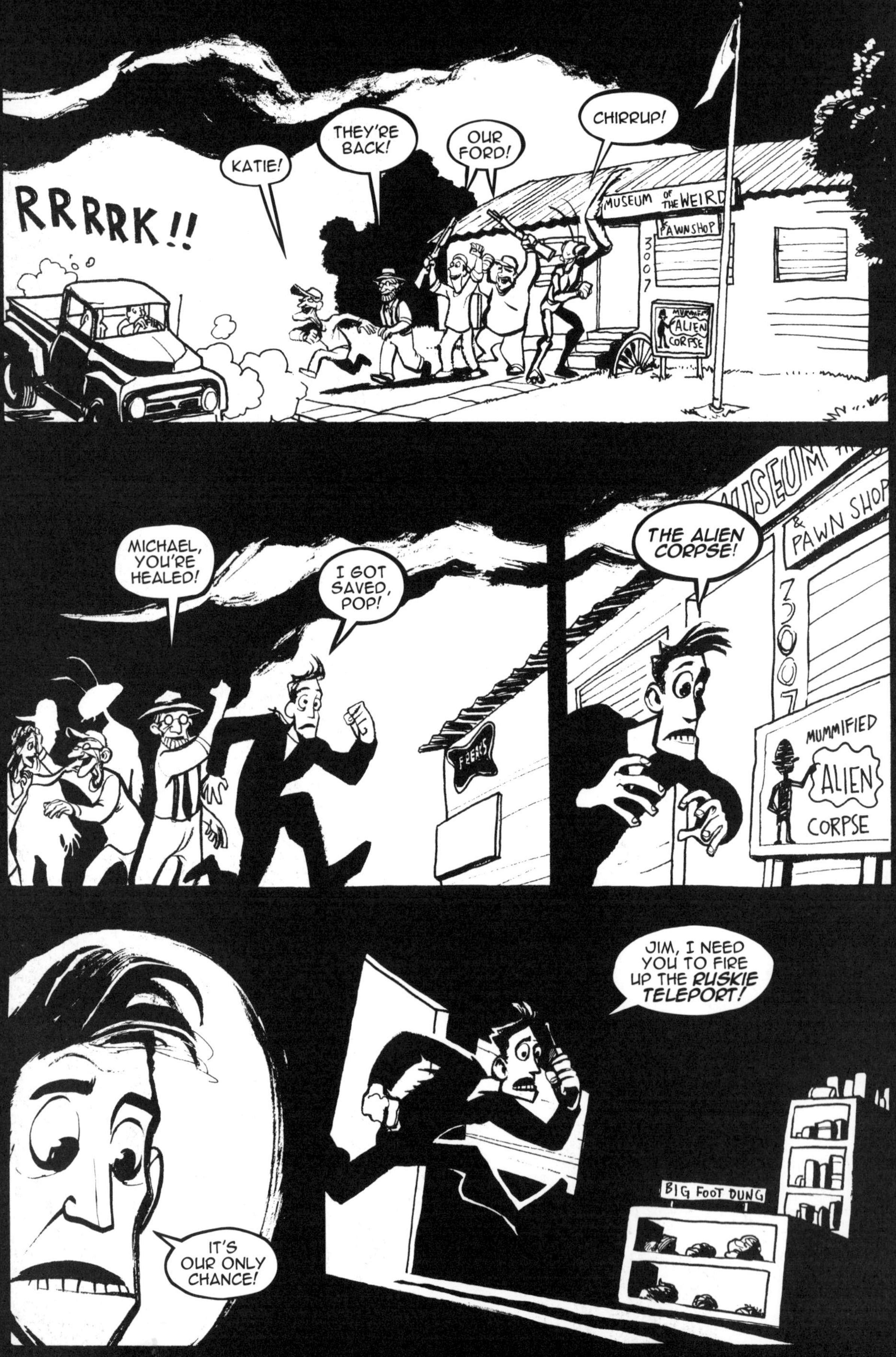
RRRRK!!
KATIE!
THEY'RE BACK!
OUR FORD!
CHIRRUP!
MUSEUM OF THE WEIRD
& PAWNSHOP
3007
ALIEN CORPSE
MICHAEL, YOU'RE HEALED!
I GOT SAVED, POP!
FREAKS
THE ALIEN CORPSE!
PAWN SHOP
3007
MUMMIFIED ALIEN CORPSE
JIM, I NEED YOU TO FIRE UP THE RUSKIE TELEPORT!
IT'S OUR ONLY CHANCE!
BIG FOOT DUNG

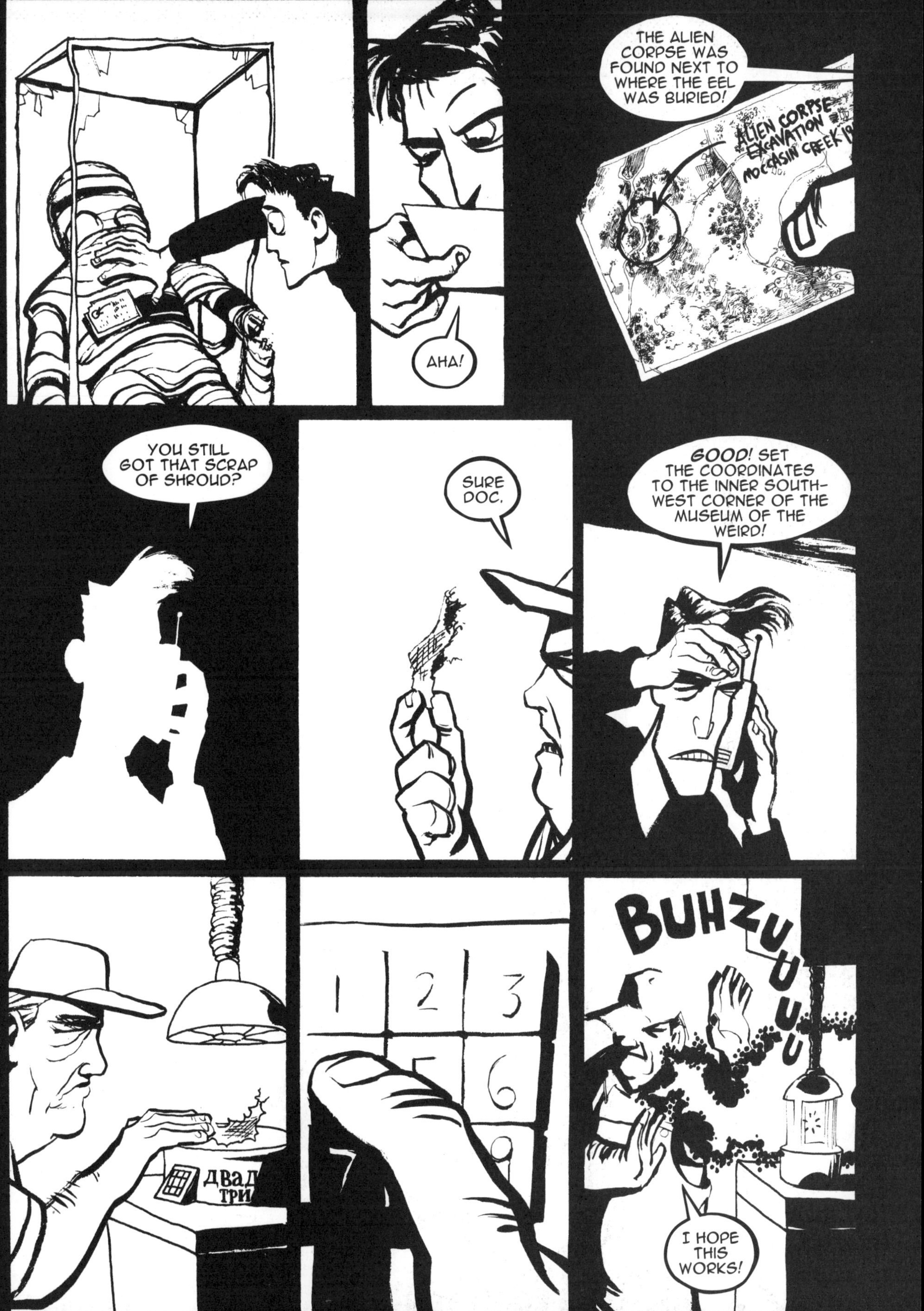
THE ALIEN CORPSE WAS FOUND NEXT TO WHERE THE EEL WAS BURIED!
AHA!
ALIEN CORPSE EXCAVATION MOCCASIN CREEK
YOU STILL GOT THAT SCRAP OF SHROUD?
SURE DOC.
GOOD! SET THE COORDINATES TO THE INNER SOUTH-WEST CORNER OF THE MUSEUM OF THE WEIRD!
ДВАД ТРИ
1 2 3
6
BUHZUUUUU
I HOPE THIS WORKS!

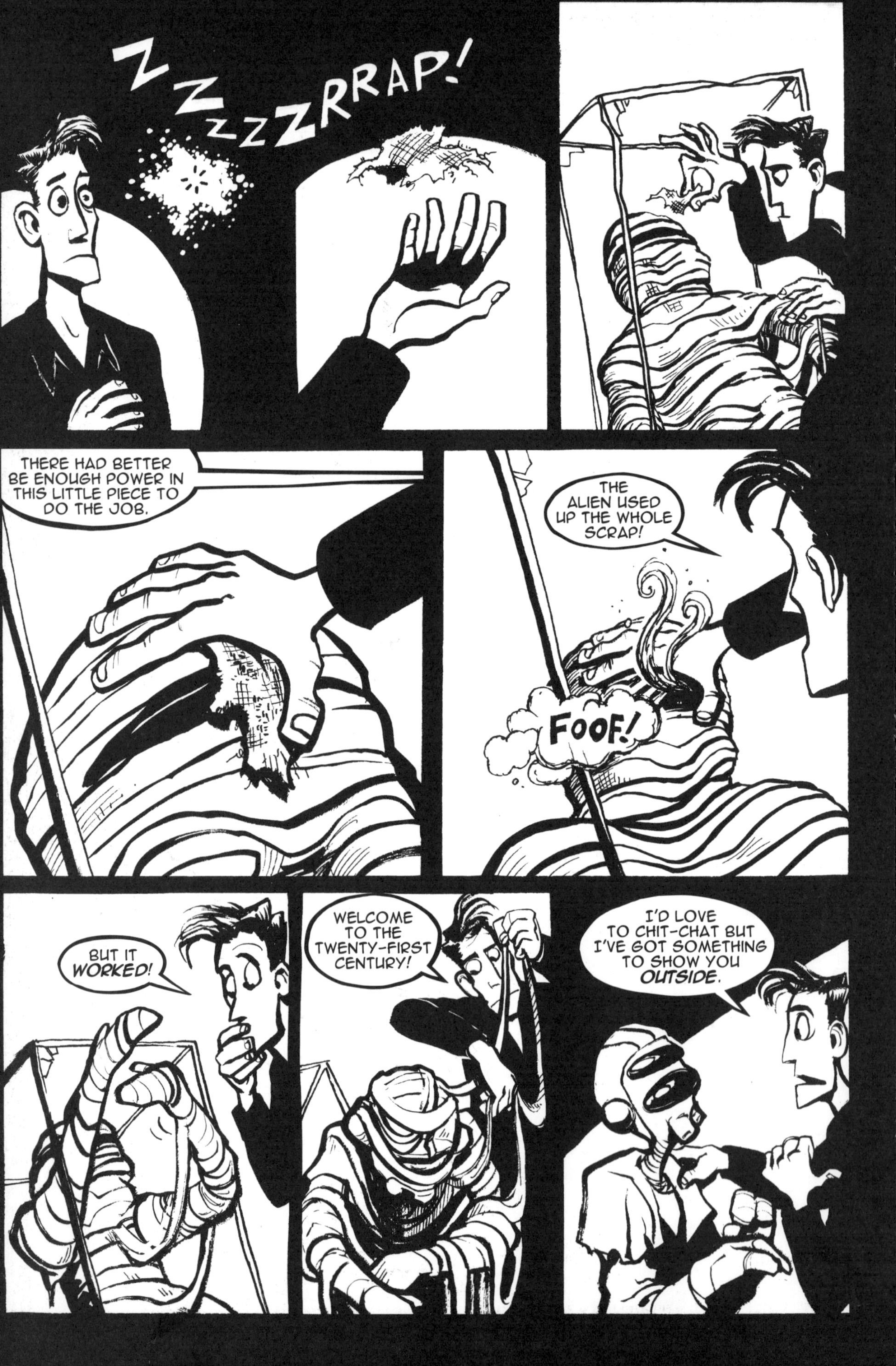
ZZZZZZRRAP!
THERE HAD BETTER BE ENOUGH POWER IN THIS LITTLE PIECE TO DO THE JOB.
THE ALIEN USED UP THE WHOLE SCRAP!
FOOF!
BUT IT WORKED!
WELCOME TO THE TWENTY-FIRST CENTURY!
I'D LOVE TO CHIT-CHAT BUT I'VE GOT SOMETHING TO SHOW YOU OUTSIDE.

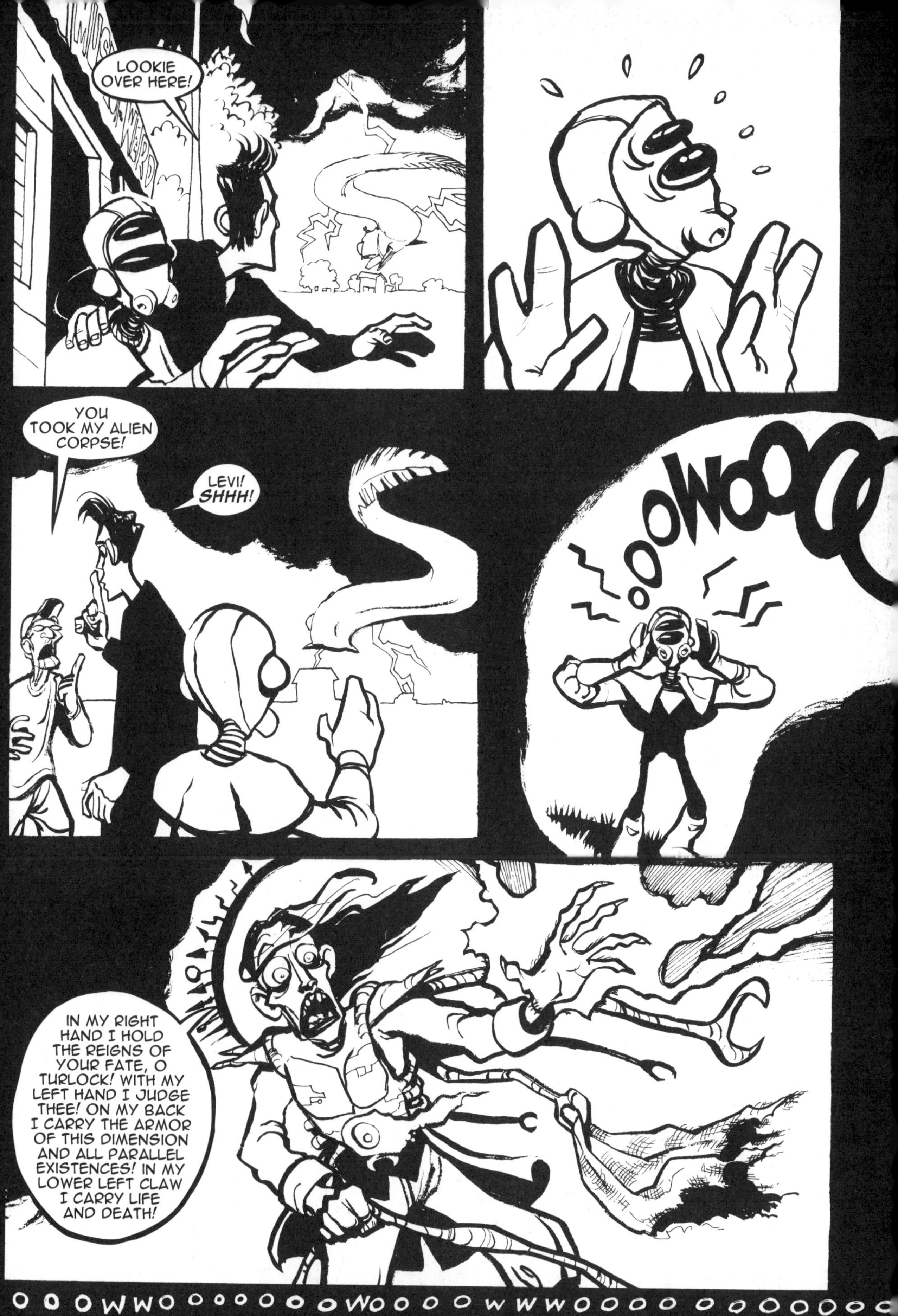

LOOKIE OVER HERE!
YOU TOOK MY ALIEN CORPSE!
LEVI! SHHH!
OOWOOO
IN MY RIGHT HAND I HOLD THE REIGNS OF YOUR FATE, O TURLOCK! WITH MY LEFT HAND I JUDGE THEE! ON MY BACK I CARRY THE ARMOR OF THIS DIMENSION AND ALL PARALLEL EXISTENCES! IN MY LOWER LEFT CLAW I CARRY LIFE AND DEATH!
OOOWWOOOOOOOOOWOOOOOWWWOOOOOOOOOOOO

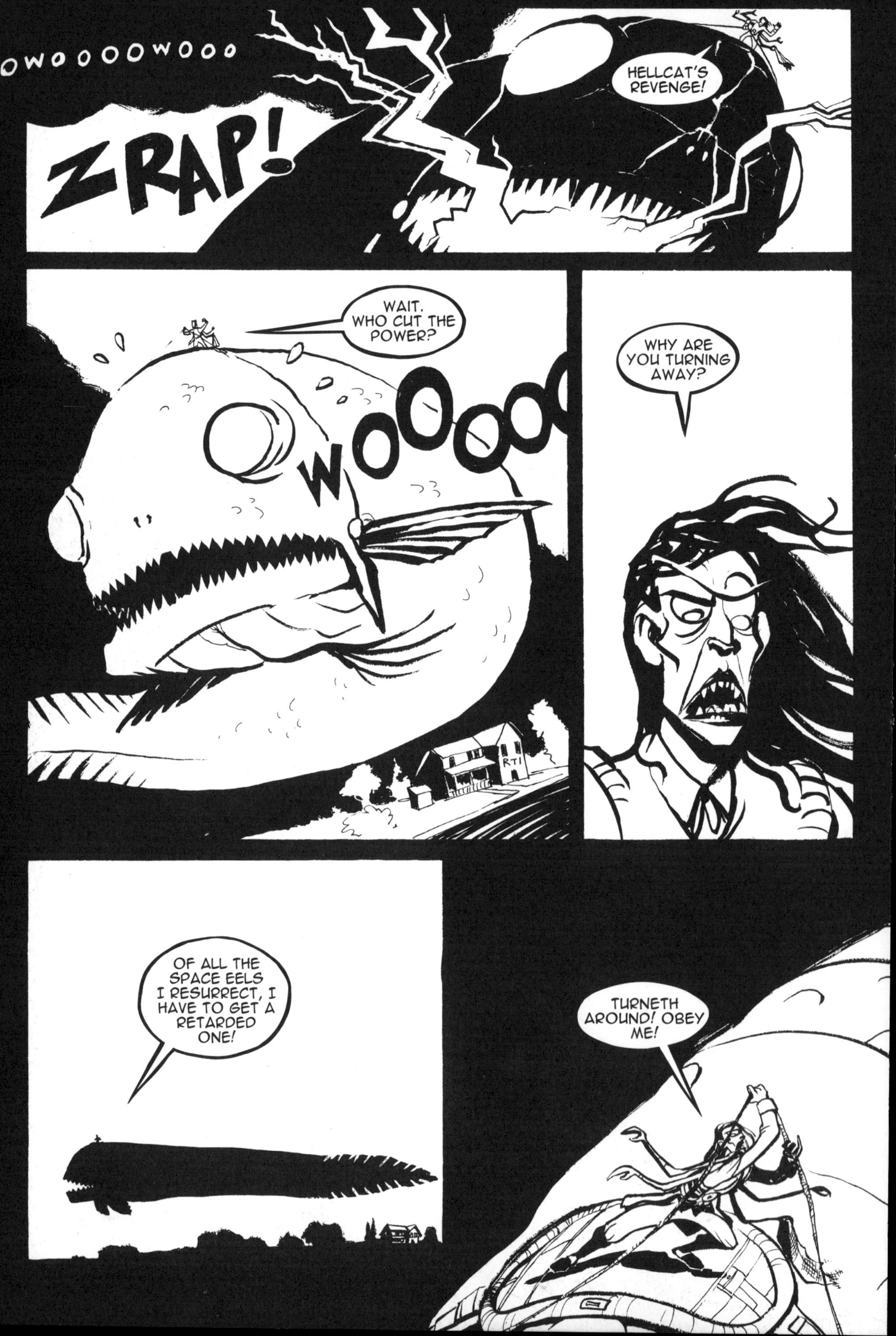
OWOOOOWOOO
ZRAP!
HELLCAT'S REVENGE!
WAIT. WHO CUT THE POWER?
WOOOOO
WHY ARE YOU TURNING AWAY?
OF ALL THE SPACE EELS I RESURRECT, I HAVE TO GET A RETARDED ONE!
TURNETH AROUND! OBEY ME!

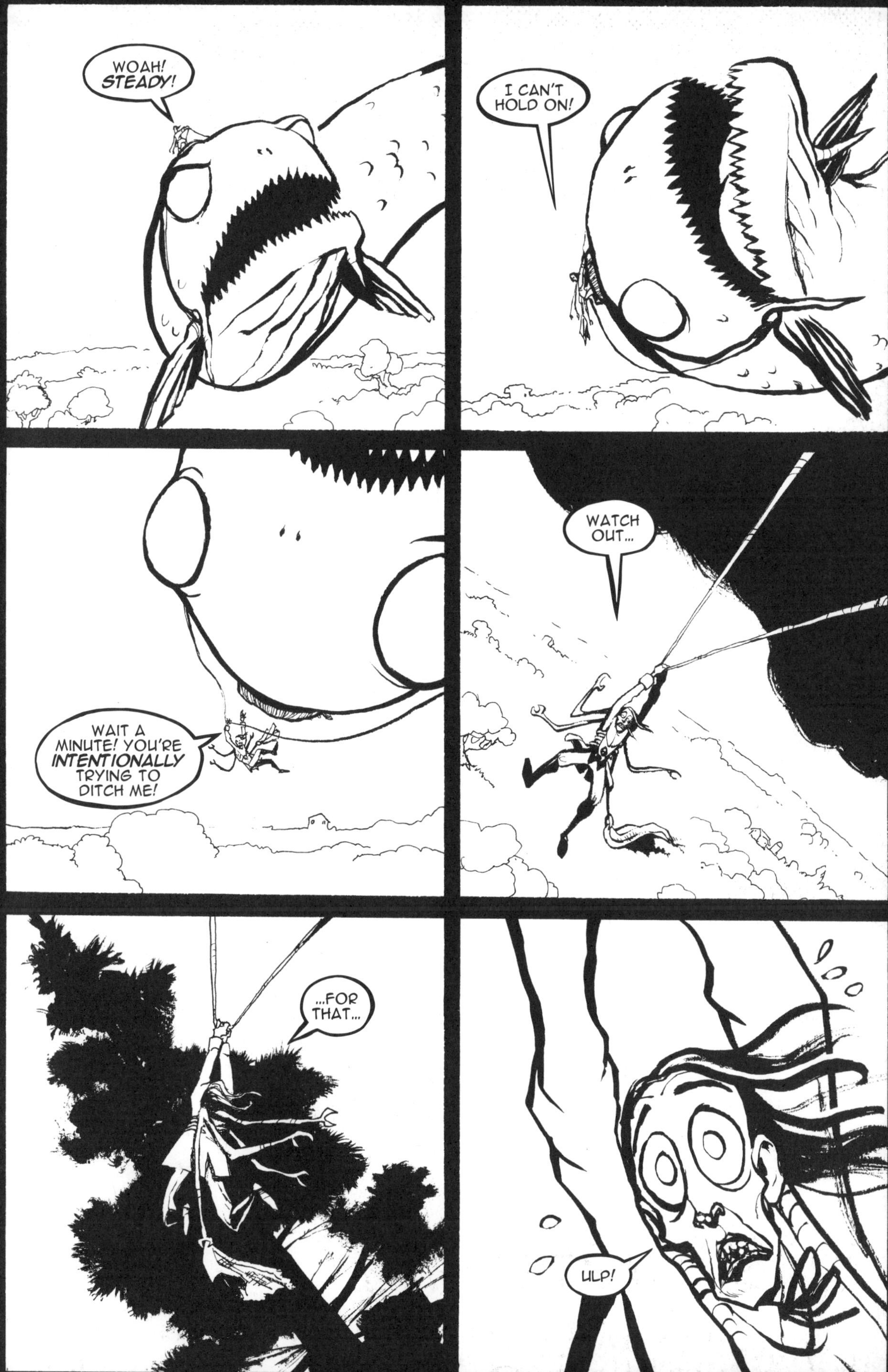
WOAH! STEADY!
I CAN'T HOLD ON!
WAIT A MINUTE! YOU'RE INTENTIONALLY TRYING TO DITCH ME!
WATCH OUT...
...FOR THAT...
ULP!

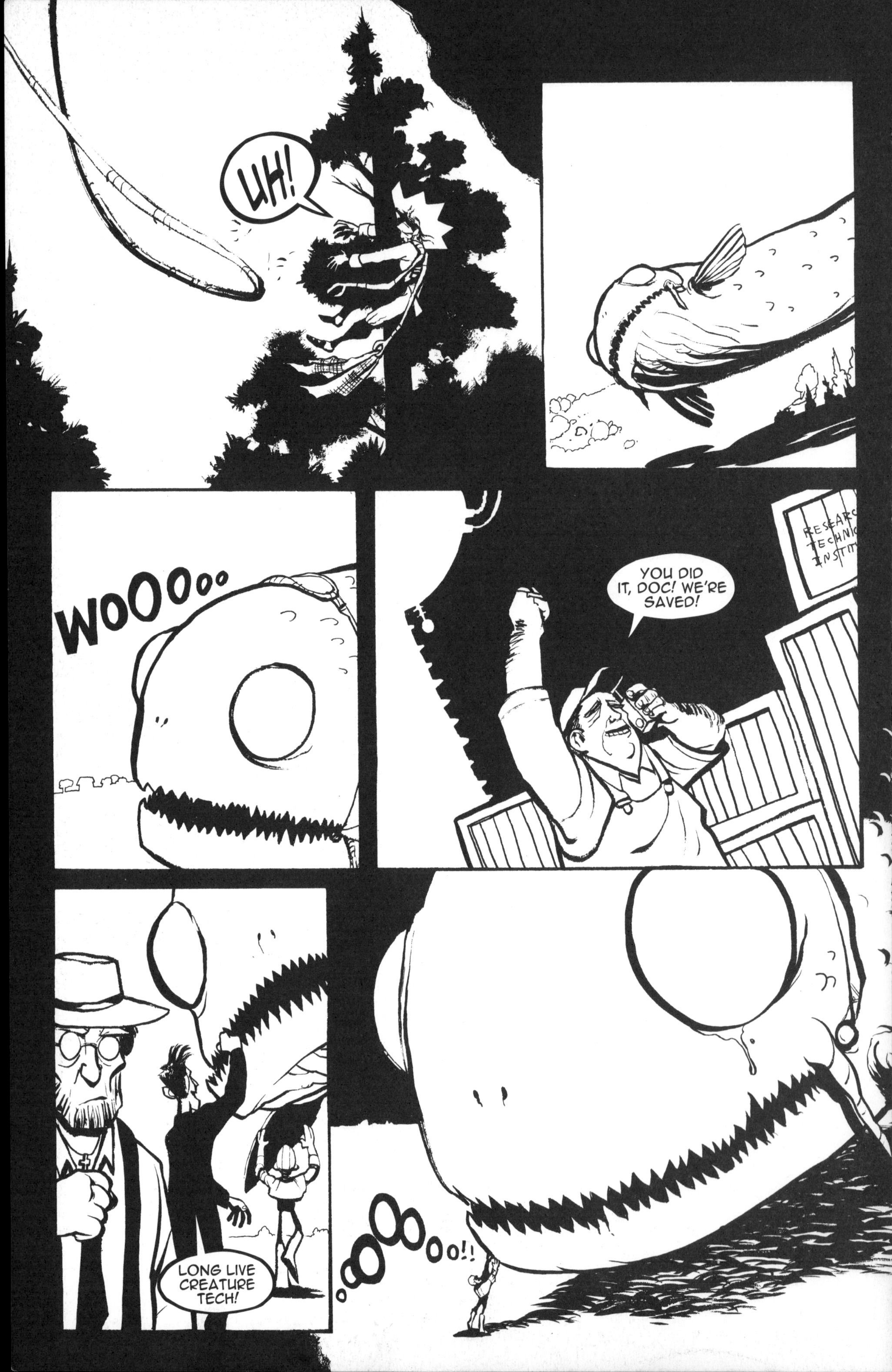
UH!
WOOOoo
YOU DID IT, DOC! WE'RE SAVED!
LONG LIVE CREATURE TECH!
oOOOOoo!!

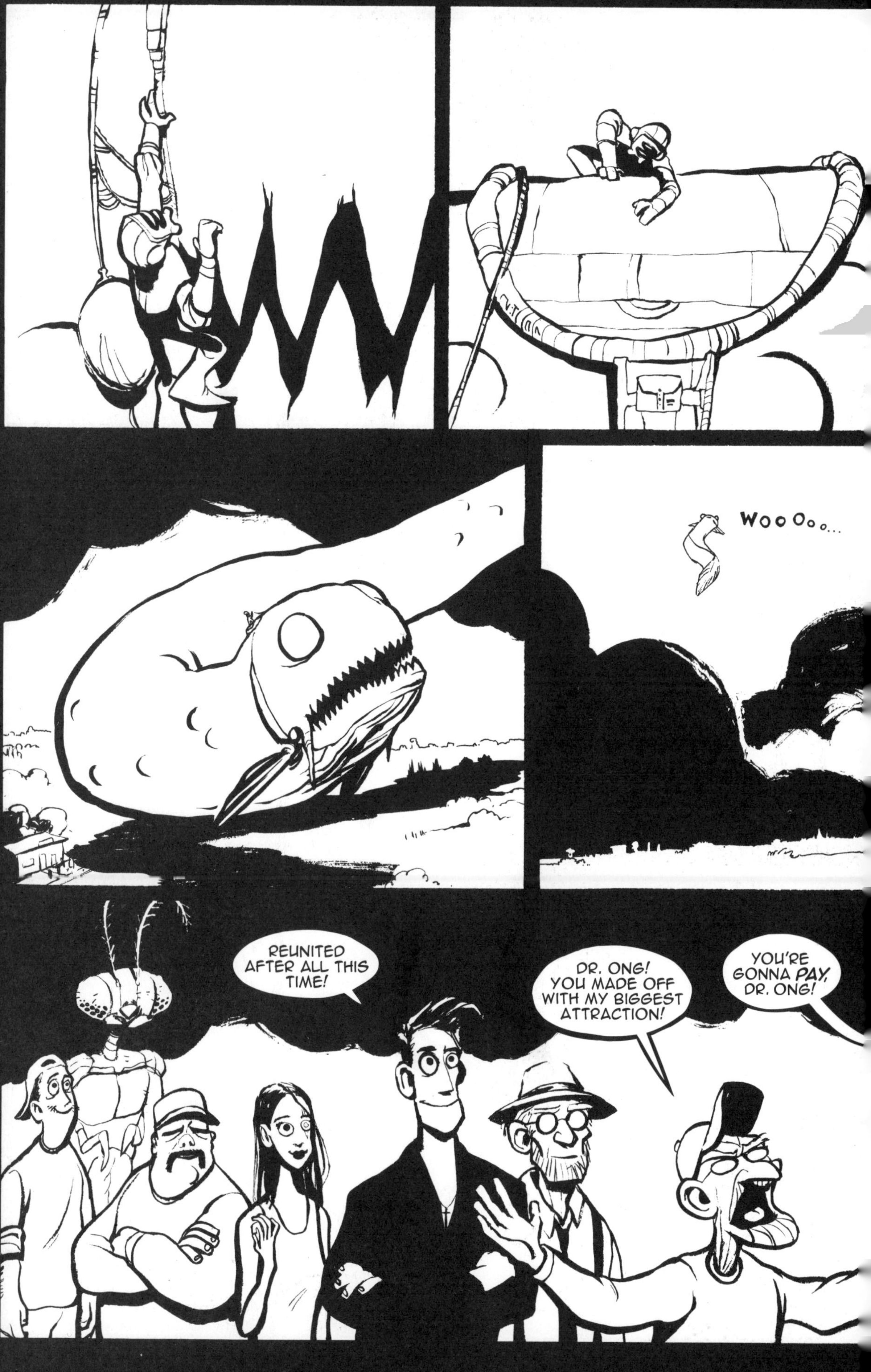
WOO Ooo...
REUNITED AFTER ALL THIS TIME!
DR. ONG! YOU MADE OFF WITH MY BIGGEST ATTRACTION!
YOU'RE GONNA PAY, DR. ONG!

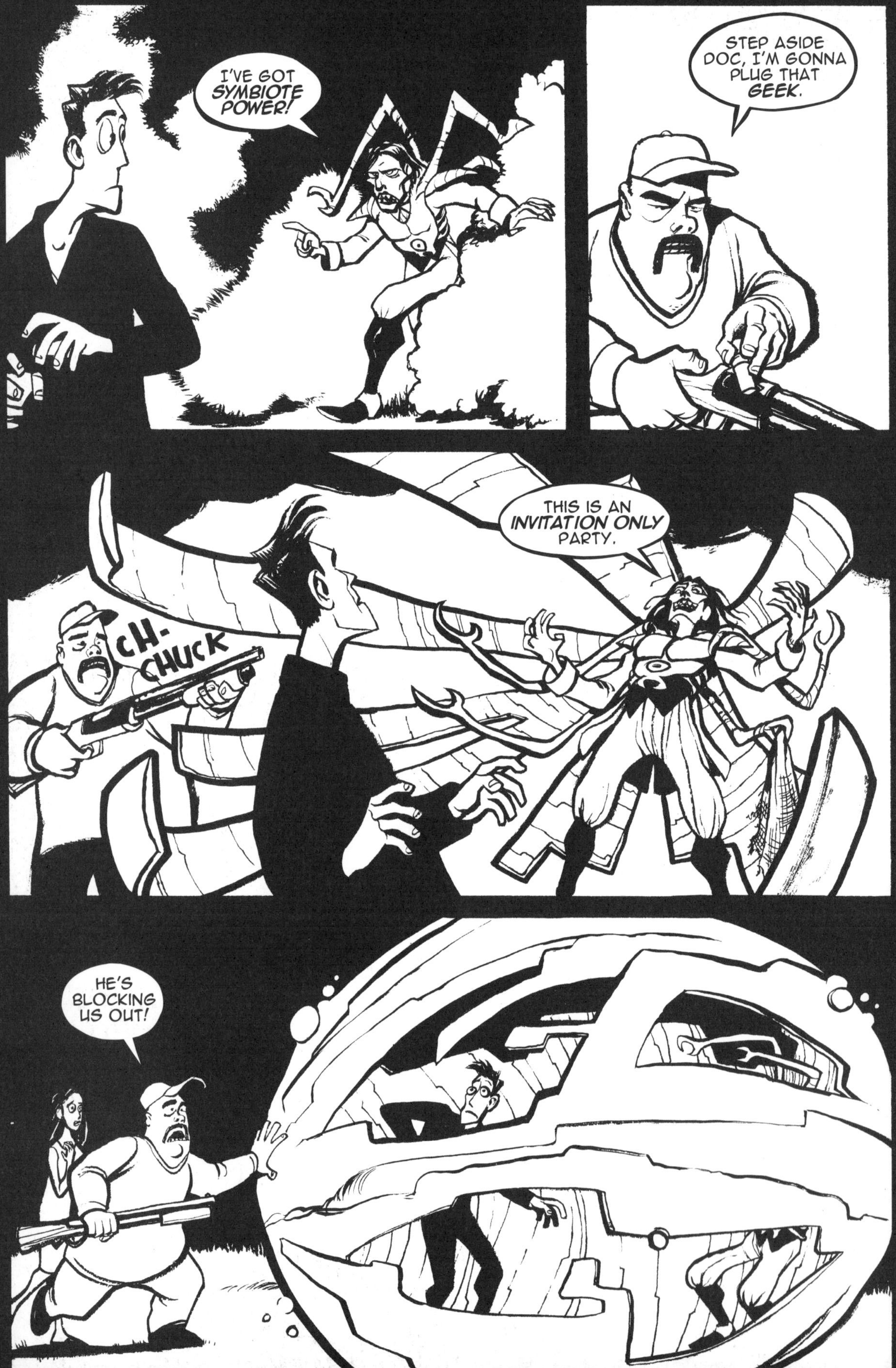
I'VE GOT SYMBIOTE POWER!
STEP ASIDE DOC, I'M GONNA PLUG THAT GEEK.
CH-CHUCK
THIS IS AN INVITATION ONLY PARTY.
HE'S BLOCKING US OUT!

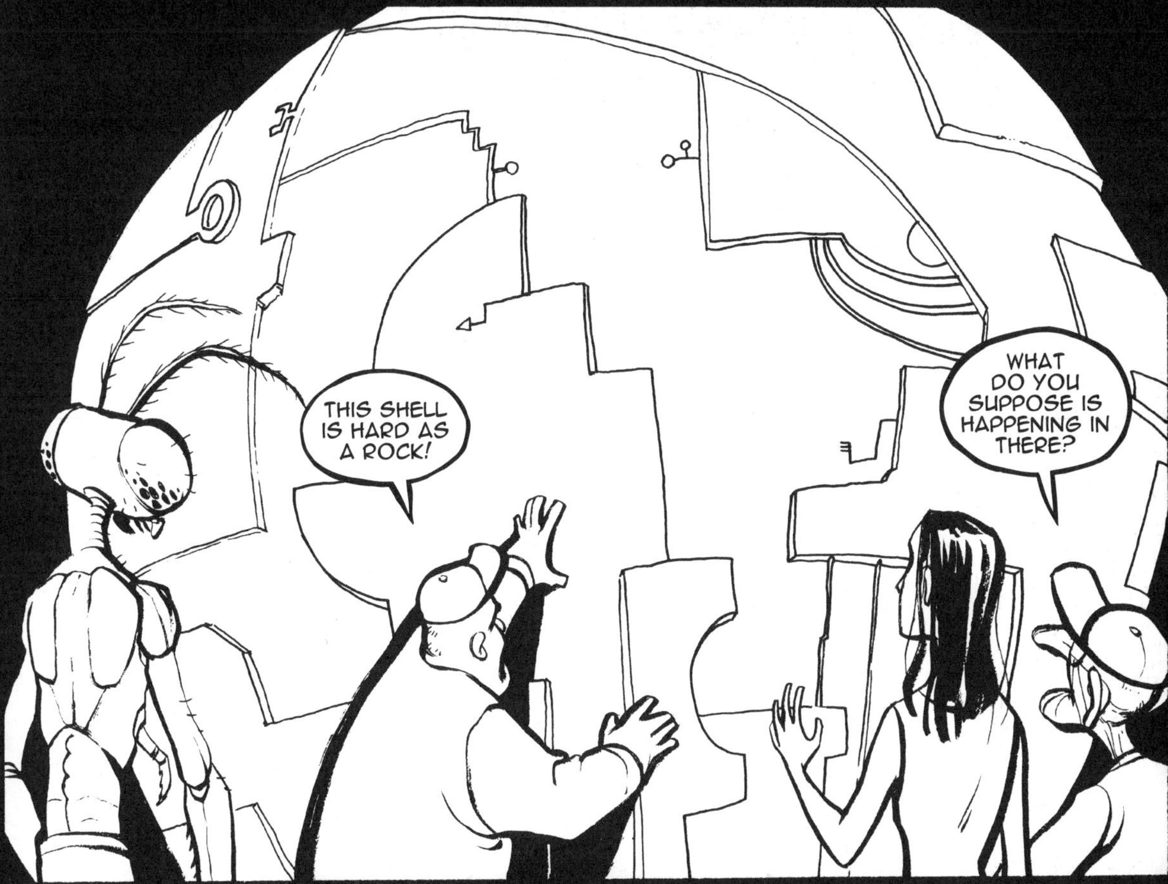
THIS SHELL IS HARD AS A ROCK!
WHAT DO YOU SUPPOSE IS HAPPENING IN THERE?

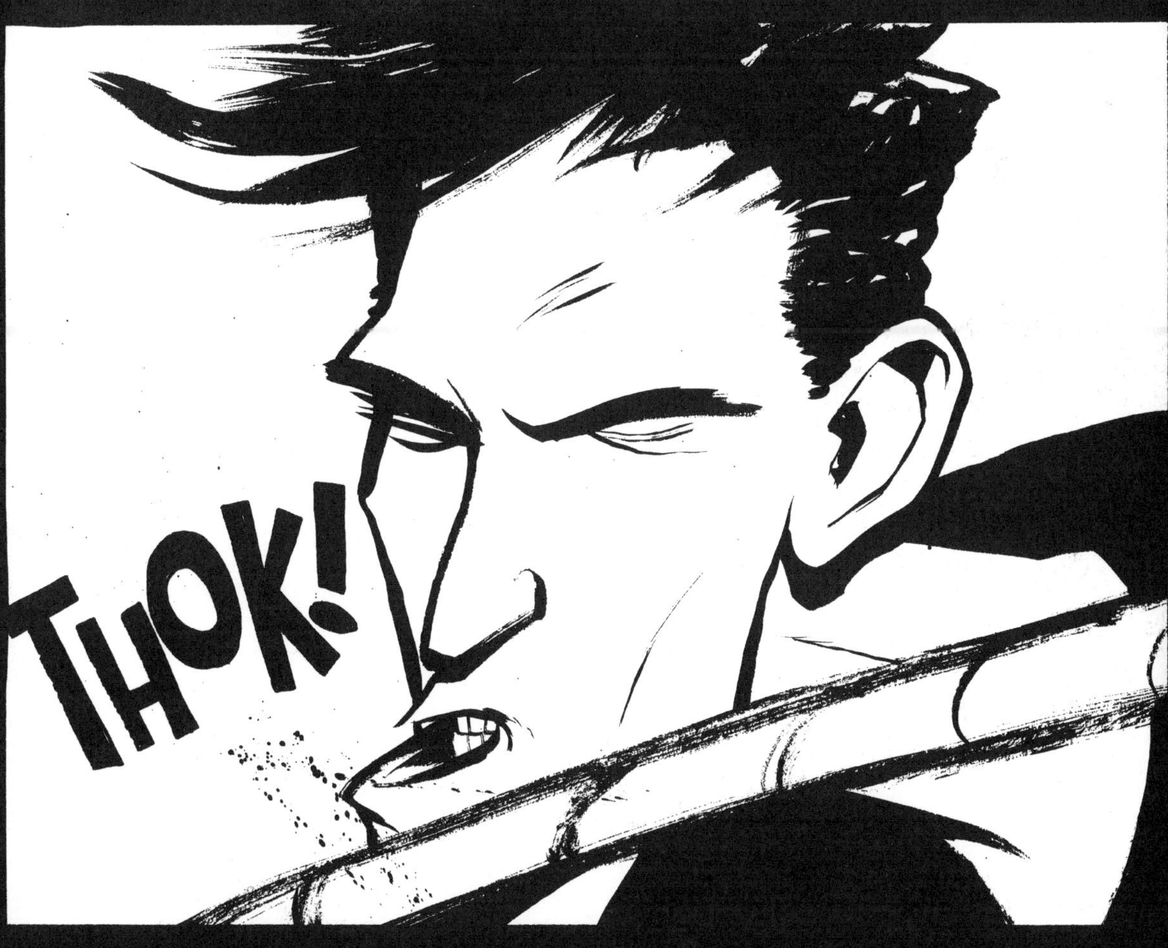
THOK!

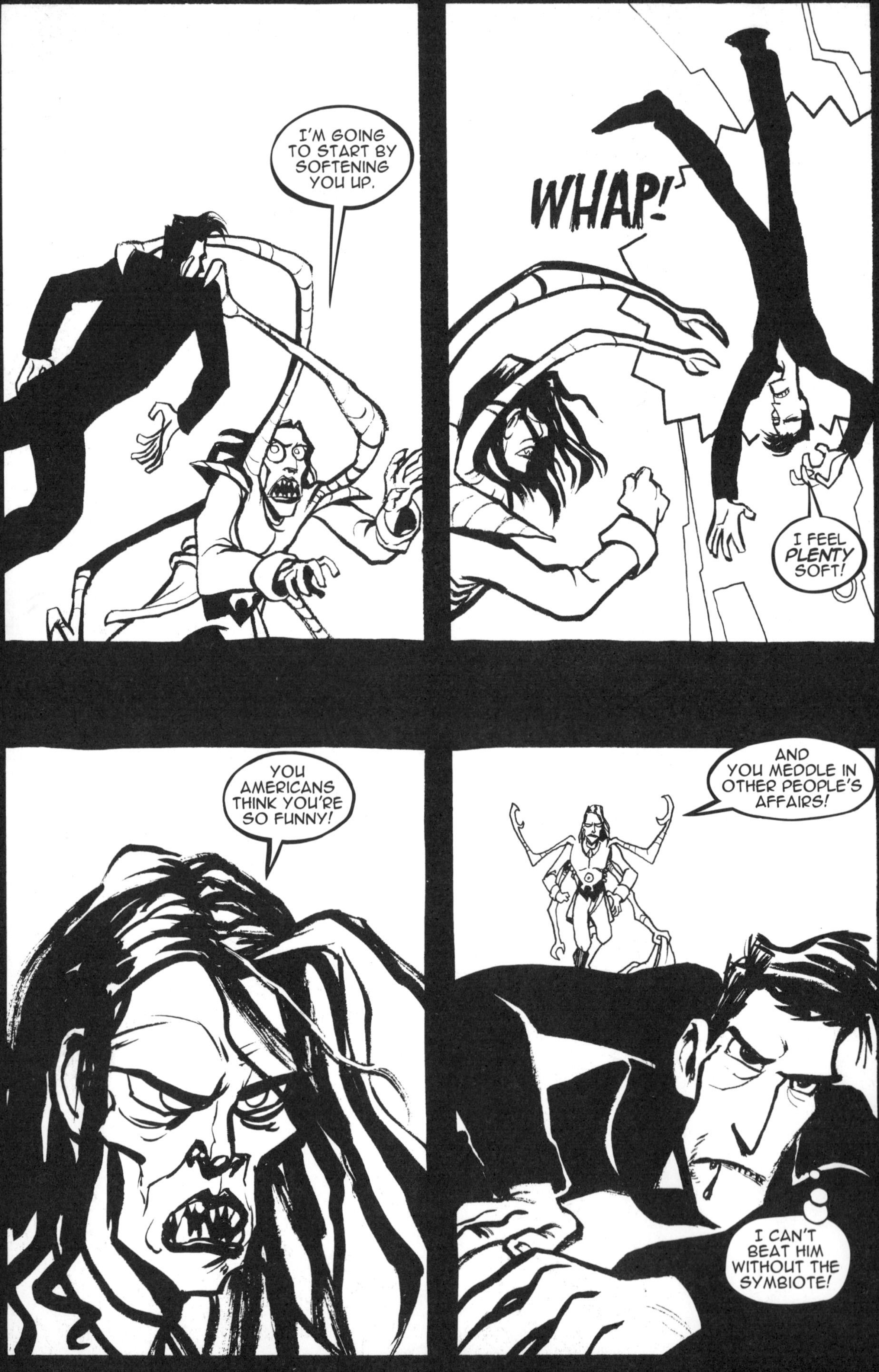

I'M GOING TO START BY SOFTENING YOU UP.
WHAP!
I FEEL PLENTY SOFT!
YOU AMERICANS THINK YOU'RE SO FUNNY!
AND YOU MEDDLE IN OTHER PEOPLE'S AFFAIRS!
I CAN'T BEAT HIM WITHOUT THE SYMBIOTE!

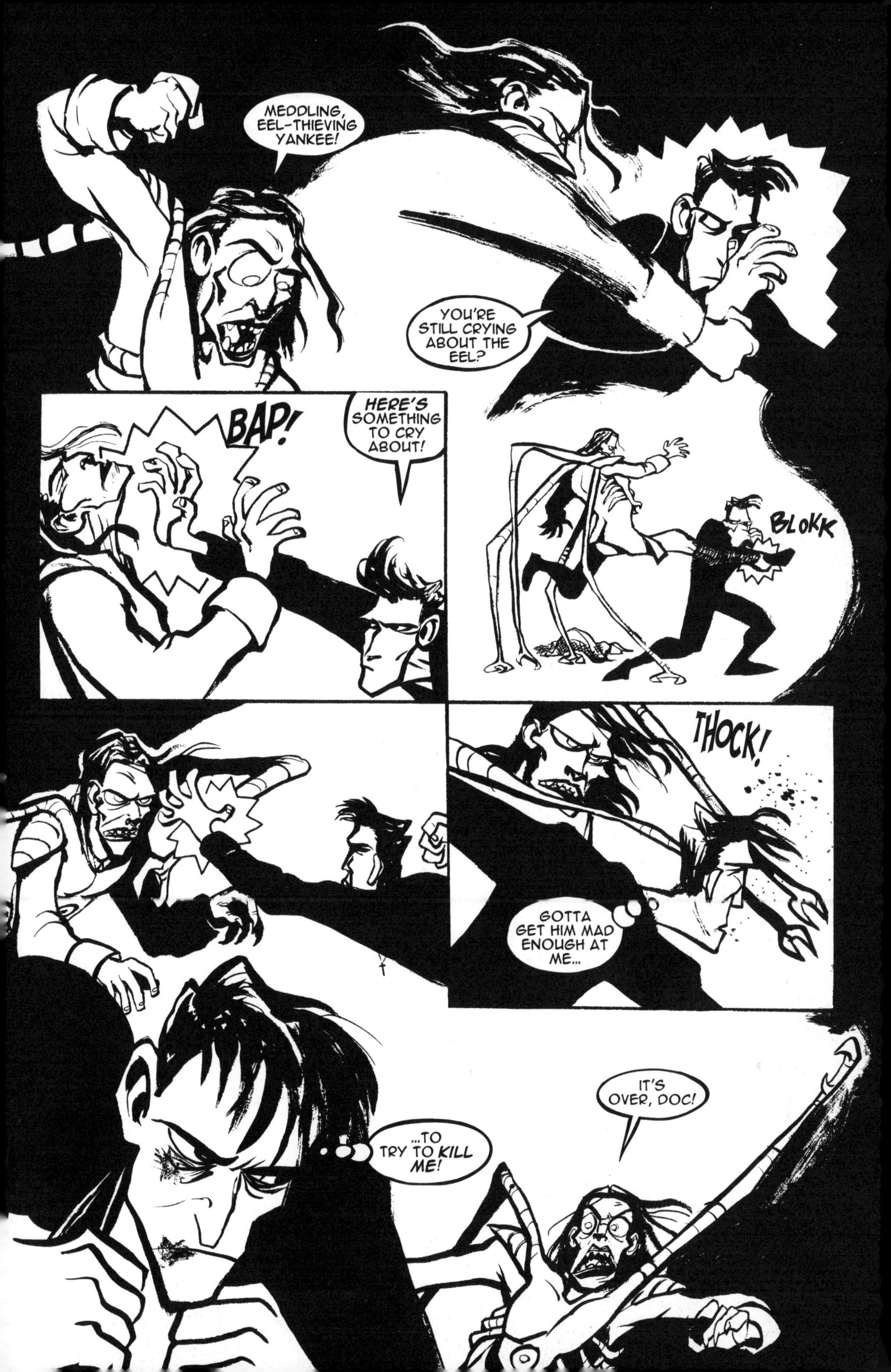
MEDDLING, EEL-THIEVING YANKEE!
YOU'RE STILL CRYING ABOUT THE EEL?
BAP!
HERE'S SOMETHING TO CRY ABOUT!
BLOKK
THOCK!
GOTTA GET HIM MAD ENOUGH AT ME...
...TO TRY TO KILL ME!
IT'S OVER, DOC!

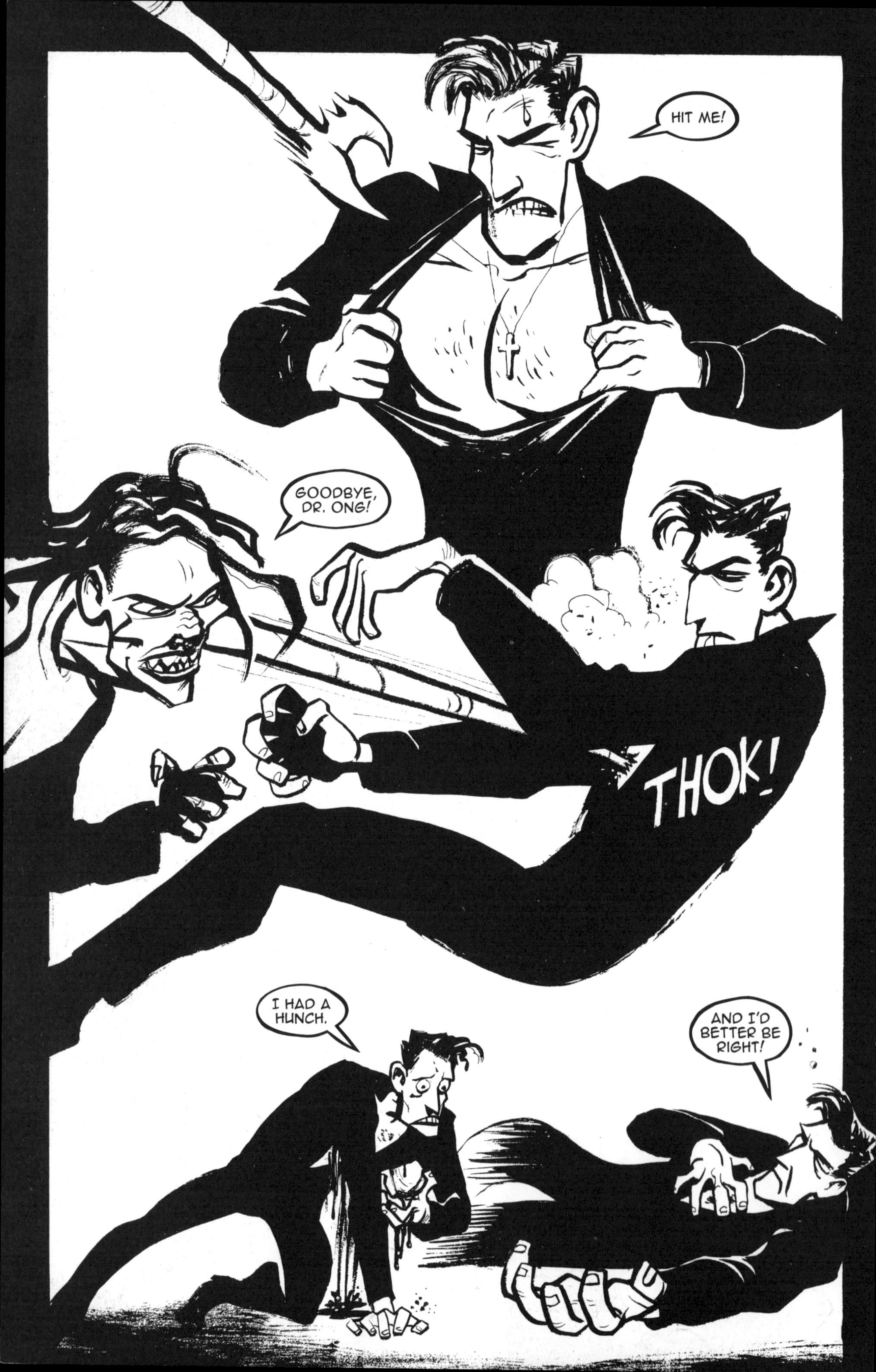
HIT ME!
GOODBYE, DR. ONG!
THOK!
I HAD A HUNCH.
AND I'D BETTER BE RIGHT!

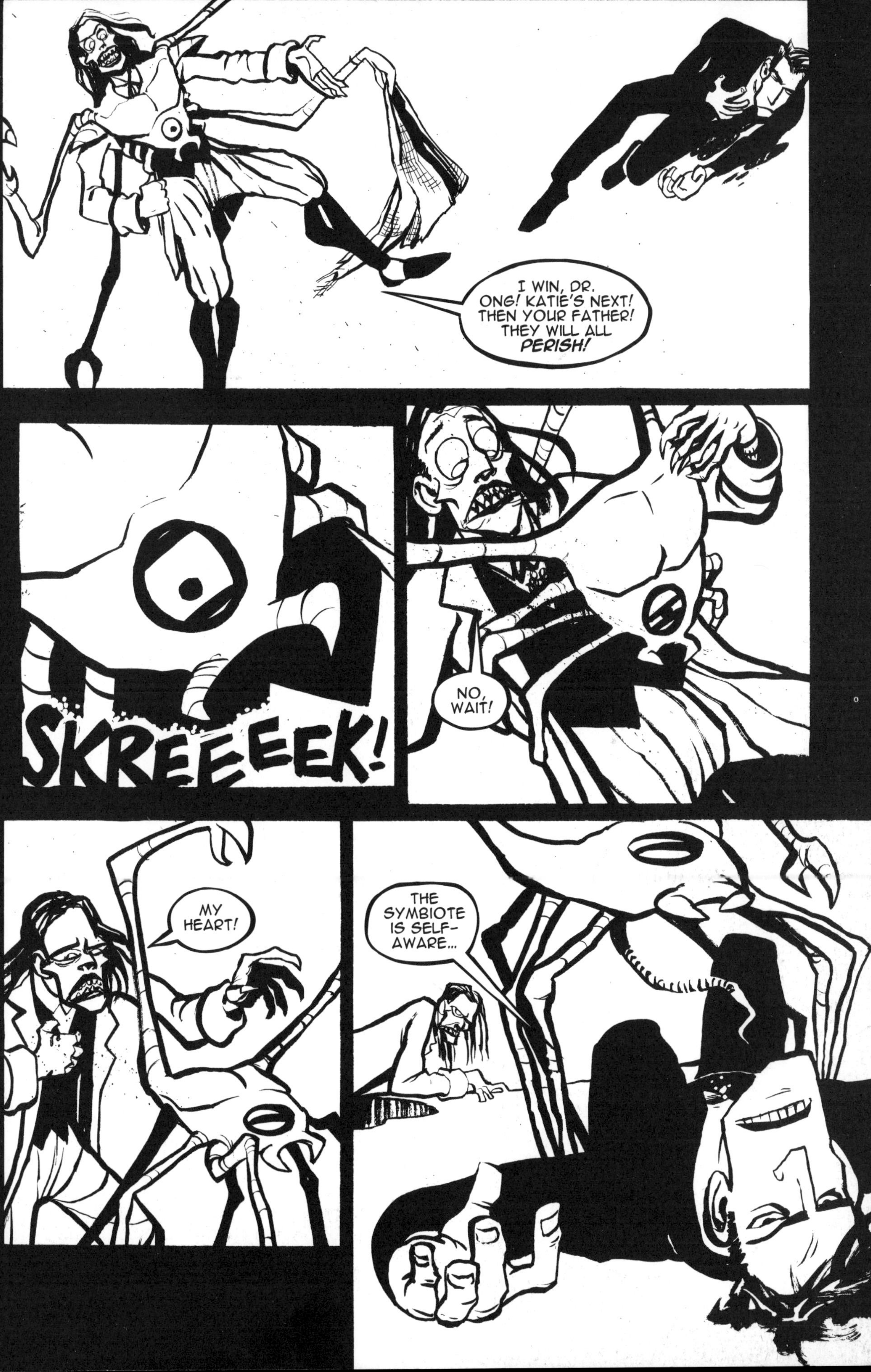
I WIN, DR. ONG! KATIE'S NEXT! THEN YOUR FATHER! THEY WILL ALL PERISH!
SKREEEEK!
NO, WAIT!
MY HEART!
THE SYMBIOTE IS SELF-AWARE...

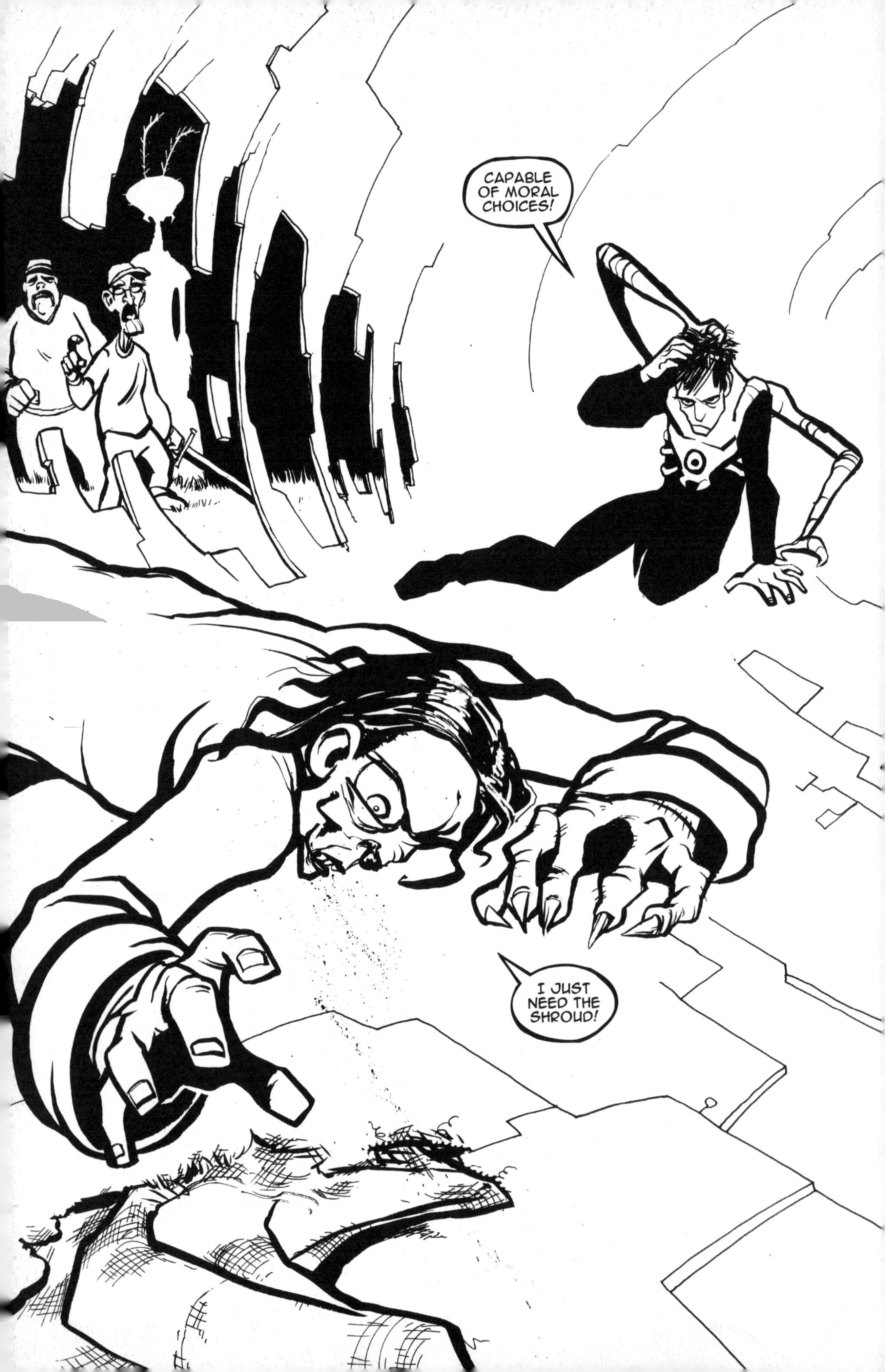
CAPABLE OF MORAL CHOICES!
I JUST NEED THE SHROUD!

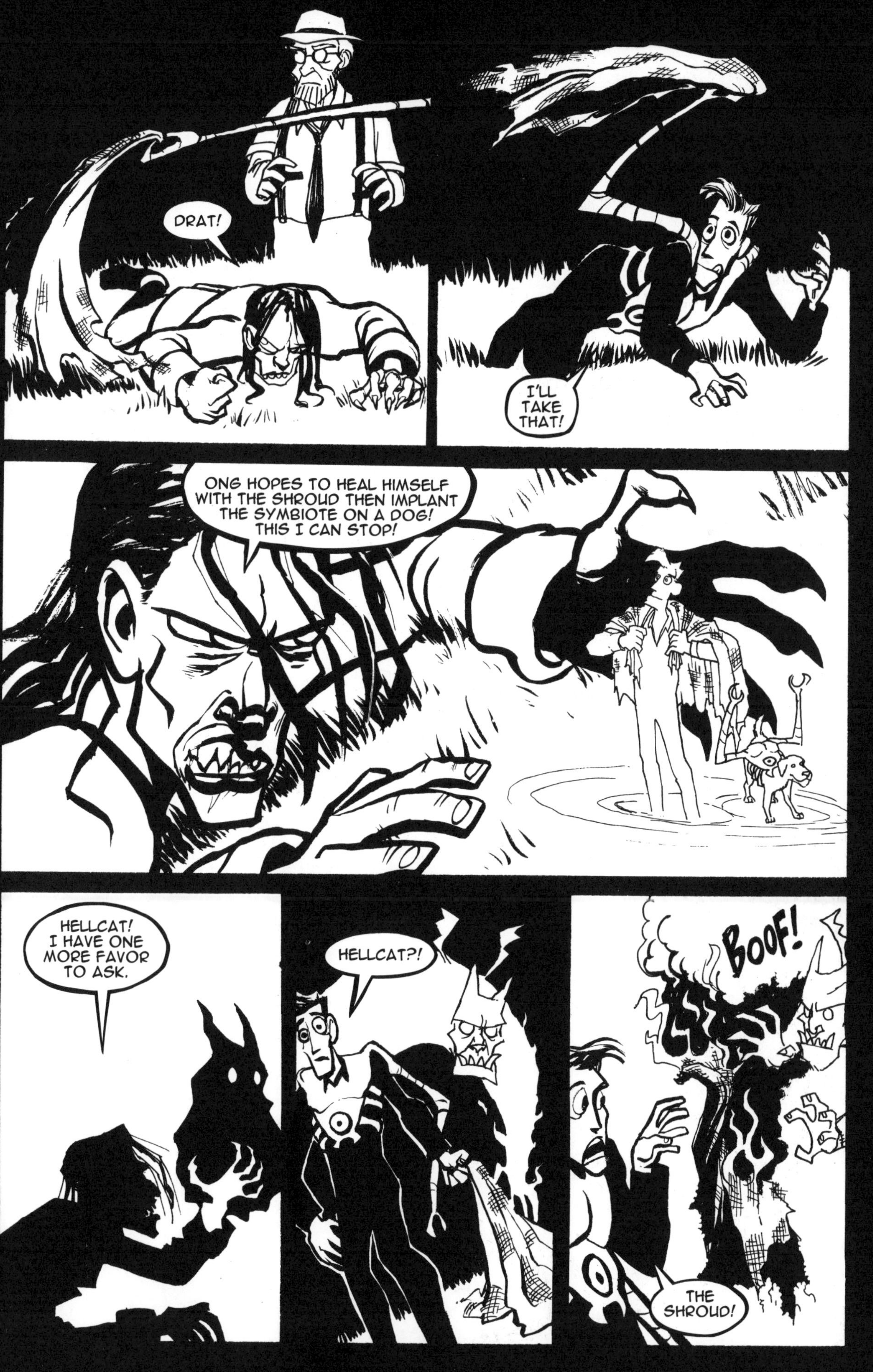
DRAT!
I'LL TAKE THAT!
ONG HOPES TO HEAL HIMSELF WITH THE SHROUD THEN IMPLANT THE SYMBIOTE ON A DOG! THIS I CAN STOP!
HELLCAT! I HAVE ONE MORE FAVOR TO ASK.
HELLCAT?!
BOOF!
THE SHROUD!

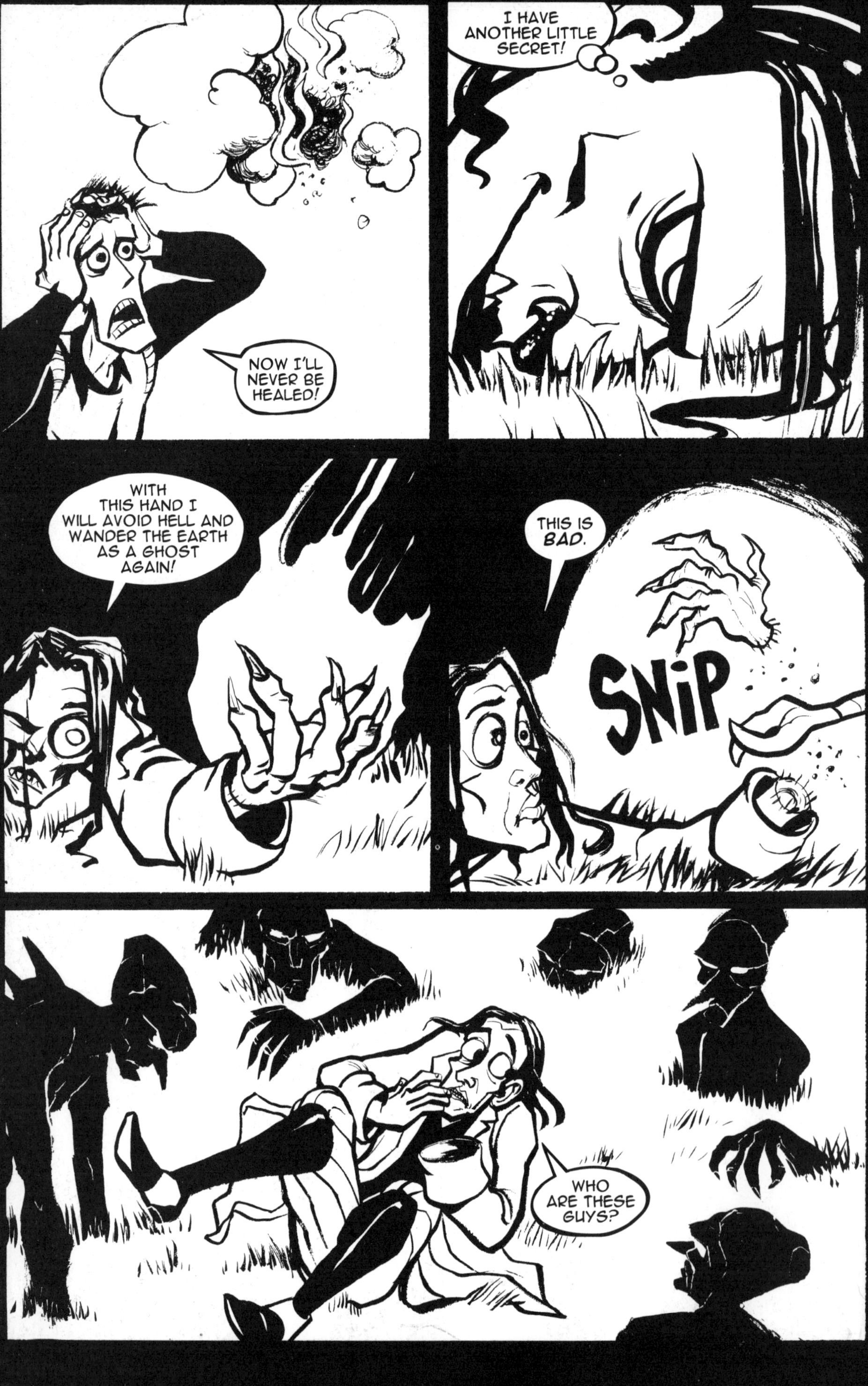
NOW I'LL NEVER BE HEALED!
I HAVE ANOTHER LITTLE SECRET!
WITH THIS HAND I WILL AVOID HELL AND WANDER THE EARTH AS A GHOST AGAIN!
THIS IS BAD.
SNIP
WHO ARE THESE GUYS?

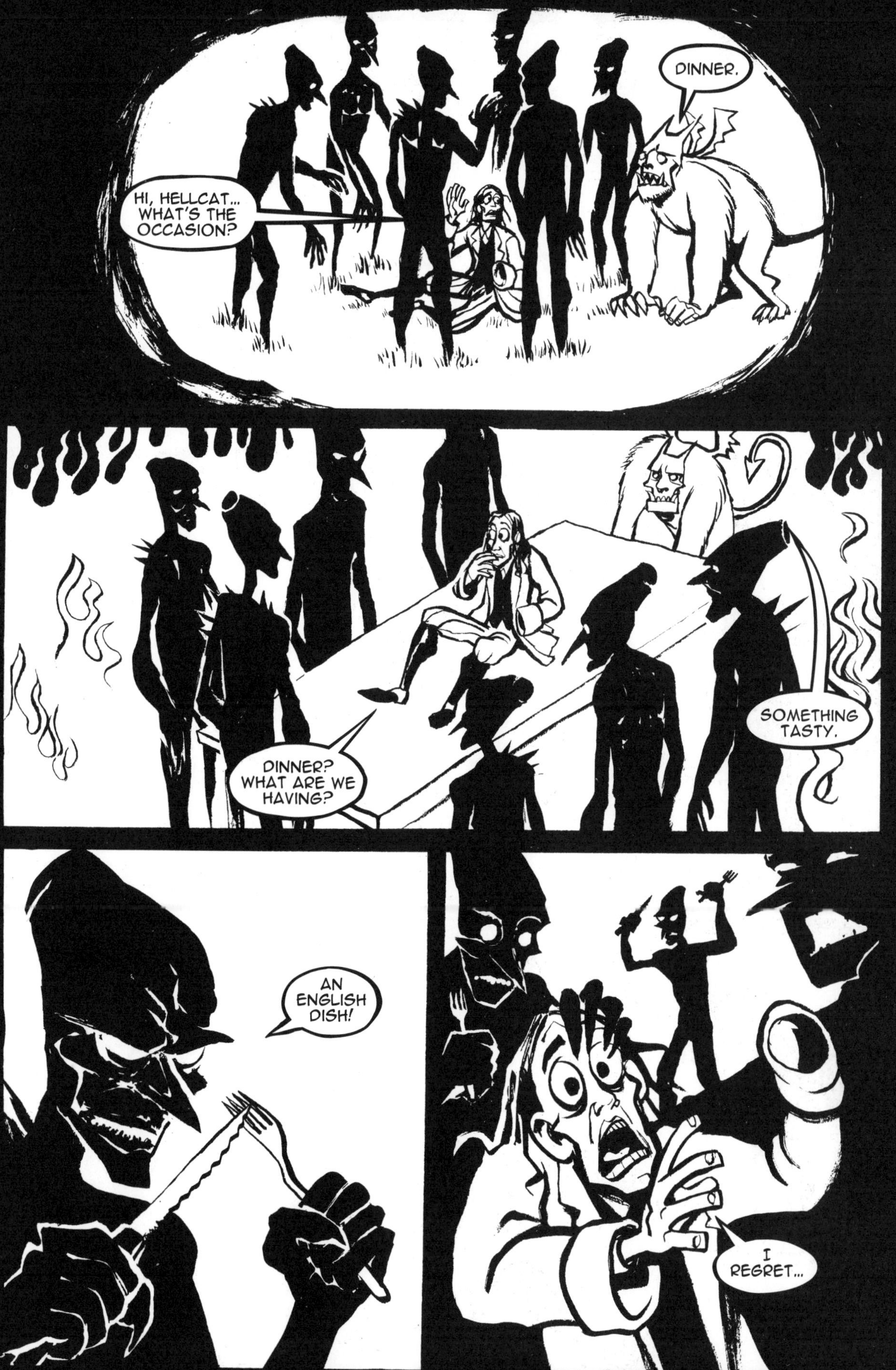
HI, HELLCAT... WHAT'S THE OCCASION?
DINNER.
DINNER? WHAT ARE WE HAVING?
SOMETHING TASTY.
AN ENGLISH DISH!
I REGRET...

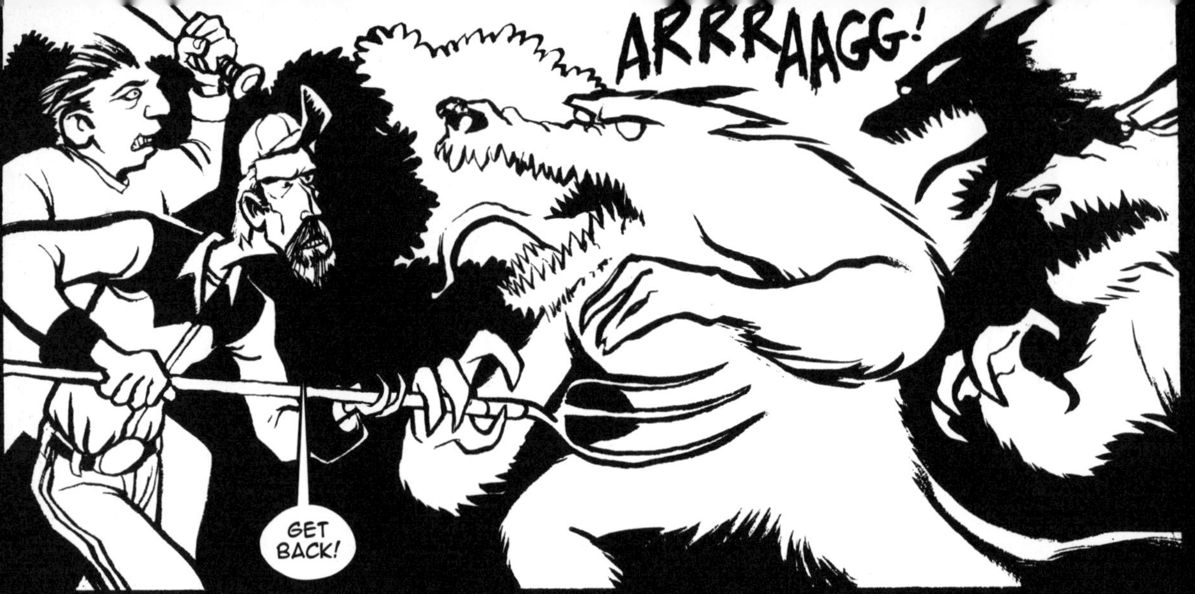
ARRRAAGG!
GET BACK!

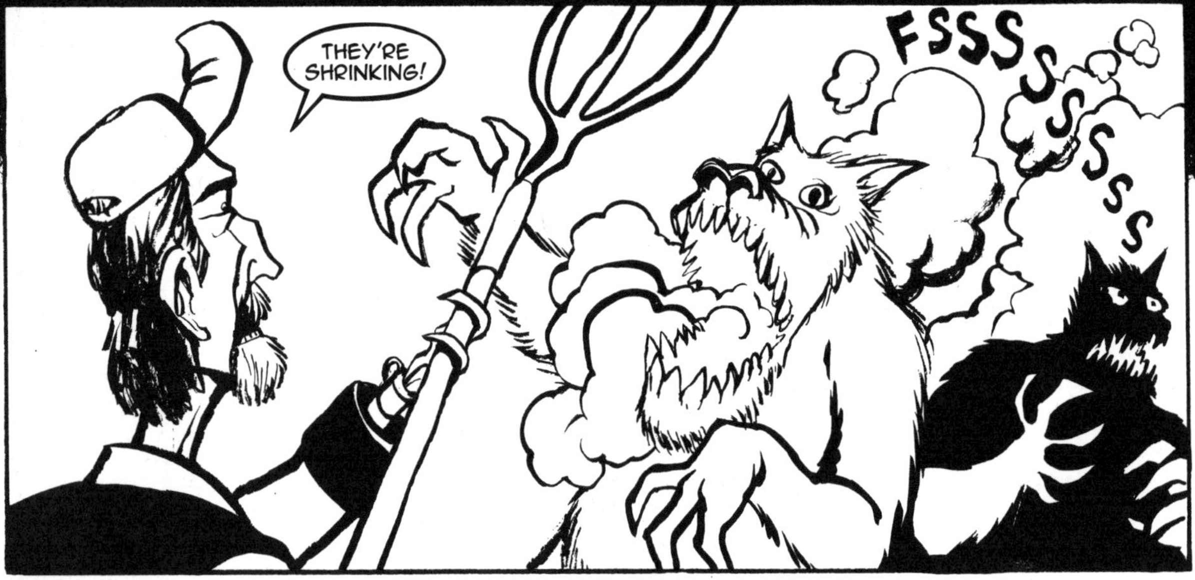
THEY'RE SHRINKING!
FSSSSSSSSSS

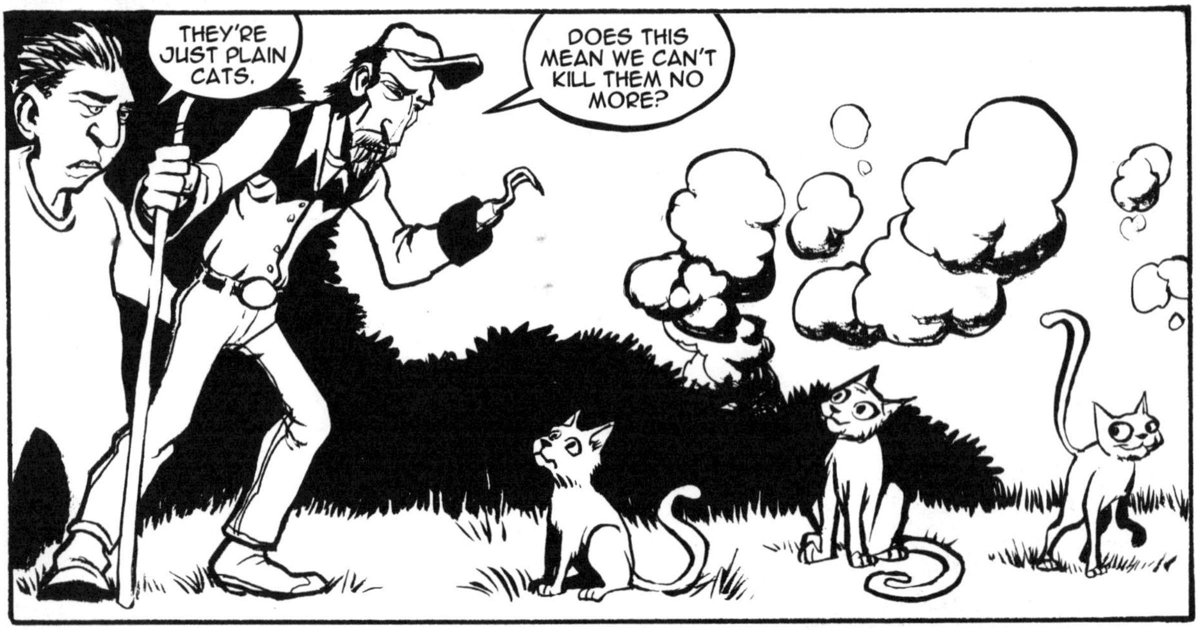
THEY'RE JUST PLAIN CATS.
DOES THIS MEAN WE CAN'T KILL THEM NO MORE?

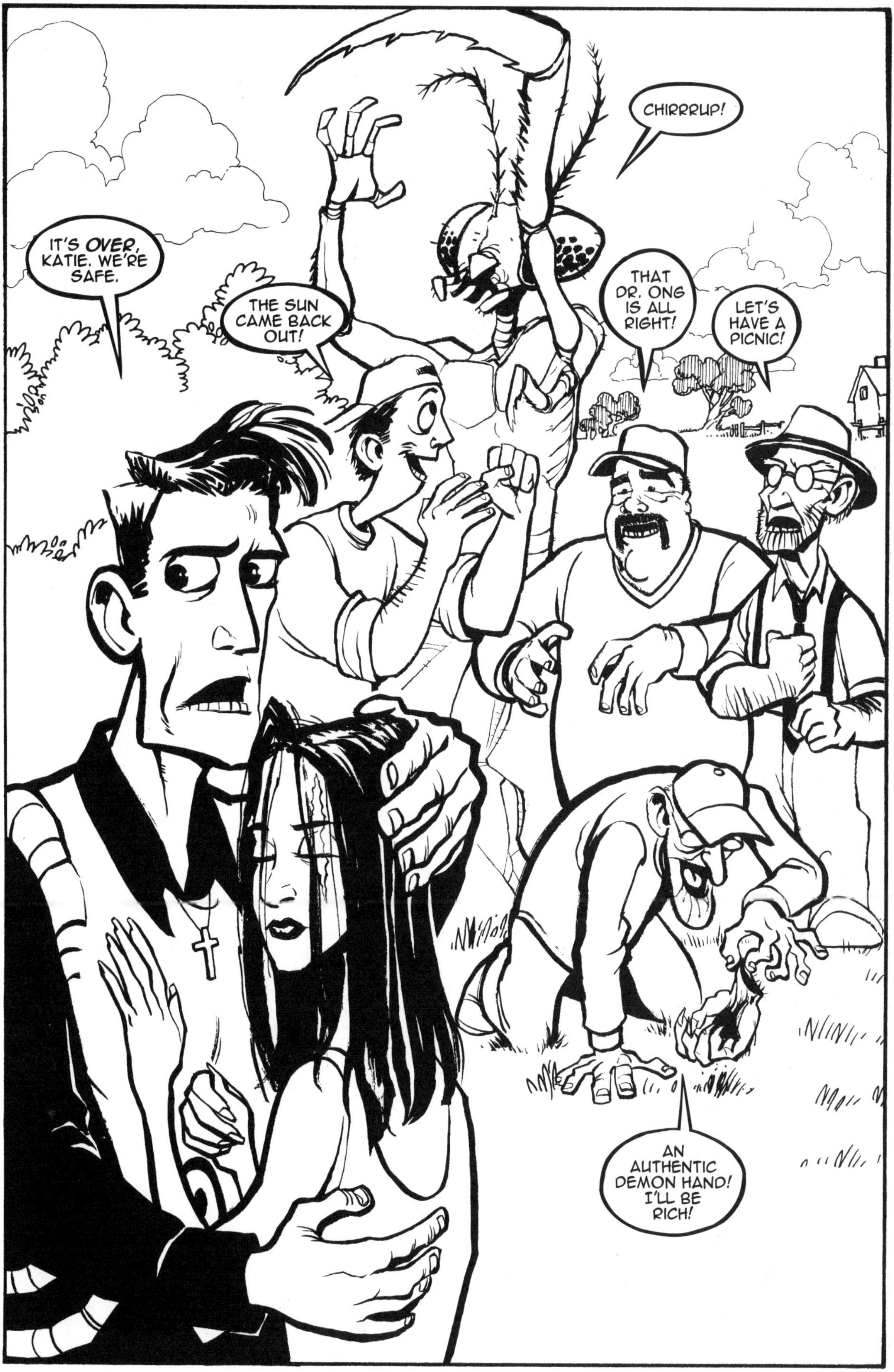
IT'S OVER, KATIE. WE'RE SAFE.
THE SUN CAME BACK OUT!
CHIRRRUP!
THAT DR. ONG IS ALL RIGHT!
LET'S HAVE A PICNIC!
AN AUTHENTIC DEMON HAND! I'LL BE RICH!

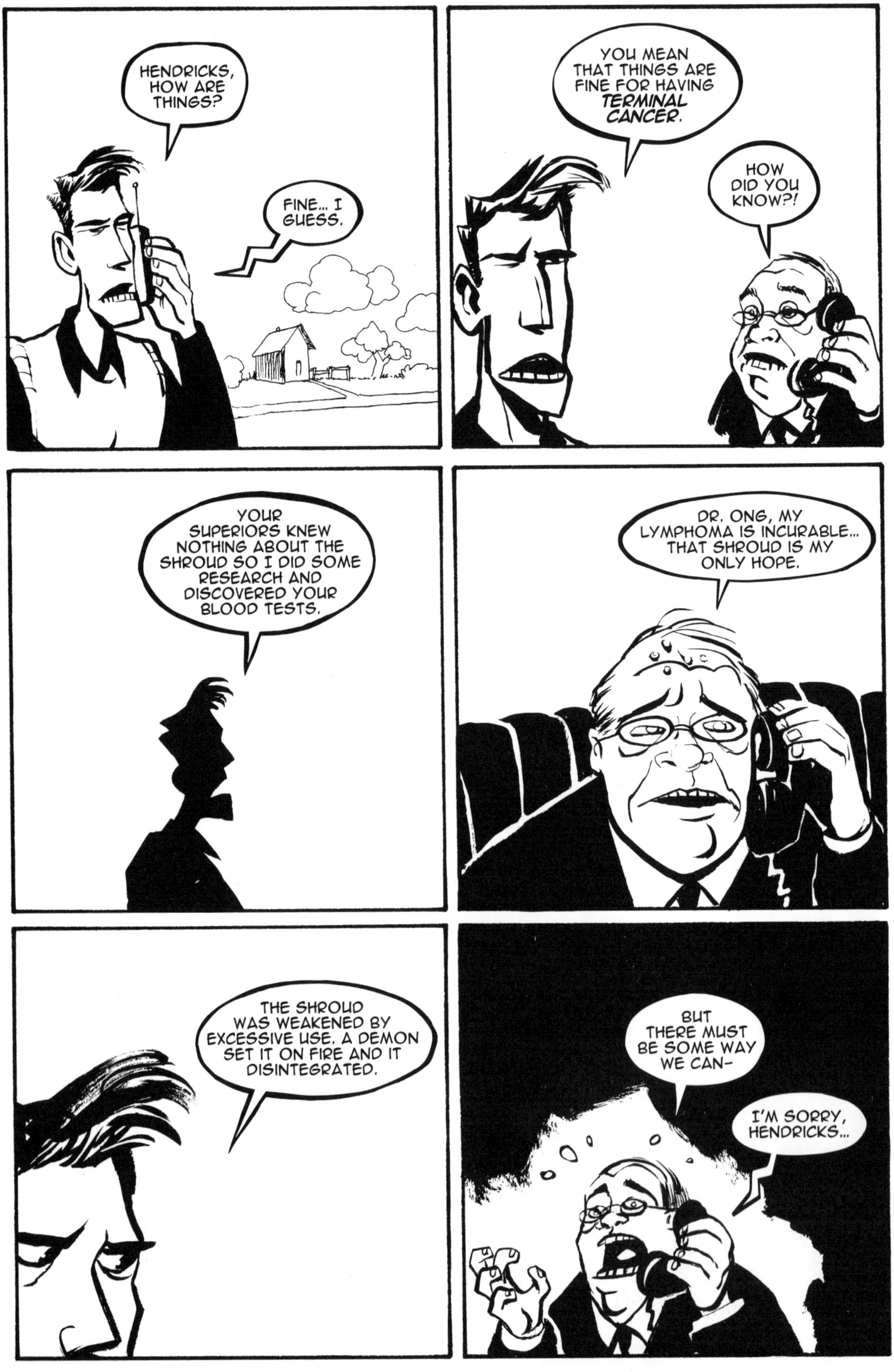
HENDRICKS, HOW ARE THINGS?
FINE... I GUESS.
YOU MEAN THAT THINGS ARE FINE FOR HAVING TERMINAL CANCER.
HOW DID YOU KNOW?!
YOUR SUPERIORS KNEW NOTHING ABOUT THE SHROUD SO I DID SOME RESEARCH AND DISCOVERED YOUR BLOOD TESTS.
DR. ONG, MY LYMPHOMA IS INCURABLE... THAT SHROUD IS MY ONLY HOPE.
THE SHROUD WAS WEAKENED BY EXCESSIVE USE. A DEMON SET IT ON FIRE AND IT DISINTEGRATED.
BUT THERE MUST BE SOME WAY WE CAN-
I'M SORRY, HENDRICKS...

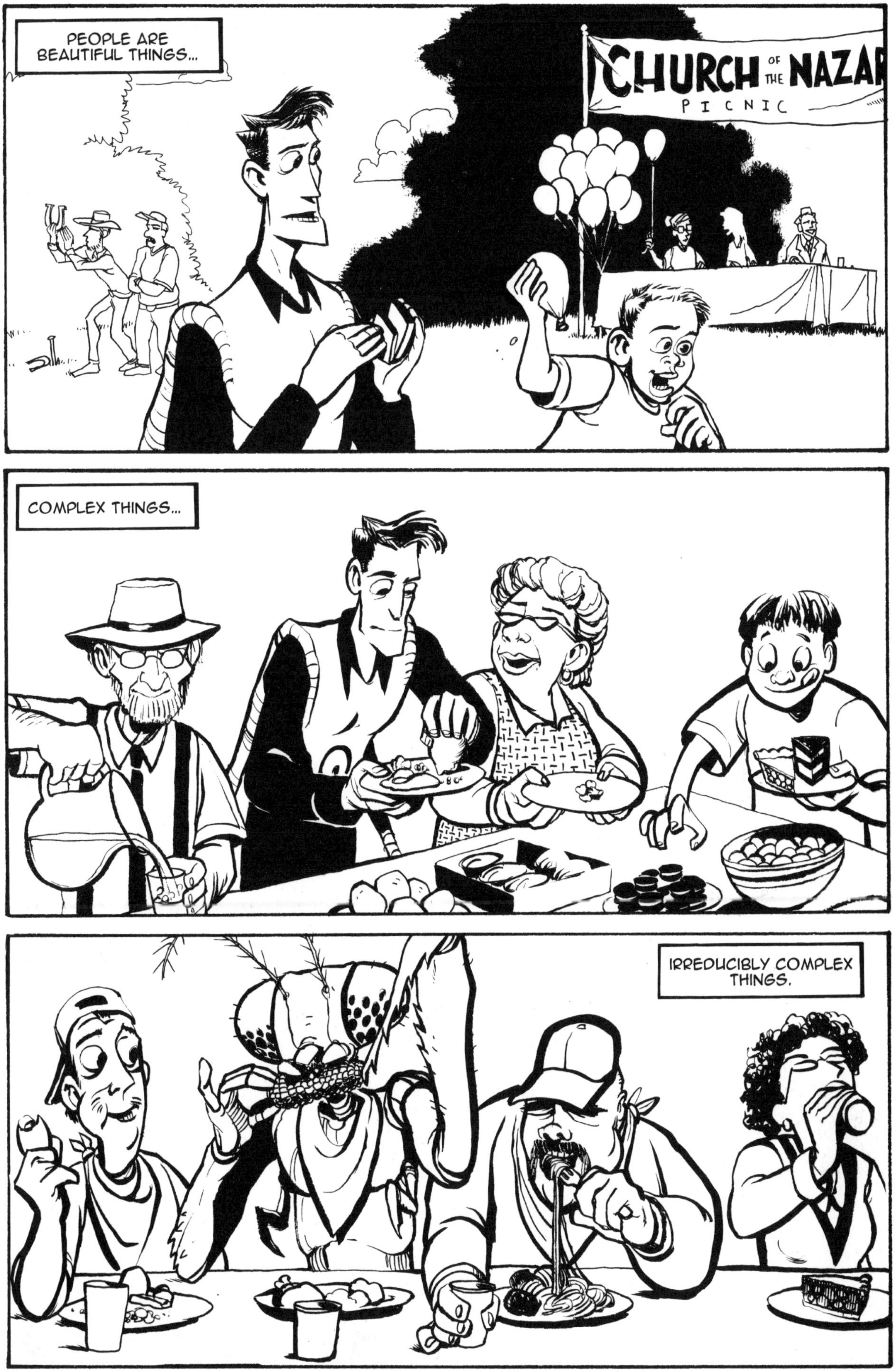
PEOPLE ARE BEAUTIFUL THINGS...
CHURCH OF THE NAZAR
PICNIC
COMPLEX THINGS...
IRREDUCIBLY COMPLEX THINGS.

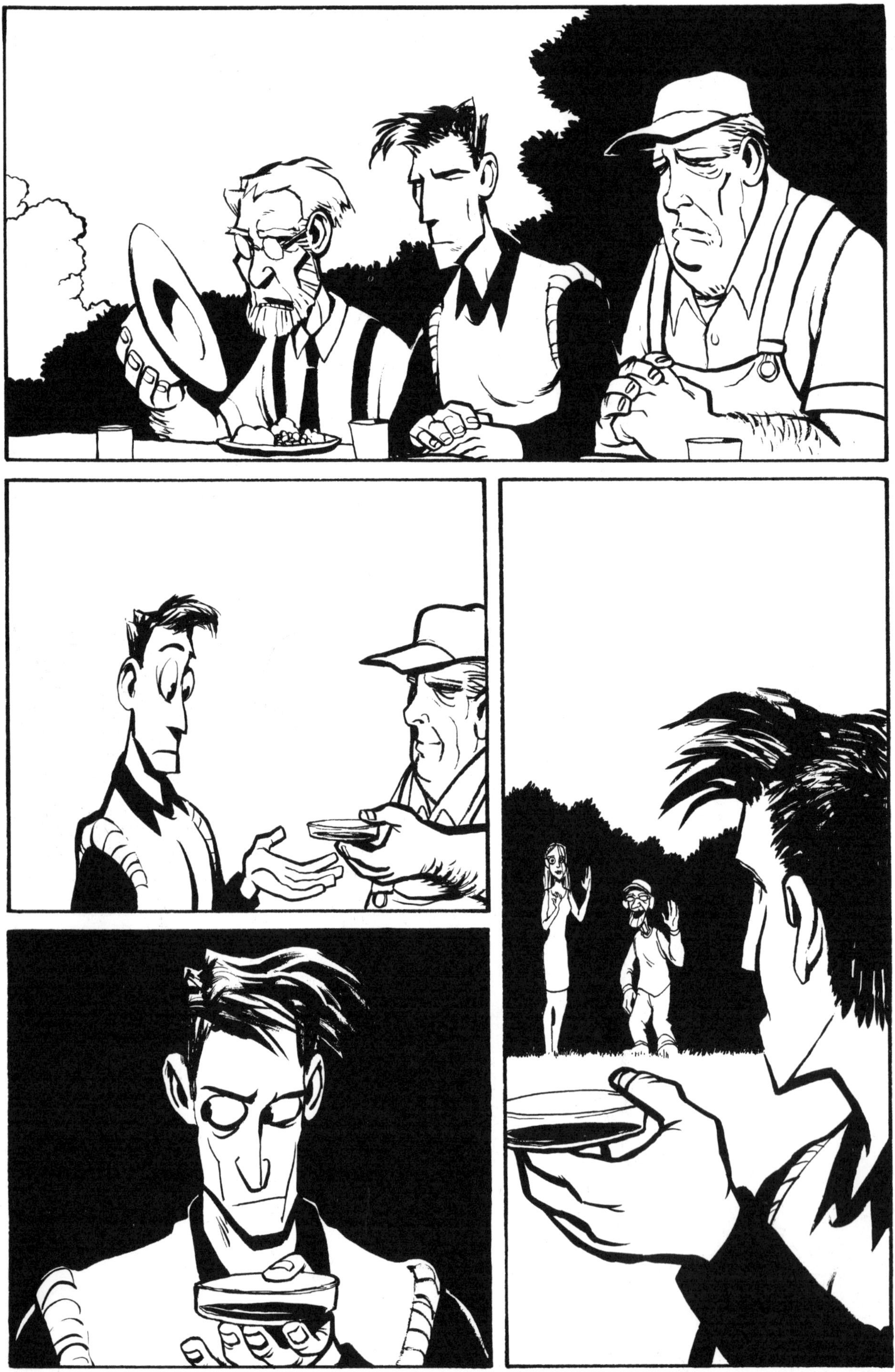

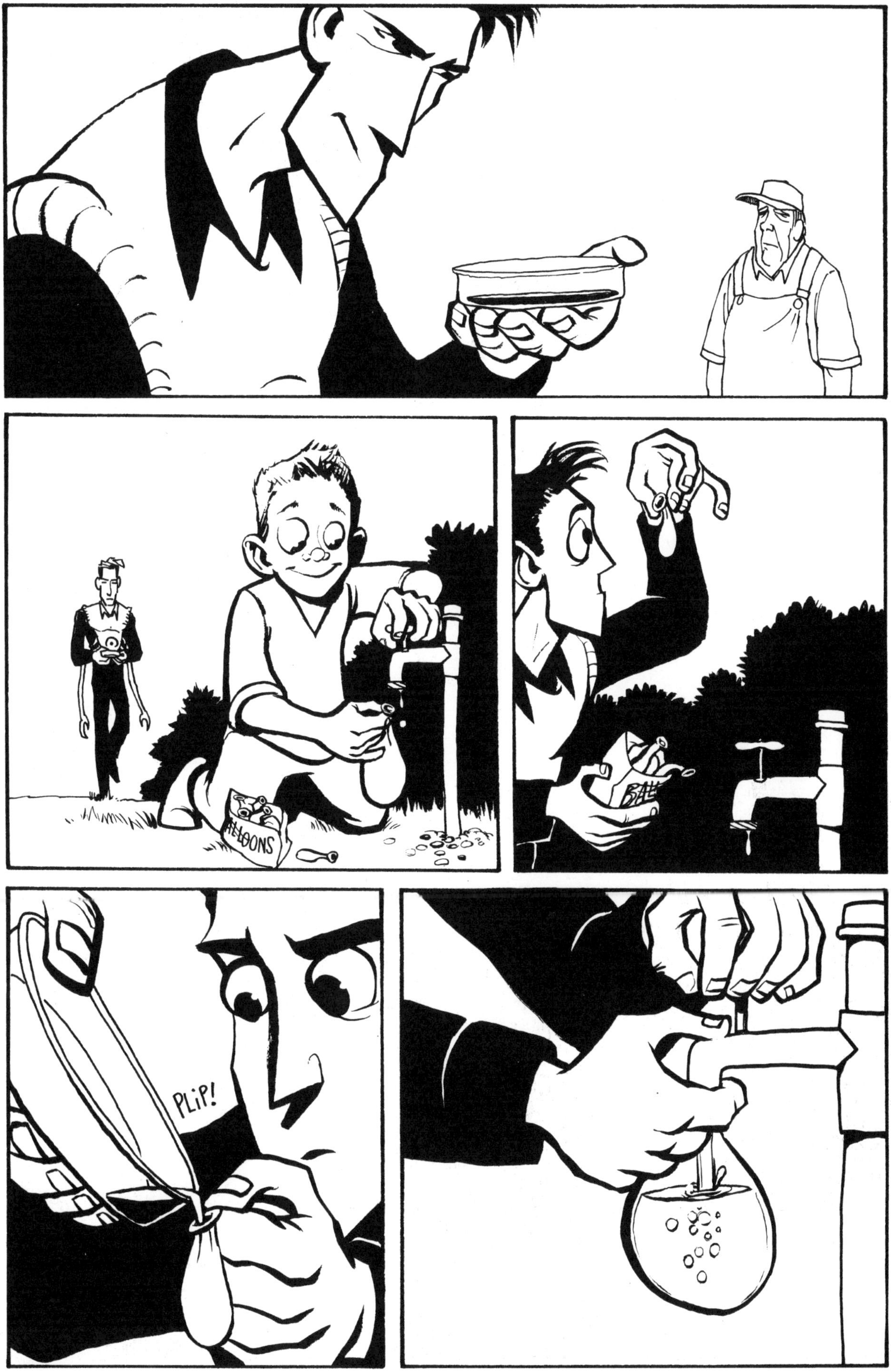
ALLOONS
PLIP!

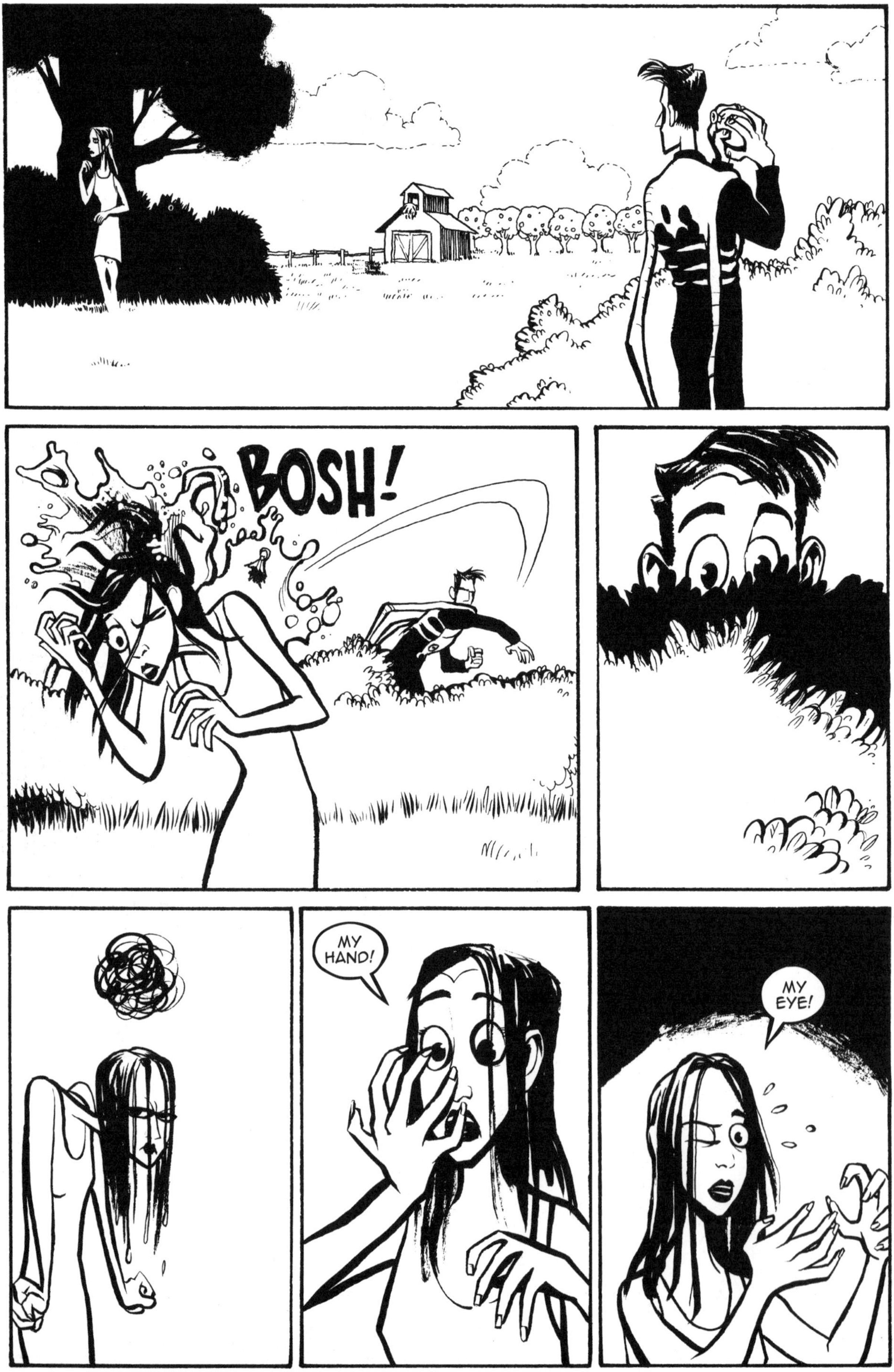
BOSH!
MY HAND!
MY EYE!

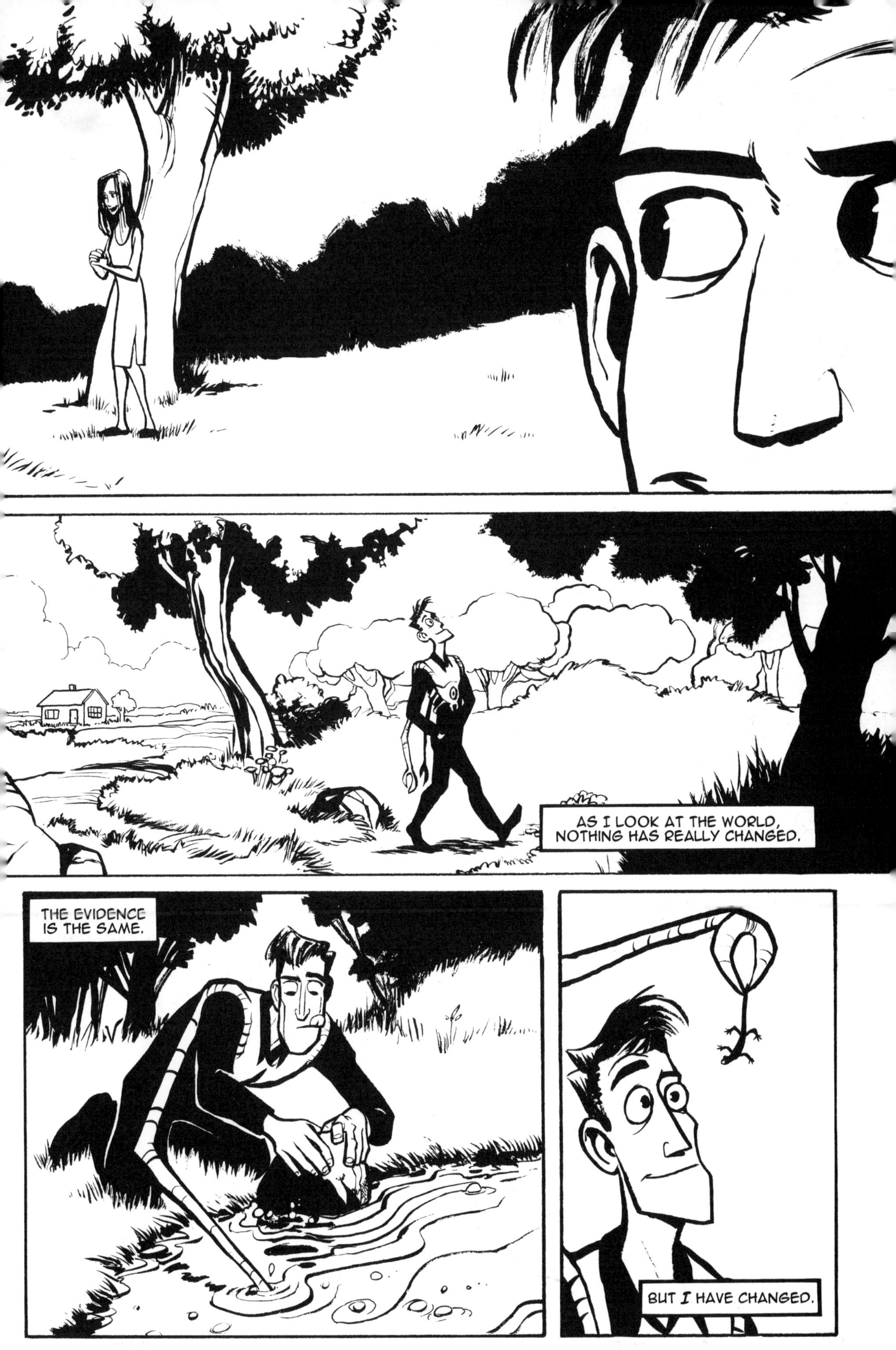
AS I LOOK AT THE WORLD,
NOTHING HAS REALLY CHANGED.
THE EVIDENCE
IS THE SAME.
BUT *I* HAVE CHANGED.

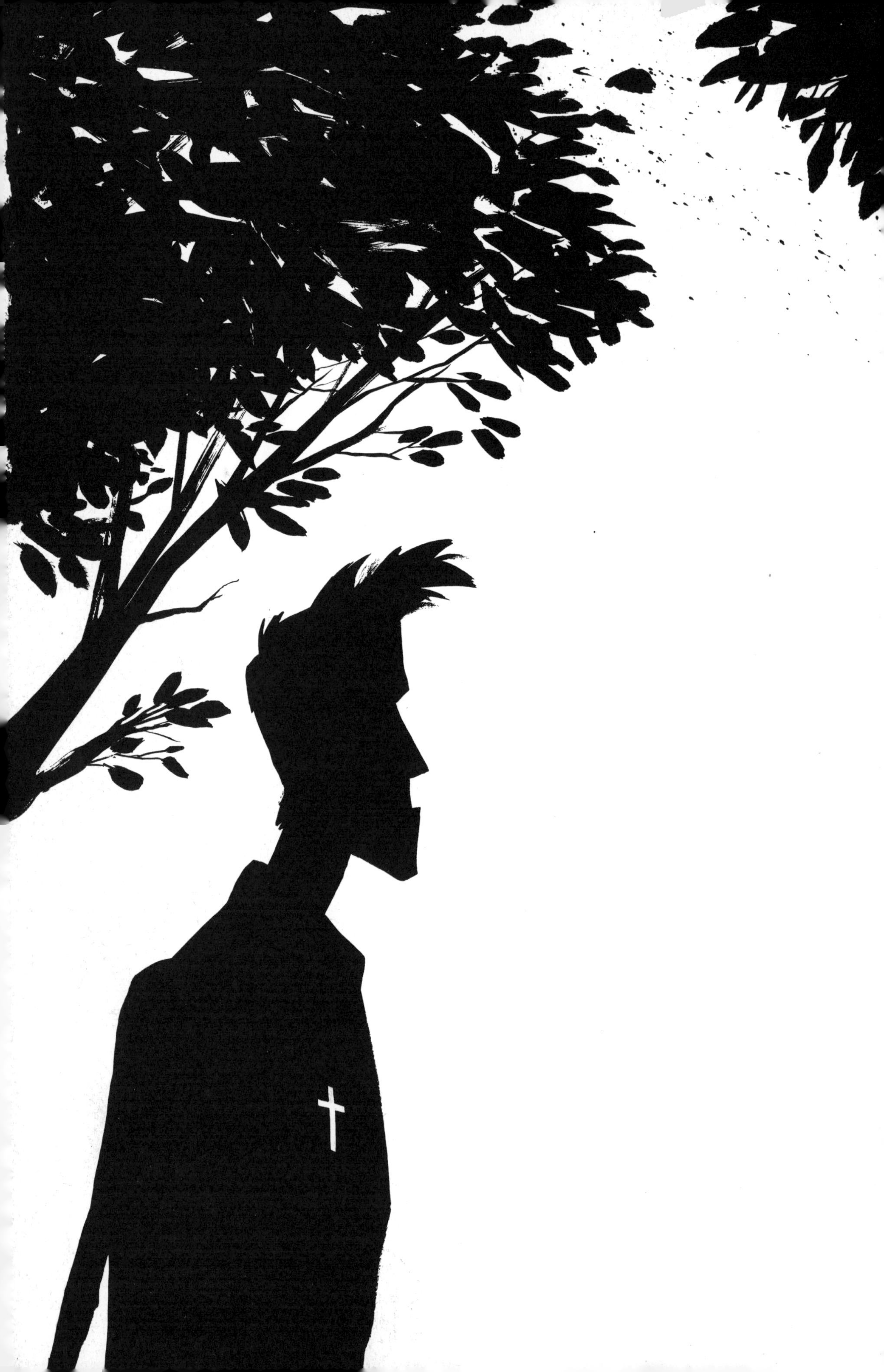

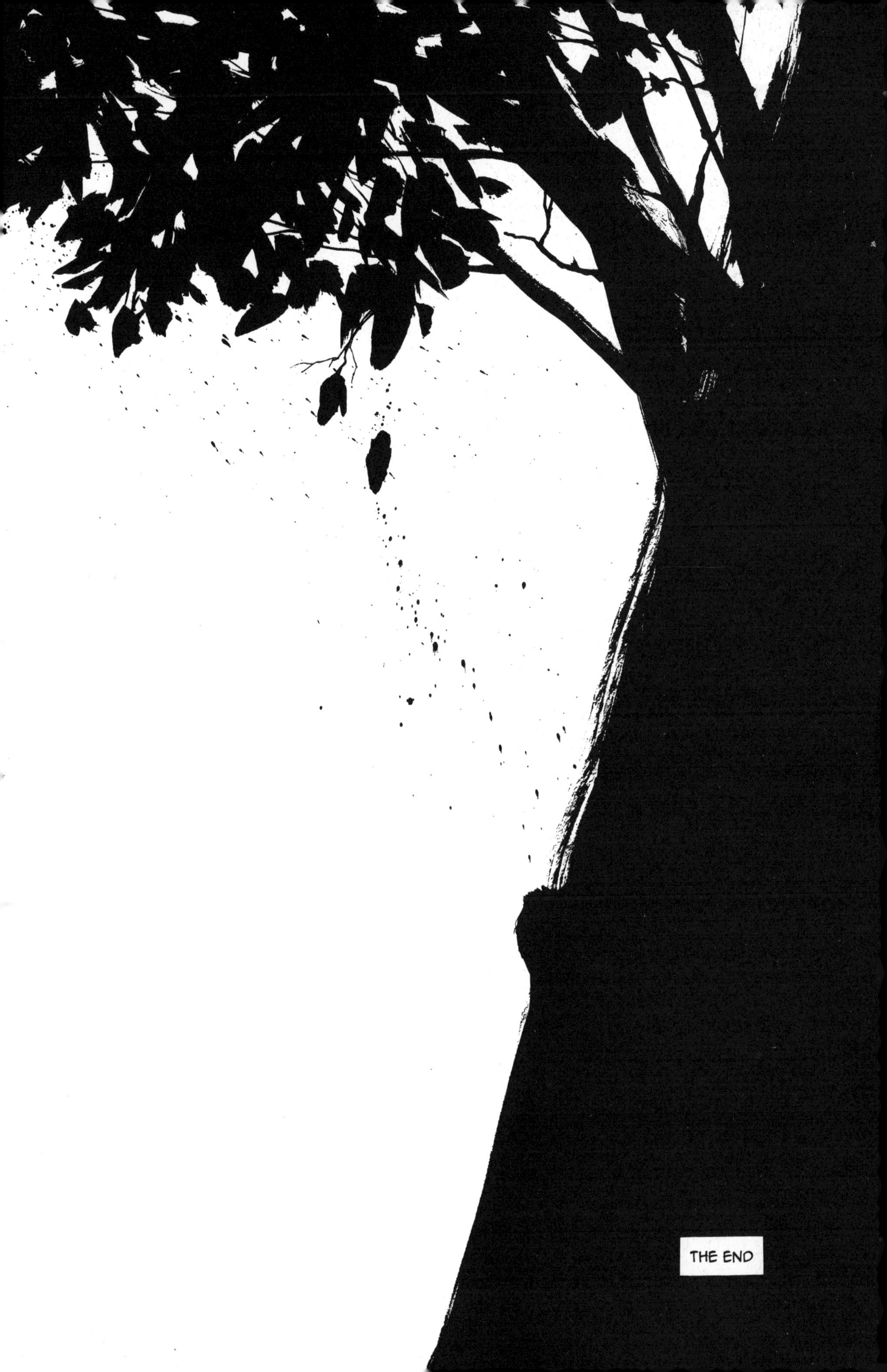
THE END

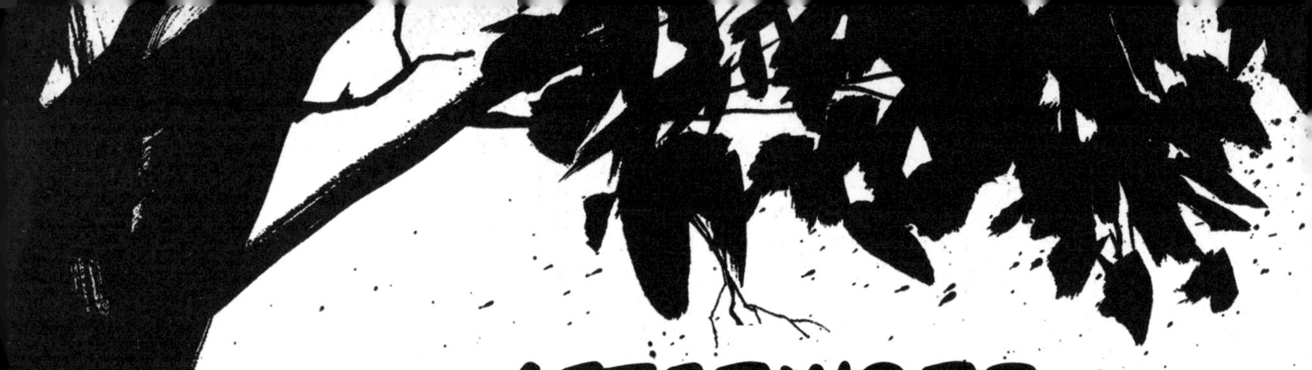

AFTERWORD

IT'S BEEN TEN YEARS SINCE I STARTED WRITING A SCRIPT FOR CREATURE TECH. THE GRAPHIC NOVEL HAS BEEN AROUND FOR SO LONG THAT IT SEEMS TO HAVE ALWAYS BEEN FINISHED, AS IF THE LEGEND OF THE FLYING SPACE EEL WAS ALWAYS HOVERING AROUND TURLOCK, CALIFORNIA. BUT, JUST OVER TEN YEARS AGO I HAD A STREAM OF DETAILS WITH NO HOME FOR THEM. LIKE PIRANDILLO'S SIX CHARACTERS IN SEARCH OF AN AUTHOR I HAD THESE FREAKY ICONOCLASTIC ELEMENTS IN SEARCH OF A PLOT.

THE FIRST TO COME ALONG WAS THE HERO, DR. ONG. HIS NAME LIKELY CAME TO ME FIRST, SINCE I'VE ALWAYS LOVED THAT NAME. DR. MICHAEL ONG. AFTER THE BOOK WAS PUBLISHED I GOT AN EMAIL FROM A REAL LIFE DR. MICHAEL ONG WHO WAS TICKLED TO COINCIDENTALLY HAVE HIS NAME IN A BOOK. I HAD A NUMBER OF VISIONS OF A GIANT, MILE LONG, FLYING SPACE EEL. HE WAS A FLOATING HARBINGER OF DOOM, WANDERING INTO OUR GALAXY FROM SOME OTHER GALAXY WHERE HE MIGHT EVEN BE CONSIDERED A SMALL CREATURE.

I'VE BEEN ACCUSED OF BEING CREATIVE BUT I'M NOT CONVINCED. A CREATIVE PERSON COULD PROBABLY WRITE A FEW STORIES WITHOUT HAVING TO RESORT TO A GIANT FLYING SPACE EEL AS THE CLIMAX BUT NOT ME. I WOULD PUT THAT GIANT EEL INTO EVERY SHORT STORY, COMIC STRIP AND VIDEO GAME DESIGN FOR YEARS. SAME WITH THE BUG MAN ON A MOTORCYCLE. AFTER SEEING THE WHISPY GIRL WITH A GIMPY HAND APPEAR IN SO MANY OF MY DAYDREAMS I KNEW IT WAS TIME TO BRAIN DUMP THEM INTO A STORY. IT WAS TIME FOR CREATURE TECH.

APPARENTLY, MY IMAGINATION AND OBSESSIONS ARE SHARED WITH LIKE MINDS EVEN IN THE SCIENTIFIC COMMUNITY BECAUSE ON MARCH 9TH OF 2006 I WAS SHOCKED TO FIND THIS HEADLINE ON THE NEWSCIENTIST WEBSITE: "COSMIC 'EEL' PREYS ON SPIRAL GALAXY". THE ARTICLE REFERENCES AN IMAGE IN SPACE, "A GIANT SPACE "EEL" APPEARS TO BE CHASING AFTER A SPIRAL GALAXY IN THIS NEWLY RELEASED IMAGE FROM THE VICTOR M. BLANCO TELESCOPE IN CHILE."

WHEN I DECIDE TO CREATE ANYTHING I FEEL LIKE I'M FILLING A VOID. AS IF WHAT'S WRONG WITH THE UNIVERSE IS THAT THERE AREN'T ENOUGH STORIES THAT INCLUDE ATHEISTS WITH CREATURES ATTACHED TO THEIR CHESTS AND GIANT FLYING SPACE EELS. IT'S NICE WHEN THE UNIVERSE RESPONDS TO THE SAME CONTENT DEFICIT BY PRODUCING REAL LIFE IMAGES OF GIANT MILE LONG SPACE EELS. I'M STILL WAITING FOR A REDNECK MANTIS, BUT I'M CONFIDENT MY VISION WILL BE VINDICATED. IT'S JUST TOO NEAT-O TO BE IGNORED BY THE UNIVERSE.

DR. DEAN NELSON WAS MY CREATIVE WRITING PROFESSOR IN COLLEGE AND HE WARNED ME ABOUT PUTTING SEVEN-FOOT-TALL INSECTS AMONG NORMAL HUMANS INTO TOO MANY OF MY WRITING ASSIGNMENTS. HE KNEW IT WAS SOMETHING I WAS DOING AS A REFLEX AND NOT AS A CREATIVE IMPULSE. THAT OR I FEARED MY OWN SKILLS WEREN'T UP TO TASK TO WRITE ABOUT REAL MOMENTS WITH REAL PEOPLE. EITHER WAY, I NEEDED TO DUMP THE GIANT INSECT MAN SCHTICK, AND CREATURE TECH WAS THE BEST RECEPTACLE.

I SPENT MOST OF MY LIFE BEING 6'8" AND NOT FEELING VERY COMFORTABLE IN MY OWN SKIN. I WAS ALWAYS THE TALL SIDE KICK, AND HAVE BEEN ASKED IF I PLAY BASKETBALL MOST DAYS OF MY LIFE. IT FEELS A WHOLE LOT LIKE BEING A SEVEN-FOOT-TALL INSECT MAN IN TURLOCK, THE HOMETOWN WHERE I WENT THROUGH PUBERTY. IF I IDENTIFIED WITH ANY CHARACTER, IT WAS WITH BLUE. NOW YOU KNOW.

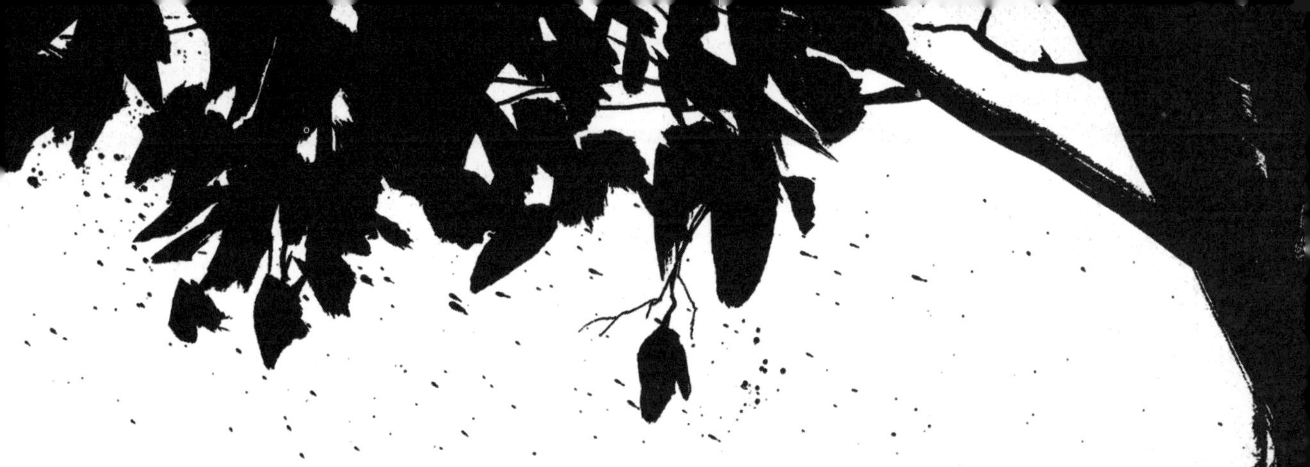

THE ODD BALL CHARACTERS COMING TOGETHER IS JUST THE BEGINNING OF MY CAR WRECK, BECAUSE I WAS BORN IN NORWALK, CALIFORNIA BEFORE MOVING TO MY SMALL FARMING COMMUNITY. SO THERE IS A LITTLE L.A. MIXED IN WITH MY FARMING COMMUNITY. I HAVE A DEEP LOVE FOR SCIENCE AS WELL AS A GREAT RESPECT FOR SMALL TOWN CHRISTIAN EVANGELICALS. THAT'S ODD ENOUGH, BUT I'M ALSO A GRAPHIC NOVELIST... PERHAPS THE ONLY PRO LIFE, CHRISTIAN, GRAPHIC NOVELIST WHO HAD ALSO SPENT TWELVE YEARS BATHED IN THE WRITINGS OF DARWIN, DAVID HUME AND NIETZSCHE. I LOVED STUDYING ART BUT ALSO LOVED TAKING PRE-MED HUMAN ANATOMY. I STUDIED THE OCCULT AND DEMON POSSESSION BUT ALSO RAISED AND ATTEMPTED TO BREED 15 SPECIES OF AMPHIBIANS. ALL OF THESE ELEMENTS WOULD BE THROWN INTO THE SOUP. I DIDN'T THINK IT WAS PARTICULARLY UNIQUE, I THOUGHT IT WAS AMERICAN.

THEN THE BOOK CAME OUT AND A FEW, VOCAL, SKEPTICS WERE FURIOUS THAT I DIGNIFIED CHRISTIANITY WITHIN THE PAGES OF A GRAPHIC NOVEL. EVEN TODAY, I'M AMAZED AT HOW HALF OF THE COMMENTS CLAIM, "IT'S NOT EVEN PREACHY" WHILE THE OTHER HALF SAY, "IT'S JUST TOO PREACHY". I KNEW I WAS ONTO SOMETHING GOOD WHEN THE STORY AND SUBJECT MATTER HIT A NERVE. IT'S A TOUGH TIGHTROPE TO WALK, AND IT'S IMPOSSIBLE TO WRITE SOMETHING GOOD AND HAVE EVERYONE IN THE WORLD THINK IT'S ON IDEOLOGICAL NEUTRAL GROUNDS. TO THIS DAY I STILL DON'T KNOW OR CARE IF IT'S PREACHY. I'M FAR MORE CONCERNED IF MY READERS LIKE IT AND GIVEN IT'S ONE OF MY FEW BOOKS THAT IS ON ITS FOURTH PRINTING I'M GOING TO CALL IT A SUCCESS.

STRANGER STILL IS THE SUCCESS CREATURE TECH HAS FOUND IN THE MOVIE INDUSTRY. I ORIGINALLY TOOK THE SCRIPT AROUND HOLLYWOOD AND COULD BARELY GET A READER TO NOTICE IT. BUT AFTER THE GRAPHIC NOVEL WAS ANNOUNCED ON AINTITCOOLNEWS BY DREW MCWEENY WE HAD SCORES OF REQUESTS TO READ IT. WITHIN TWENTY FOUR HOURS THERE WERE MOVIE OFFERS. THE RIGHTS WERE PICKED UP BY FOX/NEW REGENCY. I PAID A PERCENTAGE TO MY THEN PUBLISHER TOP SHELF, WHO MADE A GOOD SUM BEFORE THE BOOK EVEN HIT THE SHELVES. I MADE A GOOD CHUNK OF CHANGE OFF THAT MOVIE DEAL, BUT AFTER ALL THESE YEARS THERE IS STILL NO MOVIE. WE HAD JON HEDER ATTACHED TO PLAY DR. ONG, AND VARIOUS WRITERS, INCLUDING MYSELF, TOOK A CRACK AT THREE VERSIONS OF THE SCRIPT BUT NOTHING HAPPENED. IT'S HARD TO MAKE A MOVIE, AND REQUIRES SOMETHING MORE THAN GREAT SOURCE MATERIAL TO MAKE IT HAPPEN. BUT ONE THING I LEARNED FROM THE CREATURE TECH MOVIE DEAL, THAT EXECUTIVES HAVE A MUCH EASIER TIME ENVISIONING A GIANT, FLYING SPACE EEL IN A GRAPHIC NOVEL THAN IN A SCRIPT. SOME THINGS JUST HAVE TO BE SEEN.

TO MOST OF US WHO FULLY GET CREATURE TECH IT ALREADY IS A MOVIE. THE CHARACTERS ARE ALIVE AND WELL IN THE MIND OF THE READER. DR. ONG IS IN A SMALL FARM TOWN WORKING ON THOSE CRATES AND BLUE THE GIANT MANTIS-MAN IS PROBABLY BEING BAPTIZED AT THE LOCAL NAZARENE CHURCH BY NOW.

IN CASE YOU HAVEN'T GUESSED, THIS STORY WORKS BECAUSE IT'S A TRUE STORY. DON'T LET THE DETAILS DISTRACT YOU, BECAUSE WE'VE BEEN TRAINED TO REJECT SOME OF THE MOST IMPORTANT TRUTHS KNOWN TO CIVILIZATION BY PICKING AT MOLECULE-SIZED DOUBTS. AS I LOOK BACK ON THE HISTORY OF THIS UNIVERSE I ASK IF GIANT SPACE EELS ARE RESURRECTED FROM THE DEAD BY THE SHROUD OF TURIN OR DO GIMPY GIRLS REGAIN THEIR SIGHT BY THE MIRACULOUS SACRIFICE OF ONCE SELFISH PEOPLE? DO ATHEISTS HAVE RELIGIOUS ARGUMENTS WITH THEIR DADS? DOES A SEVEN-FOOT-TALL MANTID OUTSIDER SIT AMONG THE REDNECKS AT A SMALL TOWN CHURCH PICNIC? EVERY DAY. ALMOST EVERY DAY.

DOUG TENNAPEL
APRIL 21, 2010

the making of creature tech

STUDYING FREAK SHOWS & THE SHROUD OF TURIN.

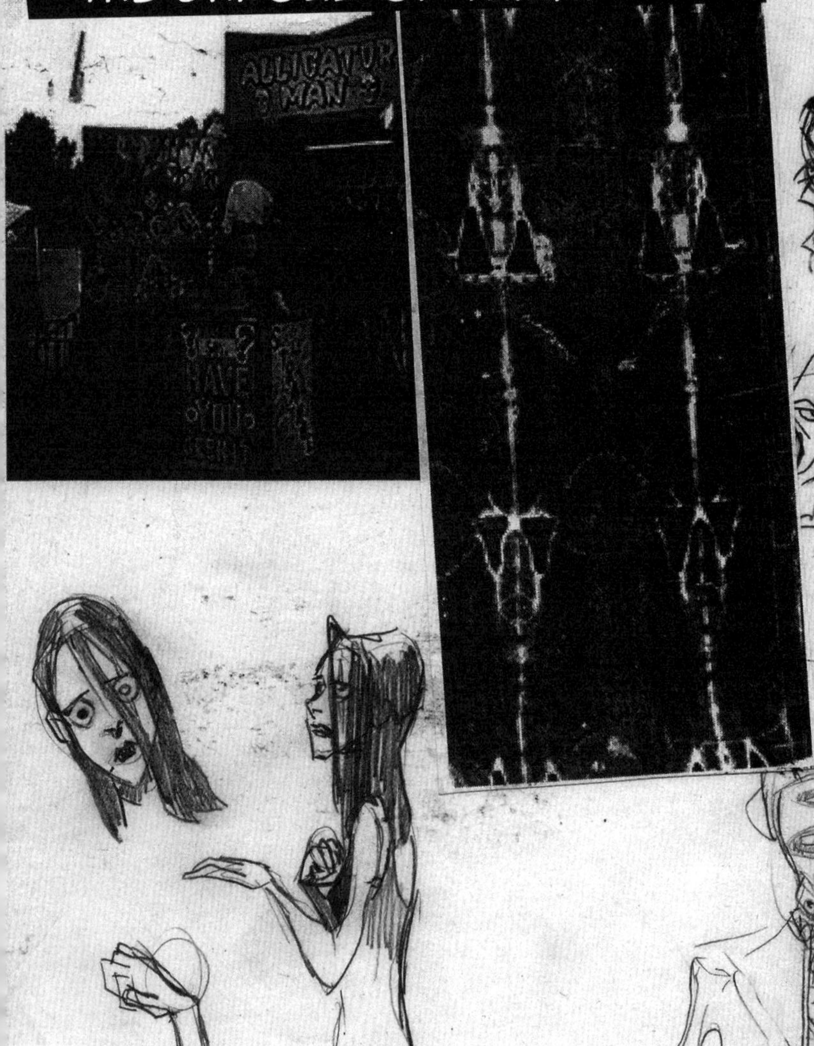

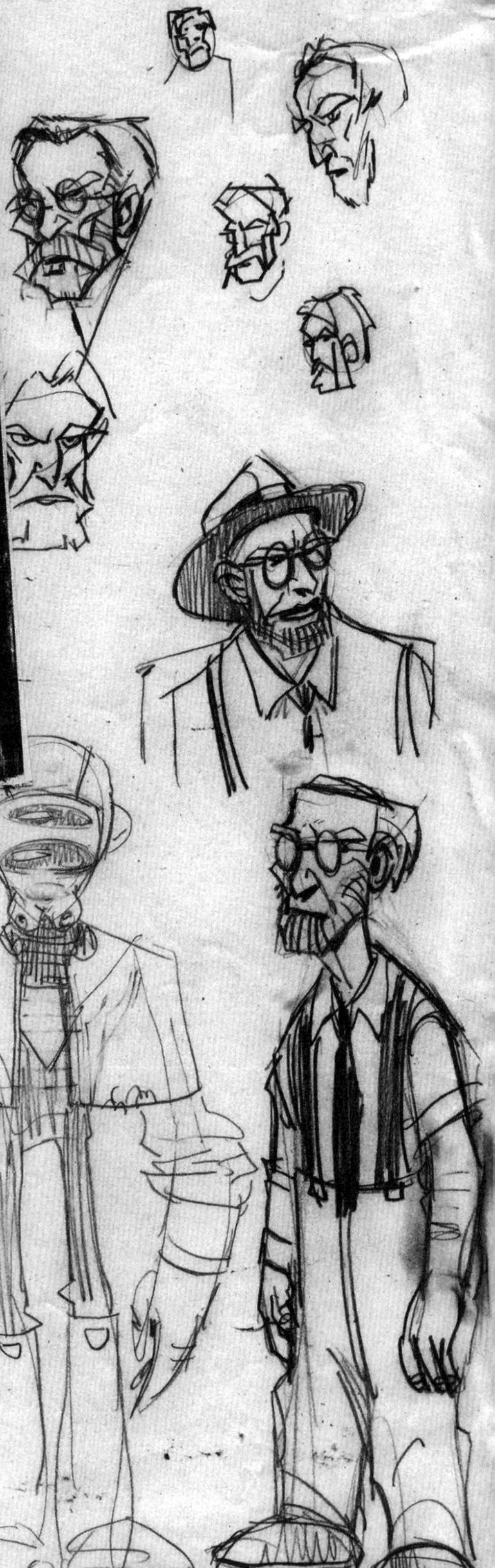

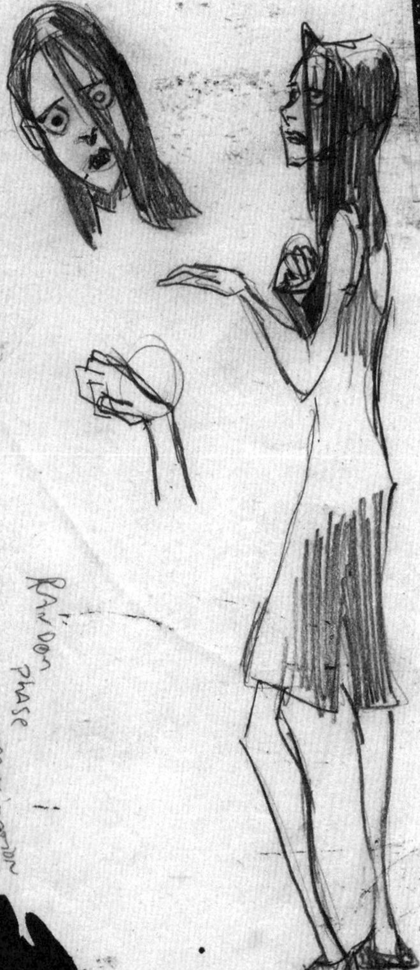
RAndom phase approximation

MY FIRST SKETCHES OF KATIE.

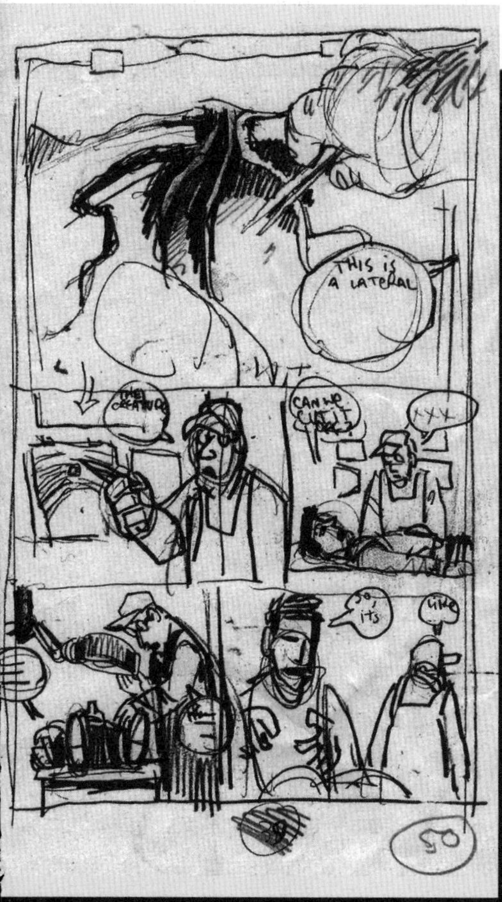
THIS IS A LATERAL
THE CREATURE

This is how it's done, folks.

I THUMBNAIL THE PAGES TO WORK OUT BASIC COMPOSITION, BLOCKING, LIGHTING AND TEXT BALLOONS.

IN GENERAL, IF A PAGE LOOKS CLEAR AT THIS 3" X 5" SIZE THERE'S A GOOD CHANCE IT WILL BE CLEAR WHEN DRAWN AND INKED FOR THE FINISHED PAGE.

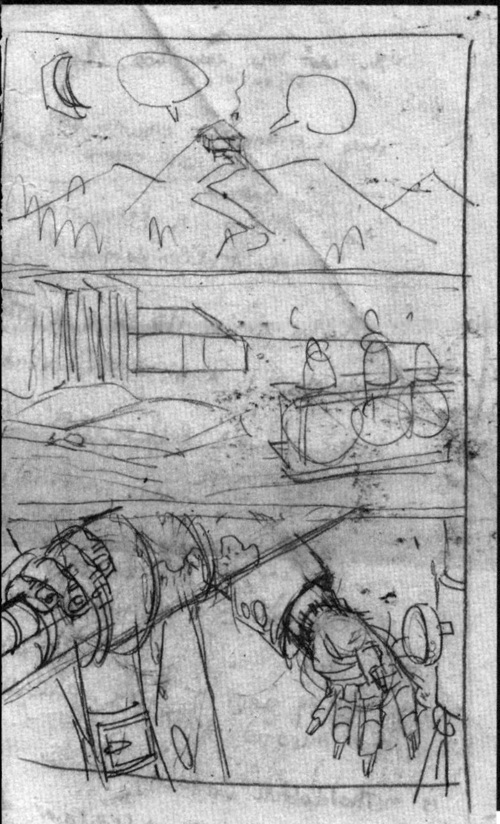

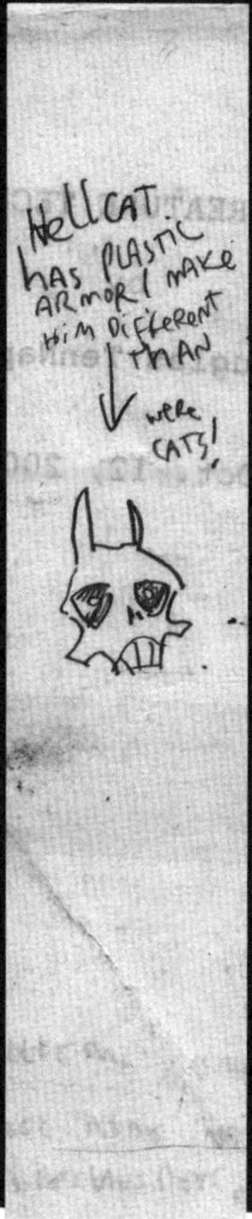
Hellcat has plastic armor / make him different than were cats!

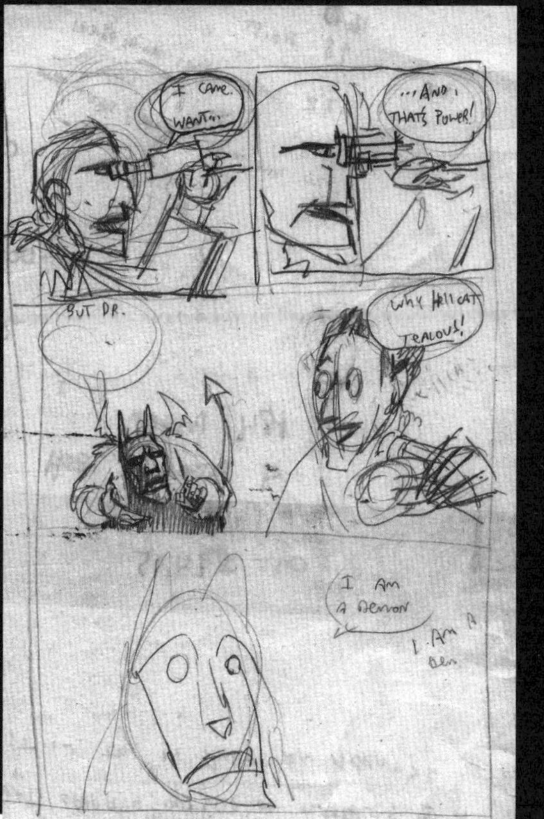
I came. Want...
...And, that's power!
But Dr.
Why Hellcat Jealous!
I Am A Demon

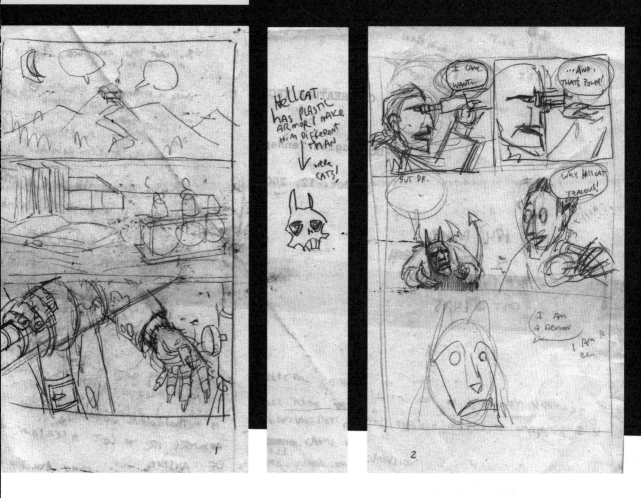

THIS IS MY PAL, ED. I BASED DR. ONG ON HIS BODY TYPE. ED RIDES A JAPANESE MOTORCYCLE AND IS AN ACCOMPLISHED ANIMATOR SO HE STRIKES GREAT POSES.

I DIDN'T FEEL CONFIDENT IN MY ABILITY TO DRAW THE HUMAN FORM BEFORE STARTING CREATURE TECH. I TOOK PHOTO REFERENCE, SIGNED UP FOR SOME FIGURE DRAWING CLASSES AND STUDIED KYLE BAKER'S WORK BEFORE I WAS READY TO START THE BOOK.

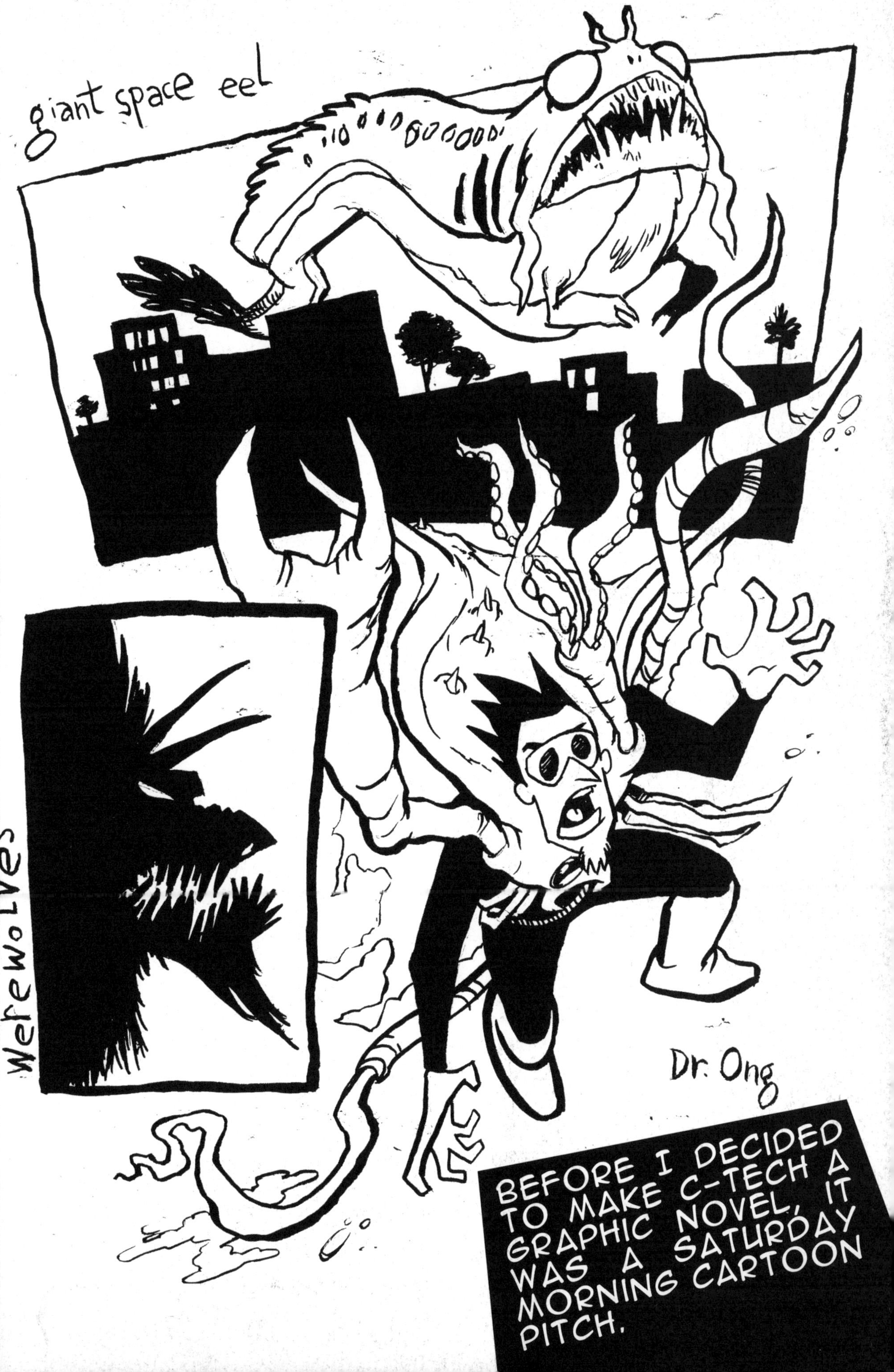
giant space eel
Werewolves
Dr. Ong
BEFORE I DECIDED TO MAKE C-TECH A GRAPHIC NOVEL, IT WAS A SATURDAY MORNING CARTOON PITCH.

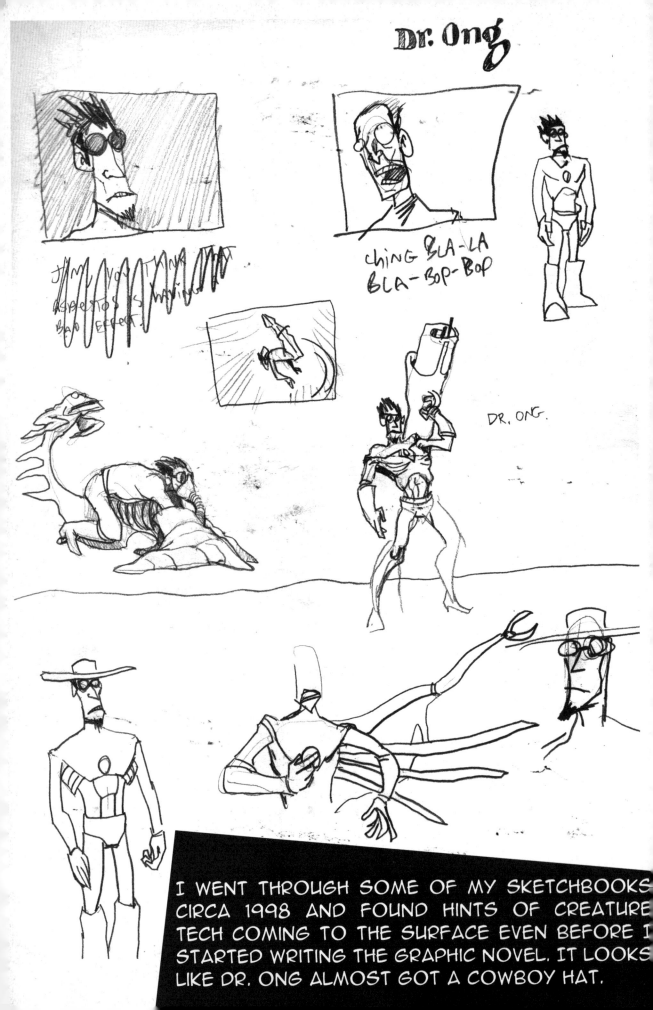

Dr. Ong

JIM
ASBESTOS
BAD EFFECT

CHING BLA-LA
BLA-BOP-BOP

DR. ONG.

I WENT THROUGH SOME OF MY SKETCHBOOKS
CIRCA 1998 AND FOUND HINTS OF CREATURE
TECH COMING TO THE SURFACE EVEN BEFORE I
STARTED WRITING THE GRAPHIC NOVEL. IT LOOKS
LIKE DR. ONG ALMOST GOT A COWBOY HAT.

PIN-UPS

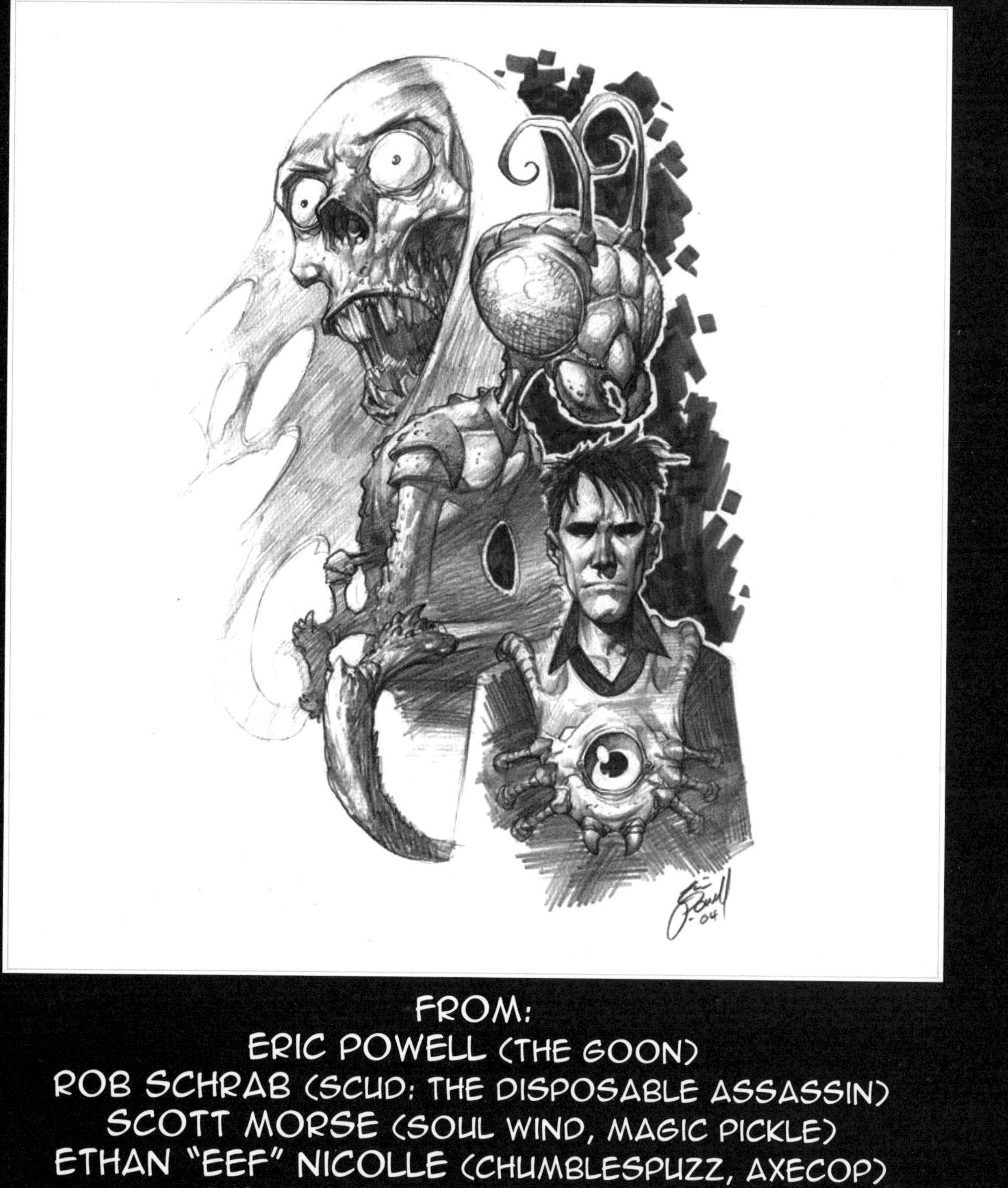

FROM:
ERIC POWELL (THE GOON)
ROB SCHRAB (SCUD: THE DISPOSABLE ASSASSIN)
SCOTT MORSE (SOUL WIND, MAGIC PICKLE)
ETHAN "EEF" NICOLLE (CHUMBLESPUZZ, AXECOP)
JIM MAHFOOD (STUPID COMICS)
DANIEL BRADFORD (R13)
SKOTTIE YOUNG (WIZARD OF OZ)

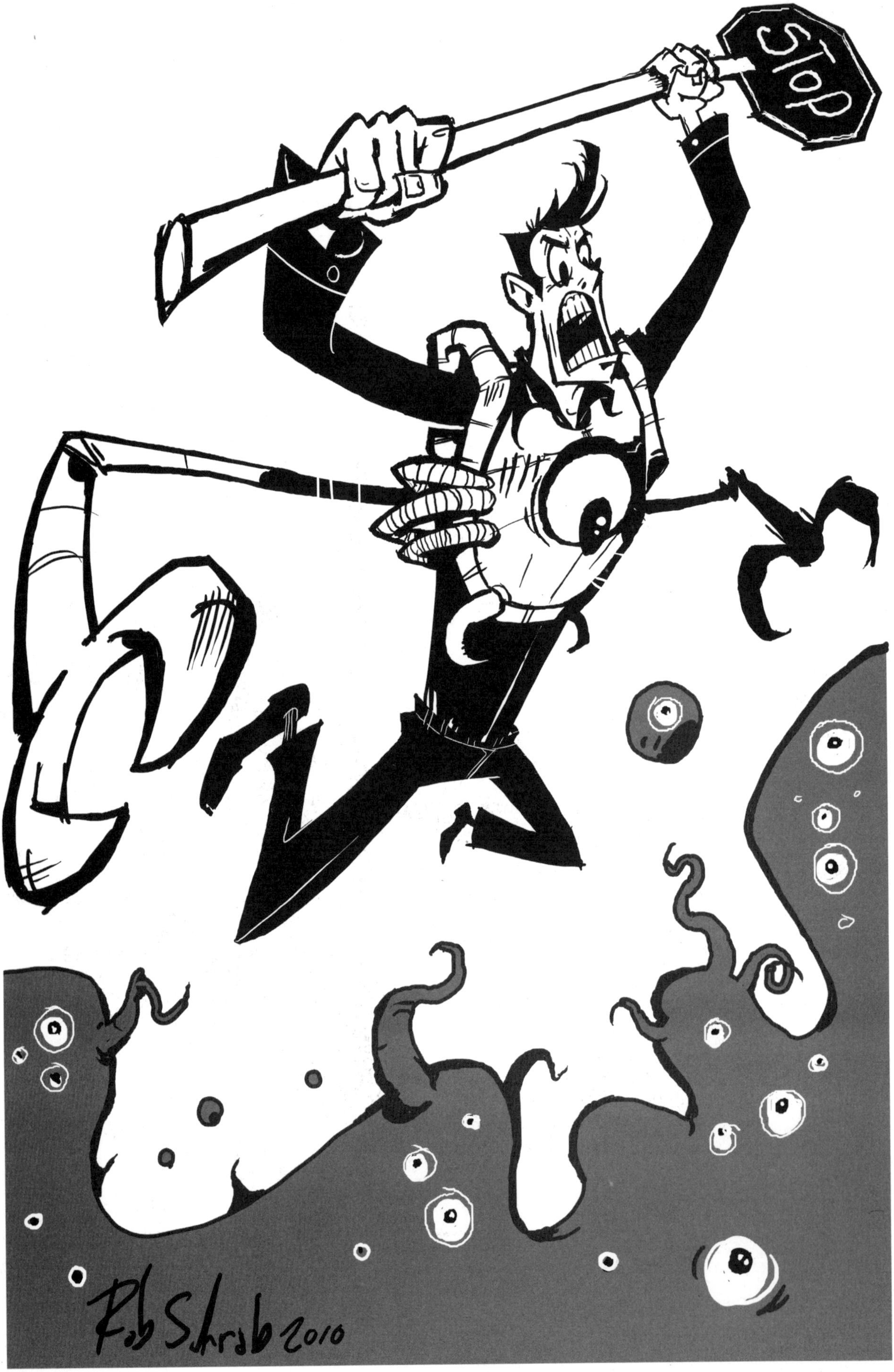
STOP
Rob Schrab 2010

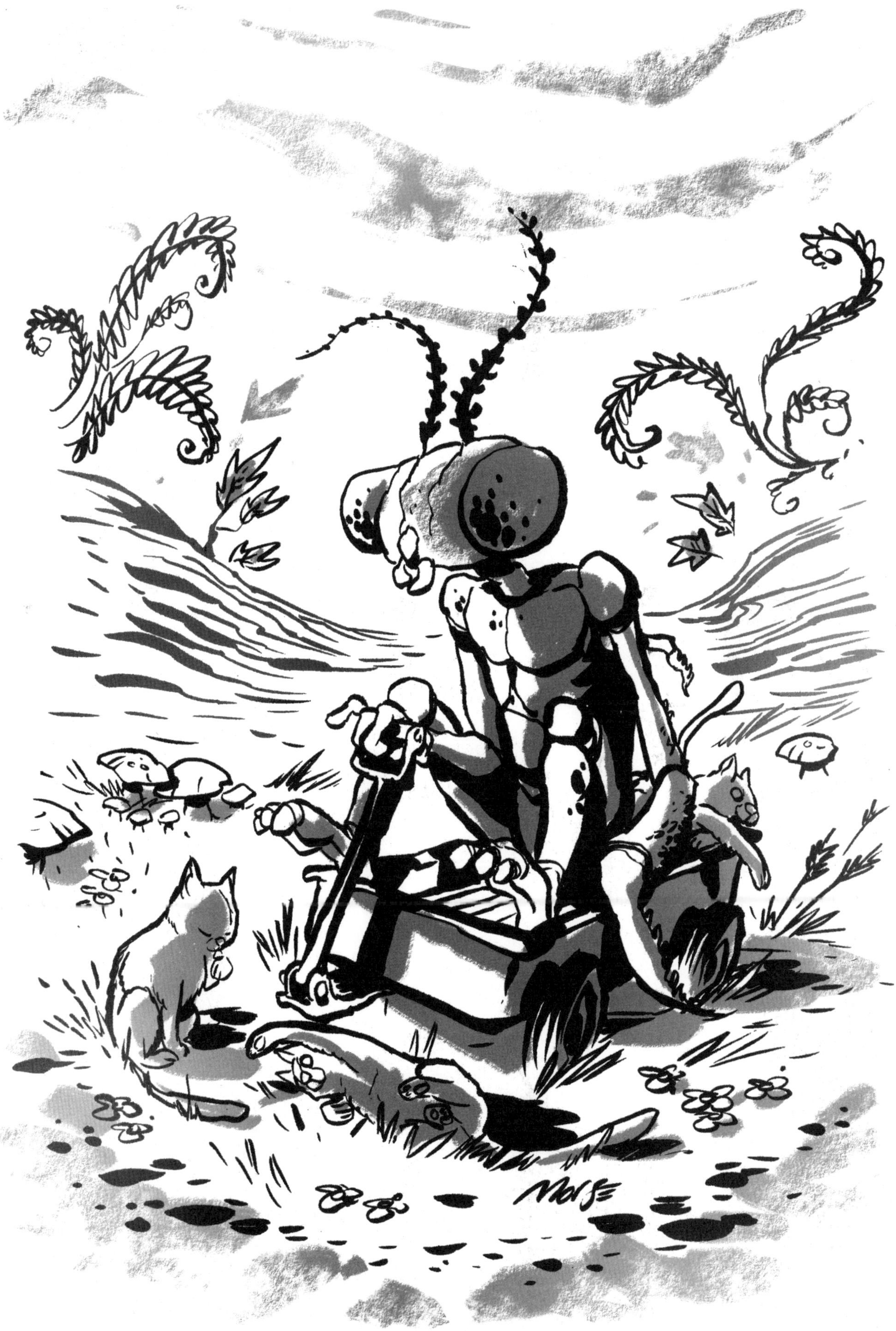
Morse

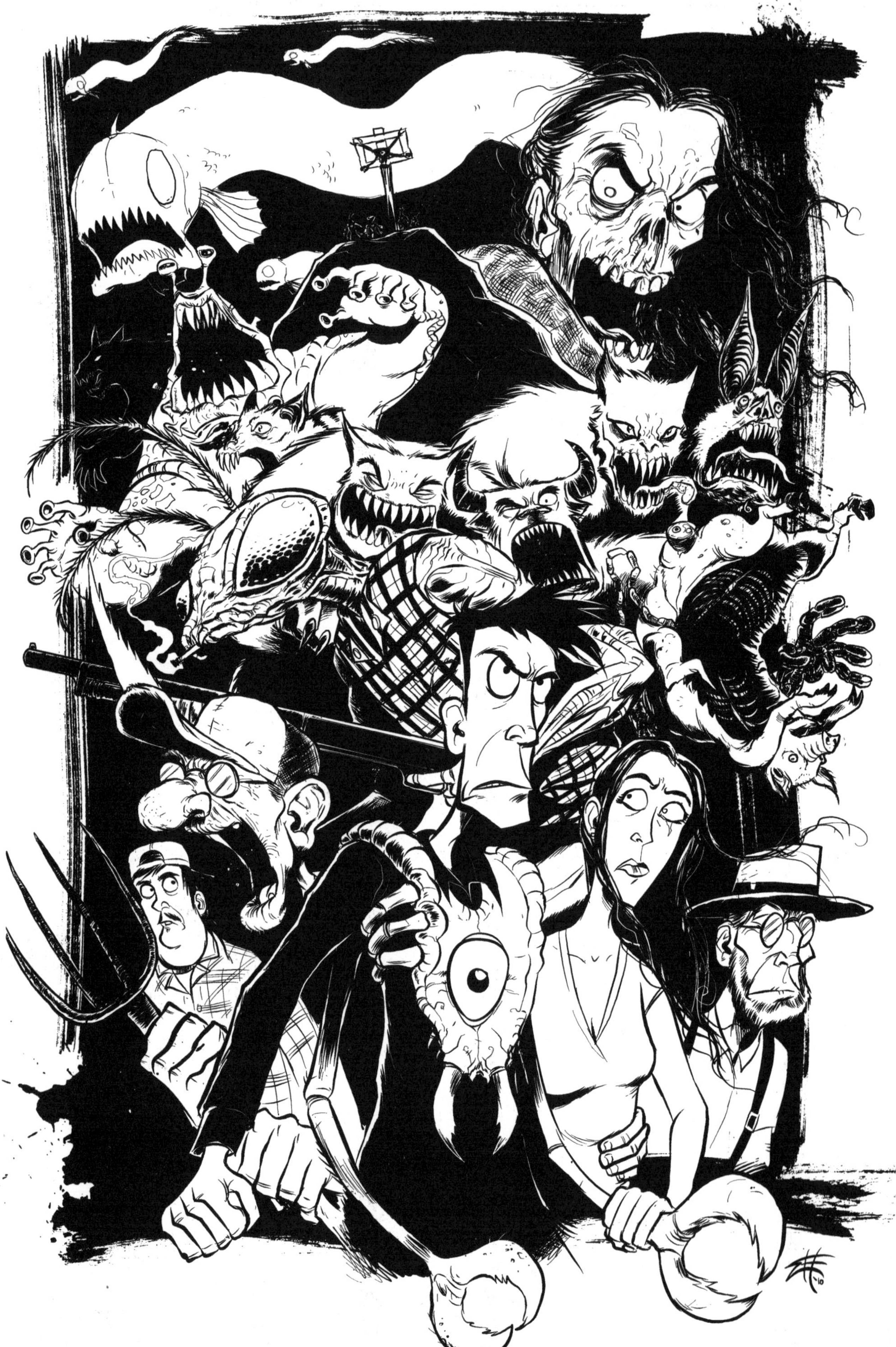

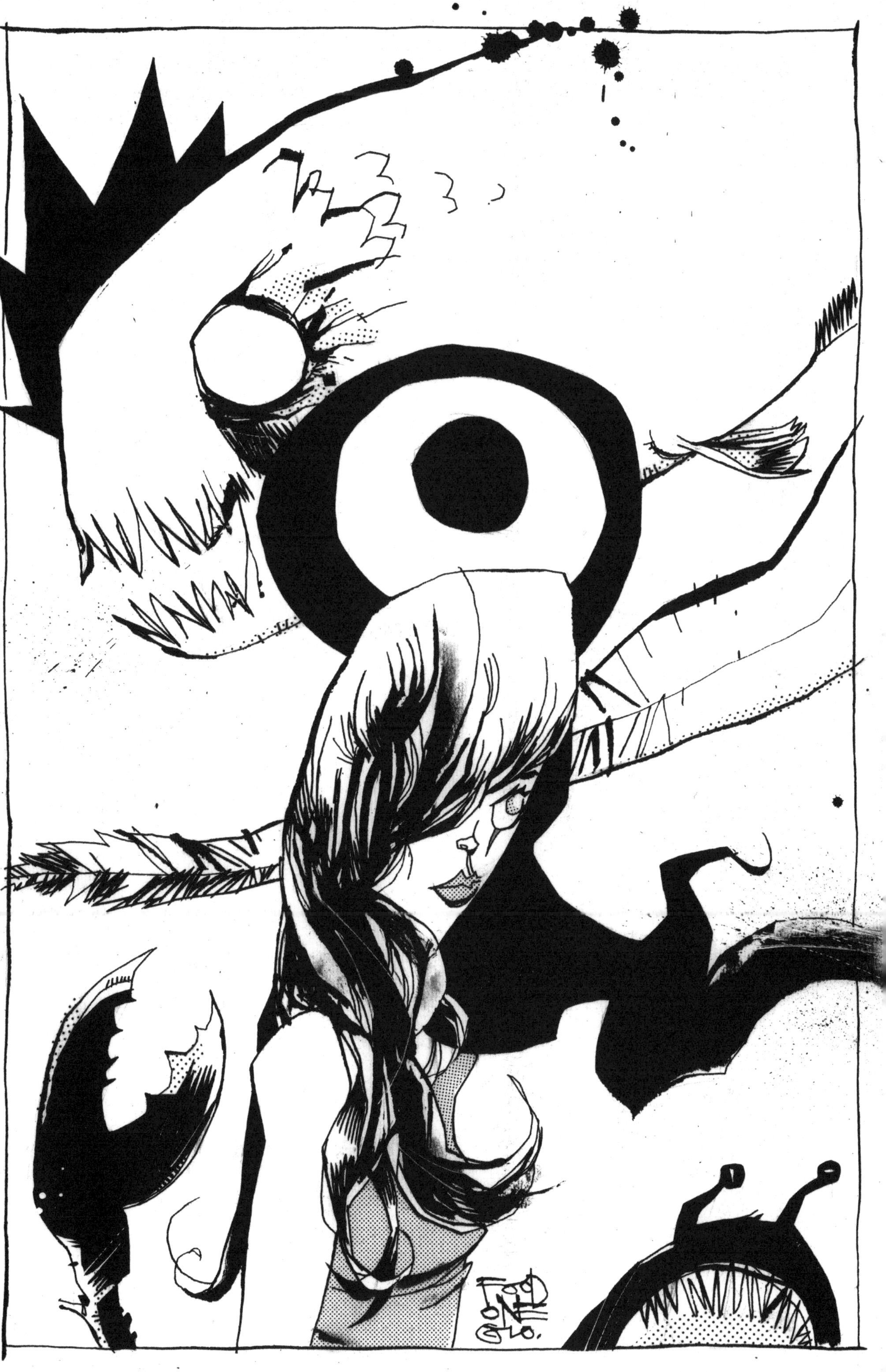

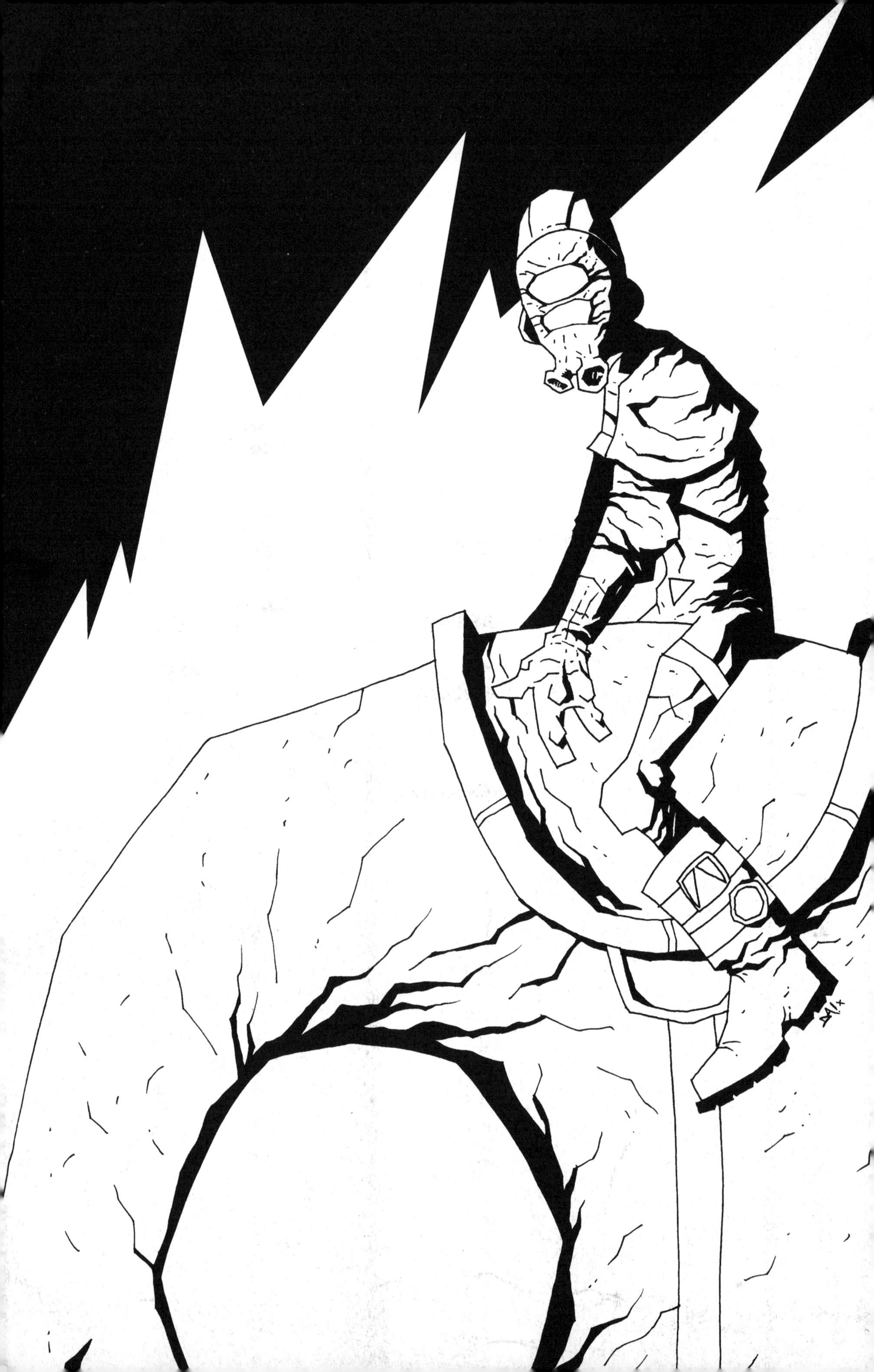

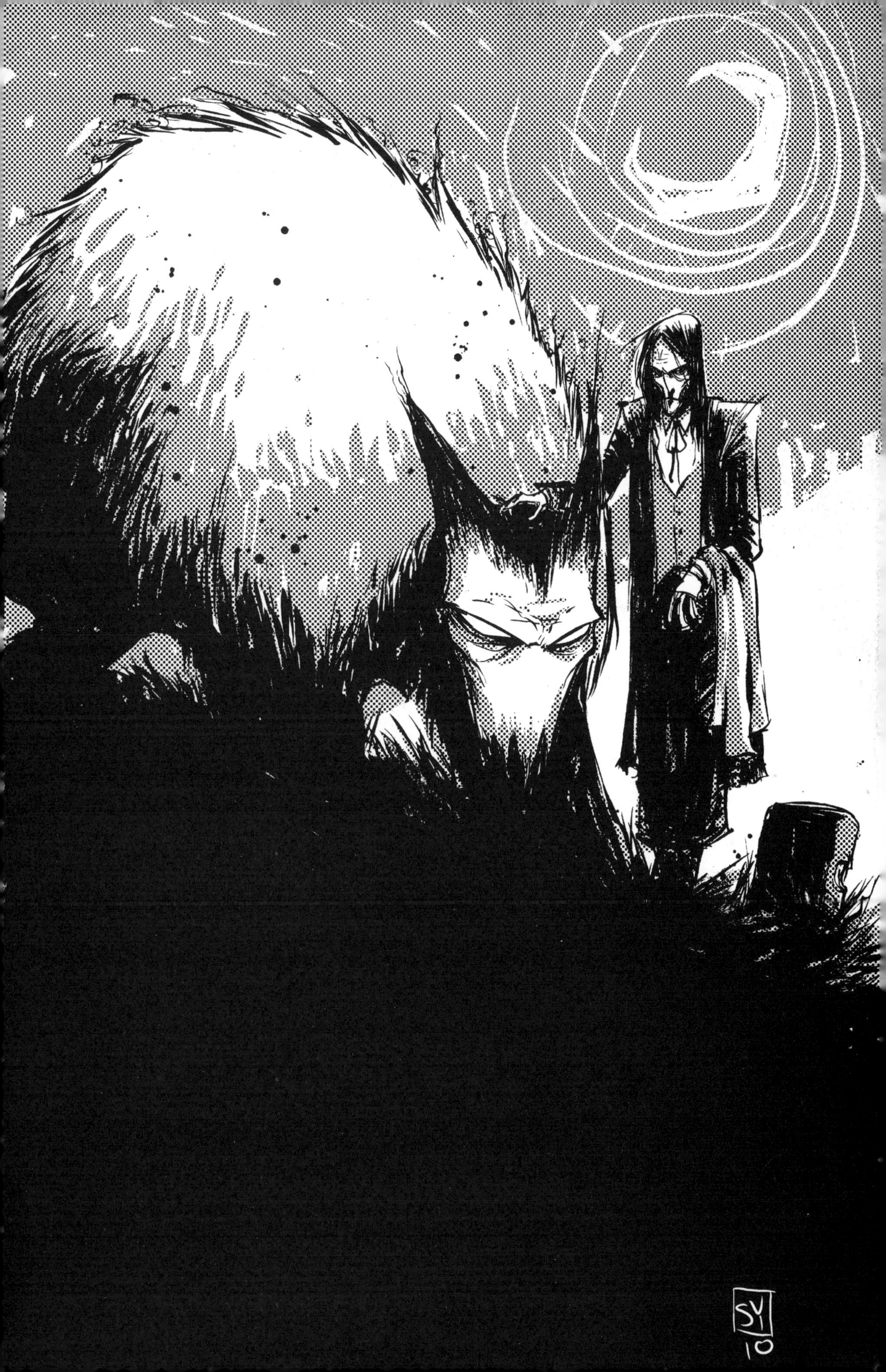
SY
10

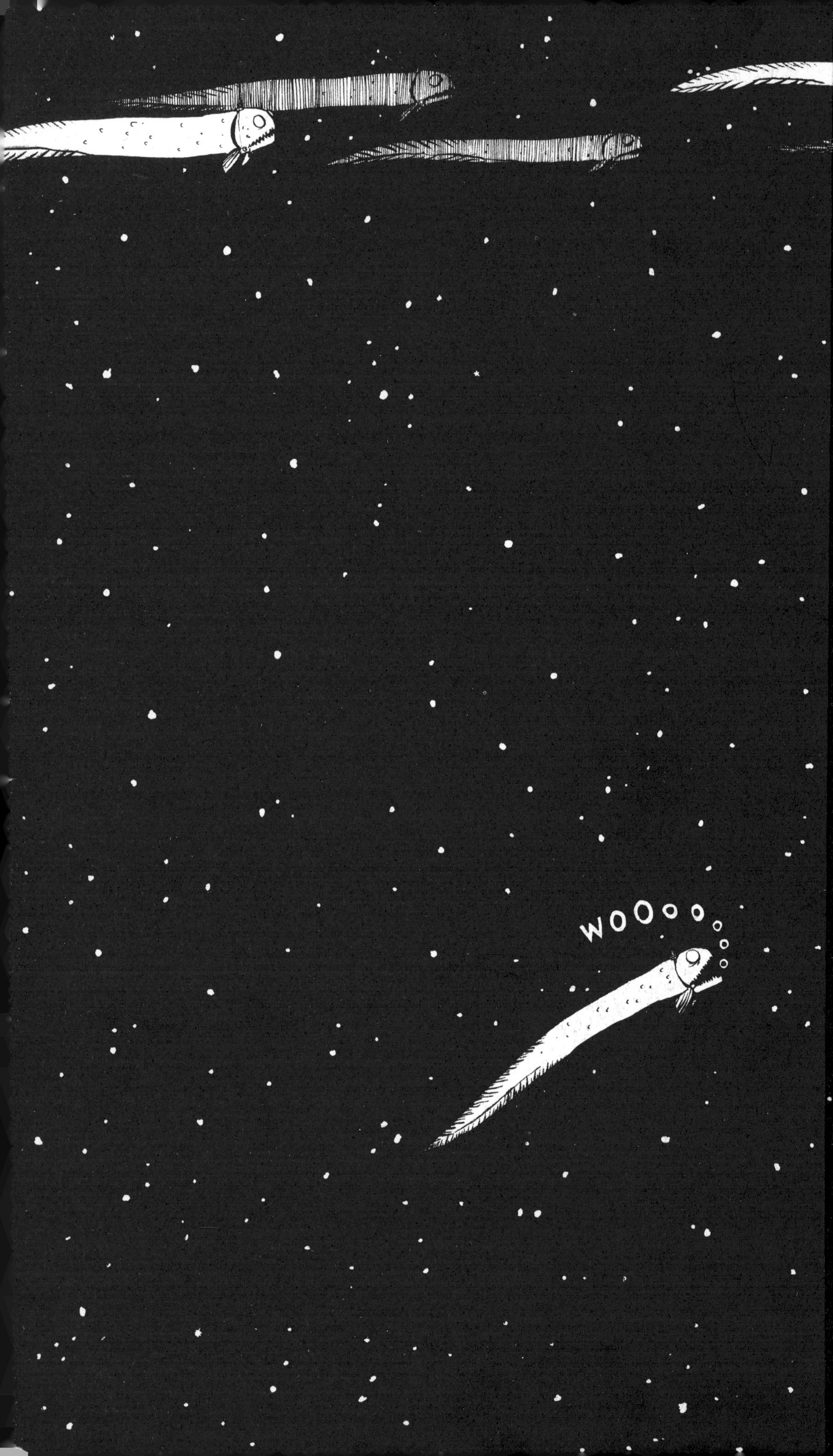
WOOooooo